SHOULDERING THE BURDENS OF DEFEAT

SHOULDERING THE BURDENS OF DEFEAT

West Germany and the Reconstruction of Social Justice

by Michael L. Hughes

The University of North Carolina Press ▪ *Chapel Hill and London*

© 1999 The University of North Carolina Press

Publication of this work has been supported through
the generosity of the Research and Publication Fund
of Wake Forest University.

Set in Adobe Minion by Tseng Information Systems, Inc.
Manufactured in the United States of America

⊗ The paper in this book meets the guidelines
for permanence and durability of the Committee on
Production Guidelines for Book Longevity of the
Council on Library Resources.

Library of Congress Cataloging-in-Publication Data
Hughes, Michael L.
Shouldering the burdens of defeat : West Germany and
the reconstruction of social justice / by Michael L. Hughes.
p.   cm.
Includes bibliographical references and index.
ISBN 0-8078-2494-1 (cloth : alk. paper)
1. Lastenausgleich (1949-) — Germany (West)
2. Capital levy — Germany (West) — History.
3. Currency question — Germany (West)
4. Germany (West) — Economic policy.
5. Germany (West) — Politics and government.
6. Germany — History — 1945-1990.   I. Title.
HJ4133.G3H84   1999
338.943 — DC21   98-49536
                                         CIP

A portion of this work was previously published, in
somewhat different form, in "Hard Heads, Soft Money?:
West German Ambivalence about Currency Reform,
1944-1948," *German Studies Review* 21, no. 1 (1998): 309-27,
and is reprinted here by permission of the journal.

03   02   01   00   99   5   4   3   2   1

To Geoffrey and Sean

CONTENTS

ACKNOWLEDGMENTS

In the course of this project I have incurred many debts to many people.

In pursuing the research for this book I benefited from a Z. Smith Reynolds Research Leave and from research grants from the American Philosophical Society, the German Academic Exchange Service, the Archie Fund, and the Griffin Fund. A second Z. Smith Reynolds Research Leave allowed me time to prepare a draft of this manuscript. I used numerous archives and libraries in the United States and the Federal Republic of Germany. I would particularly like to thank the staffs of the Bundesarchiv Koblenz, the Parlaments-Archiv, and the Friedrich Ebert Stiftung.

Over the last decade I have discussed aspects of this project with many different people. Participants in the Social Science Research Seminar and Economics Department Workshop of Wake Forest University, the conference on the culture of rights at the German Historical Institute in 1997, a panel on victim identities at the German Studies Association conference in 1995, and the Research Triangle Economic History Colloquium read and commented on drafts of various articles and papers. Dr. Christoph Buchheim discussed currency reform and Lastenausgleich with me early in the project. Professors James Diehl, Kevin Doak, Joshua Landis, Harold Marcuse, Maria Mitchell, Robert Moeller, Perry Patterson, Greg Schroeder, Yuri Slezkine, and Alan Williams read and discussed drafts of my articles and papers on the Lastenausgleich. Going above and beyond the call of duty, Professor Helga Welsh read the entire manuscript. Dr. Gloria Fitzgibbon provided substantive suggestions and encouragement beyond anything I can adequately acknowledge.

To all these people and any I have inadvertently omitted, many thanks. I am, of course, responsible for any errors, inconsistencies, or omissions.

ABBREVIATIONS

The following abbreviations are used in the text.

ACC	Allied Control Council
BdL	Bank deutscher Länder
BHE	Block der Heimatvertriebenen Deutschen
BVD	Bund der vertriebenen Deutschen
C-D-G Plan	Colm-Dodge-Goldsmith Plan
CDU	Christlich-Demokratische Union
CDU/CSU	Christlich-Demokratische Union/Christlich-Soziale Union
CSU	Christlich-Soziale Union
DM	Deutsche Mark
FDP	Freie Demokratische Partei
GB	Gesamtdeutscher Block
RM	Reichsmark
SPD	Sozialdemokratische Partei Deutschlands
ZvD	Zentralverband vertriebener Deutschen
ZvF	Zentralverband der Flieger- und Währungsgeschädigten

SHOULDERING THE BURDENS OF DEFEAT

INTRODUCTION

The Nazis fought World War II on credit. They ran up debts of hundreds of billions of Marks to individual German citizens that the German state and people would somehow have to repay. Some of those debts were to finance war production. Yet the Nazis also believed that the "racial community" must balance out war's burdens as fairly as possible among its members. The regime hence gave Germans who suffered war-induced property losses an entitlement to full restitution. It thereby created the legal category of "the war-damaged."

Adolf Hitler was totally indifferent to the level of war debt Germany was incurring. He believed that life was a struggle to the death among the world's different nationalities. As he told his cronies in May 1942, "he contracted today all the debts for the Reich in firm confidence in our victory and in the conviction that — if this war should not come to a satisfactory end — then it's all over for us anyway." He was also convinced that a state could print as much money and run up as much debt as it wanted — as long as it secured the productive assets and·labor to back those debts. Yet he did not expect the German people to work to pay off the bill for his extravagant war. Rather, he expected non-Germans to pay that bill through their forced labor for his "master race."[1]

Looming German defeat made it ever less likely after 1942 that Hitler could force Germany's enemies to pay its war bills. The Germans themselves were going to have to redeem Hitler's extravagant promises, including any recompense for the horrendous losses individual Germans were suffering. Yet who in German society was going to get stuck with the bill for the madness of World War II? Would the burden be imposed on one segment of the German population, as after World War I? Or would it be distributed more or less equally — or equitably — among all Germans? Indeed, did Germans have a right to support an aggressive war conducted with unspeakable brutality and still expect recompense for damages suffered?

Yet scarcely anyone in wartime Germany dared to discuss postwar finances. To suggest that Germans would be stuck with the bill was, the Nazis said, defeatism, a crime punishable by death. The fear was real and powerful, as the later economics minister and chancellor of West Germany, Ludwig Erhard, discovered. Erhard scarcely hid his contempt for the regime. Even though he had some protection from his well-placed brother-in-law, industrial official Karl Guth, his position was risky. In 1943 he began work on a memorandum, "War Finance and Debt Consolidation," predicated on the assumption that Germany would lose the war. Theodor Eschenburg reports that in 1944 Erhard prepared and distributed to various individuals a summary of the memorandum. When Eschenburg finally nerved himself to read his copy of that summary, he discovered that it opened with the bald statement, "Once it had become indisputable that the war was lost, the most urgent task would be to reform Germany's currency." Eschenburg admits that he was so terrified that the secret police might catch him with this defeatist summary that he went immediately to Erhard's dwelling—in the middle of the night. He pounded on the door until he roused a disgruntled Erhard from bed. He insisted that Erhard take the summary back, and he implored him to be more circumspect in the future.[2]

Given such fears, only after Germany's defeat and the Nazi regime's collapse did Germans begin publicly debating a *Lastenausgleich*, a just allocation among different segments of the German people of the material losses from brutal war and crushing defeat. "Lastenausgleich" has been translated as "equalization of burdens," but few Germans favored an equal burden for every German. Rather, Germans wanted a "balancing out of burdens" among all Germans, a burden for each individual proportional to his or her current need or earlier wealth and status. Financing such a Lastenausgleich would involve confiscating half or more of the wealth of those lucky enough to have kept any property, to provide assets to distribute to those unlucky enough to be war-damaged.[3]

All European nations granted some compensation for citizens who suffered war damages, but only one approached the scale of West German efforts. European states usually offered only minimal and often grudging aid for securing a new livelihood or preventing starvation, not restitution for lost wealth. Funds to finance aid almost invariably came out of general revenues. Only Italians, Austrians, West Germans, and Finns recognized fellow ethnic nationals expelled from another country as entitled to some assistance. Only West Germans and Finns proposed and partially implemented a Lastenausgleich imposing massive capital levies (50 percent and more) to redistribute the nation's private wealth to restore the prewar distribution of property. Finland, though, was a small, primarily agricultural nation with substantial amounts of uncultivated land to redistribute. Given West Germany's size and socioeconomic structure, its Lastenausgleich legislation was unique in nature and scope.[4]

The Lastenausgleich is important because it vividly illuminates postwar German economic, social, and political attitudes. Uninterested in restoring anyone's private property, the Communist East German government contented itself with social aid to needy war-damaged. West Germans, though, seeking to rebuild a private property–based socioeconomic order, struggled for years to construct a Lastenausgleich that would reconcile the rights of former and current property holders, meet the hopes and needs of individual Germans, and prove compatible with a social-market economy. They were forced to articulate, in thousands of documents, what social justice might mean, what rights and obligations private property has, how the economy should operate, who should foot the bill for Germany's aggressive war, and how liberal democracy could produce legitimate outcomes from vehement political conflicts.

The Lastenausgleich struggle is also important because it would have fateful consequences for the character and stability of future German societies. After World War I, German governments had left holders of paper assets to bear the costs of defeat while sparing the wealth of those who held real assets. That policy had affected the distribution of wealth, subsequent savings and investment rates, and economic development. Crucially, anger over it had fueled opposition to Weimar democracy and had bolstered support for the Nazis.[5] Postwar Germans knew that, similarly, their choices in the Lastenausgleich struggle would determine which Germans were going to bear the staggering costs of World War II, what (West) Germany's future economic structure would be like, and whether any second German democracy would flourish or perish.

The Lastenausgleich was an issue because of events that had happened before the Federal Republic of Germany was created, and its development illuminates the continuities and discontinuities in German history. The Lastenausgleich reflected the property losses Germans had suffered because of their support for Hitler's aggression, and it developed under the impact of Nazi legislation and Nazi communalism. It also reflected longer-standing German ideas about the rights and obligations of property and of the community. Nonetheless, it developed in a new historical context, brought about by longer-term structural changes in Germany's economy and society and by more recent developments during the war and after.

Nazi legislation and wartime and postwar events created a category of the war-damaged, but they could not determine who would belong to that group psychologically or politically. How much and what kind of losses would motivate an individual to perceive him- or herself as war-damaged varied enormously, depending not only on the individual's alternative resources and options for rebuilding a viable livelihood but also on social and political views.

Those who had suffered relatively minor losses would often have other concerns that would make them relatively or totally uninterested in seeking any Lastenausgleich. Moreover, Germans made choices about whom they would acknowledge as a (deserving) victim of war or persecution and whom they would ignore.

In this and other contexts, the Lastenausgleich illuminates the tension between discourse on the one hand and institutional, structural, and material forces on the other. War-damaged Germans secured a Lastenausgleich, as opposed to modest aid from general revenues, because they could draw on a discourse about individual virtue, social responsibility, and economic realities that "undamaged" West Germans found compelling. Yet the war-damaged could not get all the restitution they demanded, because undamaged Germans outnumbered them and could argue that West Germany could not afford to overburden the economy with enormous in-kind capital levies without deleterious consequences. West Germans generally perceived the latter assertion as an accurate reflection of inalterable realities, not as just another discourse.

Although this narrative is primarily a tale of West German successes, the history it reconstructs was not one of inevitable modernization or unblemished progress. West Germans' creation of a stable liberal democracy is hard to characterize as anything but an improvement over what had come before. Nonetheless, historians have rightly become suspicious of naïve concepts of progress and modernization. Nazism, however barbarous, was partially both reflection and agent of modernity. The Lastenausgleich reflects this two-edged nature of modernity. It grew out of brutal modern war and Nazi communalism, and its development illuminates the complex processes by which the war-damaged and other West Germans parlayed nonmodern values and some of the more emancipatory aspects of modernity into a new social order that provided a modicum of individual security, autonomy, and status for most — but not all — West Germans.

Chapter 1

INFLATION, DESTRUCTION, EXPULSION

World War II devastated Europe. Between 1939 and 1945, well over 30 million Europeans lost their lives; millions more suffered injury, torture, or privation; and few Europeans escaped the loss of some loved one, friend, or acquaintance. The war also imposed enormous material losses. Land, sea, and air warfare destroyed business premises and inventory, public buildings, homes, and personal property. Expropriation, plunder, and expulsion deprived millions of Europeans of much or all of their property. Wartime monetary and fiscal policies shifted wealth from citizens to the state and even among citizens. Moreover, the costs did not end in May 1945, because states had to rebuild, recompense wartime losses, and support the disabled and impoverished.[1]

Although Germany started the war and devastated its enemies, Germans also suffered. Seven million died because of the war. Total German war costs were 716 billion RM from 1933 to 1945, with a similar sum in Deutsche Mark paid out since 1948 to cover war-related costs. Support payments from the German government to various war victims and their survivors will not end until well into the twenty-first century.[2]

One important subset of German war costs was "war damages"—material losses of real and paper assets that Germans suffered as a result of the war and defeat. Losses of real property were approximately 105 billion RM. Some 18 million West Germans, more than one-third of the population, had lost most or all of their real property, leaving them at best poorer but more usually impoverished. West Germans would also lose 90–93.5 percent of their paper assets, including hundreds of billions of Reichsmark in savings, to suppressed inflation and currency reform.[3] Based on popular expectations that society should protect citizens from arbitrary war damages, Germans identified and

Nazi legislation defined a category of war-damaged with a widely acknowledged entitlement to recompense.

LEGAL RECOMPENSE FOR WAR DAMAGES

Before the eighteenth century, people scarcely imagined anyone might secure recompense for war damages. They generally assumed that they had little control over their lives and must accept whatever fate or the gods laid upon them. Job, who ultimately submits to a God who has devastated his life as part of a wager with Satan, exemplifies such human resignation. For Christians, everything that happened, no matter how small, was part of God's larger plan, even if it seemed arbitrary and callous to human beings. War was one of the Four Horsemen of the Apocalypse, whose visitations humankind had to endure as God's will, trusting in the hope of a better life hereafter.[4]

In the eighteenth century, some Europeans, the philosophes, began to suggest that human misery was not inevitable. They believed not that every particular event was part of God's plan but rather that a benevolent God had created a rational universe and had placed human beings within it as autonomous agents who would have to make their own decisions. The philosophes and many other Europeans therefore began actively to pursue happiness as something subject to human design and effort, not divine will. "The upshot," Paul Hazard writes, "was that happiness became a right, something to which we were entitled." Any human misery that did not result from individual fault was unreasonable and unjust. Indeed, it implicitly called into question the new moral order of the rational, benevolent universe. People must make whole again the victims of such unmerited suffering — not only to help those victims but to restore the moral order. Not surprisingly, then, the French Revolutionary and Napoleonic Wars sparked the first tentative proposals that a state should recompense its citizens for war losses.[5]

Economic and social developments in nineteenth-century Europe strengthened citizens' claims to recompense. The state came to have an interest in recompense to help rebuild national economic assets. Greater material security, consequent on economic growth and medical advances, increased people's expectations and society's ability to compensate individuals for the consequences of life's disasters. Some measure of security came to seem the norm. Further, Europeans increasingly recognized a social right to some guaranteed minimum for workers and other poor citizens, making it difficult to deny compensation for those devastated by war damages. A West German journalist writing in 1948 exaggerated only a little when he asserted, "People in the 19th century thought they had come so far that they could erect and maintain a protective wall between war and the civilian population."[6]

That wall, though, still rested on the shaky foundation of government acquiescence. Germany first granted compensation for war damages after the brief and successful Franco-Prussian War. The relevant legislation denied any *right* to recompense by stating that compensation must be by special law. The citizen could hope only for social assistance at the grace of the state. War damages resulted from sovereign acts, and one still could not sue the sovereign, who was the monarch and not the people.[7]

In the twentieth century, popular leverage on the German state increased. The state could not easily ignore citizen soldiers and voters, especially when total war required that it draw into its war effort people from all social classes. When war broke out in 1914, the German common soldier received 53 Pfennige (about 13 cents) per day—nowhere near enough to support a wife and children left behind. The war soon produced other victims, such as disabled veterans and war widows and orphans. To allow these victims to tumble into poverty would have devastated the soldiers' morale. The German government hence quickly introduced a number of measures to assist these people. It explicitly distinguished those measures from the widely despised welfare, to avoid humiliating the recipients and the soldiers on whom they had depended.[8]

German war-damage compensation nonetheless proved minimal after World War I, even though Germany escaped most of that war's enormous direct devastation. German wartime legislation did entitle individuals to have their damages officially registered. Yet it also denied any entitlement (*Rechtsanspruch*) to compensation, which remained subject to governmental discretion. War and postwar governments did grant partial compensation for material losses and for loss of an economic existence for the self-employed (but not for their employees!). Inflation and hyperinflation, though, eroded or obliterated the value of that compensation. Subsequent legislation did offer up to 10–20 percent compensation, but with substantial delays that eroded its value.[9]

When World War II began, the Nazis hesitated to commit themselves on the issue of war-damages compensation. They could not be sure how successful German arms or how expensive German war damages would be. Although insurance policies normally excluded war damages, the government did order private insurers to cover war losses up through July 1940, asserting that damages had been minimal enough that the companies could afford it. Further, on 8 September 1939, the Nazis issued a War-Damages Registration Decree that provided for the registration of war damages to real property but that explicitly postponed compensation against a future decision. The decree did, though, provide for prepayments in special cases, particularly to forestall economic ruin for the self-employed.[10]

This decree began the process of giving a legal identity to a subgroup of Germans who might be denominated the war-damaged. "War-damaged" was not a purely arbitrary construct. Some 1940s Germans would suffer significant material losses, and others would not. Some would see military action, especially bombing, destroy their homes, businesses, or personal property; some would flee in terror or be expelled from their homes, forcing them to abandon all their possessions; some would see the value of their paper assets slashed by inflation. Those who suffered such losses came out of the war with a different set of experiences and a different situation than did those who had not suffered such losses. Both the damaged and the undamaged were conscious of those differences. Nonetheless, how many Germans would suffer war damages, how many would come to perceive themselves as war-damaged, and which the society would recognize as war-damaged and with what consequences, remained to be seen.[11]

Germany's rapid, cheap run of victories in 1939 and 1940 produced an overweening optimism in Germany and a generous attitude toward war damages. On 30 November 1940 the Nazis issued the War-Damages Decree. The decree provided in principle for full compensation for war damages, including those from the loss of use of destroyed property. Compensation was not to be interest bearing, and the state would disburse compensation only when the individual could replace the lost property or when payment was indispensable to ensure life's necessities. Eventually, the regime ruled that individuals would have to cover minor losses from their own resources.[12]

Implicit in this legislation was Hitler's expectation that final victory would enable him to extract any compensation costs from the conquered. As Lastenausgleich expert Walter Seuffert (SPD — Social Democratic Party, the moderate socialists) put it in 1951, "this [compensation] law was a very generous discounted bill by the National Socialist regime, one that was to be redeemed by the enemy through the subjugation of several peoples, who would pay the bill." No one at the time, he went on, had expected Germans to have to settle these costs among themselves.[13]

One notable aspect of this war-damages legislation was the extent to which the Nazis failed to give it a purely National Socialist character. Certainly the exclusion on racial grounds of Jews and other "non-Aryans" from compensation reflected Nazi ideology. Nonetheless, the civil servants who drafted the War-Damages Decree drew its fundamental principles from the compensation practices of the Second Empire and the Weimar Republic. The decree hence reflected liberal values by being structured around the principle of compensation for individual property losses, including loss of the use of property, but not for the loss of a job. The timing and priority of compensation were to be based on national-economic considerations, but no government could afford to do otherwise. Indeed, the Wilhelmine and Weimar governments had acted similarly.[14]

Ideologically, though, the Nazis were promoting during the war an anti-individualistic notion of social obligation. No compensation was really possible for loss of one's own life or, despite survivors' pensions, for that of a loved one, and the exigencies of the war economy would long delay compensation payments for most material losses. Maintaining the morale of the troops, the armament workers, and their relatives required an emphasis on selfless sacrifice for the community. *Meyers Lexikon,* in a volume published in 1940, defined sacrifice as the "voluntary, self-evident, silent setting into action of one's strength and personality for the achievement of communal goals . . . without the expectation of sacrifice from others." This definition directly reflected both the needs of a state at war and the communalist strain in Nazism. Nazi wartime propaganda actively promoted the need for sacrifice. For example, in his famous "Total War Speech" of 18 February 1943, Goebbels asserted, "The *Volk* wants to take on all, even the *heaviest,* burdens and is prepared to make *any* sacrifice if it serves the cause of victory." Even the churches seconded such calls. Moreover, wartime propaganda emphasized revenge on Germany's enemies, not compensation to German war-damaged.[15]

Even the Nazis, though, felt compelled to soften extravagant demands for selfless sacrifice with a more communal ideology of shared sacrifice. Already in April 1941 Goebbels suggested that the German people expected "to distribute *justly* the burdens that are now as a rule associated with war and to make them bearable for everyone." An official commentary on the War-Damages Decree asserted, "According to the National Socialist conception, the individual citizen is not a subject whom the sovereign or state can dispose of at will. Rather, the individual is a member of the racial community with the rights thereto pertaining, and from that follows the obligation of the racial community on its side to step in for the racial comrade who has made a sacrifice for it, and to at least take from him the burdens where his sacrifice exceeds substantially what has been expected of the majority of other racial comrades."[16]

Germans' new status as citizens or "members of the racial community," not subjects, presumably played an important role here. When the prince was the sovereign, the subjects could not sue him for the consequences of his actions. Yet now the people were the sovereign, explicitly under the Weimar Constitution that officially remained in force in Nazi Germany and implicitly in Nazi ideology of the leader as the apotheosis of the racial community. Hence, they could more easily make claims on a state that was in principle their agent, not an overweening ruler with implicitly absolute power.

The Nazis also moved away rhetorically, if not legally, from the individual recompense that the War-Damages Decree offered toward a more communally defined recompense. In their limited public discussions of war damages, they preferred to gush over how much "more beautifully and opulently" German cities would be rebuilt after the war. Even as Goebbels emphasized revenge, he reassured the war-damaged, "In thanks for their currently proven heroic resolution it will be an obligation of honor of the whole *Volk* to rebuild the cities and the buildings in the air war areas *more beautifully* than ever." Significantly,

Goebbels and company were not promising to replace as private property each individual's losses. One of the great historical unknowns is how communalistic a victorious Nazi Germany would have been. As in other areas, the Nazis remained during the war committed to apparently opposing conceptions, here legally individualistic but rhetorically communal.[17]

Unfortunately, the sources are not available to explore systematically how wartime Germans responded to the mixed messages of Nazism. When it came to material losses, wartime and postwar actions suggest that they overwhelmingly rejected Nazi calls for selfless sacrifice. They remained committed, not surprisingly, to having their lost property, *all* of their lost property, restored. A German government had, after all, acknowledged their entitlement to restitution. Yet the Nazis had also reinforced the idea that the community as a whole had an obligation to share the burdens of war equitably rather than leaving unlucky individuals to bear them alone.

INFLATION

The first "war damages" that struck large numbers of Germans were losses in the *value* of their paper assets: their savings deposits, bonds, war-damages compensation claims, and so on. The Nazis financed much of their war effort with the hidden tax of inflation, which left paper assets formally in existence while substantially eroding their purchasing power. Average Germans had few opportunities for evading this inflationary policy. Efforts to compensate inflation losses hence played a role in the Lastenausgleich.

Because governments must strive to maintain popular support for their war efforts, they have found it difficult to impose stiff taxation that would soak up large chunks of people's earnings to finance the war. Instead, governments have tended to rely on the sale of government paper (war bonds, treasury notes, and the like) to their citizens, to divert people's purchasing power away from current consumption and into the government's coffers. Yet there are limits to how much people are willing to save, to how much they are willing to forego consumption. Governments have then introduced economic controls to allocate resources directly to war-related, and away from consumer-goods, production. They have also printed more money to finance the war. To prevent an immediate inflation of prices from consumer-goods shortages and the increased money supply (especially for vital goods such as food, rent, and clothing), wartime governments have also eventually introduced price controls and rationing.[18]

Germans had experienced such inflationary war finance during and after World War I. The Wilhelmine Reich had run up enormous war debts while more than doubling the money supply. It had weakened the economy's ability to service those debts by foregoing investment to divert resources to immediate war needs. Postwar democratic governments faced massive costs for demobilization, reparations, social programs, and interest on the massive government debt they had inherited. The Weimar Republic became trapped in inflationary policies that resulted in a 100 trillion percent inflation, 1914–23, effectively destroying the value of the government's debts and of all other paper assets, including people's life savings. German governments had shifted the costs of World War I almost entirely to one social group—the holders of paper assets.[19]

Desperate to recoup their losses, creditors (savers) demanded a revaluation of debts—their forced repayment at least partially in Gold Mark instead of worthless paper. Bolstered by a favorable 1923 decision by Germany's Supreme Court, creditors argued that principles of equity and good faith required that debtors pay back the real value of the loan, not some merely nominal sum. Unfortunately, imposing a 100 percent revaluation would have meant trying to reverse a decade of economic development and would almost certainly have been economically disastrous. The government, which was the biggest debtor, hence sought in December 1923 to ban revaluation outright. When that proved politically impossible, it drastically limited private-debt, and banned government-debt, revaluation.[20]

Outraged by government actions, creditors mounted a partially successful, but to them disappointing, campaign to expand the revaluation. In the 1924 parliamentary election campaigns, most political parties had promised substantial, often implicitly 100 percent, revaluation. The new governing coalition broke those promises when it promulgated final legislation in July 1925 offering 15–25 percent revaluation of private debts and 0–12.5 percent revaluation of public debts. Yet even though economic realities limited the revaluation the Weimar Republic could offer, it had more than doubled the revaluation amount creditors would be entitled to receive. Creditors, though, remained unshakably convinced that substantial, perhaps even 100 percent, revaluation was possible—and were properly outraged at the demagoguery of the political parties.[21]

The creditors' bitter disillusionment had important political consequences. The revaluation conflict left most creditors anticapitalist and antidemocratic. Although they were themselves "capitalists" (they wanted their capital, their lost savings, back), they reserved the term for the often economically powerful businessmen-debtors who had paid them off in paper currency and then opposed any revaluation. The free-market economy seemed to these creditors inhumanly unjust because it constituted their life savings as mere speculations that government policies could capriciously destroy. They further concluded that parliamentary democracy had proved itself in the revaluation struggle to be merely a corrupt facade behind which powerful but unscrupulous interests could expropriate honest German citizens. Many creditors, probably a majority, ended up voting in the early 1930s for Adolf Hitler's Nazi Party, which promised (though it did not deliver) 100 percent revaluation. Bitter memories of the 1920s ensured that post–World War II Germans would be determined that this time Germans would distribute the burdens of war equitably among different segments of the society.[22]

Despite Germany's horrific 1920s experience of hyperinflation, the Nazi regime pursued increasingly inflationary policies. It continued to run budget deficits and a loose monetary policy after 1935, even though full employment made such policies inflationary. Wartime production required massive expenditure increases, but the regime refused to increase taxes substantially, for fear of weakening popular morale. Tax revenues covered only about one-third of Germany's enormous wartime expenditures, and exactions from other countries an additional 14 percent. Government paper, primarily short-term, covered the remaining 55 percent. By April 1945, the Nazis had run up more than 400 billion RM in certificated debt for the German people. They also expanded currency in circulation from 10.9 billion RM in September 1939 to 70.3 billion RM at war's end.[23]

Because memories of Germany's World War I inflation and its consequences were still vivid, the Nazi regime sought to mask the nature of its policies, pursuing what Germans later called the "silent inflation." The government made its budget a state secret, to conceal its deficits. It avoided public bond sales because it feared giving citizens an opportunity to "vote" against the regime and its war by refusing to buy its bonds. Instead, it forced people to save by limiting their access to consumer goods and services, primarily through cuts in consumer goods production and through rationing, and by imposing rigid price controls. Despite the absence of desirable goods at official prices, the Gestapo was able to dissuade most Germans from offering goods and services for more than the state-mandated prices by imposing draconian punishments, including execution, for such black-market activities. Individuals had little choice but to deposit their unspendable income with savings banks and other financial institutions. The government then forced financial institutions to use the deposits to buy government paper. These polices created substantial suppressed inflationary pressures and drastically eroded, for the second time in a generation, the value of people's life savings.[24]

Despite government efforts, Germans came to recognize the inflationary implications of these policies. Already in 1939, the security forces reported, Germans were expressing fears of another inflation. Meanwhile, one could read descriptions of monetary and fiscal policies in the financial pages of the daily press. From early 1942, government spokesmen acknowledged the dangers of inflation. Nonetheless, like Hitler, they argued that the debt was being invested in expanding Germany's living space and productive assets and that the availability to a victorious Germany of cheap raw materials and labor from all of Europe would enable it to carry that debt, just like a successfully expanding private company. Yet after 1942, that gamble on victory seemed decreasingly likely to pay off, and investing in paper assets was hence becoming extremely unwise. Germans were increasingly unwilling to accept paper money, and some sellers began to demand that buyers pay them with in-kind supplements to inflated paper currency (despite the risks).[25]

Most Germans were in an unenviable quandary because so few could act to limit their losses. When the Nazis forced the powerful industrial magnate Alfred Hugenberg, who had no confidence in the currency, to sell his publishing empire for 64 million RM, he had the leverage to insist on being paid in shares of stock in various firms. The average citizen, though, could not easily find similar investment opportunities. Moreover, hoarding real goods as an inflation hedge — if you could find anyone foolish enough to sell them to you — was problematic. It was illegal and dangerous black marketeering, and falling bombs could destroy or invading soldiers might plunder your cache of goods anyway. Germans were forced to do what they ought to have known, and often did know, was foolish — invest in paper assets. Much of the postwar talk of the Nazis' silent inflation was just an attempt to mask this painful reality.[26]

Savers were a concretely identifiable group. They all possessed some legally binding claim to a share of the society's assets: a savings account, bond, or other debt instrument. They all shared the experience of seeing the value of that legal claim eroded by suppressed inflation, even though prices legally remained fixed. They hence suffered a creeping, de facto expropriation of their property. After the experience of the 1920s, Germans took it as a matter of course that savers were entitled to protection from such insidious attacks on their wealth. The form and degree of protection, though, remained unclear. Moreover, the implications of that identity as saver varied, depending on how much savings individuals had lost and how dependent they had been on them.

German economists knew early on that the Reich would face a difficult task in dealing with its soaring debt. As the bombing war spread, the government acknowledged ever new compensation claims for war damages. The Reich also promised generous future support to the increasing number of disabled veterans, war widows and war orphans, and disabled bombing victims. Such claims, while uncertificated (not formally embodied in debt instruments and not tradable), constituted an enormous additional obligation that any future German government would have to service. Moreover, from 1943 the prospect of total defeat loomed. That defeat would preclude access to foreign resources to finance German recovery, debt, and war-damage claims. Some German economists were discussing these issues among themselves. Nonetheless, most were unwilling to acknowledge the full scope of the problem or openly to entertain radical solutions, given the risk of arrest for defeatism. Indeed, that risk, the wartime struggle for survival, and inadequate information kept all but a few Germans from addressing postwar fiscal problems at all.[27]

One of the most painful aspects of Germany's World War II experience was the horrific bombing campaign that the Western Allies unleashed against Germany's cities and civilians. When precision bombing failed to work, the Britons and Americans resorted to area bombing: indiscriminate carpeting of German cities with incendiaries and high explosives, a practice Goebbels denounced, with some justice for once, as terror bombing.

Although the British and American governments initially repudiated any intention of attacking civilian targets from the air, both gradually shifted to unrestricted bombing. The German bombing of Warsaw, Rotterdam, and British cities provided some justification for widening the bombing campaign, but the main motives were expedient. Some Allied leaders seemed to believe that aerial bombardment could quickly break civilian morale or shatter the economy, forcing Germany to surrender. Most leaders, though, saw it as part of a larger strategy of draining Germany's ability to fight by soaking up scarce German resources in air defense, securing Allied air supremacy for a whole range of military purposes, and slowing and eventually strangling German war production.[28]

To minimize loss of life and conserve increasingly scarce resources for vital war workers, the Nazi regime encouraged and eventually compelled "nonessential" persons to leave the cities. They first evacuated children and mothers with young children. Later, they also evacuated older and unemployable individuals, often against their wills. These "evacuees," some 8 million by war's end, found themselves in villages and small towns whose inhabitants often saw these urbanites as the noxious carriers of alien corruption. The government forced those inhabitants of the villages and small towns who had "extra" rooms to accept these evacuees into their homes — a "temporary" solution that not infrequently dragged on for years. The need to share kitchens, baths, and toilets forced individuals into unwanted intimacy. Despite efforts by both evacuees and their unwilling hosts to make the most of an unfortunate situation, friction was inevitable and occasionally vicious. The evacuees were often desperately homesick and in some cases ignored Nazi regulations and returned to their home cities. Those who remained in the villages and small towns could only dream of an eventual return.[29]

Despite the evacuations, the effects of area bombing on German civilians were horrific. From 1942, German cities faced the horror of carpet bombing. By 1945, thousands of planes flew unopposed support missions for the Allied armies pouring into Germany. Inured to the use of force against a dehumanized enemy, many Allied pilots proved willing to attack virtually anything in Germany. Even tiny villages, farmsteads, columns of refugees, or individuals on foot could become targets for Allied planes. Within the 31 December 1937 area of the Reich, aerial attacks killed some 537,000 civilians (including refugees) and wounded some 762,000. An additional 32,000 foreigners and prisoners of war and 24,000 police and military personnel also died in the bombing war. The experience of being bombed, of cowering impotently in some darkened cellar or exposed doorway or under a bed, was terrifying. Postwar polling suggested that 41 percent of West Germans had experienced severe bomb attacks and that 21 percent had been bombed out.[30]

The loss of property was also enormous. In Germany's big cities, the loss of dwellings was in the range of 51 to 70 percent. In some smaller cities in the path of advancing armies, artillery attacks added to the destruction, with losses running as high as 99.2 percent of prewar dwellings. For all of West Germany the loss of dwellings was more than 20 percent, leaving millions of people homeless. The total destruction of a dwelling or business usually meant loss of all personal possessions or goods as well, and even partial destruction could devastate household goods and other property. Cherished mementos could never be replaced, but in wartime conditions neither could mundane but vital items: warm clothing, a bed, a stove, cooking pots, and so forth. Bombing also destroyed the livelihoods of millions of Germans. Not only did shopkeepers and artisans lose their business premises, inventories, and tools, but their employees were often left without suitable employment as well.[31]

While the "bomb-damaged" (*Ausgebombte* or *Fliegergeschädigte*) had the shared experience of loss, certain common problems, and a legal identity under the War-Damages Decree, they were not homogeneous. Their material losses might or might not have been accompanied by physical injury or the terror of dodging falling bombs. Moreover, the degree of loss varied enormously, from minimal to total. The government denied legal recognition to minor losses and to losses by "non-Aryans." As with the savers, the relative importance of the lost property to the individual strongly influenced the individual's attitude. The loss of a business could be economically, psychologically, and socially devastating. The loss of a home—even of a rented dwelling—often had a devastating psychological, as well as material, impact, even if one managed to salvage many possessions. Indeed, a renter who salvaged most possessions but had no place to sleep or a worker who lost a workplace might not count legally as bomb-damaged but could have experienced a worse loss than a bombed-out homeowner or businessman with other resources. Indeed, even substantial losses could seem relatively unimportant to someone who had other assets or the youth or talent to begin again. The first West German chancellor, Konrad Adenauer, for example, lost a house in Cologne to Allied bombing, but he had another house in Rhöndorf, a civil service pension, and a budding postwar career as a politician. He never expressed any public self-perception as war-damaged. These variations in the implications of the shared experience of material loss would play themselves out in the Lastenausgleich debate.[32]

Germans reacted to the bombing primarily with resignation. Insurrection against the Nazi regime seemed impossible. The very real danger of painful death loomed over any would-be rebel or even defeatist. Beyond that, Nazi propaganda worked to deny Germans any sense of alternatives except victory or annihilation. By late 1944, Goebbels could convincingly emphasize that German policies meant that a defeated Germany could expect only a brutally vengeful peace. Germans fought on, at the front and in the factories, hoping somehow to escape the worst.[33]

Some Germans did see the bombing as divine retribution. Bishop Theophil Wurm, head of the Evangelical Church in Württemberg, had in December 1938 written the Nazis, acknowledging "the state's right to fight Jewry which is a dangerous element." Yet by December 1943 he asserted that the "annihilatory policy against Jewry" was "a fateful injustice for the German people. . . . As does every conscious transgression of God's commandments, this too revenges itself sooner or later. Our *Volk* often perceives the sufferings that it must bear from enemy air attacks as retribution for what has been done to the Jews."[34]

This appeal to divine Providence to explain Germany's misery seems, though, to have had little resonance. Perhaps Wurm was right that many Germans shared his view during the war, though they more frequently spoke of the bombing as an inexplicable act of fate. Yet his view would only very infrequently be repeated during the Lastenausgleich debate. Most strikingly, Wurm himself had already changed his tune by May 1945, telling American military officials, "The heart of the German people beat for peace; the war was a [Nazi] Party war. And therefore one should not hold the whole German people responsible for the violence and terror methods of a system that was inwardly rejected by an exceedingly overwhelming majority."[35]

One of the Nazi regime's most criminal aspects, from the perspective of its own citizens, was the callous indifference to Germany's future with which the regime — and the officer corps — prolonged the war to the bitter end, long after they had to have known that defeat was inevitable. Hitler had ordered that every city, town, and village be defended to the death, so that from the autumn of 1944 total destruction threatened even the tiniest hamlet. Some fanatical Nazis did fight to the bitter end, causing thousands of deaths and additional destruction in a hopeless cause. Moreover, Hitler was convinced that Germans had failed in the great struggle for survival that he thought characterized life; in March 1945 he ordered that the retreating German forces destroy all means for the future existence of the German people. German troops proved less willing to carry out those orders than they had been to destroy property in other people's countries. Indeed, by March 1945 all but a few Germans were fed up with war and convinced defeat was inevitable; they sought only to surrender themselves and their places of residence — to the Western Allies if at all possible.[36]

As defeat approached, Nazi behavior served to discredit the party and its ideology. After 1942, the party took increasing responsibility for all aspects of German life, as it sought to mobilize the society more completely for total war. It thereby made itself responsible in the eyes of its subjects for the increasing misery and terror they were experiencing. When the party committed itself to defense to the death while the overwhelming majority of Germans sought only peace, it distanced itself from its popular base. As Allied troops arrived, some individual Nazis insisted on defense to the death, bringing or threatening to bring death and destruction to their neighbors. More frequently, however, they fled ignominiously or committed suicide, to escape the arrest and possible execution they feared at Allied hands. In doing so, they delegitimized themselves and the ideology that they represented. Hitler's suicide then discredited him and sealed the fate of Nazism.[37]

The scope of the Nazi debacle also precluded the kinds of delusions about military and political responsibility that had plagued German politics after World War I. German troops had still been on foreign soil when Germany negotiated the 1918 Armistice, and a revolution had broken out before the Armistice was implemented. Hence, the German military and German conservatives had been able to claim that their country had been undefeated in the field and had only had to surrender because of a "stab in the back" by traitorous prodemocratic forces. The Allies' 1940s insistence on unconditional German surrender, the Nazis' ability to maintain near total control until their defeat, and the total Allied occupation of the country meant that no one could blame Germany's democratic forces for defeat.[38]

EXPULSIONS

The stream of ethnic Germans who poured into rump Germany in 1944 and afterward was but one branch in a twentieth-century flood of human migrations. The rise of nationalism has changed governments' attitudes toward minorities, making them seem less exploitable subjects than potentially subversive outsiders and encouraging efforts to force people either to adopt the dominant national identity or to leave. The use of minority populations by foreign enemies as an excuse for intervening in a country's internal affairs has only strengthened the conviction that getting rid of foreign nationals, especially in exchange for one's own nationals, could be a useful policy. The period 1912–22 hence saw no less than eighteen refugee movements in the Balkans alone, including both spontaneous and planned exchanges of population.[39]

The Nazis made the mass expulsion of peoples on expedient nationalist grounds into a principle of statecraft. Hoping to purge Germany of "non-Aryans," they pursued policies that induced about half of Germany's Jewish population to emigrate from 1933 to 1939. After conquering Poland in 1939, they expelled ethnic Poles from some areas that had been Polish for centuries. To Germanize those areas, the Nazi regime negotiated with countries farther east to compel ethnic Germans living in those countries to abandon their ancestral homes and come "Home to the Reich." Many of these "Germans" had no desire to return to a "home" they had never seen. Nonetheless, they were forced to sell their assets and set off, usually on foot, for Greater Germany, where the Nazis resettled them in homes that had been confiscated from expelled Poles.[40]

By making systematic use of German minorities to the east to justify expansionist foreign policies, the Nazi regime encouraged other countries to eliminate those minorities. Most notoriously, the Nazis in 1938 annexed the Sudetenland, an area of Czechoslovakia occupied by ethnic Germans, and in 1939 invaded Poland, to "protect" German minorities. Yet the Nazis also used such minorities as a lever in dealing with other Eastern European countries. Having seen a German minority exploited to attack their sovereignty, exile Poles and Czechs in the early 1940s were already proposing to expel all Germans from their territory. When the Allies decided to compensate Poland for territorial losses to the USSR with the annexation of German territory, the Poles assumed that expelling the resident Germans would be necessary to ensure Polish control. Having seen Hitler use German minorities to start a horrifically destructive war, the Soviet government, and even some British and American officials, could also see expulsions as the easiest way to "tidy up" the potentially dangerous ethnic mixing that characterized Eastern Europe.[41]

The experience of German atrocities clinched the determination of Eastern Europeans to expel ethnic Germans from their territories. The Nazi regime considered the Slavs subhuman, and it ordered German occupation forces to treat them accordingly. German military personnel overwhelmingly cooperated in the systematic extermination of local elites and in draconian reprisals against occupied peoples who patriotically resisted German conquest. These policies were most barbarous in the Soviet Union, Poland, and Czechoslovakia but extended to Yugoslavia and even, near war's end, to nominal allies such as Romania and Hungary. From 1939 to 1945 Poland, for example, lost fully one-fifth of its population to Nazi-ordered German brutality. By war's end, Germans could expect little sympathy and much hatred from their eastern neighbors.[42]

Although Germans had varying degrees of knowledge of Nazi-ordered brutality, virtually all knew that German forces had done "terrible things" in the East and that they could expect no mercy from the invading Red Army. Soviet troops were often ready for revenge in any event, but the Soviet leadership sponsored a propaganda campaign urging them to brutalize the German population in retaliation for all that happened in the Soviet Union since 22 June 1941. A substantial number of Red Army troops proved ready to follow this advice. For example, during the Red Army's first, temporary, occupation of easternmost East Prussia (in October 1944), Soviet troops took a cruel revenge, brutally raping German women and murdering German civilians—elderly, women, children, even infants. Goebbels broadcast this evidence of the threat of Soviet vengeance, to stir Germans to greater resistance.[43]

Consequently, as the Red Army approached in 1945, millions of Germans fled their homes, usually in horrific circumstances. The "treks" by fleeing Germans took place in winter and early spring, in what was often brutally cold weather. Elderly people, women, and children loaded up carts with their most prized possessions, but people usually had to walk for hundreds of miles, especially as the carts often were stolen by Russian or German troops or had to be abandoned when the horses died or were confiscated. If Soviet troops overtook the refugees, women were raped, men were often killed, and German property was plundered. Hundreds of thousands of Germans died, from enemy attacks, cold, exhaustion, or starvation. By May 1945, some 5 million Germans from the East had fetched up in "rump Germany" (German territory west of the Oder and Neiße Rivers), usually with little more than the clothes on their backs.[44]

These spontaneous flights were only the beginning. The Poles and Czechs were determined to expel their German minorities. The Soviet government was quite willing to assist because of its own sympathy with brutalized fellow Slavs and because such expulsions would perpetuate German-Polish and German-Czech enmity, leaving Poles and Czechs dependent on the Soviet Union for protection. Soviet commanders hence looked the other way in May and June 1945 when Polish units began driving out, often most brutally, Germans who had remained in the territories east of the Oder-Neiße line that were to come under Polish administration.[45]

The Americans, Britons, and Russians had declared forced population transfers by the Nazis, 1939–44, to be war crimes, and Britain and the United States generally opposed such expulsions when directed at Germans. Yet British and American leaders thought they had little choice but to accept the 1945–48 expulsions of Germans by Eastern European states. They lacked the military forces and political will to attempt to reverse by force Soviet policy in Eastern Europe, especially as other issues seemed more important than the fate of former enemies. Besides, after the exposure of Nazi atrocities, they and their citizens felt little sympathy for Germans. Britons and Americans hence acquiesced in the expulsions, not only from Poland and Czechoslovakia, but also from the Soviet Union, Romania, Hungary, and Yugoslavia.[46]

Britons and Americans did seek to ensure, as the Potsdam Agreement declared, that such expulsions should "be effected in an orderly and humane manner," but they were unsuccessful. Eastern European governments sought to be rid of the Germans as quickly—and as profitably—as possible. Germans were loaded onto freight cars and sent off, usually without food or water, toward Germany. They were seldom allowed to take anything more than a single suitcase, and that and other possessions were frequently stolen from them. Their trains had the lowest priority and often took days to reach German territory. More than 16 million Germans had lived in the areas that Eastern European governments sought to clear of Germans, but fewer than 13 million German refugees fetched up in rump Germany. An indeterminate number remained in Eastern Europe, held back because their labor was too valuable to dispense with or choosing to melt into the local population by virtue of some Slavic ancestry. Nonetheless, more than 1 million and possibly as many as 2.25 million Germans died as a result of flight and expulsion.[47]

The shared experiences of expulsion, exile, and discrimination gave expellees a real and vivid sense of group identity. They had all been compelled by force or the threat of force to abandon their homes, and they were prevented by force from returning to those homes. They had lost their *Heimat* (their home and homeland), their livelihood, virtually all of their personal possessions, their social connections, and almost always one or more close relatives. No one could deny their emotionally devastated, homeless, and almost always impoverished situation in western Germany. They also faced substantial discrimination from the locals in that region. For example, expellees were not only the last hired and first fired, but western German villagers not infrequently denied them burial in the hallowed ground of the local church cemetery.

Yet, as with savers and the bomb-damaged, the experiences of individual expellees varied enormously. Some expellees had relatively easy journeys, whereas others suffered brutally. Many male expellees who had been prisoners of war did not personally experience expulsion, even if they could not return home. Those who had lost property usually had more at stake than did those who had had few material possessions. Those with relatives or other connections in the West had a far easier time of it than did those who were dumped in some village or camp with no friends or relatives to help them get back on their feet. Such differences would have crucial implications for the Lastenausgleich's development.[48]

The expellees faced a painfully uncertain future in a truncated, devastated Germany. Rump Germany, meanwhile, faced a herculean task in trying to integrate them — and all the other war-damaged — economically and socially.

For most Germans, the war's end proved to be relatively unimportant because dramatic change had begun in early 1943 and came to an end in 1948 and 1949. Mobilization for total war, from 1943 on, substantially eroded traditional socioeconomic relationships and laid the groundwork for Germany's postwar economic and social transformation. Defeat brought an end to combat, but the chaos that war produced, with its uncertainty, physical immiseration, malnutrition, separation of families, and breakdown of traditional communities, intensified in some ways with defeat and began to abate only in mid-1948.

Finally, the fundamental economic and political institutions that would characterize West (and East) Germany took form only in 1948 and 1949.[49]

The Lastenausgleich conflict reflects this complex development. Despite price controls, irresponsible fiscal policies began to pinch, in the form of black markets and shortages, in 1943, as the Nazis diverted more and more resources to the war effort. The bombing began to shatter German cities and destroy traditional livelihoods in earnest in 1943 as well. The chaotic mixing of Germans into new homes and homelands began with the evacuations of 1943–44 and the refugee treks of 1944–45, not with defeat in May 1945. Moreover, flight and expulsion continued — and in many places only began — after defeat, and they persisted on a systematic basis for three years and on an individual basis for more than a decade and a half. Finally, the paper assets that had been battered by inflation (including war-damages claims) still existed, if only formally, until mid-1948. Germans could only begin imagining, let alone implementing, a Lastenausgleich after 1945.

Crucially, the Lastenausgleich was only one among a plethora of burdens the Nazis had bequeathed. Into the mid-1950s, German taxpayers had to pay "occupation costs" to support Allied armies in Germany. Those payments would absorb over half of West German central government revenue in 1950. Germans would feel politically compelled to provide assistance to millions of people who had been racially and politically persecuted, the "war-injured" (disabled veterans and civilian casualties of military action), war widows and orphans, returning prisoners of war (POWs), expellees and refugees from the East (including from the Soviet Occupation Zone/German Democratic Republic), displaced civil servants, savers, and Reich debt holders. In addition, the society would finance massive housing construction, the costs of rearmament against the menace of Soviet attack, renewed servicing of Germany's prewar foreign debt, and steps to allow war victims to share in the economic growth the society enjoyed in the 1950s. The war-damaged would face serious competition in the struggle over shares of the economic and fiscal pie.

Chapter 2

OBSTACLES AND OPPORTUNITIES

Germany's devastating defeat created both obstacles and opportunities. Germans certainly did not have an "Hour Zero," as many of them imagined, in which they could start completely fresh—with either a totally new beginning or a restoration of the "good old days" that had existed before 1933 or 1914. Too much remained of their own distant and recent past, and angry enemies-turned-occupiers also limited their freedom of action. Yet Nazi totalitarianism and total defeat had swept away much of their traditional culture and institutions, so that they had both the need and the opportunity for some fundamental rebuilding.[1]

As the war-damaged cast about for recompense amid the chaos of defeat, they too faced obstacles and opportunities. Massive destruction made paying for compensation difficult, and the disappearance of the German state left them without any obvious source of aid. Yet traditional German values such as the sanctity of private property, certain elements of Nazi ideology, and the need to include all Germans in some stable new economic, social, and political order gave the war-damaged the bases on which to construct a convincing claim to recompense.

POLITICAL CONSTRAINTS, POLITICAL OPTIONS

Postwar Germans, including the war-damaged, initially faced a highly unfavorable political context for dealing with their problems. They had the opportunity, though, to struggle to reestablish a political identity and to define the contours of a Lastenausgleich.

Convinced, with considerable justice, that Germany had started two devastating wars within a generation, the Allies (Britain, France, the Soviet Union, and the United States) were determined to deny Germans the opportunity to start a third. They foresaw a long-term process of reeducating Germans to become peaceful, democratic members of the civilized community of nations. They declared on 5 June 1945 that the German state had ceased to exist and that they were assuming its sovereign powers. They initially banned all political activity by Germans, to prevent Nazi activity and to ensure absolute Allied control over German life. In the process, they undercut potentially important grassroots German efforts at democratization. Germans would until 1949 be almost entirely dependent on the occupying powers to initiate solutions to Germany's problems.[2]

The Allies planned in 1945 to rule Germany as a unit through an Allied Control Council in Berlin, but irreconcilable conflicts among them soon paralyzed joint Allied policy making. Long-standing Anglo-American mistrust of Soviet Communism was only exacerbated by Soviet determination to impose friendly, Communist governments on its neighbors in Eastern Europe and by Soviet probing for advantage elsewhere. Within Germany, the Soviets took steps in their zone that were perfectly logical in terms of their ideology and goals but that contradicted the policies of their "partners." The blocking of most bank deposits, the replacement of private banks with a state banking system, and the nationalization of most large firms were only the most obvious sources of divergence. Meanwhile, fearful of yet another German invasion, the French effectively vetoed any Allied steps toward centralized institutions in Germany. Reparations proved particularly divisive. The Soviets and French sought enormous reparations from all zones to help rebuild their devastated countries. Britons and Americans resisted because they feared reparations would weaken their zones' economies, compelling their taxpayers to subsidize their German enemies. General Lucius D. Clay, American commander in Germany, became increasingly frustrated by Soviet and especially French resistance to joint measures to promote a German economic recovery that might ease U.S. occupation burdens. In May 1946, as a bargaining ploy, he unilaterally halted reparations deliveries from the American Zone, a step that poisoned relations with Moscow and strained relations with Paris.[3]

Nonetheless, the alliance initially held—at the cost of stalemate. None of the occupiers wanted to provoke any new, costly international conflict so soon after the devastation of World War II or to assume the onus of having divided Germany and Europe. Each hoped for some satisfactory settlement in Germany that would maximize its security and minimize its costs. They limped along, searching in vain for common ground and leaving many problems in Germany unaddressed.[4]

Meanwhile, Germany's economic and social context had been transformed. The Nazis, intentionally and unintentionally, had speeded up the complex processes of secular change that had been transforming Germany's economic and social institutions and relationships for generations. The Nazis' efforts to assert totalitarian control and their emphasis on equal opportunity for and maximum performance from all "racial comrades" had eroded traditional values and social relationships. Economic recovery and rearmament had spurred social and geographical mobility, further eroding traditional ties and attitudes. The war economy had strengthened big business at the expense of agricultural and artisanal sectors. Defeat and occupation had discredited the military elite, and the Soviets had eliminated East Elbian landed elites. Forced shifts of Germany's population had dissolved traditional communities in the East and transformed communities in the West with floods of refugees. These developments had strengthened Germany's industrial and Western orientations. Finally, the Nazi and Allied elimination of virtually every existing social organization had left more or less cleared sites on which Germans would have to create new institutions or re-create old ones in changed circumstances.[5]

Germans struggled desperately to regain their footing politically. Most Germans had in the 1930s and 1940s come to accept the legitimacy of the Third Reich — or at least of its leader, Adolf Hitler. Catastrophic defeat and Hitler's suicide had then delegitimated that political order. Revelations about the horrors of Nazi concentration and death camps only added to the revulsion and confusion Germans felt. They had thought of themselves as civilized people, perhaps even the master race. Now they were not only defeated and occupied but had become an object of international scorn for the barbarous acts committed in their names and by many of them.[6]

The dismal failure and criminal consequences of the political choice Germans had made in 1933 did seem to some Germans to cry out for a complete reassessment of Germany's political system, economic structures, social relationships, and cultural assumptions and for a fundamentally new beginning. They reacted to the horror of Nazi crimes and the devastating thoroughness of defeat with a real, if often temporary, sense that Germans had no choice but to start over because past solutions had failed so dismally and because the destruction had been so total. Such people were most important in the immediate postwar years because they tended to be among the politically most active.[7]

Supporters of a "forward-looking" Lastenausgleich often favored such a far-reaching break with the corrupted German past and creation of a fundamentally new German future. Such a Lastenausgleich would not compensate lost assets but would assist needy war-damaged to build for themselves, and the West German economy, a solid future. The SPD and the trade unions, not surprisingly, preferred a more forward-looking Lastenausgleich. As expellee and SPD politician Pastor Heinrich Albertz asserted, "What interests me is what is possible now and what is necessary for the renewal of Germany, and what interests me is just this presentness, so that I can set on their feet people who, on the day . . . they can . . . return to Silesia, will not be living — in their political views — in the year 1914." Other groups, including the business community and various Catholic social groups, were also attracted to such a Lastenausgleich.[8]

Most Germans reacted in 1945 not with a commitment to reassessment and transformation but with apathy and a denial of responsibility. Nazi politics had been all-pervasive but had proved to be a disastrous lie. Perhaps more important, the crimes were so horrific and the destruction so shattering that genuine reflection was painful — and often potentially dangerous for compromised individuals who could face severe punishment for Nazi activities or war crimes. Forgetting was much easier, as Germans preferred to focus on getting on with their lives, on somehow surviving what they liked to think of as the blows of an inexplicable, and undeserved, fate. Memory generally kicked in again at the moment at which one could start describing oneself as a victim — of bombing, expulsion, or something else. Indeed, to the extent that Germans did talk of Germany's victims, they almost invariably did so only to highlight their own suffering, relativizing that of non-German victims.[9]

Most surprising, but most important, was the near absence of support for a return to Nazism after April 1945. The Allies had been deeply fearful of an underground resistance movement by fanatical Nazis, the so-called Werewolves. No such movement appeared. In fact, virtually no one in postwar Germany was willing to identify him- or herself as a Nazi. Doing so publicly could well have brought prosecution, but available evidence suggests that Germans were generally unwilling to do so even privately. To the contrary, Germans overwhelmingly sought to distance themselves from the Nazi movement. All those former Nazis had certainly not become liberal democrats overnight, and expressions of authoritarian attitudes would resurface periodically. Nonetheless, at no time after 1945 was Nazism an acceptable political alternative for most Germans.[10]

Overall, the Allies' de-Nazification policies contributed to anchoring this repudiation of Nazism. For all their problems, the Nuremberg war-crimes trials of Nazi leaders demonstrated to all but the most obtuse Germans that their country had engaged in an aggressive war and brutal crimes against humanity. Similarly, de-Nazification processes revealed the egoism, brutality, and corruption that had characterized Nazi rule. In the crucial years 1945–49, the Allies also banned from political and interest-group activity former Nazis and anyone who articulated antidemocratic attitudes. The most compromised and presumably most authoritarian Germans were hence unable to influence developments when political life in Germany was beginning anew. In addition, the experience of internment for Nazi activities for up to two years seems to have been so painful and humiliating that former Nazis either did not resume political activity or, if they did, distanced themselves from neo-Nazism.[11]

The Allies not only blocked some people from political activity, they also promoted others whom Germans initially might not have chosen. West Germans seemed likely to adopt some form of democracy, because of both the failure of "totalitarian dictatorship" and the desires of the democratic Western occupying powers, but they would not necessarily have adopted parliamentary democracy. Postwar Germans generally saw the Weimar Republic more as a mistake to be learned from than as a model to be emulated. The Nazis had secured power because of a widespread belief that the "Weimar system"—parliamentary democracy and free-market economics—had failed. Germans in the late 1940s, from all across the political spectrum, expressed serious concern about the German people's susceptibility to demagogues; they also often denounced political parties as divisive and parliamentary democracy as inefficient or corrupt. Many postwar Germans promoted corporatist forms of democracy based not on individual voters but on the elected representatives of key socioeconomic groups. Yet when the Western Allies licensed newspapers and political parties in the late 1940s, they sanctioned those formed primarily by Germans who had been politically active in the pre-1933 Weimar Republic and who, except for the Communists, were committed to parliamentary democracy. Allied choices guaranteed supporters of liberal, parliamentary democracy at least a second chance.[12]

The form of Germany's economic system was also uncertain. For most post-1945 Germans, 1929 marked the end of the era of capitalism. The weak economic recovery of the mid-1920s and the horrendous unemployment and catastrophic drops in industrial production of the early 1930s had only been overcome through often substantial government intervention in the economy. Indeed, the Nazis had introduced an arguably noncapitalist economic system. The brutal postwar shortages suggested that only the most careful organization and planning, to exclude waste, would allow German recovery. Most Germans were in 1945 convinced that the postwar period would be marked by some kind of socialist, or at least social, economy. The Social Democrats had long been committed to socialism, and the newly founded Christian Democratic Union inclined toward "socialism," toward some significant social direction of the economy between 1945 and 1948. Even businessmen often hoped that economic guidance (preferably through business groups, cartels, and business-government cooperation) would allow them to manage economic development to some degree independently of competitive forces.[13]

Central to postwar German efforts to position themselves in the world was the desire to find a "Third Way" between heartless capitalism and brutal Communism. Germans have often seen themselves as holding a middle position, for example between the rationalistic West and the mystical East. Now they found themselves quite literally in the middle of the Cold War between the Soviet Union and the Western Allies. Most Germans hoped to synthesize the individual freedom of the West and of free markets with the communalism of the East and the social direction of Communism. Historians have tended to emphasize the Marxian and Christian Socialist element in this desire for a Third Way, but understanding immediate post-1945 German politics means understanding the desire among nonsocialists for some Third Way of their own. Although the CDU dropped its early socialism, the party's strong trade-union wing, the long German statist tradition, and Catholic social teaching limited the appeal of laissez-faire and kept the party committed to a significant government role in the economy. Even the liberal Free Democratic Party acknowledged in the immediate postwar period that some degree of planning, preferably organized through business groups, would be inevitable.[14]

Postwar neoliberals such as Ludwig Erhard offered another nonsocialist new beginning, the "social-market economy." Their ideas have often seemed the restorationist element par excellence because of their commitment to free markets and private property. They did reject government intervention in production because of its inefficiency and of the threat to individual choice it entailed, preferring as much free competition as possible on the production side, bolstered by the widest ownership of capital. Yet the lesson they learned from interwar German history was that capitalism could not survive in a laissez-faire form. The economic crises of the 1920s and 1930s had thrown millions of people into bankruptcy, unemployment, and misery — and into the arms of anticapitalist radicals of the Right and Left. Neoliberals concluded that Germans were simply not going to support a system that could condemn them so easily and so capriciously to misery. They hence accepted the need for social programs to moderate the often enormous income inequality and the occasional desperate misery that free competition could generate. Nonetheless, they expected that state policies to maximize competition would minimize the necessity for social programs and that whatever social programs proved necessary would be "market conforming."[15]

The war-damaged argued for recompense in the context of this debate about West Germany's future socioeconomic order. The demand for a Lasten-ausgleich was rooted in the desire to escape the consequences of the unrestrained operation of material — including market — forces, often while preserving property and hierarchy against the demands of Marxian socialism. The bomb-damaged called in 1946 for a "socialism of the deed" and "a strict guidance of the reconstruction" by the government. Generally speaking, wider-reaching proposals to transfer wealth to secure a Lastenausgleich presupposed a greater degree of public intervention in private economic decisions, to ameliorate the shocks from such transfers. Conversely, narrower limits on government intervention in private decisions would tend to limit the amount of wealth one could force people to transfer without risking economic difficulties. Moreover, funneling all Lastenausgleich levies into a single, government-controlled fund would create significant potential for government intervention in the economy. Germans, war-damaged and undamaged, were conscious of these implications.[16]

The near complete ideological triumph of the social-market economy in Germany has tended to obscure the contingency and limited nature of that outcome. Postwar West Germans were not predestined to accept the social-market economy. They contemplated various alternatives after 1945, and most Germans were still not committed to it in 1951. Since then, West German markets have been much less free than social-market economy ideology demands. Moreover, other postwar Western Europeans successfully adopted several variants of a free economy, with varying degrees and types of government intervention. West Germany could well have chosen another model besides the social-market economy. From the perspective of the 1990s, the more radical Lastenausgleich proposals may seem to have been totally infeasible; they did not seem infeasible to most Germans in the late 1940s—and in the right circumstances might have been introduced.[17]

ECONOMIC CHAOS, ECONOMIC HOPE

The Nazi regime had left Germans a devastated economy whose extreme weakness would complicate future efforts to finance recompense for the war-damaged and other war victims. That economy barely functioned in May 1945. Systematic destruction of transportation, plus the exhaustion of many stocks in the last months of the Nazi war effort, had deprived the economy of necessary inputs, including food for workers. Labor shortages were severe because millions of former forced laborers departed, while Russia and France initially kept millions of able-bodied German prisoners of war to help rebuild their economies. Allied occupation policies interfered with the free flow of vitally necessary commodities. By December 1945, German industrial production had recovered to only about 20 percent of its 1938 level.[18]

The functioning of the German economy had been predicated on an ability to export that scarcely existed in 1945. Germans needed to import food and raw materials to have the physical energy to work and the inputs for manufacturing and economic recovery. Yet they could earn such commodities only by first manufacturing goods for export—even though they lacked many of the necessary inputs for production. They faced a long, painful crawl back to prosperity through rigorous squeezing of domestic consumption, unless they could somehow get foreign assistance to prime the pump.[19]

The legacy of Nazi controls created severe problems. By war's end, an elaborate system of controls determined the allocation of resources, not the market. Given the desperate postwar shortages and disruptions, each occupying power, even the free-market Americans, believed they had to continue the Nazi economic system, at least temporarily. The jumble of controls had been improvised piecemeal over a decade to manage a wartime economy embedded in a European economic network. They now had to function for a devastated peacetime economy cut off from its traditional markets. Furthermore, they were now being administered not by a national government for national purposes, but by foreigners for their own purposes. Germans sought to evade the controls they often considered illegitimate, compounding their inherent inefficiency.[20]

The overhang of purchasing power that the Nazis had created was another serious obstacle to German economic recovery. In relying on inflationary means of war finance, they had given German citizens hundreds of billions of Reichsmark in claims to the society's wealth and future production. More than 300 billion RM of those claims were in savings accounts that Germans could turn into a flood of cash on short notice. As Germans began doing so, to deal with postwar problems, they seriously distorted economic activity. Germany could only eliminate controls and reestablish free markets if it could eliminate that overhang of purchasing power through open inflation or a currency reform, thereby allowing the reemergence of a meaningful price structure.[21]

Many Americans and Europeans so mistrusted Germans, after two world wars in a generation, that they wanted to block German recovery to prevent future German aggression. The notorious Morgenthau Plan, which sought to limit German industrial production drastically, was never implemented, but its supporters initially blocked overt U.S. efforts to promote German economic recovery. Hoping to prevent future German rearmament, punish Germans for past aggression, and (in some cases) limit German competition, the Allies in March 1946 imposed the Level of Industry Plan. The plan limited German economic capacity to 75 percent of the 1936 level, with special limits and some outright bans on arms-related industries. "Excess" capacity was then to be dismantled and transferred as reparations to Germany's former enemies. The German economy was so weak in the late 1940s that it never actually bumped up against the plan's limits, especially after they were raised in 1947. Moreover, changing Anglo-American attitudes assured that relatively little dismantling would take place in their zones. Nonetheless, the psychologically depressing impact of the limits hampered investment and slowed German recovery.[22]

At war's end, much of Germany's received social structure and relationships had simply dissolved, and Germans had no way of knowing what would take their place. Millions of German men were prisoners of war, millions of Germans, perhaps half the population, were on the road in flight from bombs and enemy troops, and millions were dead as a result of the war, so very few German families remained intact. Inflation, bombing, expropriations in the Soviet Zone, and expulsion had destroyed the livelihoods of millions. De-Nazification was driving millions of middle- and upper-class men from their traditional occupations and, often, into internment camps. Massive shortages so characterized the society that virtually all Germans had experienced downward social mobility. Usually, class is the single biggest determinant of life chances, but for Germans it had become, at least temporarily, the whims of war.[23]

As Martin Enssle and Michael Wildt have shown, scarcity was the central fact of Germans' postwar experience. Shortages had begun in wartime, but the devastated postwar economy could not even meet the most basic needs of the German population. Official food rations, for example, never rose above 1,600 calories per day—if one could even find those rations in the shops. A desperate scramble to survive characterized Germans' lives, and the experience of scarcity would mark Germans into the 1950s. The focus on work and performance that became the hallmark of West Germans had roots before 1945, but this experience of desperate need made productive work seem especially crucial.[24]

The economy's long-term prospects were much better than 1945 circumstances suggested. Despite the devastation Germany had suffered, its productive machinery proved hard to destroy. The country had also devoted substantial resources to expanding productive capacity during the war, with annual net investment of 5.8 percent, 1940–45. Thus, even after reparations and dismantling, West Germans disposed of 11 percent more productive capital in 1948 than they had in 1938, and that capital was newer and of higher average quality. Meanwhile, the Allies had to begin repairing the worst-hit sectors, transportation and coal mining, in order to supply their own troops and peoples. Furthermore, the labor market was extremely favorable for reconstruction. The average human capital of the surviving German workforce was among the highest in the world. Millions of Germans, especially expellees, desperately needed to build a new existence, forcing them to be flexible and cooperative. Through its investment and labor policies, and the unintended consequences of defeat, the Nazis had left behind a more "modernized" productive plant and workforce while shattering any delusions of German autarky. West Germany had the prerequisites for an economic "miracle" after 1946.[25]

Further, the forces in American and British society that sought to punish Germany would eventually be overmatched by forces that sought to help Germany recover so that it could contribute to European prosperity and help contain Communism. American forces arrived in Germany with a can-do attitude. They were inclined to build, not hold the Germans down. They certainly did not want to watch Germans, especially women and children, starve. Moreover, the destruction in Germany was so great that Americans quickly concluded that the problem would not be to keep Germany down but to help it rebuild so it could pay its own way. Similar concerns would come to influence British officials.[26]

Germans could not foresee this glowing economic future in the late 1940s and early 1950s. Recovery after World War I, when Germany had experienced much less destruction and disruption, had been slow and had been followed scarcely a decade later by a disastrous depression. The degree of insecurity that postwar Germans experienced was unprecedented, with over half the population affected by one or another of the major blows war and defeat had imposed. West Germans could not be at all sure how much wealth they would have in the future out of which to rebuild their own lives, recompense war damages, and deal with the many victims (e.g., the politically persecuted, disabled veterans, war widows) the Nazi regime had left behind. On the one hand, considerable pressure existed to focus on increasing future production and reestablishing some degree of personal security, not compensating past losses. On the other, redistributing surviving wealth, including its limited capital stock, could seem the only way quickly to help the immiserated.[27]

DEALING WITH PAST DEBTS

In the context of political and economic weakness, one relic of the past, the problem of the Reich (central government) debt, including war-damages claims, loomed especially large after 1945. That debt represented hundreds of billions in claims against the former German state that constituted property for millions of German citizens. Germans could never meet all those claims, but they could not ignore their fellow citizens' property rights, either.

Aside from imports or seizures in occupied territories, which played a secondary role, Germany's wartime consumption could come only from prewar or wartime German production. By 1939 the Nazis had not accumulated even a fraction of the matériel necessary to fight a total war. Nor could they fire in 1943 an artillery shell produced in 1956. So the Nazis had supplied their war effort primarily out of wartime national production, by drastically squeezing current consumption in Germany to free up resources for the war effort. Germans had already paid for war between 1933 and 1945, by working longer and harder and by accepting a drastically lower standard of living—however grudgingly.[28]

To strengthen wartime morale and to assure citizens of a more acceptable distribution of the costs of war, however, the Nazis had provided Germans with hundreds of billions in *future* claims on the economy, with generous promises of extra shares of future national production. They had done so partly by selling government paper to savings institutions to cover the forced savings of the citizenry. They had also promised recompense for wartime damages and injuries, creating additional uncertificated government obligations that constituted property. That is the real nature of war finance through (domestic) debt—to recompense some citizens for wartime sacrifices after the fact, at the expense of others, by shifting the distribution of future national income. Whether individual Germans came out ahead in that shift would depend on how much in state obligations they had accumulated during the war or had inherited or purchased speculatively after the war; how much they owed in taxes after the war; and how their particular claims fared in the inevitable currency reform. Some (not all born after the war) would pay more in taxes than they received for their claims against the state and would be net losers, whereas others (not all of whom would have been alive during the war) would pay less in taxes than they received in payments and would be net winners.[29]

In 1945, though, the claims the Nazi regime had guaranteed, the property rights it had recognized, far exceeded the German economy's current wealth or future ability to pay. Postwar estimates of the Reich's total obligations started with the certificated debt of 420 billion RM and rose to as high as 1 trillion RM when one included uncertificated debt. Worse, contemporaries estimated remaining real wealth in Germany at less than 200 billion RM. Existing real property invariably had owners who would defend their property rights vigorously against efforts to tax them to realize the property claims of Reichsmark creditors and the war-damaged. Future German governments would in practice find it impossible to extract sufficient revenue from the citizenry to service all of the enormous debt that the Nazi government had created.[30]

Germans, or the occupying powers, hence had to decide how much debt to service and then *choose* which promises to honor and which to break. That set of choices would determine whose private property the state would seize (through currency reform, debt repudiation, or taxation) to meet the costs of defeat. It would also determine how much each individual and each stratum in German society would ultimately contribute to financing war and defeat. Most 1940s Germans recognized that the way in which Germany consolidated its war debt would constitute the primary policy for distributing the costs of World War II within German society. They also knew they did not want to repeat the 1920s policy of allowing inflation to impose these costs one-sidedly on paper-asset holders.[31]

That realization played a central role in the precocious organization of the bomb-damaged and savers. On 30 March 1946, school administrator Adolf Bauser founded the Federation of Savers and Bomb-Damaged, in Stuttgart. Having organized the main savers group during the 1920s hyperinflation and the main creditor political party thereafter, Bauser understood that the 1940s debate over currency reform and Reich debt revolved around the same issues of who would bear war's burdens as had the revaluation struggle of the 1920s. He was determined that in the 1940s he and his fellow bombed-out and savers should not lose their compensation claims and savings (a second time) to inflation or "unsocial" currency reform. Consciously seeking to learn from the 1920s creditors' mistakes and failures, he repeatedly admonished the bomb-damaged and savers that they would have to organize effectively to secure generous solutions to the war-damage and currency-reform problems from the undamaged majority. Drawing on the prestige and contacts he had developed as a prewar leader of the creditors, Bauser soon succeeded in uniting virtually all bomb-damaged groups in western Germany under his leadership in the

Central Association of Bomb- and Currency-Damaged (Zentralverband der Flieger- und Währungsgeschädigten, the ZvF), which would successfully claim to represent all bomb-damaged and, to a lesser extent, savers, in the western zones.[32]

The war-damaged were at great pains to identify themselves as expropriated, impoverished, declassed citizens who could become radicalized—just as had 1920s creditors. In a 1946 speech, Bauser reminded his listeners, "The false solution after the First World War had politically catastrophic consequences, for, as a result, millions of expropriated savers fell victims to the enticements of the inflammatory and deceitful propaganda of the Nazis." Failure to provide a just balancing out this second time would, he contended, be politically even more fateful. Wilhelm Mattes, who served as Hessian finance minister in 1932 and 1945–46 and who succeeded Bauser as ZvF head in 1948, also warned, "If a balancing out of capital that corresponds to just claims does not come about, then it is our firm conviction that the death knell for private property in Germany will have sounded. Great segments of those robbed of their assets without their own fault will turn to political radicalism and join the ranks of those who are fundamental opponents of private property."[33]

Significantly, the undamaged were inclined to accept that the danger of radicalization was real. Remembering the 1920s, they agreed that the revaluation conflict had had devastating consequences for Weimar democracy and that Germany had to act more justly this time to prevent a second radicalization. In calling for measures to integrate the expellees into West German society, including a Lastenausgleich, the liberal Free Democratic Party (FDP) argued, "It must be prevented . . . that a self-enclosed 5th estate develops, which, if it is not integrated into the people as a whole, can easily develop into a revolutionary and revolutionizing estate." Even neoliberal economists, who sought to reorganize the nation's finances most efficiently in a currency reform, recognized that war damages claims represented a legal and moral debt no German government could ignore. They usually agreed with Erhard (whose parents had lost their life savings in the 1920s hyperinflation) that a just distribution of war burdens was a prerequisite to establishing legitimacy for free markets.[34]

The war-damaged were favorably positioned to win some sort of compensation, but they could not expect smooth sailing. Their sheer numbers did make them a political force that Germans could not ignore, and memories of the "unsocial" and radicalizing currency stabilization of 1923/24 gave them a powerful tool for shaping public discourse about how to distribute this war's costs. Nonetheless, other German war victims were also demanding assistance and warning of the danger that they would be radicalized if ignored. The war-damaged faced often vigorous competition for minimal resources, and they would have to work to justify their particular demands in a complex environment.[35]

The war-damaged, especially those who were organized, often looked backward. They wanted to anchor their compensation claims by arguing that the claims were still legally binding under the 1940 War-Damages Decree, and they hoped to shift enough assets to restore the prewar distribution of wealth. Unfortunately, they could neither make their legal claim stick nor ignore the impact of a decade of history.

The war-damaged repeatedly sought to root their claim in the 1940 decree. Virtually all of the bomb-damaged had registered their losses with government officials; like the savers, they had an official, if uncertificated, legal claim, recognized by a German government, to a specific Reichsmark sum. The expellees had also suffered war-related material losses, such as the decree had covered. All war-damaged would have preferred simply to (re)assert their clear legal status — and the right to full payment of their Reichsmark claims.[36]

Unfortunately, Germany's defeat was so thorough that the war-damaged arguably lacked any legally enforceable claims. On 5 June 1945, the occupying powers dissolved the German state, announcing that they "assume supreme authority with respect to Germany." The risk of legal uncertainty was so great that the Allies did allow all but egregiously racist or fascist Nazi legislation and judicial decisions to stand, and after 1949 the Federal Republic of Germany would consider itself the legal successor to the German nation-state (whenever it proved convenient to do so). Most of the war-damaged hence insisted that their legal claims against the "German state" were still fully binding. Nonetheless, laying claims against a no-longer-existent state was problematic, as some war-damaged individuals acknowledged, especially when those claims had been predicated on conquering and exploiting other peoples.[37]

More important, the Nazi regime had left behind so many claims and such a devastated economy that German society was insolvent in 1945. The maintenance of price controls meant that the value of war-damage claims continued to exist formally. Yet, as Federal Finance Minister Fritz Schäffer later argued, in practice "the claims against the Reich have lost their inherent economic worth" because any successor to the Reich would lack the assets to pay them all. In deciding which claims it could meet, any new German state would have to look to the nation's future, not to an individual's past claims, because the whole life of the people depended on reestablishing stable monetary and fiscal conditions. Even to the extent one acknowledged that a legal claim had once existed, a Finance Ministry official later argued, this claim "would have to be regulated anew statutorily," as in a bankruptcy, with the legislator free to choose to "provide compensation or aid or to eliminate the claim." Crucially, the Constitutional Court of the Federal Republic of Germany would in 1962 rule that this line of argumentation was constitutionally correct.[38]

The Allies further eroded war-damage claims when they blocked compensation payments to the war-damaged. In spring 1945 German *Länder* (state) administrations generally took over payments to war-injured and war-damaged individuals, in place of the now defunct Reich, but by autumn 1945 each of the occupiers had banned compensation payments to war-damaged in its zone. They apparently sought to ensure that Germans suffered directly for the consequences of German aggression. The Allies did allow the continued registration of war-damage claims, but they had de facto repealed the payment provisions of the War-Damages Decree. If the war-damaged wanted restitution, they were going to have to find some new entity from which to obtain it — and some new basis on which to justify it.[39]

The expellees did not even have a notional legal claim. The Nazis' 1940 decree applied only to damages that occurred *during* hostilities. Yet none of the refugees had officially lost their property until the Allies agreed at Potsdam in July 1945 to sanction the expulsion of Germans from Eastern Europe, that is, until after hostilities had ended and the German state whose legislation promised recompense had ceased to exist. Further, more than 40 percent of expellees came from areas that had only briefly become German by virtue of conquest or that had never been legally part of the German Reich; they would be trying to claim compensation from a formerly existing state based on its brutal conquest of its neighbors or from a state of which they had never been citizens.[40]

Some Germans were quite willing to say that no *legal* claim had ever existed for the expellees. For example, the first official German Lastenausgleich proposal called for recompense for expellees from outside Germany "even though until now no claim against the Reich existed for them." These ethnic German refugees, a Finance Ministry official noted, had never been German citizens, "have contributed nothing to the national well-being, and also have never been under the protection of the Reich." Moreover, Walter Seuffert said that one must state plainly that there was no law anywhere making the new Federal Republic legally obligated for the disastrous Allied policies that had led to the expulsions. This willingness of some Germans to acknowledge a legal claim for the bomb-damaged while denying one to (many) expellees was particularly galling for expellees.[41]

Absent a convincing legal claim against the state, the war-damaged could in theory have identified a specific victimizer from whom to demand compensation, as is common practice when an individual suffers an injury. As a finance official later commented, "Claims to restitution for damages or for recompense are directed, according to general principles, against that person who culpably has caused the damage."[42] The war-damaged deployed this argument, but it proved ineffective.

In a private-law context, the war-damaged could have tried to sue the Allies for damages. Allied acts — military action (especially bombing), sanction of expulsions, and, later, currency reform—were the immediate causes of the damages that the Germans suffered because of the war. Yet neither the British nor the American, let alone Eastern European, governments were going to ask their taxpayers to help pay for the war damages Allied forces had caused in defending their countries against German aggression and atrocities.[43]

The Nazi regime had started the war that had provoked the Allies to self-defense, making the "Nazis" (party leaders or members) another potential victimizer. Through 1948, a number of individuals and groups, damaged and undamaged, proposed forcing the Nazis to help make good the damages from "their" war. SPD head Kurt Schumacher argued in summer 1945, "Above all, the consequences [of the war] should be borne by those whose policies brought about the catastrophe." A finance official noted the logic in principle of dunning the "war criminals, [Nazi] activists, etc." for restitution. As one impoverished bombing victim wrote, "It should be self-evident that all [Nazi] party comrades shall bear their own burdens, and moreover that their capital shall be seized for the Lastenausgleich. They cannot expect to be compensated for troubles they themselves brought on."[44]

While such attacks on the Nazis did not disappear after 1948, they would tail off dramatically. In 1946 and 1947 the Allies passed legislation seizing and redistributing the assets of the Nazi Party and related organizations, eliminating that source of revenue. Also, during the period 1945–48, de-Nazification tribunals had fined many Germans for their activities under the Nazi regime, reducing the assets of former Nazis and limiting the returns from any special levies on them. Moreover, combining fines on Nazi activities with punitive Lastenausgleich levies did raise troubling questions of double punishment.[45]

Just as important, German attitudes toward de-Nazification changed. Most postwar Germans hoped to shift all the blame for German aggression and atrocities onto a narrow circle of party leaders. They asserted a dubious distinction between honorable Nazis, who had acted decently (at least toward their German neighbors) even if they had been party members, and dishonorable Nazis, who had acted brutally or exploitatively. Nonetheless, the Allies insisted on humiliating and often punitive de-Nazification procedures that assessed the culpability of all the numerous middle- and upper-class Germans who had chosen to join the Nazi Party or Nazi organizations, often for careerist reasons. Those procedures soon acquired a partially justified reputation for arbitrariness. This was the era of the *Persilschein,* the carefully crafted testimonial of political purity from one's cronies, to gull the de-Nazification authorities into letting you off lightly. Moreover, German de-Nazification judges feared being too severe on "Nazis" who were their neighbors, whose expertise Germany often needed, and whom they could see as "upstanding." The net result was a mass political rehabilitation of most former Nazi supporters. The level of cynicism became so high that—not surprisingly, even if deplorably—

the political will to pursue former Nazis disappeared in West Germany. In the Lastenausgleich that loss of will would express itself in a disinclination to pursue special levies against former Nazis and Nazi supporters.[46]

Furthermore, so many Germans had been compromised by some degree of collaboration that discriminating against "Nazis" in the Lastenausgleich would create substantial political difficulties. Proposing special levies on them or excluding them from compensation would make enemies of millions of fellow citizens, citizens whose support the war-damaged would need to push through their demands. As Eugen Kogon, a concentration camp survivor, argued more generally, the sheer number of former Nazis meant that Germans would have to kill them all or win them over for democracy, and the former was unthinkable in a democratic and Christian state. In the Lastenausgleich, too, it would prove much easier to invite former Nazis into the process. Whereas the first two leaders of the bomb-damaged, Adolf Bauser and Wilhelm Mattes, had records of opposition to Nazism, the third, Wilhelm Ziegler, had been a high official in Goebbels's Ministry of Propaganda. Whereas early expellee leader Linus Kather had defended German Catholics in Nazi political trials, Waldemar Kraft, a major expellee leader in the early 1950s, had served in the Nazi administrative apparatus in occupied Poland and had been a member of the SS.[47]

Absent any secure legal basis for compensation, the bomb-damaged and expellees had to adopt a new terminology to describe themselves, in comparison with what the creditors in the 1920s had used. Those creditors had won a German Supreme Court ruling that the Civil Code required (partial) revaluation; they hence could and did appeal repeatedly to the widely accepted principle of the *Rechtsstaat,* the state based on law and justice, and to their rights within it. The bomb-damaged of the 1940s, though, could not convincingly pursue their claims in this context, given the disappearance of what even Bauser had to describe as the "former German Reich" and the doubts that any legal claim still existed or would survive currency reform. Despite Bauser's reference to the *Rechtsstaat* in a 30 March 1946 speech, and even though appeals to justice in the abstract would be a staple of war-damaged rhetoric, appeals by the war-damaged to the legalistic concept of the *Rechtsstaat* were infrequent. Despite a lingering nostalgia for the 1920s, the war-damaged were going to have to fight for recompense on post-1945 terms.[48]

INVENTING THE LASTENAUSGLEICH

Unable to rely on legal arguments to ground a claim against the state or some victimizer, the war-damaged had to find some new entity from which to obtain restitution. Only the community of Germans, in one way or another, could be that entity. Nonetheless, as useful as an appeal to communalism proved to be, it also generated an ongoing tension with individualistic claims to recompense.

Future leaders of the bomb-damaged recognized early that the German state's collapse presented problems. In late summer 1945, Mattes identified the taxpayers, not the no-longer-extant German state, as the source of funds to service Reich obligations, including the uncertificated war-damages claims. He saw capital taxes (not levies) as the best revenue source. Having been concerned since 1942 with the ultimate fate of the Reich debt (including war-damage claims), economist Robert Nöll von der Nahmer (later a parliamentarian for the FDP) wrote in early 1946, "Therefore, in the interests of the creditors, in place of the debtor incapable of paying (the German Reich), a debtor capable of paying must take over the debt. . . . The new debtor can only be the mass of German capital holders."[49]

To justify burdening these more or less innocent bystanders, the war-damaged called on communalist notions that had long existed in German society and that the Nazis had actively promoted. They did not abandon claims to individual entitlement, but they asserted the existence of a *Gefahrengemein-schaft*, a community of risk, that bound all Germans to mutual aid in a "joint liability community" that must share out war's burdens through a Lasten-ausgleich. They maintained that Germans had fought the war in common, would have shared the fruits of victory in common, and must now bear the burdens of defeat in common. Two of those three statements were patently false. On ideological and "racial" grounds, the Nazi regime had forbidden various Germans to share in fighting the war and would have forbidden them to share in the fruits of any victory—if it had allowed them to live. Besides, one can scarcely expect that every German in a hierarchical society could have benefited equally or even proportionally from victory. Yet the war-damaged could ground their claim of joint liability in traditional values, Nazi rhetoric, and Germans' recent experiences.[50]

Although the notion of a Lastenausgleich and the term itself appeared during World War II, Germans (especially the war-damaged) preferred to think the idea only appeared in 1946, presumably to distance it from the Third Reich and its crimes. The Nazis apparently never used the specific term "Lasten-ausgleich." Nonetheless, they did use the term *Ausgleich* (balancing out) to describe the process by which the burdens of the war should be distributed among German "racial comrades," and they did promote the idea of a Lasten-ausgleich, that those burdens should be balanced out proportionally among the different members of the community and not left to the vagaries of war. The first use of the term "Lastenausgleich" that I have found was by the paragon of neoliberalism, Ludwig Erhard. He was no supporter of any radically redistributionist Lastenausgleich, but in his 1943/44 memorandum on war-debt consolidation he proposed a "just balancing of burdens [*gerechter Lasten-ausgleich*]" and thereafter would favor some equitable redistribution of war's burdens among the German people.[51]

Erhard's support for a Lastenausgleich reflects its deep roots in pre-Nazi German culture. Human beings seem to find the sense of identity and security that community can provide reassuring. Notions of (usually local) community had had a powerful role in German political discourse for centuries. The erosion of traditional ties has turned Germans' loyalty from local communities toward the broader level of the nation. Yet the late appearance of a German nation-state, the broad spread of Germans across Central and Eastern Europe, and the power of race-thinking in turn-of-the-century Europe gave a suprastate thrust to German national identity. When the German Empire promulgated a new citizenship law in 1913, it rested German citizenship on German descent, confirming a notion of German community rooted in (putative) genetic interrelationship. The turn-of-the-century youth movement had actively promoted German communalism, and by the 1920s community was "one of the magic words" in Germany, touted by virtually all segments of the society. The notion of community of risk had been implicit in 1920s complaints that inflation was unjust because it imposed World War I's burdens on only one segment of society. The Nazi emphasis on community had been a significant element in their pre-1933 appeal.[52]

The Nazis promoted this sense of community, indeed radicalized it with their notions of race, during twelve years in which they controlled all public media, drastically curtailed private expression, and specifically promoted a balancing out of burdens among all Germans. Central to Nazi beliefs was a notion of racial community that inextricably bound all Germans together biologically. The regime explicitly tied that principle to war-damage claims, as Goebbels promised Germans that the regime would ensure that "the burdens of war are justly distributed" because "only in that way will we be a true racial community, which today bears *in common* the sacrifices of the war and at its end will harvest *in common* the fruits of victory."[53]

The shared experience of war and defeat tempered and strengthened that nationalism and sense of community. All Germans' lives and property were at risk, even for those who opposed the war, and that risk did create a sense of community. Even though the "undamaged" may have escaped major damages, virtually everyone had lost relatives, friends, property, or all three to war's havoc. Amid heightened wartime nationalism, even neoliberals could emphasize the communal obligation of Germans to share the war's burdens. Defeat, too, brought shared misery to all West Germans. The food and other shortages affected all, even those who managed to avoid the worst, and the Allies were imposing collective punishments on Germans as Germans. (West) Germans were, perforce, all in it together.[54]

Expellees often argued that their losses constituted a prepayment of Germany's reparations bill that entitled them to a Lastenausgleich at the expense of other Germans. As one expellee complained in September 1948, "Through our capital losses [we] have not only paid but overpaid the reparations demands of the eastern states. [We] have taken over from the German people, and in particular the people of the western zones, obligations that must be borne by the whole German people." Expellee leaders, though, were generally circumspect about making this argument because it could be construed as legitimating the expulsions and precluding any expellee claim against the expelling states. Further, the Federal Republic implicitly repudiated this argument in the preamble to the Lastenausgleich Law.[55]

On balance, virtually no one in postwar West Germany disputed the notion that Germans constituted a community of risk obligated to offer some Lastenausgleich. The major political parties and *all* federal-level economic interest groups explicitly or implicitly accepted that notion. Thus, Herbert Kriedemann (SPD) argued, "At issue here is the fact that ultimately all Germans lost the war in common, and it cannot be allowed that a portion of the German people should bear in full the whole burden of the war." Even those who opposed any significant Lastenausgleich could acknowledge some joint responsibility. One newspaper commentator, for example, rejected the war-damaged's more extravagant demands but added, "Certainly a community of fate of all members of our people exists; we have all conducted and lost the war, even though with very differing feelings."[56]

An opinion poll in the American Zone in November 1948 illuminates the breadth of support for a Lastenausgleich. Of those asked, 74 percent supported a Lastenausgleich. Not surprisingly, 95 percent of refugees did — but so did 68 percent of native western Germans. Among political partisans, 63 percent of Christian Democrats (center-right), 82 percent of Social Democrats, and 81 percent of Free Democrats (liberals) favored a Lastenausgleich. Ninety percent of those with nine years or more of education supported a Lastenausgleich. Moreover, a bare majority of those expecting to have to pay into a Lastenausgleich, 51 percent, explicitly supported it. A Lastenausgleich did not enjoy universal support, but it had a solid base.[57]

As John Connolly has pointed out in another context, the Nazis created a real community with real consequences, even if not the community they had intended. War-damaged individuals were successfully deploying Nazi-promoted notions of communal obligation to compel the undamaged to acknowledge the need for postwar sacrifices. Yet the focus for formerly propertied war-damaged was clearly not the shared sacrifice for the racial community that Goebbels had touted during the war. Instead, the war-damaged were successfully instrumentalizing Nazi communalism to secure sacrifices by the undamaged to finance *individual* recompense for war-related material losses.[58]

The notion of communal responsibility for Germany's war losses was crucial for efforts by the war-damaged to secure recompense. War-damaged Germans might have seemed weakly placed to demand recompense. The state against which they pressed their legal claim had ceased to exist. Moreover, almost all other twentieth-century nations insisted that refugees, including fellow ethnics, had no legal claim against the country to which they fled, even when their numbers made them a serious social problem. The best such refugees could expect was minimal assistance to forestall starvation and varying opportunities to seek work. West Germany would be one of just a few countries to offer its fellow nationals automatic citizenship and some legal claim to compensation.[59] Meanwhile, the enormous devastation Germany had suffered meant that the scope of claims far exceeded the society's ability to provide recompense. The willingness of undamaged Germans to entertain the war-damaged's demands rested not on legally dubious Nazi legislation but on a widely accepted communalist argument that even neoliberals were unwilling to reject. West Germany's unique Lastenausgleich legislation reflected uniquely German conditions and traditions.

Even though West Germans generally agreed on the need for a "Lastenausgleich," they discovered that they did not agree on what that meant in practice. Various Germans proposed a social, a quotal/individual, or a productive Lastenausgleich. A social Lastenausgleich would be based on the current needs of war-damaged individuals, not on their earlier status or the specific amount of material damages they had suffered. It would focus on social-support payments to the unemployable and on loans, grants, or other measures to integrate the employable as quickly as possible into the West German economy. An individual or quotal Lastenausgleich would be based on the amount of material losses formerly propertied war-damaged individuals had suffered, not on their current needs. It would exclude formerly unpropertied individuals (though such folk might be granted some public assistance) and would seek to recompense individual losses proportionally, so as to re-create on a lower level the prewar distribution of wealth. A productive Lastenausgleich would be based on the needs of the West German economy, focusing on job creation (often by undamaged firms), housing construction near unfilled jobs, and loans and grants to war-damaged individuals seeking to start a new business.[60]

The wartime tension between individualistic legislation and communalist rhetoric would resurface in postwar debates over these competing visions of a Lastenausgleich. A communal basis for claims to recompense would suggest communally oriented forms of compensation, a social or productive Lastenausgleich. Yet an influential minority of the war-damaged, and all the major organized war-damaged groups, preferred an individual Lastenausgleich. Reconciling a communalist justification for recompense with demands for individual restitution would be difficult. Organized war-damaged used the rhetorics of legal claim and of Lastenausgleich simultaneously, but they would also attempt, periodically but unsuccessfully, to move from a claim to a "Lasten-ausgleich" to a claim of legal entitlement based primarily on Nazi war-damages decrees.[61]

Much, obviously, had gone painfully wrong for Germans since 1914. They had suffered a horrible war, revolution, hyperinflation, deep depression, a totalitarian regime, a second, even more horrible war, and foreign conquest and occupation. They consciously tried to understand where Germany had gone astray between 1919 and 1945 and to profit from that knowledge. The most famous example of this desire to learn from the past is the way West Germans crafted the Basic Law of the Federal Republic of Germany to avoid perceived flaws in the Weimar constitution. Postwar West Germans did make different choices after 1945 than before. They may have adopted a particular policy not because they had drawn suitable lessons from the past but for other reasons. Yet one can agree with Hans-Peter Schwarz that the disasters of 1914–45 had so discredited past solutions that Germans were open to new ones, even if their grounds for choosing one new solution over another may be more complex than a simple reference to "learning" might suggest.[62]

The Lastenausgleich debate constitutes a striking example of the intention to learn from the past. Nöll von der Nahmer, for example, demanded, in dis-cussing the 1920s revaluation and the 1940s currency reform/Lastenausgleich, "Let us begin at last to learn from experience!" Not only did West Germans say repeatedly that they were looking back to the revaluation conflict as an ob-ject lesson, but in the thousands of documents I have seen, only one German questioned the validity of the historical analogy (and then only partially). West Germans from all walks of life and all political persuasions then altered their behavior, supporting in principle, and to varying degrees in practice, a more generous, and more sensitively presented, policy for reforming the currency and dealing with the burdens of war and defeat. The final Lastenausgleich Law reflected more than "lessons learned," but the effort to learn lessons from the past reflected an openness to new solutions and defined the issue in ways that bolstered some possible solutions at the expense of others.[63]

The post-1945 context offered war-damaged Germans both advantages and disadvantages as they struggled for adequate recompense. The openness to reform, the strong sense of communal responsibility, the doubts about free-markets, the apparent lessons of the past, all bolstered demands for a radical Lastenausgleich. Doubts about the economic risks attendant on a radical inter-vention in current property relations certainly existed. Nonetheless, as Allies and Germans began debating currency reform and Lastenausgleich in 1946, considerable scope existed for the kind of generous resolution of the govern-ment debt/Lastenausgleich issue that the war-damaged sought.

Chapter 3

CURRENCY REFORM PREJUDICES THE LASTENAUSGLEICH

Economic and political developments in Europe provoked Britain and the United States to take a series of crucial decisions, from mid-1946, on Germany's future. Both countries faced continuing costs for subsidizing their occupation zones because of Germany's weak economic recovery; both hence favored policy changes, including a currency reform, that would make the zones self-supporting. Further, as the Cold War deepened, their fear that a unified Germany would end up under Soviet domination made them more willing to accept a divided Germany that was partially under their influence. To ensure West German recovery, they then imposed a swingeing currency reform in the western zones that effectively divided Germany, structured West Germany's socioeconomic order, and prejudiced the distribution of war's burdens within German society.

ALLIES DISAGREE

On geopolitical grounds, the Soviet Union and the United States each feared that the other could become so powerful as to dominate the world. Possession of Germany's industrial might by one side or the other could decisively shift the economic and military balance between the two sides. Allowing German unification entailed the risk that the other side would gain control of the whole country. The United States was tempted to allow Germany to become divided to be sure of controlling at least one portion of it.[1]

On ideological grounds, too, the two sides were likely to squabble because each saw reason to expand its sphere at the other's expense. The United States was committed to a world free-trade order. The Soviets, though, could join that order only if they abandoned central planning, a key element in their ideology.

Meanwhile, after the horrors of the German invasion of 1941, the Soviet Union was determined to establish a glacis of friendly, Communist neighbors on its western border. Yet (as the Americans hoped) a free-trade order would tend to draw Russia's neighbors away from it and into the orbit of the economically most powerful state, the United States.[2]

Soviet actions in Europe and the Middle East may have been primarily defensive, but they exacerbated American, British, and French fears. Soviet attempts in 1946 to expand their influence in neighboring Iran and Turkey might have led to Soviet domination over the vital Middle East. Meanwhile, Communist parties in Eastern European states, bolstered in some cases by the presence of Soviet troops, were expanding their influence in 1946 and 1947.[3]

Certain developments in 1945 and 1946 were pushing Germany toward division, exacerbating the East-West conflict. The Soviets were nationalizing banks and big enterprises in their zone, while American opposition, and influence over France and Britain, prevented any socialization measures from coming into force in the west. Also in the Soviet Zone, the forced merger of the Communist and Social Democratic Parties and Communist control of important organizations, such as the trade unions and the youth organization, seemed designed to establish the base for a Communist government for any unified Germany. Some Germans, including future West German chancellor Konrad Adenauer, had predicted already in 1945 that the fundamental differences in ideology between the Soviets and the Anglo-Americans would lead to the creation of two separate Germanys with two separate socioeconomic systems. Events were suggesting they might be right.[4]

As growing friction with the Soviet Union made the Germans seem less threatening than they had in 1945, Anglo-American policy toward Germany began to change. The French were blocking American and British efforts to create some central German institutions that might accelerate German economic recovery. Yet if Allied policies prevented Germans from supporting themselves, then British and especially American taxpayers were going to have to pay to feed their defeated enemy. The purchasing-power overhang was a major factor inhibiting an economic recovery that could enable Germans to earn the foreign currency necessary to buy imported food. Despite their disinclination to help a former enemy and aggressor recover quickly, American officials found that national self-interest was driving them to take steps to reform the German currency.[5]

In May 1946, General Clay officially proposed to the U.S. government the Colm-Dodge-Goldsmith Plan (C-D-G Plan), the root of West Germany's future monetary and fiscal structure. After gathering data and expert opinion in Germany, the German-American economists Gerhard Colm and Raymond Goldsmith, along with the chief American financial official in Germany, Joseph Dodge, had drafted the plan, which was intended as the basis for a currency reform and Lastenausgleich for all Germany that the Allied Control Council (ACC) would promulgate.[6]

The C-D-G Plan was draconian, on economic and political grounds. It proposed to introduce a new currency (the Deutsche Mark, DM), convert private debts at 1 DM:10 RM, and cancel the Reich debt (including war-damages claims). Doing so would wipe out much of the property of millions of German creditors and the war-damaged. The Americans chose the 10:1 conversion ratio to squeeze all inflationary pressures from the German economy. They sought a speedy currency reform to show Germans that "these sacrifices . . . are a direct result of the Nazi regime and its policies." They explicitly promoted an Allied-sponsored currency reform to free German democratic politicians of the onus of the unavoidable cancellation of Reich debt.[7]

Colm and Goldsmith realized that currency reform could not simply obliterate Germans' hard-earned savings and cherished war-damages claims. Having lived through the Weimar Republic's economic and political failures, they argued that a currency reform plan "would bear the seeds of serious trouble in the future if it repeated the mistakes of the stabilization which liquidated the great inflation after World War I with its one-sided penalization of small savers, the old and the poor." To ensure that the burdens of war and defeat would be distributed fairly among all Germans — paper- and real-asset holders, rich and poor — their plan included provisions to balance out those burdens. It established a War Losses Equalization Fund financed from a 50 percent "public mortgage" on all real property in excess of 1,000 DM and from a capital-gains levy. The fund would issue War Loss Certificates to all who suffered losses because of the currency reform, including the war-damaged. Each family would receive full compensation for up to 500 RM in savings. The remaining certificates would all eventually be redeemed in whole or in part to provide recompense, as the War Loss Equalization Commission determined was appropriate.[8]

These certificates offered the authorities (Allied or German, as events might dictate) considerable discretion in manipulating the Lastenausgleich and the economy. The plan envisioned a "forward-looking" Lastenausgleich. Past assets would offer some general claim to assistance but not a legal claim to restitution of lost individual wealth. Instead, government officials would decide which claims to meet and when. Such discretion would allow the most "social" possible settlement of the war- and currency-damages problem, through early redemption "in hardship cases." Furthermore, it would allow the government to manipulate certificate redemption to control the overall level of credit, counteract inflationary or deflationary pressures, and promote socially desirable investment and production. A fund with such wide discretion about expending so many assets would have enabled — and tempted — any government to influence substantially the allocation of resources in the economy.[9]

Early implementation of the C-D-G Plan could have built on interventionist forces in the United States and Germany (and Britain, France, and the Soviet Union). As an economic adviser to President Harry Truman, Colm sought to introduce some governmental economic planning into U.S. domestic policy. While he became a minority voice in the increasingly Cold War–consumed United States, his support for planning did have roots in both pre-1933 German traditions and the American New Deal. Moreover, he could easily propose governmental manipulation of war recompense in Germany because of widespread post-1945 German expectations that some economic controls and planning would be necessary and that the Lastenausgleich might offer one means for constructive state intervention in the economy.[10]

Clay vigorously supported the whole C-D-G Plan. He recognized that, absent a balancing of burdens, a currency reform would embitter many Germans, who might then become radicalized, as millions of Germans had in the 1920s and 1930s. He also feared that a German government that had to tackle the onerous Lastenausgleich problem would lose all popular support.[11]

Clay had to fight to win Washington's support for the C-D-G Plan. Some Washington policy makers, especially State Department officials, supported the C-D-G Plan. Others, though, thought the complex plan could prove an embarrassing fiasco. More important, they viewed any Lastenausgleich as dangerously radical. Wesley Haraldson of the War Department, for example, complained that the capital levy "virtually socializes or communalizes all wealth and places tremendous power in the hands of the Government . . . and creates a situation similar to that which the Soviets are attempting to develop in their zone." Only by appealing to his friend, Secretary of State James Byrnes, was Clay able to secure Washington's grudging approval.[12]

Ironically, American critics of the C-D-G Plan sought to save private property in Germany by opposing a measure that most 1940s Germans thought necessary to preserve private property. American elites had long feared that in a democracy a poor and immoral majority might threaten the rights of the virtuous propertied. The capital levies and government control of the C-D-G Plan were hence a red flag to late 1940s Americans worried about statism and collectivism, especially in the context of the widespread support for "socialism" in postwar Europe. Most Germans, though, even those who supported private property, believed that the distribution of property in the aftermath of Nazism and war was so arbitrary as to delegitimize the institution of private property. Germans, and not just the war-damaged, would insist that the only way to relegitimize property was to confiscate some of it, to redistribute wealth so that its distribution accorded more closely with higher moral and social principles. Clay, Colm, and Goldsmith sought to explain this to Washington officials — but with limited success.[13]

Four-power discussions of the C-D-G Plan failed to produce agreement. Some of the Allies wanted to leave the Lastenausgleich measures aside. The

Soviets in particular made an "impassioned plea" not to let German cities be rebuilt before the cities Germany had destroyed. German aggression and atrocities were simply too recent for most other Europeans to welcome any steps that might advance war-damages compensation to Germans. The Soviets also wanted to ensure that they retained the right to issue enough new currency in their zone to finance reparations and their occupation costs, a potentially inflationary option that the Americans and Britons were unlikely to accept. The French remained opposed to anything that might foster the reestablishment of a unified Germany, including a four-zonal currency reform. Despite eventual general agreement on the need for a currency reform and Lastenausgleich, the various powers continued to have such widely differing views on the substantive details, rooted in differing national interests, that early consensus was unlikely.[14]

THE GERMANS SEEK A GERMAN ALTERNATIVE

The C-D-G Plan's exact provisions remained secret until 1955, but Germans soon knew its broad outlines — and seldom liked them. Leaders of the Federation of Savers and Bombed-Damaged, for example, proposed an alternative to the plan in April 1947. They vehemently rejected any drastic write-down of private-law debts or cancellation of Reich debt (including war-damages claims) as a betrayal of solemn promises by German society to its members. They would accept only the temporary blocking of savings accounts and claims against the Reich. They were willing, in 1947, to propose an initially productive and forward-looking Lastenausgleich, to spur economic recovery. Nonetheless, once the economy had grown enough, the government was to use capital-levy revenues to service all the Reich debt (even if at low interest), thereby offering individual recompense. The bomb-damaged wanted to preserve the Reich debt, even if in name only, both to preserve hope for some unknowable future and to provide a marker of social status in the present.[15]

The bomb-damaged and other Germans were generating hundreds of currency reform plans (usually with some Lastenausgleich measures), but such plans initially remained dead letters. Each occupying power was gradually creating new, German-run political institutions that might have implemented a currency reform in a single zone. The Allies, though, reserved important decisions, such as currency reform, to themselves. Moreover, Allies and Germans hesitated to impose a currency reform in just one zone. Doing so would separate that zone economically from the remainder of Germany, and no one wanted to take responsibility for any step that might contribute to the permanent division of Germany.[16]

Increasingly frustrated at the ACC's inability to craft common policies that might spur German economic recovery, the Britons and Americans announced in July 1946 that they were ready to unify economically with any other occupation zone, to ease economic strains and to accelerate the restoration of German unity. Neither the French nor the Soviets were ready to agree to economic unity on Anglo-American terms, so the Americans and British merged their two zones economically, effective 1 January 1947. For this "Bizone," the United States and Britain created administrative bodies, including the Economic Council with members elected by the state parliaments. They insisted that the latter was merely an advisory body, but as the highest-level body of democratically legitimated German representatives, it became a quasi-parliament within which Germans began developing a greater role in their own governance. Both countries denied any intent to promote the division of Germany, but this step made division more likely.[17]

These German-run institutions also provided an opening for more German involvement in currency reform discussions. Germans increasingly believed that a speedy currency and finance reform was crucial for German economic recovery, but they disliked the C-D-G Plan. Hence, in summer 1947, the Economic Council established the Special Agency for Money and Credit, which it charged to develop a German alternative to deal with currency reform, Reich debt, and the Lastenausgleich. The agency, headed by Ludwig Erhard, officially included eight financial experts, co-opted nine others, and solicited outside opinion.[18]

The Special Agency faced a painful dilemma in trying to place Germany's money and credit on a sound footing. After horrific experiences with hyperinflation in the 1920s and with suppressed inflation and black markets in the 1940s, Germans demanded a currency reform draconian enough to ensure that no third inflation erupted. Yet after losses of often painfully accumulated savings in the 1920s, most Germans also insisted that any currency reform had to be "social" enough to protect the weak and to distribute war's burdens fairly. Moreover, after the brutal deflation and mass unemployment of the early 1930s, they sought in addition a monetary policy "elastic" enough to forestall any deflation. Constructing a currency reform and Lastenausgleich package that was simultaneously draconian, elastic, and social would be comparable to squaring the circle.[19]

Economic historians have expressed doubts that the overwhelmingly neoliberal Special Agency members could have been serious about any Lastenausgleich. Yet neoliberals sought to create a political-economic order most conducive to the effective functioning and *survival* of a market economy. In 1947 and 1948, most Germans favored interventionist social and economic policies and vociferously demanded a currency reform that prevented new social hardships. If Special Agency members wanted their currency reform to be politically viable, they had to meet popular expectations, so they did try to provide some real Lastenausgleich.[20]

Contrary to post-1948 West German experience, the Special Agency experts had difficulty committing to a hard-money policy. They proposed to allow Germans immediate access in a new currency (to be issued by a new central bank) to only 5 percent of their Reichsmark holdings, a harsh 20:1 conversion ratio. Another 15 percent of each individual's Reichsmark holdings, though, would be credited to a blocked account and could be released as the authorities thought prudent. Further, to ensure that economic life could continue, the experts proposed that individuals and businesses should be able to secure credit almost automatically, especially against those blocked-account holdings. Indeed, their draft foresaw that "during the transitional period credit institutions [would] readily accept normal commercial paper and indeed fully independently of the amount of blocked account funds the discounter possesses." Moreover, needy individuals were to be allowed to tap their blocked accounts, perhaps in full, to avoid destitution. Germans saw this as a rational way to meet urgent social needs and to adjust money supply to economic needs gradually, as no one could know in advance what percentage of the Reichsmark money supply the economy would need in new currency.[21]

American and British experts feared, with some justification, that German authorities would prove unable to resist political pressures to free much of the blocked funds as social aid or bank credits, producing a conversion ratio more like 5:1 than 20:1 and introducing inflationary pressures. They debated these issues with the German experts from November 1947 through March 1948, but the Special Agency's final proposal—the April 1948 Homburg Plan—was not draconian. It proposed making only 5 percent of an individual's Reichsmark assets freely disposable in the new currency, but an additional 15 percent of Reichsmark assets would be posted as new marks in a blocked account, potentially available to businessmen against commercial bills and to the destitute. In a nod to Anglo-American concerns, the Germans did suggest that discounting of commercial bills would be subject to central-bank limits on the money supply.[22]

The Special Agency experts rejected canceling the remaining 80 percent of Reichsmark savings accounts and Reich debt (including war-damages claims), which represented private property. Instead, they proposed to preserve them as non-interest-bearing, unamortized certificates. The certificates were to have no inherent value and would constitute no claim to recompense but would merely be a "unit of account" for calculating each individual's future capital-levy obligations and compensation claims. The society would redeem only as many of the certificates as it could in future afford. Yet the agency proposed that in cases of social hardship the state could repurchase these certificates at up to 100 percent of face value. Beyond that, the society would choose which certificates to redeem, and when, on the basis of broader economic, monetary, and fiscal considerations. This policy would open the door to pressure from certificate holders for their (nearly) full repayment and would tempt government officials to intervene aggressively in the economy by manipulating the redemption process.[23]

The Special Agency had great difficulty dealing with the losses of the expellees. Most expellees lacked any documentation on their earlier wealth, and trying to establish concretely what their losses had been would be costly, time-consuming, and open to fraud. The experts were inclined to divide the expellees into a limited number of groups according to their earlier socioeconomic status, with the amount of each individual's compensation dependent on the group to which he or she belonged. In the Homburg Plan, though, they contented themselves with promising the expellees that they would be given compensation claims comparable to those of other war-damaged Germans, with details to be settled in future legislation.[24]

As did the C-D-G Plan, the Homburg Plan proposed on the expenditure side a social and productive, a forward-looking, Lastenausgleich. Both plans provided that decisions about the timing and amount of compensation would be made on the basis of each individual's current social need and the society's overall economic needs. Whatever hopes some war-damaged individuals might entertain, neither plan even suggested that the amount of each individual's compensation would be proportional to losses. At this time, the communalist basis of any Lastenausgleich was trumping the individualistic desires of the formerly propertied war-damaged — in a neoliberal plan.[25]

On the revenue side, Special Agency experts had to respond to the widespread, vociferous demand that this time, unlike in the 1920s hyperinflation, real- and paper-asset holders should bear war's burdens equally. Acknowledging that "a currency reform will hence only be judged as socially just if the sacrifices associated with it are divided equally between money assets and real assets," the experts proposed levies on post-1935 capital gains (realized and unrealized) and on real assets to ensure that currency reform was fair as between holders of paper and of real assets. A capital-gains levy might be difficult to implement, but it would assuage popular anger at profiteering and extinguish large chunks of excess purchasing power. As for a capital levy, Erhard stated early on that "the principle of justice must be placed in the foreground. Thereby one could contemplate burdening real assets immediately, so that holders of paper assets do not feel themselves disadvantaged."[26]

Only the Finns shared the West German focus on massive capital levies to finance war-damages compensation. West Germans chose such levies out of a determination not to repeat the 1920s policy of imposing war's burdens on paper-asset holders while letting real-asset holders escape any share. Yet that choice also reflected the absence in the immediate postwar years of other lucrative revenue sources to finance recompense. Moreover, the organized war-damaged demanded capital levies in order to lower the wealth of the undamaged enough to make it possible to raise the war-damaged to the same level, restoring the relative prewar distribution of wealth and, hence, of status.

Although the Special Agency experts never abandoned the principle that some capital and capital-gains levies must accompany currency reform, they agreed that any transfer of real capital was, as Erhard put it, "extremely problematic." As neoliberals, they disliked the interference in private economic activity and property rights that capital levies, especially any attempt to transfer real assets, would entail. Further, property holders, especially big businesses, were already pressing them to avoid excessive burdens on the economy. The experts initially proposed making the capital levy payable in installments, but they soon inclined to making all the levies payable in the certificates that individuals would receive for their Reichsmark assets. The central bank would destroy the paid-in certificates, eliminating them as potential money and reducing the government's obligations. The experts were making the certificates something more than a mere unit of account.[27]

Payment in certificates, though, threatened to make the Special Agency's Lastenausgleich provisions meaningless. Instead of having to transfer real assets to meet their obligations, real-property holders would have the opportunity to pay off their levies with the certificates, that is, with inflated and now worthless wartime currency. In fact, the experts discovered that most businesses would be able to pay all of their levies with their own certificates, without having to "sell" real assets to war-damaged individuals to get certificates. Hence, almost no new currency or real assets would have been available to provide any meaningful compensation to the war- or currency-damaged.[28]

Nonetheless, the Special Agency experts remained convinced that, no matter what their economic qualms, they had to reassure Germans that the war's burdens would eventually be distributed justly. The agency hence decided in early April 1948 that the levy on real assets would be "due in principle in new money." As Special Agency expert Curt Fischer noted, they ensured thereby that "an obligor cannot be relieved of the burden on those of his real assets subject to a levy by the surrender of demonetarized portions of his former money assets." Recognizing the paper character of most war and postwar profits, the agency did allow payment of the capital-gains levy in certificates. The agency's final bill also made the capital levy due immediately. Obligors could petition to pay the latter in installments, with 4 percent interest, but the Special Agency experts assumed that the interest rate was high enough "that only in infrequent, economically specially situated cases will use be made of the alternative of payment in installments." Hence, many debtors would have had to sell real assets on open markets, presumably to the war-damaged, to meet their sizable levy obligations. Despite their monetary and fiscal conservatism, the experts had, under political pressures, produced a very generous currency reform–Lastenausgleich plan.[29]

Politics does sometimes trump economic expertise and economic "necessity." Instructive in this regard is the 1990 currency union between West and East Germany. Economic experts overwhelmingly agreed that exchanging East German marks for Deutsche Mark at any rate more favorable to East Germans than 2:1 would cause serious monetary, fiscal, and economic problems for both East and West Germany. The West German government imposed a 1:1 exchange ratio for wages, pensions, social benefits, and much of East Germans savings anyway (with less favorable rates for higher levels of savings) — primarily for political reasons.[30]

The Homburg Plan met with a very positive response. The Economic Council's Currency Committee, the German minister presidents of the western German states, and the Bizone's upper house of delegates all voted to request the Allies to implement that plan in full. Even business leaders favored joining currency reform and Lastenausgleich, if only to give all Germans a clear view of where they stood financially. Germans could not ignore the deep wounds left by the stabilization and limited revaluation of 1923–25 and by the deflation and mass unemployment of 1929–34. If the Allies had allowed the Germans to design currency reform in the spring of 1948, the Germans would almost certainly have implemented a policy that was less draconian than the Anglo-American policy of 1948 and that included a Lastenausgleich more generous than the Federal Republic's legislation of 1952.[31]

POLICY SHIFTS

Events in early 1947 provoked crucial shifts in American policy. The unusually severe winter of 1946/47, which paralyzed much of Europe for weeks, made obvious the fragility of Europe's economic recovery. Western Europeans were running down their reserves to rebuild rapidly from war's destruction. American officials worried that any economic slowdown could batter such weak economies, spreading misery, opening the way for Communism, and cutting the United States off from important trading partners. A capitalist United States isolated in the Western Hemisphere would, most Americans officials feared, face a return of 1930s-style economic stagnation and might be unable to survive. Simultaneously, Britain's postwar economic difficulties made it impossible for that country to continue providing economic and military aid to a Greek government threatened by Communist insurrection. The United States responded with the Truman Doctrine, which provided economic and military support for governments threatened by subversion, and the Marshall Plan, which was intended to aid in the recovery of Europe.[32]

The Truman Doctrine, which was primarily defensive, certainly did not warm Stalin's heart, but the Marshall Plan seemed a direct threat to Soviet interests. American officials offered aid under the Marshall Plan to any European nation willing to cooperate in expanding free trade — including those countries in Eastern Europe that the Soviets sought to incorporate into their buffer zone of friendly neighbors with more or less planned economies. Although Soviet officials contemplated accepting the plan if they could secure American concessions, they forced their Eastern European neighbors to refuse to participate when it became obvious the United States would not bend.[33]

Central to the new American economic policy toward Europe was a determination to promote German economic recovery. Despite the efforts of some Americans to block Germany's revival, a strong contingent of American officials had long argued that an economically prosperous Germany was a prerequisite to an economically stable Europe. Germany had been a crucial source of coal, steel, and capital goods for other European countries (much of which they now had to obtain from the United States) and an important market for their exports. As European recovery slowed in early 1947 because of a shortage of U.S. dollars to finance vital imports, those Americans who insisted Europe needed German inputs and markets got the upper hand. Moreover, American officials feared that an impoverished Germany would again become a breeding ground for radicalism, perhaps this time for Communism. The U.S. government hence changed its policy to emphasize rebuilding in Germany and offered Marshall Plan aid to any part of Germany whose occupation authorities would cooperate. The Allied-imposed limits on German industrial production were not yet abandoned, but a decisive policy shift had occurred.[34]

Fearful that the Soviets had no interest in monetary reform in Germany, American officials began to prepare for a bizonal or trizonal (with the French Zone) currency reform. The closing of banks in the Soviet Zone in 1945 had reduced the money supply sufficiently to reduce the need for currency reform there, while further currency reform could make it harder for the Soviets to squeeze occupation costs and reparations out of their zone. Furthermore, some American officials concluded that the Soviets were ideologically opposed to currency reform because reestablishing a functioning monetary system was a prerequisite for reestablishing free markets in Germany. Yet economic recovery in Germany hinged on currency reform, and the Americans did not want to be held hostage to Soviet willingness to cooperate. In the autumn of 1947, the United States unilaterally took the crucial step of having bank notes for a German currency reform printed, a secret that soon leaked. These notes were now available to be used for a separate Western currency reform or as leverage to pressure the Soviets.[35]

Americans nonetheless continued negotiating over a unified currency reform into early 1948. Western Germans seemed increasingly to agree that a successful currency reform could come only in the three western zones because the Russians might sabotage any plan they joined. Even so, actually taking a decisive step such as a separate currency reform that precipitated division could outrage Germans against the power that did so. American officials feared that not going the extra mile for a currency reform for all four zones would undercut support in western Germany for wider American policy goals. Hence, at a December 1947 Anglo-American conference, "It was agreed," a participant wrote, "that a further effort should be made to obtain four-power agreement in the [Allied] Control Council regarding a new German currency."[36]

Hoping to secure Russian agreement, Clay introduced a stripped down version of currency reform at the ACC meeting on 20 January 1948. He proposed a write-down of the old currency, the issuance of a new currency, and the cancellation of Reich debt — and nothing more. Clay hoped that by limiting currency reform to the bare essentials he could maximize the chances of four-power agreement. The other elements of the C-D-G Plan could be negotiated and implemented later. Despite significant Soviet concessions in mid-February, negotiations on technical issues dragged on, not least because the Soviets still feared the effects of any quadripartite currency reform on their ability to finance reparations and their occupation costs.[37]

In the second half of February, though, before these negotiations could bear fruit, a Soviet-backed Communist coup overthrew the democratically elected government in Czechoslovakia, sending shock waves through Western capitals and alarming Western peoples. Czechoslovakia had been Hitler's first victim, a scant decade before, so Stalin seemed to be following in that other totalitarian's brutal footsteps. After three years of growing suspicion of Soviet motives, most Europeans and Americans — even many on the Left — now became convinced that the Soviets were aiming at expanding their sphere of influence, by force if necessary, and that the Communists would be unscrupulous in their tactics and were not to be trusted.[38]

The Americans and Britons then decided to push through a separate currency reform. On 10 March 1948, Deputy to the Assistant Secretary of State Frank Wisner argued that the Soviets might exploit nominal agreement on a currency reform for all of Germany as an opportunity to "frustrate further the economic recovery of western Germany by the use of obstructive and delaying tactics." He also noted that stripped-down currency reform would deprive the Western Allies of important monetary policy tools (e.g., a central bank) for promoting economic recovery. He concluded, "It is recommended that General Clay be instructed that the policy of this government is no longer to reach quadripartite agreement on currency and financial reform in Germany and that, accordingly, his objective should be to withdraw from quadripartite negotiations." The Western Allies faced the embarrassing prospect of having to take responsibility for dividing Germany economically — and perhaps eventually politically.[39]

Fortunately for the United States and Britain, the Soviets let them off the hook. At the London Conference, which ended on 6 March 1948, the Western countries discussed German policy without Soviet participation, and Britain, France, and the Benelux powers negotiated the Brussels Treaty, a mutual-defense pact implicitly aimed as much at the Soviets as at the Germans. The Soviet government resented negotiations that assumed it was a hostile power. Soviet representatives therefore walked out of the ACC on 20 March 1948, thereby disrupting unified government of Germany. The Western Allies could now pursue separate currency reform with less fear that Germans would blame them for any resulting division of the country.[40]

FORMULATING AMERICAN-STYLE CURRENCY REFORM

Having abandoned hopes for four-power action, the United States was in a position to shape a currency reform more to its liking. It could not ride roughshod over the (West) Germans, Britons, and French, who favored a less severe, though potentially more inflationary, currency reform. Those countries, though, depended economically on U.S. aid and politically and militarily on U.S. support against the newly threatening Soviet Union. Determined to provide a solid monetary-policy basis for future growth, the United States pushed through a currency reform that effectively expropriated the millions of German holders of paper assets, including the war-damaged, and that repeated the consequences of inflationary war finance that had so outraged Germans in the 1920s.[41]

The degree of support for a Lastenausgleich with currency reform was remarkably broad in early 1948. German politicians and financial experts were committed, even against U.S. resistance, to a Homburg Plan that included a Lastenausgleich. Clay and U.S. State Department officials feared that any currency reform without a Lastenausgleich would be so obviously unjust as to discredit the occupying powers who implemented it; the latter urged that any "financial plan for western Germany be a comprehensive plan embodying the equalizing features at the outset." The British, though always dubious about a capital levy, also remained committed to an early Lastenausgleich. Hence, State Department officials were confident the United States and Britain could include some balancing measures in a joint Anglo-American currency reform. If the French proved reluctant, "the original agreement might embody as much common ground as possible, with any differences left to subsequent settlement."[42]

Opposition in Washington to any Lastenausgleich measures was, though, stronger than it had been in 1946. Given the urgency of currency reform, most American officials preferred a relatively simple version of currency reform—without a Lastenausgleich—to limit the scope for disagreement among the three Western powers. Moreover, the U.S. government had become more conservative, as new president Harry Truman replaced New Dealers with more moderate individuals and as American officials reacted to the growing anti-

Communism in the United States. The new secretary of the army, conservative Southern Democrat Kenneth Royall, instructed Clay to leave Lastenausgleich measures to the Germans.[43]

To be successful, American occupation officials thought, currency reform had to be draconian, to eliminate completely the danger of any future inflation. Many financial experts believed that only a sharp shock could convince Germans that inflation was over and get them to alter their behavior in ways that would promote stability. The Americans were also determined to cancel old Reichsmark assets, including the Reich debt, and to limit the Germans' ability to expand the money supply, to squeeze inflationary pressures from the West German economy. Jack Bennett, chief U.S. financial official in Germany, asserted scathingly, "Recognition of the Reich debt is not merely a political blunder, but is also a sure commitment to future inflation." He recognized that a currency-reform plan must provide some degree of justice as among "various classes of the citizenry." Nonetheless, he warned, "too great an emphasis on justice would lead to minimizing nominal losses to the point which might leave an excess of money or of politically enforceable claims to money in the economy, and thus defeat the purpose of currency reform." Some blocked accounts or certificates could easily be turned into money to meet the likely clamor from business for easy credits, while others could be unfrozen to help impoverished victims of war and currency reform. That two-barreled character, as economic and as social measure, would make unblocking harder to resist.[44]

The Americans feared that, despite painful experience with inflation, Germans were inclined to fall back on soft money whenever things started going badly. We now tend to assume that painful experience had taught Germans to prefer an extremely conservative monetary policy, as exemplified after 1950 by the rigid monetary rectitude of the West German central bank and by the extremely negative reaction of West German public opinion to any hint of inflation. In 1948, though, recent history, 1914–45, offered the spectacle of three different German political systems (authoritarian monarchy, parliamentary democracy, totalitarian dictatorship) pursuing inflationary policies. In addition, postwar Germans remembered another horrific economic experience: the depression of the 1930s; they often worried as much or more about renewed deflation as about renewed inflation. A 1946 memorandum on currency reform, for example, asserted, "The future 'creation of money' may not be so low that destructive deflationary tendencies and an excessive burdening of the economy with credit costs arise."[45]

British officials shared the German preference for a moderate currency reform. Britons had long opposed canceling the Reich debt as an attack on property and creditor rights, a position the U.S. Treasury shared. They agreed with most Germans in preferring to preserve, through blocking or certificates, the Reich debt and the legal claims it embodied. They also supported a more reflationary postreform currency regime. They worried, with some justice, that cutting the money supply too sharply might leave the (West) German economy with too little liquidity, provoking a deflationary spiral and soaring unemployment. They hence favored the Special Agency's plan because they liked the flexibility for increasing the money supply the plan provided. Britons were implicitly proposing a Keynesian system of stimulatory but interventionist fiscal and monetary policies to guarantee full employment. Similar (though less directly Keynesian) concerns were animating the Special Agency experts.[46]

One should note here the proconsumer thrust of British and German proposals. The primary goal of Keynesian fiscal expansion was to put purchasing power into the hands of consumers. Erhard's version of the social-market economy also focused on consumers. Ensuring that they had adequate incomes would provide the demand, the profits, and the savings to make investment desirable and possible. Moreover, Erhard maintained that the economy was not an end in itself but a means of enabling consumers to live and make choices on economic and noneconomic matters. The Homburg Plan would have provided some funds for investment, but it and Erhard's other late-1940s policies would have served primarily to spur economic activity through consumer demand.[47]

The Germans and the British got one last shot at pushing through a more generous currency reform in May 1948 at the Rothwesten Conclave. Currency reform would be dangerously complex and far reaching, and unless it was carefully drafted by people intimately familiar with German language, law, and economic life, it had the potential to create all manner of unintended, deleterious effects. The German financial experts at the conclave, drawn primarily from the Special Agency, were hence charged to draw up the actual German-language legislation on the basis of Allied principles.[48]

Those German experts nonetheless continued to press for an elastic currency reform. They clashed with the Americans over the "free quota," the percentage of Reichsmark holdings that would be freely available in Deutsche Mark to each individual (initially as a posting to a new Deutsche Mark savings account). The Germans objected to freeing up 10 percent of an individual's Reichsmark assets in Deutsche Mark immediately, as the United States proposed, because businessmen would have so much funds that they could delay selling off their hoarded inventories. Rapid sales from inventory were necessary, though, to hold down prices. The experts argued one should start with a low 5 percent free quota in Deutsche Mark, but post 15 percent of Reichsmark assets to blocked Deutsche Mark accounts. Monetary authorities could then release as much of the blocked amounts as necessary to fine-tune the money supply—through "an elastic credit policy with low interest rates" and through payments to address social needs. The Allies finally agreed that the free quota would be only 5 percent of each natural and legal person's Reichsmark assets and that an additional 15 percent of Reichsmark assets would be posted to blocked Deutsche Mark accounts — but the United States retained a veto on any release from the blocked accounts.[49]

The Allies and the Germans also clashed over the amount of the initial cash issue in Deutsche Mark for each West German, the "per capita quota." Germans and Britons wanted each West German to have enough cash after currency reform to meet his or her own needs and to finance economic activity, forestalling social unrest and recession. They were also concerned, on social grounds, that everyone start off at least apparently equally. The French also wanted a large initial stock of notes issued, to ensure that enough liquidity was available in their zone to enable them to finance their enormous occupation force. Determined to secure French participation in the currency reform, the United States and Britain agreed to a per capita quota of 60 DM. Unfortunately, the stock of preprinted Deutsche Mark notes was so low that the Allies would have to issue the quota in two installments, of 40 DM and 20 DM. The Germans further argued that the per capita quota should not be subtracted from the individual's free quota but should be, in effect, a gift (a policy that would have expanded the money supply substantially). The United States, though, insisted that the 60 DM per capita quota be subtracted from the free quota.[50]

Another contested issue was the conversion rate for long-term, private-law Reichsmark debts (mortgages, commercial bonds, and the like). Fearful of bankruptcies among businesses forced to repay old long-term debt in new currency, the Americans insisted on conversion at 10:1. Most Germans, though, viewed a 10:1 conversion rate as "unsocial" because it would allow real-asset holders to escape 90 percent of their debts, giving them enormous windfall profits at the expense of innocent private creditors. German experts continued to favor a 1:1 conversion to ensure that 1940s private debtors would not profiteer from the state's efforts to write down its own debt, as debtors in the 1920s had. As the Americans admitted, any currency-reform profits would have to be taxed away anyway. Yet doing so after the fact would involve substantial administrative complexity at the cost of another blow to small savers. The Americans, though, were adamant.[51]

The German experts were not soft-hearted proponents of soft money. As Erwin Hielscher put it, "It is in my view in no way a matter of a weak solution, but rather of an elastic solution."[52] They favored a stringent conversion rate to squeeze out inflationary pressures. Nonetheless, they were also highly sensitive to the political and economic imperatives to provide funds to needy individuals to prevent destitution and to business to forestall deflation. Erhard correctly predicted that currency reform would initially produce inflationary pressures, which would be followed by deflationary pressures. The Germans wanted to be very flexible in releasing money from the blocked accounts, to be able to address those deflationary pressures. They implicitly assumed that the new central bank, the Bank deutscher Länder (BdL), would successfully control overall liquidity, preventing both inflation and deflation. They were counting on the BdL, which was just beginning operations, for a great deal. Political pressures to address high unemployment with expansionary policies would be substantial, and the BdL initially pursued relatively loose monetary policies to ensure the availability of "useful and indispensable credits." Circumstances would allow tight-money forces in the BdL to push the balance toward tighter money, but an easy-money regimen was a possible alternative.[53]

Furthermore, an individual's attitude toward hard and soft money could change once currency reform had been implemented. All but the poorest Germans, including most real-property holders, had Reichsmark assets. They often hoped for a reform that would leave them with as much of the value of *their* Reichsmark assets as possible. Moreover, businesses often needed credit to maintain operations, so businessmen preferred a monetary policy that ensured easy credit. Yet, if they had sufficient profits, as German business generally did after 1948 because of a favorable tax code, they could be willing to accept a hard money policy in return for price stability. Moreover, once currency reform had been successfully implemented, most West Germans developed an interest in stable money, to provide predictable values and access to goods. Finally, as people began to accumulate Deutsche Mark assets, their interests shifted to ensuring that no new inflation would erode the value of those Deutsche Mark assets. We must not assume that Germans were as devoted to hard money in May 1948 as they increasingly became after June 1948.[54]

Although German scholars have often dismissed the efforts of conclave participants as merely technical, Michael Brackmann has argued vigorously that the participants themselves carefully contrived this impression, to escape the onus for their role in the draconian currency reform that (West) Germany required. He argues that Special Agency members had influenced Allied proposals through the participation of American and British experts in the Agency's discussions and at the Rothwesten Conclave. He also points out that the overall structure of the reform, 5 percent of Reichsmark assets available immediately as a "free quota," 15 percent blocked, and the remaining 80 percent eliminated, reflected exactly the Homburg Plan's provisions. The Americans were pressured into that structure, he argues, by the combined weight of German, British, and French opinion. Yet these notable similarities to German proposals should not blind one to the crucial differences. German experts had lost on the social aspects of currency reform, on provisions for easy business access to credit against the blocked accounts, on cancellation of Reich debt, and on inclusion of a Lastenausgleich. The American-sponsored reform was significantly more draconian than was the Homburg Plan.[55]

Anglo-American efforts to secure French agreement to a trizonal currency reform almost failed at the last minute. The Western powers had in early June decided to work to establish a West German state. The French National Assembly was soon caught up in a dramatic debate over whether France should allow a German state, even a partial one, to be created so soon after German aggression had yet again brought misery to France. Meanwhile, the French military government in Germany rejected a tax reform that the Americans, Britons, and Germans thought was crucial to spur economic recovery but that would threaten France's ability to squeeze resources from its zone. Dramatic midnight negotiations among the American, British, and (deputy) French military governors paralleled the even more dramatic midnight debate in the French Assembly. Telephone calls flew back and forth among Paris, Baden (French military government headquarters), and Clay's house in Berlin. In the early hours of 16 June 1948, the French Assembly approved the French government's support for a West German state and the French military governor approved a compromise on tax reform. A trizonal currency reform was saved.[56]

The Americans had failed to keep their printing of Deutsche Mark bank notes a secret, but in February–April 1948 (in "Operation Bird Dog") they managed to slip 23,000 unmarked crates full of crisp new Deutsche Mark bills, 500 tons of cash, into the American Zone without even their British allies finding out. On 18 June 1948, the Americans, British, and French promulgated the first three currency-reform laws for their zones. On the same day, under military guard, the Americans shipped billions of marks in notes by truck and train across the three western zones to ration-card offices. On 20 June, West Germans lined up to register their Reichsmark assets, turn in their old currency, and receive new Deutsche Mark currency. The time had come to clean up the monetary mess the Nazis had left behind.[57]

IMPLEMENTING CURRENCY REFORM

The Allied currency-reform legislation established the BdL as the central bank and bank of issue and the Deutsche Mark as the new legal tender for the Trizone. It fixed a conversion rate of 1 RM:1 DM for all recurring Reichsmark obligations (wages, salaries, rents, social-insurance contributions, taxes, short-term debts, and so on), except as otherwise provided. It converted all private long-term debt at a 10:1 rate. Each person had access to 5 percent of their registered Reichsmark holdings in Deutsche Mark as a free quota, posted to a new savings account; 5 percent was held in a blocked Deutsche Mark account; and 10 percent survived as a "shadow quota"; the rest, 80 percent, was canceled. To cover financial institutions' liabilities in the new currency (for free and blocked accounts, capital, and reserves), the legislation furnished them with new Länder (state) debt. Each person would receive 40 DM cash on 20 June and 20 DM in late July. Germans had to turn in at least 60 RM to get that amount of cash in Deutsche Mark. For those with more than 60 RM, the per capita quota was subtracted in Deutsche Mark from the free quota. Each employer also received 60 DM cash per employee, subtracted from his or her free quota.[58]

The currency legislation effectively canceled all Reich debt by excluding it from conversion into Deutsche Mark. American occupation officials, under pressure from Treasury officials in Washington, had in the end agreed not to cancel all Reich debt explicitly. Yet the Allies had legally confirmed the extinction of Germans' claims against the Reich by leaving them payable only in a currency that no longer existed. Only specific legislation could give each type of claim an existence and value in Deutsche Mark. The war-damaged would resist this conclusion, but legally it would triumph.[59]

Average Germans particularly resented the decision to subtract the 60 DM per capita quota from the individual's savings. After years of running down assets to secure vital supplies on the black market, two-thirds of West Germans found that subtracting the 60 DM wiped out their meager converted savings. They now faced life in the uncertain post–currency reform economy with no savings to fall back on. Moreover, many Germans desperately needed the savings to replace clothing, bedding, and other necessities lost because of the war. This Allied policy outraged Germans all the more because German authorities, including the Special Agency experts, had touted the need to spare small savings in any currency reform, on grounds of social equity. Even after currency reform the Germans, including Erhard, urged the Allies repeatedly, though in vain, to reverse themselves and not subtract the per capita quota from people's savings accounts—a policy equivalent to a de facto increase in the broad money supply.[60]

With prices rising in autumn 1948, the Americans convinced the French and Britons to join them in issuing the Fourth Currency Law, on 4 October. Determined to reduce inflationary pressures by reducing the money supply, the Allies canceled 100 percent of the shadow account and 70 percent of the blocked account. The Allies had, in the end, abolished 93.5 percent of individual savings. Because workers and lower-middle-class individuals had held most of their savings in savings accounts, they had lost more of their assets than the middle- or upper-class holders of mortgages or bonds (which had been converted at 10:1). Average Germans were outraged to discover that the currency reform had imposed a greater proportion of war's burdens on the less affluent than on the wealthier.[61]

Some West Germans later asserted that all West Germans started equally on 21 June 1948, so subsequent differences in wealth resulted entirely from varying individual talent and diligence. That assertion is simply untrue. Not only did real property holders start off after currency reform with often substantial assets that nonreal property holders did not have, but those who had a business on 20 June 1948 were able to secure cash and credits when money was relatively scarce and when the pent-up demand for goods offered golden opportunities for those with the assets to meet that demand. Businesses also benefited from a favorable tax code. Talent and diligence undoubtedly played a significant role in the drive for wealth in post–currency reform West Germany—but all most certainly did not start out equally. As the neoliberal historian Reinhold Schillinger has noted, "Indeed, with the one-sided liquidation of the old currency, accompanied by a sparing of real capital, the class division of German society was never more openly made the basis of a political-economic decision."[62]

In one important regard, though, the currency reform did privilege western German (but not expelled) employees, including civil servants. One of the war's major costs was the destruction by Nazi fiscal and monetary policies of the value of the assets supporting employees' social-insurance claims and civil service pensions. The capitalized value of those social-insurance rights had been the major form of capital available to blue- and white-collar workers and most civil servants. They could not dispose freely of that capital, but they had an entitlement in the event of illness, disability, or old age. The Allies, though, backed by German experts, decided to establish a (nearly) 1:1 conversion rate for western Germans' civil service pensions and social-insurance benefits, giving those entitlements additional value because they proved to be protected, by social and political pressure, against the consequences of inflation, which permanently eliminated 90 percent of the value of private savings, pensions, and insurance plans.[63]

The American-sponsored reform had required complex and painful choices about whose assets to save and whose to destroy. Canceling Reich debt hurt its creditors, including war-damaged citizens. Separating currency reform and Lastenausgleich benefited real-property holders, because delay lowered the present value of levies and led to a more modest Lastenausgleich. Converting long-term private debt at 10:1 benefited debtors, usually real-property holders and the better-off, at the expense of creditors. Converting civil service pensions and social-insurance payments at 1:1 did benefit civil servants and blue- and white-collar workers. Overall, barring a radical Lastenausgleich, the Allied currency reform imposed the burden of World War II almost entirely on holders of paper claims against the former German state, including the war-damaged and savers. As after World War I, holders of real property escaped relatively unscathed. The post–currency reform Deutsche Mark balances of corporations suggest that they preserved, on average, 96 percent of their real assets (though much less of their paper assets), while savers had preserved only 6.5 percent and mortgage and commercial bond holders only 10 percent of their paper assets (and had usually had no real assets).

Despite currency reform's reputation as a glorious success, Germans were in 1948 outraged that it destroyed what they considered the vested rights of German citizens and distributed war's burdens unfairly. West German officials distanced themselves from the reform by emphasizing the Nazi origins of the problem and Allied responsibility for the painful solution chosen. The Allies, especially the Americans, then reaped a whirlwind of protest for their draconian policy. One retired army officer, for example, complained bitterly, "The primitive, asocial currency dictate of the military governors has handed German legislators a hot potato, all the more as the generals have meanwhile attacked their own law by canceling 70 percent of the blocked account and have thereby sinned badly and unnecessarily against the democratic value of legal certainty."[64]

Currency reform and Lastenausgleich were arguably related issues where Allied, here primarily American, preferences played a key role in determining German policy. The Allies could not simply impose their will on West Germans, as their failures in education and civil service reform show. Yet they could decisively influence developments where they could build on German desires and create a fait accompli. Currency reform met those tests. Many Germans, including the Rothwesten financial experts, were willing to cooperate in a draconian currency reform because of their commitment to establishing a solid monetary base for future economic development — and because they thought the reform offered more scope for easy money and for a generous Lastenausgleich than events allowed. Moreover, that currency reform created a fait accompli. Despite periodic calls from various West Germans for revision, the risks of renewed inflation from any direct tampering with currency reform seemed too great.

Nonetheless, German outrage created enormous pressure for a Lastenausgleich to readjust the balance between paper- and real-asset holders. Germans were now left with the task of making good, at least in part, the (to some degree unavoidable) unfairness of Allied currency reform.

Chapter 4

FIRST AID FOR THE WAR-DAMAGED

Allied currency-reform legislation required the Germans to promulgate a Lastenausgleich law by 31 December 1948. German policy makers believed that six months was insufficient time to legislate responsibly on the complex Lastenausgleich issue, yet currency reform had plunged many individual Germans into often desperate poverty. German policy makers hence chose to pass an interim Lastenausgleich law to meet the immediate needs of the war-damaged. That decision, in the late 1948 political environment, initially privileged the social Lastenausgleich that some Germans favored.

POLITICAL AND ECONOMIC TURNING POINTS

The burgeoning Cold War was hardening the de facto division of Germany that currency reform had introduced, and West Germans faced tough choices about their future. West German leaders decided that a liberal democratic West German state was a better bet than a possibly Communist- and Russian-dominated unified Germany. Meanwhile, West Germans were moving, albeit hesitantly, toward a social-market economy. They could now begin acting on the Lastenausgleich, within limits.

Germany lay at the center of the Cold War between the Western and Eastern blocs. The occupying forces on its soil divided it physically, economically, and politically. U.S. policy makers emphasized the danger of Soviet domination of any united Germany, to mobilize West German support for a separate West German state and to bolster European support for West German economic recovery. The Cold War hence offered Germans the reality of division, the threat of renewed war on their soil, and the opportunity to squeeze concessions from the competing sides.[1]

The Soviet blockade of Berlin, which began in earnest on 26 June 1948, contributed crucially to swinging West German opinion behind the Western Allies and their proposals for a separate West German state. In blocking all rail, boat, and road traffic from the western zones to Berlin, the Soviets were attempting to compel a change in U.S. policy in Germany—by starving 2.5 million Berlin civilians into submission. Such brutality shocked most Germans. Moreover, the policy suggested that the Soviets would not allow a unified Germany to live in peace but would instead attempt to dominate it. Most West Germans, though, wanted independence for their country and opposed the introduction of Communism. Memories of Red Army atrocities in eastern Germany in 1944 and 1945 only strengthened opposition to Russian and Communist expansion among western Germans, especially the expellees. The successful U.S. and British commitment to supply the city with an airlift reassured Germans that the Western Allies, and the United States in particular, would stay to defend them against Soviet aggression. Meanwhile, American and British pilots were risking their lives day after day in often brutal weather to fly vital supplies to German civilians, transforming Americans and Britons from enemies to saviors in the eyes of most West Germans.[2]

Determined to promote (West) German economic recovery and to tie the industrial Ruhr to the Western alliance, the American and British governments demanded in July 1948 that West German politicians create a West German state. Virtually no West German wanted to assume responsibility for dividing Germany or abandoning 17 million Germans in the Soviet Occupation Zone to Russian and Communist rule. Nonetheless, West German politicians of almost all stripes realized that an independent, unified Germany was not likely any time soon. Most were coming to prefer a (semi)sovereign, liberal, Western-oriented West Germany to either an occupied and dependent Germany divided into four zones or a unified but Communist- and Russian-dominated Germany. West German politicians therefore agreed, in July 1948, to take steps to create a provisional parliamentary-democratic state in western Germany.[3]

In retrospect, West German economic growth after currency reform seems a tale of unbroken success based on neoliberal policies. Erhard did seek to liberalize the economy, and industrial production and overall output did grow in every year into the 1960s. Nevertheless, economic policy and economic change between 1948 and 1953 were both complex and variegated.

By spring 1948, Germans could contemplate some revision of Nazi-era economic controls, to take account of postwar realities and to free up entrepreneurial initiative. The neoliberals had not convinced Germans that they could dispense with all guidance of the economy, but most Germans were fed up with the hodgepodge of controls that still constrained the German economy. Given the desperate shortages that plagued postwar Germany, those controls were becoming associated with redistributing misery. The availability of goods on black markets that were unavailable through rationing provided a kind of "education" for the market economy that left even many workers open to a removal of controls. The discretion the controls gave to government officials led to widespread complaints, even from Social Democrats, against bureaucratic arbitrariness, while insufficient personnel meant the controls could only be administered inefficiently. Even the SPD announced that it was against the "controlled economy," though it still favored a "planned economy." Moreover, the CDU could most easily distinguish itself from the SPD, amid the growing tensions of the Cold War, by emphasizing entrepreneurial initiative against "Soviet-style" economic controls.[4]

The United States and Britain allowed Germans to create an opening for revolutionary change in West Germany's economic order. After currency reform, the Germans would need to adjust prices and controls to take account of a decade of substantial economic change. On 18 June 1948, the CDU and FDP pushed through the Bizone's Economic Council a law that gave the director of the Administration for the Economy—Erhard—extraordinarily broad discretion in revising price and other controls. Morally committed to liberalizing the economy as much as possible, Erhard moved decisively, freeing most consumer goods from price and other controls and scaling back the controls on most remaining consumer goods. He did leave controls in place on the most important raw materials, essential foodstuffs, wages, and rents. In a radical reversal of policy, Erhard had established a reconstruction policy that favored consumer-goods producers at the expense of industrial- and capital-goods producers, whom he expected to recover by filling orders from consumer-goods manufacturers and securing Marshall Plan funds.[5]

Erhard was pushing his powers to the limit. He had presumably counted on backing from the United States, and he got it from Clay. After a day-long debate at U.S. headquarters in Frankfurt, the Americans and (less willingly) the Britons approved Erhard's decontrol policy. Erhard helped build that debate into a legend of his (and implicitly Germany's) self-assertion against outside interference, but he could not in 1948 have imposed such far-reaching decontrol on his fellow Germans without American support.[6]

The Economic Council also introduced policies that provided de facto recompense to business for war losses and that spurred economic growth. West German business had preserved much of its productive capital, but it had still suffered substantial war losses of buildings, inventories, working capital, and the like. Rather than try to recompense such losses directly, the West Germans granted business favorable initial access to credit. They also constructed a tax code that favored self-financing by business of reconstruction. That code offered substantial depreciation allowances on fixed assets and essentially exempted from taxation profits that a firm reinvested in the business. That tax policy enabled most firms to rebuild; it also concentrated much of the additional wealth that West German recovery would generate in the hands of those who already had wealth.[7]

The combination of currency reform, decontrol, and tax breaks did produce a short-term boom. Industrial output soared, as firms found it easier to obtain factor inputs and could now produce and sell goods for solid Deutsche Mark. Improved workforce productivity through better nutrition and increased raw-materials supplies played a role, too. Hard money released a flood of goods on 21 June 1948. German businessmen, large and small, had been hoarding goods for months, in hopes that currency reform would offer an opportunity to sell the goods for hard currency, rather than for nearly worthless Reichsmark. Such hoarding was illegal, but Allied and German authorities (including Erhard) had tacitly supported such actions to ensure that sufficient goods would be available to prevent a new round of inflation. West Germans were thrilled that they finally had access to desperately needed goods that had been unavailable for years—but they were outraged that business was profiting enormously from illegal hoarding, rising prices, and a favorable tax code.[8]

As Erhard had predicted during the war, inflationary pressures developed right after currency reform—helped along by Erhard's decontrol of most prices. After a decade of destruction and enforced renunciation, the demand for goods was enormous. People spent their Deutsche Mark as quickly as they earned them, and the velocity of the money supply soared, to some 2.5 times the 1938 rate by the autumn of 1948. Meanwhile, financial institutions expanded bank money substantially through lending to businesses. The money supply hence rose rapidly, more than tripling from June to December 1948. Prices soared, with textile prices, for example, rising 40 percent.[9]

These inflationary pressures imperiled neoliberalism. Erhard initially refused to decontrol wages, even as he decontrolled prices. The policy did temporarily dampen inflationary wage pressures, but workers' standards of living fell even as business profits soared. Support for Erhard's policies eroded rapidly, forcing him to decontrol wages on 3 November 1948. Nonetheless, wage increases lagged because the loss of savings and soaring unemployment shifted bargaining power on labor markets decisively in favor of employers. Popular anger at soaring prices provoked a twenty-four-hour general strike on 12 November 1948 and continued grumbling.[10]

Anti-inflationary rectitude still had to struggle against anxieties about unemployment and individual misery. In September 1948 the Economic Council proposed releasing some blocked Deutsche Mark funds before Christmas, to counteract rising unemployment and allow the poorest to prepare for the rigors of winter. Objections from the BdL and the Allies blocked that proposal. The BdL refused to raise the discount rate, in response to inflationary pressures, because that "would in any case hit the legitimate credit needs for production." In November, though, with Allied backing and over vigorous Economic Council objections, the BdL did introduce credit controls to rein in inflationary pressures. Central-bank officials remained divided, but tight-money advocates did limit reflationary credit-easing measures. Although industrial production and GDP rose from mid-1948, prices fell in 1949, unemployment remained high, and many businesses saw profits plummet.[11]

The war-damaged were often particularly bitter because the post–currency reform environment was so difficult for them. They had the least resources because of their war losses. The currency reform had then wiped out their last reserves. With minimal assets and the weakest ties to customers, expellee firms in particular were least able to survive when the central bank restricted credit. Moreover, expellee workers were usually the first fired.[12]

Even well-established German businessmen had their doubts about neoliberalism in 1948–50. The long tradition of state intervention in the economy, going back centuries, still influenced most German businessmen. The pressures they now faced from currency reform and restrictive monetary policies seemed deeply threatening. They often attacked neoliberal policies and demanded easy money, with any deleterious effects to be ameliorated by government intervention or business self-administration. Even the academic economists on the Economics Ministry Advisory Board were anxious about deflation and proposed easing credit. Neoliberal thinkers, backed up by American officials, had obtained the upper hand in mid-1948, but it was not at all clear they would keep it.[13]

German authorities were under sharply conflicting and growing pressures as they sought to promulgate a Lastenausgleich law. West Germans could not be sure how much of a Lastenausgleich they could afford. Meanwhile, formerly propertied war-damaged Germans vigorously opposed any diversion of possibly limited Lastenausgleich funds from recompense for property losses to assistance for the formerly unpropertied. Yet millions of impoverished war-damaged Germans desperately needed immediate aid, whether they had formerly owned real property or not.

A SOCIAL LASTENAUSGLEICH

Even though the Allied currency reform had effectively extinguished any statutory right to compensation for the war-damaged, they still insisted that their Lastenausgleich claim was a right and that it was not a gift at the discretion of the state or the society. They rooted that right in notions of communal obligation, though it also had sources in natural rights and Christian ethics. The undamaged, surprisingly, often agreed. The Joint Chambers of Commerce of the Bizone announced, "The claims to expenditures from the Lastenausgleich are legal claims against the German state," a state that at that moment did not exist. Similarly, the participants from the major political parties and charitable organizations at the important Karlshöhe meeting on the Lastenausgleich, in August 1948, agreed that a legal claim to a Lastenausgleich existed.[14]

Crucially, though, at that meeting, Gerhard Weisser (SPD) pointed out that "it did not mean leaving the basis of rights if the content of the legal claim was established without reference to the amount of earlier capital." The organized war-damaged very much wanted to establish that connection to individual earlier wealth, as events would show. Yet, for most Germans, the underlying communalist logic of the Lastenausgleich and the desperation of impoverished war-damaged pushed any recompense away from individual restitution for specific losses and toward broader, more social measures to help all who had suffered economically because of war and its consequences. These Germans perceived social justice as demanding a social Lastenausgleich, even if one took some secondary account of past wealth or social status in establishing compensation.[15]

Mid-twentieth-century Germans (like many other people) have tended to argue that the essence of justice is equality, that is, to treat like things alike. The war-damaged also perceived justice in those terms. For example, in 1951 the ZvF called the government's draft Lastenausgleich law "a pinnacle in the area of injustice if one sees treating like factual situations legally alike as an essential precondition for justice." The ZvF clearly did assume that justice demanded such equal treatment of equal circumstances. Yet as Aristotle recognized twenty-three hundred years ago, people often disagree about what constitutes equal or like: "[people] dispute about the equality of the persons. . . . For the one party, if they are unequal in one respect, for example wealth, consider themselves to be unequal in all; and the other party, if they are equal in one respect, for example free birth, consider themselves to be equal in all." Not surprisingly, West Germans disagreed about what "equal" meant for the purposes of a Lastenausgleich, equal as Germans or unequal as Germans of unequal prewar wealth—and virtue.[16]

For those people who favored a more social Lastenausgleich, the key criterion was that all Germans were equal in that they were all human beings, or at least all German human beings. As such, they deserved an existence worthy of a human being, *ein menschenwürdiges Dasein*. Public policy generally, and the Lastenausgleich in particular, should therefore be structured to ensure that each German could enjoy such a life.

The damaged themselves did complain quite bitterly that their losses had left them in such abject poverty—and often in such geographical and social isolation—as to deprive them of the possibility of a humanly worthy life. One expellee, for example, denounced a currency reform that wiped out the last savings of the war-damaged after those battered individuals had suffered "an already years-long period of vegetating while trapped in a daily guerrilla war for a humanly decent dwelling, for an even so modest job, and for one's daily bread." The war-damaged demanded, and most Germans were willing to accord them, the right to material assistance that would restore to them the ability to live a life of some minimal human dignity.[17]

Authorities in the Soviet Occupation Zone and the German Democratic Republic saw the war-damaged as equal to all other Germans and equally entitled to some decent existence, but not to any special Lastenausgleich. The Communists had no intention of re-creating capitalist private property, and the Soviets had resisted the C-D-G Plan's Lastenausgleich proposals on the grounds that Germany's cities should not be rebuilt before the cities Germany had destroyed. When Communist leader Wilhelm Pieck discussed rebuilding Germany's bombed cities, he completely ignored the issue of war-damages compensation and proposed giving the community an ownership share in private buildings to the extent that tax revenue was used to finance their reconstruction. The German SBZ officials in charge of refugee affairs did respond to war-damaged pressure for a Lastenausgleich with a draft bill, but the Soviets banned all such initiatives. Instead, the East German regime integrated the war-damaged into the East German economy as workers, to the same degree as all other East Germans. The regime did seize Nazi goods and redistribute them to expellees, and it did offer grants to unemployable refugees, yet in both programs—which apparently assisted less than 10 percent of expellees—it based benefits on need, independent of the amount of property losses. Philipp Ther has aptly characterized this policy as "egalitarian-socialist."[18]

West German social thinkers, politicians, and even businessmen could agree on the need for a social Lastenausgleich, separate from the despised "welfare," that would enable *all* war-damaged Germans to live an existence worthy of a human being. They implicitly assumed that the unusual blow the war-damaged had suffered entitled them to more generous treatment than traditional welfare recipients. They based that claim on current need, however, not prior property ownership. As an SPD publication stated, "It is the first goal of the Lastenausgleich to provide a new securing of their livelihood through a [monthly] benefit for all who cannot support themselves from their own work. Under this viewpoint all are equally entitled—regardless of whether they formerly had only a subsistence or more." The social activist Anton Wopperer wanted to put special emphasis in the Lastenausgleich on providing household goods and clothing rather than compensation for the loss of business property: "To have one's own farm does not belong to the dignity of the person; to be clothed, to sit on a chair and at a table, to sleep in a bed, even if it's only a sack of straw, does."[19]

Germans had drawn powerful conclusions from the experience of Nazi dictatorship. The essence of Nazi racial policy had been to deny the humanity of whole classes of human beings, to define them as "lives unworthy of living" or "subhuman." The horrors of war, defeat, and expulsion had confronted virtually all Germans, directly or indirectly, with the devastating impact that abject misery could have on an individual's ability to function as an autonomous, honored person. Middle- and upper-class Germans had discovered for the first time just how dehumanizing poverty could be, even for once-solid citizens like themselves. When West Germans came to draft the Basic Law of the Federal Republic of Germany, they chose as its first article the proviso that "the dignity of the human person is inviolable. To respect and to protect it is the duty of all state authority." [20] A vivid sense of the fragility of that human dignity also dominated most people's attitude toward the Lastenausgleich.

Proponents of a social Lastenausgleich argued that a devastated, truncated, occupied West Germany had such limited resources that it must structure any Lastenausgleich so as to neither overburden the poorer nor disburse funds disproportionately to the relatively well-off. As one observer noted, "The apparent justice of restoring previous . . . circumstances must give way before the higher justice of helping the weak." The bottom line was providing a decent living for all Germans, and that could not be done if funds for a Lastenausgleich came from the less well-off strata through high levy rates on modest property holdings or were exhausted through large payments to a few formerly well-to-do damaged. The SPD, the unions, and most war-damaged Germans who had owned little real property were firmly committed to this principle, but center and right-of-center supporters of a social or productive Lastenausgleich also made this argument. As one chamber of commerce put it, "only in few and urgent cases can compensation claims be satisfied. . . . Only that program can have any hope of feasibility that attempts to help somewhat the worst affected and for the rest to ameliorate the perceptible losses and to maintain the strength of the economy's substance, including that of the damaged." Further, Johannes Kunze (CDU) later asserted, "I would not be able to recognize it as a Lastenausgleich if I were to give today even only a Pfennig to someone who is already in a good position, just because he lost some capital over there, so long as the person who still has nothing has not found his way forward again." [21]

The proponents of a social Lastenausgleich usually saw a job as an economically valuable — and recompensable — possession. People in market economies do not usually think of a worker's employment as part of his or her capital, but some Germans argued that the loss of a job could be just as devastating a blow to the employee's economic future as the loss of business premises would be to a businessman. As one Social Democrat declared firmly, "The loss of a livelihood or the loss of the ability to work is a greater injury than the loss of even . . . a substantial fortune if in the latter case the possibility remains of founding a new livelihood through one's own work." Its loss was hence just as deserving of recompense as the loss of a farm, rental property, or business.[22]

Some actually saw a quotal, property-based Lastenausgleich as immoral. All property losses might be formally equal, but differing losses could have widely differing material consequences. A white-collar worker who lost a 10,000 RM house to bombing but kept his job would be much better off than an artisan who lost 500 RM in tools necessary for her livelihood or a worker left unemployed when his workplace was destroyed. For some opponents of a quotal Lastenausgleich, all healthy individuals had an obligation to contribute by their labor to the society that nurtured and protected them. Substantial Lastenausgleich payments to formerly wealthy but currently able-bodied individuals, Gerhard Brandes (SPD) said, "would merely put the big creditors in a position to lead a carefree and workfree existence as a rentier, instead, as must others, of applying productively their own ability to work." Not just socialists took this view. Kunze rejected in July 1949 any substantial Lastenausgleich payments above subsistence, saying "capitalist do-nothings are out of place" in the new Germany.[23]

As even supporters of private property and economic self-reliance could recognize, the experience of Germans from 1914 to 1948 had called into question traditional assumptions that personal security lay in ownership of private property. Two inflations had shown that paper assets were a speculation whose value the state (authoritarian monarchy, parliamentary democracy, fascist dictatorship, or liberal democratic occupier) was quite willing to sacrifice to national fiscal expediency, leaving their owners impoverished. Germany's catastrophic economic collapse in the 1930s had driven millions of working- to upper-middle-class Germans into unemployment or bankruptcy — and into the arms of the anticapitalist Nazis. Further, bombing and the expulsion of Germans from their homes and businesses had shown that real property could be destroyed or confiscated in an instant, leaving individuals and their families penniless. Whatever moral or natural rights people might have to property, it had proved in practice to be only a bundle of rights guaranteed by a specific society under certain circumstances. When society could not or would not uphold those rights, the individual and his or her property were surrendered to the whim of the more powerful.[24]

A number of Germans were hence willing to argue that the organized war-damaged were deluding themselves in seeing property as the basis of security in a modern economy. Certainly some individual war-damaged could recognize this. An ad hoc group exploring a currency-reform plan in 1947 declared, "Experience has already taught us that the best real property can suffer just as much a disappearance of value as all other 'values,' when the economy is ailing or collapses." An annuitant wrote her insurance company, "I trusted the insurance company; nonetheless, for the second time in my life [presumably after the inflation of the 1920s] I experience the *in*security of such capital investments."[25]

If the ownership of property could not provide security, an alternative basis could be human capital, the knowledge and skills an individual possessed and the opportunity to exercise them. The SPD emphasized that such intangibles could be more important than capital, and even a business journal such as *Handelsblatt* could in 1948 assert, "A family that has lost its breadwinner in the war is far worse stricken than a family that has indeed lost its capital but kept its breadwinner." Further, the expellees and their children apparently chose to live this lesson in their own lives, as events would show.[26]

More broadly, though, some Germans argued that, given the inability of property ownership to guarantee security, one would have to demand that society provide that security. For example, Bauser argued that Germany's relative narrowness, geographically and economically, meant that its citizens could not depend on rebuilding from a disaster as Americans, "with their broad lands and unlimited opportunities," could. Rather, he wrote, Germany needed "a larger social sector than the USA" and a Lastenausgleich to protect its citizens. The goal of a Lastenausgleich, August Haussleiter, argued, "must be a new social order . . . to give back to people the necessary social security" that ownership of real property had failed to provide.[27]

Despite the provisional triumph of Erhard's neoliberalism, many Germans in 1949–51 still sought a more communal, more egalitarian social order. Any Lastenausgleich that focused on restoring past property would scarcely be compatible with such an order. More broadly, the continued strong desire for some degree of economic direction suggested a less individualistic Lastenausgleich. Finally, the scope of misery suffered by the war-damaged seemed to demand the socially most efficient use of the resources available for balancing the burdens of the war. A social Lastenausgleich had good prospects of becoming law.

THE FIRST LASTENAUSGLEICH LAW

German legislators and, significantly, the war-damaged themselves quickly concluded that some kind of "immediate aid," at least for needy war-damaged, was indispensable. The Lastenausgleich, especially any individual Lastenausgleich, had such complex ramifications that legislators would need time to craft appropriate legislation. Yet the millions of people who provided the base for war-damaged politics were often in such desperate straits that they could not wait. Many had gone for years without adequate housing, clothing, or nutrition. In Düsseldorf alone, 13,000 bombed-out residents still lacked beds to sleep in. Currency reform had destroyed the savings that had kept many above water, and rising prices were only making things worse. Whatever hopes the formerly propertied war-damaged might have had about a restoration of their lost property, they and the formerly unpropertied often needed food, a dwelling, a bed, a blanket *this* year. The criterion for such immediate aid, as the organized war-damaged had to agree, could not be past wealth but current need: a social Lastenausgleich.[28]

The American insistence on converting long-term debts at a 10:1 ratio had reduced debt burdens by 90 percent, creating substantial currency-reform profits for debtors and evoking bitter memories of the enormous windfall profits that debtors had secured from inflation in the 1920s. Virtually everyone, including the Allies, agreed that Germans had to tax away those profits for the Lastenausgleich, and the Economic Council passed in mid-August 1948 a law that established a special levy in Deutsche Mark equal to 90 percent of the Reichsmark mortgage. Interest and amortization payments, however, went to the states. An implementation decree directed the states to devote 85 percent of the income to Lastenausgleich purposes, such as housing construction for war-damaged individuals, and to transfer 15 percent to the central authorities for "supra-regional balancing out."[29]

The Economic Council's rapid, decisive response to the issue of mortgage profits shows how powerfully the memory of 1920s injustices still affected Germans, including policy makers. Yet the council failed to move decisively to secure other currency-reform profits that had redounded to the benefit of big business. This distinction shows the growing influence of the business community and the growing desire to protect firms whose productive investment would be crucial to future economic well-being.

The war-damaged initially sought immediate aid through a partial reversal of the currency reform. They believed that they had a legal right in their savings and in their war-damages claims, and they demanded that German authorities correct the Allied "error" in imposing an unsocial currency reform. Bauser, the leader of the bomb-damaged, pointed out that it would be ridiculous to destroy capital in the currency reform just so that one could compensate the losses later; the sensible thing to do was to re-create some of the Reichsmark assets, up to 50 percent for the needy, while blocking as much as necessary temporarily. Expellee savings accounts had not been converted into Deutsche Mark because the expellees usually lacked proof of their holdings and because their savings institutions had not been legally domiciled in West Germany. Expellee leaders still demanded in August that expellee savings accounts up to 2,000 RM be converted at 1:1, with 2:1 conversion for savings of 2,000–5,000 RM, and 4:1 for amounts above 5,000 RM (as opposed to the 10:1 that then prevailed for western Germans).[30]

Such proposals proved impossible to implement. The Economic Council was sympathetic, particularly because reviving some preexisting balances would provide aid to the needy without the delays that would be involved in transferring state funds through the governmental bureaucracy. The BdL and the Allies, though, refused to countenance such proposals because they were determined to restrict the money supply to control inflationary pressures. Indeed, as discussed above, they canceled the shadow quota and much of the blocked savings the damaged sought to have released.[31]

Meanwhile, the Economic Council needed nearly the full six months to come up with even the First Lastenausgleich Law, which won Länderrat and Economic Council approval on 14 December 1948. The states of the French Zone passed virtually identical legislation.[32]

The law would generate more than a billion Deutsche Mark per year to assist the war-damaged in meeting their most immediate needs. The initial draft had imposed a capital levy of 2 percent, but at SPD instigation the law established an annual levy of 3 percent on the assessed value of property in West Germany as of 21 June 1948 (though with a 2 percent rate for rental property assessed at less than 15,000 DM and for agricultural property). The bill also imposed special levies on inventories to capture hoarding profits.[33]

In April 1948, Erhard had urged German business to flout the law by hoarding goods in anticipation of currency reform. Experts from the Special Agency for Money and Credit had consistently favored such hoarding. They believed that goods could not be justly distributed in the monetary and moral confusion of postwar Germany. More important, the enormous pent-up demand for consumer goods would provoke sharp price increases after a currency reform unless a cushion of hoarded goods was available to meet that demand and hold prices down. Businesses were already hoarding goods in anticipation of getting a hard-value new currency for their goods instead of the worthless Reichsmark. Given the vehement popular outrage at hoarding, though, Erhard's open support for such activities was risky.[34]

Six months later, Erhard surprised, nay stunned, virtually everyone by proposing as part of the First Lastenausgleich Law a 25 percent levy on all inventories held on 20 June 1948, payable in one lump sum on 10 January 1949. He had warned before the currency reform that some levy would be necessary to seize the unfair currency-reform profits inventory holders would win. As he said in November 1948, "Whoever on 20 June had a legal or illegal hoard of goods secured a currency profit as against that person whose capital was at that point in cash balances. When the category of currency-damaged is created, then on the other side the currency profits must be seized." Such profits were all the greater because his decontrol policies allowed sharp price rises. Moreover, to generate revenue from which to pay the levy, many retailers would have to sell off inventory, exerting downward pressure on prices (and perhaps forestalling any need for tight credit).[35]

Subsequent observers have tended to ignore or, metaphorically, to shake their heads at this curious proposal by a probusiness neoliberal, but Erhard was acting in accordance with his late 1940s neoliberalism. He argued for as much freedom for markets as possible, but he considered some governmental action necessary to establish the necessary framework for free markets and to legitimate such markets by ensuring some fairness in the distribution of the goods. An inventory levy served both purposes. It allowed him to encourage hoarding before currency reform in the knowledge that he could use fiscal policy after currency reform to promote both destocking and a fairer distribution of society's burdens.[36]

Erhard's inventory levy faced a storm of opposition. Thousands of West German businessmen, businesses, and business interest groups flooded policy makers with telegrams, letters, and telephone calls denouncing the proposal as a dire threat to the survival of German business. Many argued that they had had large inventories because they could not obtain the inputs needed to finish up production until after currency reform. Others objected that the nature of their business meant that they had to hold large inventories as a normal part of doing business. The latter claim became particularly popular when politicians proposed two levy rates, one for "necessary" inventories for a given branch and a second, punitive rate for "unnecessary" inventories that presumably had reflected efforts to hoard.[37]

Erhard, though, held firm, to the deep annoyance of his political friends. Faced with enormous pressure from business, the FDP and CDU abandoned Erhard and sought to limit the inventory levies, especially because Erhard wanted them to be due on a single day. As Schillinger has pointed out, the result was that the only party that supported the "archcapitalist" Erhard's proposal for a 25 percent levy was, ironically, the Communists. Erhard stuck to his guns, urging the Lastenausgleich Advisory Commission that they "not be too timid in setting the rate for burdening inventories." He and others reiterated that, whatever a firm's reasons for having a large inventory on 20 June, it had in fact secured substantial windfall profits.[38]

Legislators dared not simply quash Erhard's proposal, but they modified it in crucial ways to address business's concerns. First, they set the levy on necessary inventories at 4 percent, a very modest burden for firms that had almost always been able to raise prices substantially since currency reform; they did set the levy on unnecessary inventories at 15 percent. To alleviate the weight of the levy, lawmakers provided for payment in three installments. They also allowed firms to petition for relief if they had suffered serious war damages or if they could demonstrate that the particular nature of their business demanded high levels of necessary inventories.[39]

The conflict over the inventory levy illuminates the contradictory pressures on the Economic Council in late 1948. Popular revulsion at the unsocial currency reform and at profiteering by holders of real capital created enormous pressure for government intervention in existing property relationships to secure what most citizens saw as a just distribution of burdens. Nonetheless, the complaints of the economically vital business community were too strong to ignore. The result was another compromise that imposed greater burdens on business than the latter wanted but less than public opinion demanded. Further, Erhard's role illustrates how in late 1948 even neoliberals could still favor a rigorous Lastenausgleich that would compel real-property holders to sell off assets.

Despite their deep concern about the inventory levy, business leaders, in a significant move, wrote in late November 1948 to support the First Lasten-ausgleich Law. Recognizing that "those damaged by the war and its conse-quences may wait no longer for the beginning of assistance," the Working Group of Chambers of Industry and Commerce of the Bizone declared that it would "set aside the serious reservations that could be raised against the planned regulation" and accept the immediate aid program, including a capital levy rate of 2.5 percent and inventory levies of 4 percent on normal invento-ries and 30 percent on excessive inventories. The necessity to do something on behalf of the war-damaged and a sense that social justice demanded it were so great that even obligors had to support significant levies.[40]

The bill provided extensive exemptions from the levies. The first 3,000 DM of each individual's assets were exempt from the capital levy. Most citizens ac-cepted this provision, though some war-damaged would have liked to see a lower and some undamaged a larger exemption. More controversial were ex-emptions for the assets of charitable organizations, trade unions, and public bodies. Private property owners complained, often bitterly, that these exemp-tions were unfair because they increased the levy rate for private property and gave a competitive advantage to nonprofit enterprises. Some war-damaged also complained that these exemptions reduced the levy funds available for a Lastenausgleich. The FDP and some in the CDU and CSU (Christian Social Union, the conservative, Bavarian wing of the CDU) sought to reduce or elimi-nate such exemptions, but the political climate in late 1948 was still too favor-able to provisions that could be labeled "social."[41]

The bill's centerpiece was an entitlement for expellees, bomb-damaged, currency-damaged, and the politically persecuted to nonwelfare assistance. Support Aid provided 70 DM a month for those war-damaged unable, through age or disability, to earn a living, with supplements of 30 DM a month for a wife and 20 DM a month for each dependent child. These amounts were 20 percent higher than the prevailing welfare payment. Expellees need only show the loss of 300 DM in assets to qualify for unlimited Support Aid, while the bombed-out and currency-damaged could not collect more than one-half of their ma-terial losses, plus 300 DM. (One should note here that the latter provision meant that in 1952 of the remaining evacuees from Würzburg, only 1.7 percent received Support Aid, while 11.5 percent had to depend on welfare.) Legisla-tors hoped to spare war-damaged citizens the humiliation of seeking welfare; they also sought to free cities of any welfare burden for war-damaged individu-als so that city authorities would repeal rules barring people from moving to the cities, where the jobs were, without official permission. Notably, the bill exempted the war-damaged from the usual requirement to support immediate family members who had become indigent, because the expellees especially could often get back on their feet only if spared the burden of supporting their relatives. This policy did undercut collective obligation and advance the individualization of West German society. Once the authorities had allotted sufficient funds to cover all Support-Aid payments, they were to distribute remaining funds as lump-sum payments to help needy expellees, bombed-out, and the persecuted replace their household goods and to assist them in starting up a new business or acquiring education or training for themselves and their children.[42]

Both obligors and leaders of the war-damaged complained that the First Lastenausgleich Law served only to reduce state budgets by moving the needy war-damaged from welfare, financed by general revenues, to a so-called Lastenausgleich, financed by capital levies. Supporters of a social Lastenausgleich had recognized that the law would ease state budgets, but they argued that this was neither the law's intention nor its main effect. Nonetheless, this consequence of the bill would remain an issue, even for relatively neutral parties such as the trade unions.[43]

German policy makers' protests to the contrary notwithstanding, the First Lastenausgleich Law prejudiced in certain respects the final form of the Lastenausgleich. The war-damaged, not surprisingly, did not want any vital options foreclosed in a provisional bill. While sensitive to this desire, policy makers also had to address the concerns of other sectors of German society, particularly of the economically vital real-property holders. As Alfred Hartmann, director of finances, pointed out, "Certain things have to be finally clarified already because the prevailing uncertainty in the economy is only bearable any longer with very great difficulty and, as we have seen, has led in certain circumstances to dangerously misguided decisions in the economy."[44]

Most significantly, the First Lastenausgleich Law provided that the valuation date for assessing the property subject to levies would be 21 June 1948. Some of the war-damaged wanted to postpone the date until the economy had recovered from its postwar depression, when increased production would result in a higher valuation of productive property and higher levy payments. The business community, though, objected that postponing the valuation date would undercut the incentive to invest because businessmen would fear that an increased bill for capital levies would eat up any profits from investment. The Economic Council agreed with the latter. One could also argue that the logic of a Lastenausgleich as a balancing out of war-related losses required a valuation date as close as possible to the time when the losses had occurred.[45]

The First Lastenausgleich Law established that the levies would be due in cash rather than in kind (though the law did promote voluntary payment in kind). Many of the war-damaged and their leadership argued that the logic of a Lastenausgleich required that holders of real property transfer some of it directly to bomb-damaged and expellees, to allow the latter to regain their socioeconomic positions. Nevertheless, the Economic Council quailed at the prospect of organizing such a far-reaching intervention in the economic life of the German people, at least in a provisional bill.[46]

Many war-damaged also concluded that the bill's social emphasis was predetermining future developments. Although the leadership of the war-damaged and many war-damaged had accepted the necessity of an emergency bill, they increasingly feared that the First Lastenausgleich Law seemed to be committing funds to social measures and job creation, leaving nothing for a future individual Lastenausgleich based on property losses. The leadership particularly denounced the provision that some Lastenausgleich funds would go to housing construction to the benefit of, but not necessarily for ownership by, war-damaged Germans.[47]

The war-damaged had relatively little leverage in 1948, because the numerous expellees were still struggling simply to build effective organizations. Having created a massive problem by sanctioning the expulsions, the Allies feared that the expellees might become dangerously radical and revanchist. The Allies banned expellee organizations, hoping to force the expellees into the regular political parties, speeding their integration and moderating any incipient radicalism. British and American occupation officials allowed nonpolitical refugee groups from 1947 but legalized expellee political groups only in mid-1949. These bans may have partially achieved their aims, but they also prevented the expellees from bringing their full weight to bear in early discussions of expellee policy, including the Lastenausgleich.[48]

The Allies could impose such bans in part because the expellees initially fixed their gaze so firmly on the past. The latter found their brutal expulsion from their ancestral homes so obviously unjust and so obviously illegal under international law that most of them assumed, at least into 1948, that the Allies would eventually come to their senses and that the final peace treaty would allow them to return to their homes. Most expellees in 1946–48 were loathe to push for a Lastenausgleich because to do so was to admit—to others and to one's self—that the prospects for a return to one's home were dim or nonexistent. As the Reverend Georg Goebel, an important early refugee leader, could declare as late as mid-1948, "We renounce a Lastenausgleich; give us back our homeland." Only the passage of time, and the deepening of the Cold War, could make the existing borders seem permanent and a return unlikely. By late 1948, most expellees were beginning to reorder their priorities away from a return to their old homeland and toward securing a new home and livelihood in West Germany—and compensation for property left behind.[49]

Such refocusing of attention presaged the creation of more comprehensive expellee organizations. In August 1948, several expellee leaders began trying to establish a trizonal umbrella organization for their various (still officially apolitical) groups. In October, increasing anxiety about the social character of the First Lastenausgleich Law provided the catalyst for the squabbling groups to create a Lastenausgleich Committee, which included representatives of the bomb-damaged and which would function relatively harmoniously. Continued infighting delayed until 9 April 1949 the creation of the Central Association of Expelled Germans (Zentralverband vertriebener Deutschen, the ZvD). This group, led by Linus Kather (CDU), would claim to represent the social and economic interests of all expellees. On the Lastenausgleich, though, it would for years speak primarily for the formerly propertied who favored an individual Lastenausgleich.[50]

A preference for a more individual Lastenausgleich also played a significant role in the FDP's decision to vote against the First Lastenausgleich Law. Certainly the party, with its ties to the business community, was not happy about the increase in the capital levy from 2 percent to 3 percent per year, and it opposed the inventory levy as impossible to implement fairly and too burdensome for business. Nevertheless, the FDP could not win electoral campaigns with such policy positions because virtually all of the war-damaged and many other Germans saw a Lastenausgleich based on capital levies as crucial and a taxing away of hoarding profits as only just. However, by demanding a more individual, property-based structure for the First Lastenausgleich Law, the FDP ranged itself on the side of important elements among the war-damaged and the still-propertied.[51]

The Lastenausgleich was one of two major issues in the history of the Bizone on which the main "bourgeois parties," the CDU/CSU and the FDP, split. A Grand Coalition of the CDU/CSU and the SPD passed the fundamental legislation on the Lastenausgleich (as on social insurance). Already at the August 1948 Karlshöhe meeting on the Lastenausgleich, Weisser (SPD) reported, there had been a real openness by "the decisively Christian-rooted Left CDU people and churchmen to a serious valuation of our socially based demands." In autumn of 1948, the left wing of the CDU/CSU (with the tacit consent of the party leadership in the Economic Council) joined with the SPD to craft a First Lastenausgleich Law whose expenditures were socially oriented and substantially independent of the personal losses that individual war-damaged had suffered.[52] This cooperation was a harbinger of things to come—and a danger to supporters of an individual Lastenausgleich.

THE ALLIES FIDDLE

Despite the desperate need of millions of Germans for the assistance the First Lastenausgleich Law promised, the Western powers would need eight months to come to agreement and to promulgate that law. Even then they would demand several changes in the bill.

U.S. secretary of the army Kenneth Royall only grudgingly approved the Lastenausgleich legislation. He seemed to perceive a Lastenausgleich as inherently radical, as many Washington officials had in 1946. Nonetheless, State Department officials and Clay successfully pressured him to respond to German needs and desires. Royall hence allowed U.S. approval of the bill, but only if the Germans renamed the capital levies "special taxes based on property," made the bill "exclusively a relief measure" that was "fully independent of any measure related to any general equalization of burdens," and renamed it the "Immediate Aid Law." Royall also insisted that the property of nationals of the World War II Allies be exempted from any levies to recompense war damages (in a bill that officially was not to be about recompensing war damages). Finally, the Germans would also have to postpone any further Lastenausgleich measures until after the establishment of a West German state.[53]

Disagreements among the Allies also delayed action. The French especially, though also some American and British officials, rejected any levies on their nationals' property in Germany to recompense war damages that had resulted from Allied efforts to stop German aggression. The French also resisted any Lastenausgleich because they feared its levies would limit their ability to keep squeezing substantial occupation costs out of their zone.[54]

Finally, on 1 May 1949, the Allies presented the Germans with the changes they would have to make to secure Allied approval of an "Immediate Aid Law" for the war-damaged. When they discovered what the Allies wanted, the Germans were outraged. The Allies had squandered four and a half months of precious time quibbling about what, to the Germans, seemed side issues. The Germans could understand, if not welcome, the Allied desire to exempt the property of Allied nationals, but they found utterly baffling American-inspired demands that they rename the bill the "Immediate Aid Law," exclude all references to a Lastenausgleich, and rename the capital levy. The Lastenausgleich was, not surprisingly, so integrally a part of the First Lastenausgleich Law that the Germans had to secure from the Allies the answers to a three-page, single-spaced list of questions before they could make the demanded changes. The Economic Council quickly amended the bill, to get the still necessary Allied approval — but it also passed a resolution stating that, irrespective of the law's form, it constituted "German Lastenausgleich law."[55]

That resolution was arguably a sign of democratic self-assertiveness by the West Germans. Rather than limply acquiescing to the cavalier demands that their rulers, the Allied occupation forces, sought to impose on them, the representatives of the German people stood up for what they believed to be the rights and needs of their constituents. The Nazi-inculcated fear of speaking up was beginning to dissipate. The Western Allies would not always be happy about Germans' self-assertiveness, especially given the negative consequences of such self-assertiveness in the past. Yet if Germans were to govern themselves, as the Western Allies insisted that they should, then they were going to have to be willing to assert themselves democratically against pressure from above.

Having extracted from the Germans the changes they wanted, the Allies proceeded to delay until 4 August 1949 before promulgating the Immediate Aid Law. Some Germans thought this delay was punishment for German temerity in cleverly meeting Allied demands in ways that preserved the bill as "German Lastenausgleich law." Nothing in the internal American documents, though, supports this notion, and thoughtless inefficiency rather than petty vindictiveness seems more likely to explain the delay. The result, nonetheless, was that desperately impoverished Germans had to wait yet another two and a half months before German authorities could begin implementing that "immediate" aid.[56]

One key effect of Allied inertia was to delay progress on implementing a final Lastenausgleich. Disinclined to invest too much effort until the Allies had revealed their intentions, the German advisory commission on final Lastenausgleich legislation effectively suspended operation. Work did continue in the Administration for Finances, but the Lastenausgleich was clearly slipping, as German officials reordered their legislative priorities. The prospect of immediate aid for the neediest only made such slippage easier to justify, to the undamaged and to policy makers, even if not to the war-damaged.[57] As a result, the expellees, who were organizing politically, would have more influence on the final legislation and that legislation would be crafted in an environment more friendly to the claims of property owners — albeit, much less open to economic experimentation.

Chapter 5

INDIVIDUAL VIRTUE, INDIVIDUAL LASTENAUSGLEICH

For the formerly propertied war-damaged, social justice required an individual, or quotal, Lastenausgleich. They believed that their prewar property ownership had reflected their inherent moral superiority and efficacy relative to unpropertied Germans, a view also held by most property holders undamaged by the war. They continued to hope that property ownership would promise security, even though society had failed to protect their property through the maelstrom of war. They believed that only an individual Lastenausgleich could restore their lost wealth and social status, their sense of individual control, and the moral order. To ensure that the final Lastenausgleich Law did not, like the Immediate Aid Law, offer only a social Lastenausgleich, they had to argue their case publicly and forcefully.

BUILDING A NEW POLITICAL ORDER

Post-1948 debates over an individual Lastenausgleich took place within the nascent political order of the new Federal Republic of Germany. The new republic lacked full sovereignty, as the Western Allies retained important powers under the Occupation Statute. West Germans explicitly saw it as a temporary expedient until Germany could be reunified. They even called its founding document the Basic Law, rather than a constitution, to emphasize its provisional character. Yet with the establishment of a new government, West Germans substantially increased their control over their own affairs, including the Lastenausgleich.

The Basic Law, promulgated on 23 May 1949, provided for the establishment of a parliamentary democracy for the now unified Trizone, despite widespread postwar German doubts about parliamentary democracy and political parties.

The Americans in particular had blocked corporatist alternatives, which did not accord with their ideas of democracy. Meanwhile, the survivors of Weimar democracy, who were more likely than other Germans to become politically active, had assumed central roles in the construction of postwar German self-administrative bodies. They had then parlayed those positions into control of the state constitutional assemblies and of the Parliamentary Council that had drafted the Basic Law. That Basic Law located political authority in a parliament whose popularly elected lower house (Bundestag) would both legislate for the Federal Republic and provide the basis for a cabinet dependent on a majority of its delegates. An upper house (Bundesrat) would represent the states and would have limited but still important legislative powers.[1]

The new republic's first federal elections constituted a referendum on the social-market economy versus a planned economy. The CDU issued a new platform that identified the social-market economy as the cause of West Germany's recent economic successes and as its hope for the future. As leader of the CDU, Adenauer courted neoliberal official Erhard because he wanted to offer voters a clear alternative to the socialist and Marxist SPD and because he wanted to constrain the left wing of his own party. Erhard agreed to run as a CDU candidate, despite his sympathies for the liberal FDP, because he too saw a need to tie the CDU to the market. Adenauer was still relatively unknown, and the election seemed more a contest between Erhard and the SPD's Kurt Schumacher than between Adenauer and his future adversary Schumacher.[2]

The elections to the First Bundestag, which took place on 14 August 1949, returned ten parties. The CDU/CSU (31 percent of the vote) was the largest, giving it a claim to form the first West German government, but the SPD (29 percent of the vote) was a close second. Adenauer and the CSU leadership preferred a right-of-center coalition, partly to offer voters a clear political choice, though mostly from a deep-dyed opposition to Marxian socialism. They insisted that voters had opted in the election for the market over planning. Influential members of the CDU did argue for a Grand Coalition of the CDU and the SPD because they favored a more interventionist, social government and wanted the strongest parliamentary base for addressing West Germany's multifarious problems. However, vigorous politicking by Adenauer and his supporters produced a one-vote margin in the Bundestag, on 15 September 1949, for an Adenauer government based on the CDU and parties to its right.[3]

Adenauer's success in forming a government and preserving a majority for it effected three fundamental decisions for the Federal Republic. First, the CDU's choice of the FDP over the SPD as coalition partner implied a turn toward the social-market economy (though not an abandonment of all government intervention). Adenauer continued to insist that the election had been a referendum on the social-market economy and that the CDU's electoral plurality required its government to implement that policy. Second, by rejecting a Grand Coalition and insisting on offering a clear choice between government and opposition (a policy also pursued by SPD leader Schumacher), Adenauer bolstered West German democracy, not least by denying the radical Right any leverage to increase its own vote as a voice against a wishy-washy coalition. Finally, Adenauer's preeminence confirmed the Federal Republic's Western orientation and its abandonment of either any immediate likelihood of unification with the Soviet Occupation Zone or any recovery of territories east of the Oder-Neiße.[4]

Adenauer's inaugural address to parliament, setting out his government's policies, was only partially encouraging to the war-damaged. He asserted early in the speech, "The striving for an amelioration of misery, for *social justice,* will be the highest guiding star for our entire work." In listing the pressing issues that the new parliament would have to tackle, he named the problems of the expellees and the bomb-damaged first, and he promised to promulgate Lastenausgleich legislation "as soon as possible." Nonetheless, he contended, "The reconstruction of our economy is the foremost, indeed the only basis for any social policy and for the integration of the expellees. Only a prosperous economy can bear over the long run the burdens from the Lastenausgleich." Adenauer did consider a Lastenausgleich indispensable, but Schillinger is right to argue that Adenauer placed capital accumulation and economic reconstruction ahead of recompense for war damages. Moreover, Adenauer did not mention private property or reveal how individual a Lastenausgleich he supported. The war-damaged knew they faced a tough fight to get what they wanted.[5]

To demonstrate his commitment to solving the problems of the expellees, Adenauer included in his cabinet a Ministry for Expellees and Refugees, one sympathetic to an individual Lastenausgleich. Adenauer and most other Germans were convinced that leaving the approximately 8 million expellees to "vegetate" would be disastrous and that the Federal Republic had to take vigorous measures to integrate them economically, socially, and politically. As expellee minister, Adenauer chose Hans Lukaschek, an expellee from Silesia. A Catholic and a former civil servant with ties to the resistance against Hitler, Lukaschek had played a leading role in early expellee efforts to organize. He was invariably a minority of one in the cabinet on Lastenausgleich issues, but he was never willing to resign over Lastenausgleich conflicts. Other expellee leaders came to see him as weak, but, as a strong believer in private property and a vehement antisocialist, he was convinced that expellees had to work with the CDU.[6]

Adenauer also appointed the man the war-damaged would come to see as their nemesis, Federal Finance Minister Fritz Schäffer. Schäffer had before 1933 served in the civil service, in Bavarian politics, and (briefly) as head of the Bavarian Finance Ministry. A vehement anti-Nazi, he had faced persecution under the Third Reich. During his brief service in 1945 as American-appointed minister-president of Bavaria, he opposed rapid democratization and "politics" in government, favoring administrative solutions instead. He also showed anxiety about the flood of refugees who were eroding traditional Bavarian identities. He was by 1949 the most powerful national-level politician in the CSU. Adenauer had to offer him an important cabinet post for political reasons.[7]

Schäffer was the target of numerous bitter and occasionally nasty attacks from the war-damaged. He was virtually the only national-level politician willing to voice even tentative doubts about the idea of a Lastenausgleich, though he insisted he favored a (feasible) Lastenausgleich. He reportedly made several apparently callous remarks about the Lastenausgleich, and his Finance Ministry took a very long time to produce what the war-damaged considered a highly unsatisfactory Lastenausgleich bill. Because this politician, of all politicians, had jurisdiction over the Lastenausgleich, he became a lightning rod for the anger of the war-damaged at the sub rosa opposition to their demands. Many war-damaged believed that if only he were replaced or some other ministry given jurisdiction over the Lastenausgleich, their worries would be over.[8]

As finance minister, though, Schäffer was, in effect, paid to tell people the government could not afford what they wanted. Under the Basic Law, any finance minister was formally charged to object to any "excessive" spending request, an objection that only an explicit vote of his cabinet colleagues could override. Schäffer was, as Hans Günter Hockerts notes, "proverbially penny-pinching," and even groups with which he sympathized, such as civil servants, faced his implacable opposition to increasing expenditures in a time of fiscal weakness. The Lastenausgleich was an enormously expensive and potentially deleterious policy that competed with other social, political, and economic needs for scarce resources. Schäffer had since 1945 insisted that a balanced budget was a prerequisite to solving the war-damages problem, but any responsible finance minister in the early Federal Republic would have been an obstacle to the kind of generosity the war-damaged expected.[9]

Personalizing the issue by attacking Schäffer was an unsurprising but ultimately counterproductive strategy. Political conflicts are often personalized, with citizens identifying various policies with specific individuals while ignoring the social interests behind those policies. Besides, the Nazis had spent over a decade telling Germans that individual political leadership was preeminent. Yet Schäffer's attitude toward the Lastenausgleich was not mere personal whim; rather, it reflected the interests and desires of important social groups, not least the disinclination of many local Germans to sacrifice *too* much to the benefit of the war-damaged, especially expellees from the East. Ultimately, Schäffer could put his stamp on the Lastenausgleich Law only where he had sufficient support to carry the cabinet and the coalition parties with him.[10]

A package of early measures suggested the Adenauer government was willing to help war victims in the name of national solidarity, despite Schäffer's fiscal concerns. The Allies had made the varying West German states responsible for benefits for disabled veterans and civilian casualties and for war widows and orphans, and benefits varied enormously. In February 1950 the Federal Republic passed a provisional law to raise benefits in the poorer states, and in December 1950 it passed the Federal War Victims Benefits Laws, increasing and regularizing benefits across West Germany. The Republic in April 1950 passed a law providing returning POWs with severance payments, assistance in securing necessary civilian clothes and personal goods, and legal protections to assure adequate access to employment. Finally, in April 1950, the Republic began a massive housing construction program to make good the devastating losses of shelter West Germans had suffered. That program, however, privileged social over privately owned housing, to make the most efficient use of available resources to build the maximum number of housing units.[11]

The creation of the Adenauer government and its early policies offered the war-damaged grounds for both hope and concern. The government quickly demonstrated its acceptance of the community's obligation to provide an entitlement to assistance to those who had made individual sacrifices during the war. Also, it had promised a Lastenausgleich, and it had the power to deliver. Its commitment to private property and its inclusion of the FDP even offered hope for an individual Lastenausgleich. Nonetheless, it initially focused on means-tested, socially oriented programs, and many Christian Democratic politicians leaned toward a social Lastenausgleich. Moreover, Schäffer's activities signaled the danger that economic and fiscal objections could predominate. Those who favored an individual Lastenausgleich would have to work hard to justify their demands.

JUST DESERTS

Formerly propertied war-damaged often simply insisted that justice was on their side. They would assert that justice or morality or Christian morality or natural law made a (quotal) Lastenausgleich necessary, with no further clarification as to what those terms might mean. Most would have agreed with the local war-damaged group in Cologne, which announced flatly, "Our demands are in no way exaggerated, but rather they correspond to the sense of justice and feelings of decency of right-thinking people."[12]

Most of the formerly propertied war-damaged, though, defined justice more concretely, as a distribution of rights and burdens among members of the community proportional to each individual's differing social contributions and inherent value. Like supporters of a social Lastenausgleich, they wanted equals treated equally. Yet they considered their contributions and value to be qualitatively different from — and superior to — those of unpropertied Germans. As Aristotle had suggested of the propertied of his day, they assumed that "if they are unequal in one respect, for example wealth," then they must "be unequal in all" — particularly in degree of virtue. These war-damaged argued that it was superior virtue, including practical abilities and knowledge, diligence, foresight, self-sacrifice, and thrift, that had enabled the propertied, including themselves, to accumulate assets. For the supporters of an individual Lasten-ausgleich, then, the equals who needed to be treated equally were the (formerly) propertied damaged on the one hand and the (still) propertied undamaged on the other. Because property ownership had reflected individual virtue before the war, and should again, one could only reestablish the moral order by restoring on a lower level the prewar distribution of wealth and status.[13]

Formerly propertied war-damaged often did possess knowledge and had shown practical talents that made them especially suitable candidates for property ownership. They had more or less successfully managed productive assets in the past and could presumably do so successfully again, to the benefit of society. Expellee leader Oskar Wackerzapp, for example, said that the damaged demanded "a starting position that enables them to utilize their intellectual, occupational, and artisanal abilities in the right place again."[14]

In demanding a Lastenausgleich, formerly propertied war-damaged occasionally emphasized their contributions to the community. As one group put it, "They have in earlier, decades-long occupational activity created opportunities for work for countless white- and blue-collar workers and have through their contributions helped create the basis of the pensions and social security for these people." They argued that they had paid the greatest part of the taxes. They also lauded their own patriotism in supporting both Germany against foreign enemies and the state against "subversive" forces. One impoverished saver, for example, tried to awaken extra sympathy for his misery after the currency reform by adding, "That is how it goes with many elderly people, who have always stood true to the Fatherland and never reached out a hand to the Social Democrats! And even more never gave the Social Democrats a single vote!"[15]

Savers who had accumulated a nest egg against disability or old age tended, not surprisingly, to emphasize their thrift and self-sacrifice. They had chosen to forego consumption, often at considerable discomfort, in order to remain independent and to avoid becoming a burden on the community when they could no longer work. Savers were often especially embittered because they had lost their savings twice, once in the inflation of 1914–23 and again in the inflation of 1936–48. One impoverished saver described how she worked twenty-nine years for 30 Pfennige per hour and managed to accumulate 3,576 RM (the fruits of nearly 12,000 hours of work) — only to have it reduced to virtually nothing by currency reform. "We've already been defrauded twice," she said.[16]

The bomb-damaged and expellees emphasized their thriftiness, but especially their diligence and foresight. A former farmer, whom the Nazis had forced to sell up and whose assets currency reform had destroyed, wrote, "That is the result of 42 years of greatest diligence and thrift, that I stand today without livelihood, home, and (nearly) assets, and all through no of fault my own." One businessman complained that he had through "untiring work" and fore-sight put together a substantial fortune and a house against old age, only to lose all through his expulsion. He was especially bitter that his white-collar workers' social-insurance benefits were higher than the Support Aid he got under the Immediate Aid Law.[17]

The war-damaged could even refer to themselves as just generally virtuous. They seemed to be generalizing, as Aristotle had suggested, from one virtue or a few to general superiority. One saver, for example, referred to the damaged as "the elevated and socially valuable strata."[18]

Particularly galling for the war-damaged was the sense that they were being punished for their hard work and self-sacrifice, through the loss of their hard-earned property, while the lazy and spendthrift had no assets to lose. As one local group of bombed-out and savers asked despairingly, ostensibly quoting the sentiments of all older war-damaged, "Why did we work so hard and hon-estly, lived, and squeezed every Pfennig and every Mark in savings from our own blood? Was that a crime, since we must now live in such misery?" One bombed-out and saver protested that "it is nonetheless not right to give him who accomplished and saved nothing the same [Lastenausgleich payments] as him who in a long life has responsibly secured for himself what was necessary for his business and social honor."[19]

Because the formerly propertied war-damaged believed in their special rec-titude, they rejected any Lastenausgleich for those who had lost only a job and not capital. Employees could be just as diligent and economically vital as busi-nessmen, and losing a job could be more devastating than losing a business. Formerly propertied war-damaged, though, insisted that the unpropertied had not accumulated through diligence and saving the resources to support them-selves. The propertied war-damaged argued that such implicitly unvirtuous individuals did not deserve any Lastenausgleich, though they might receive some public assistance to prevent starvation.[20]

The expellees made one telling exception to their dismissal of the claims of the employed—an exception on behalf of civil servants. The latter were, of course, employees of the state. Historically, though, Germans had seen civil servants as having both a special status as servants of the common good and a kind of property right in their jobs. Many civil servants had lost their positions after the war because of their Nazi past or because they had been expelled from their former place of residence and work in Eastern Europe. The Parliamentary Council, a majority of whose members had been civil servants, had included in the Basic Law a provision requiring the new West German state to pass legis-lation restoring the rights and jobs of dismissed civil servants. The expellee organizations not only supported speedy passage of generous legislation here, Kather even suggested that it had been the ZvD's top priority. The civil servants were well educated, well organized, and well represented in the Bundestag and, of course, the government. The Federal Republic hence promulgated, on 11 May 1951, a generous law that improved pensions and provided quotas for hiring dismissed civil servants. The law reflected West Germans' disinclination to punish "honorable" ex-Nazis and their continuing acceptance of an in some ways premodern ideology emphasizing civil servants' sacrifice and honor.[21]

Convinced of their superior character, the formerly propertied war-damaged contended that they had not only a property right in their material possessions but a kind of property right in their social status. Wackerzapp wrote, "The damaged have a claim to a balancing out that opens to them the way to their earlier social status." One regional expellee group asserted that the Lastenausgleich must lead to "the reestablishment of the productive social livelihood [of expellees] and indeed as much as possible on the level of the previous social worth." The war-damaged frequently asserted the need for a Lastenausgleich that would allow them "a standard of living appropriate to their status" or enable them to purchase "furnishings corresponding to their cultural level." They were insisting that, if they lost their prior social status for any reason outside their immediate control, they had a right to demand that the state reestablish it—using radical means if necessary.[22]

For many war-damaged, their very sense of self was tied up with their formerly superior positions in a hierarchical social order. A regional group representing expellee *Gymnasium* teachers (a high-status group in Germany) complained that its members had to take low-status positions in the school hierarchy in their new homes, so they suffered not merely material losses but a "devaluation of their person." A civil servant commented that "the war-damaged want not to be considered and treated as an undifferentiated mass, but rather, like the portion of the population spared [by war], to be integrated into the social order again as personalities." Seuffert (SPD) noted during a public disputation that some war-damaged Germans wanted their losses legally confirmed, even if they secured no compensation, "with the sole purpose," he asserted, "of wanting to be able to prove, because of one's honor, how rich one once had been." Expellee leader Alfred Gille (BHE) rejected Seuffert's characterization—but then tacitly embraced it a few sentences later by saying that the expellees "had a right to have confirmed, somehow, things as they were in the past, even if nothing material comes out of it."[23]

Determined to defend their moral superiority, the war-damaged vehemently rejected any payment or assistance that seemed like welfare or charity. Poor relief had been predicated on the assumption that its recipients were undisciplined individuals who needed moral elevation, an assumption that was anathema to virtually all war-damaged, formerly propertied or not. The latter believed that they deserved more than welfare because they were more virtuous than the "typical" welfare recipient or charity case. "Everyone must see,"

Kather asserted, that one could not offer a war-damaged farmer, artisan, or businessman, whose lost assets "as a rule were the result of a long and strenuous life's work, a so-called full support payment that was scarcely more than a standard welfare payment." The German Federation of Rentiers complained that compensation for savers ruined by currency reform "scarcely exceeds the level of welfare payments for those who did not save through self-renunciation and are rewarded for that behavior."[24]

The war-damaged found it particularly odious that they—the virtuous—had lost all, while other, nefarious individuals had "profiteered" in the midst of the German people's war or postwar misery. Mistrust of middlemen and profit in general had a long history in Germany. Already in World War I, this mistrust had been married to the nationalist conviction that all must subordinate their private interests to the shared need to support the national war effort, making profiteering among the most heinous crimes. Despite similar feelings during World War II, some Germans, especially military contractors, had enriched themselves enormously. Even worse in most Germans' eyes were the sharp operators who had made fortunes by speculating in desperately needed but scarce goods on black markets. Many war-damaged particularly disliked the farmers in whose villages and even houses they had to live. Food shortages between 1943 and 1948 had allowed farmers to charge illegally high prices and to secure substantial incomes while the evacuees and expellees were often abysmally poor—and sneered at by the farmers as disreputable paupers. The war-damaged repeatedly attacked all such profiteering and demanded that its beneficiaries be made to pay their "immoral" profits into the Lastenausgleich. "It may never be allowed," one war-damaged wrote indignantly, "that, for example, some kind of black marketeer, speculator, or human question mark, who lived high on the hog at the expense of his fellow humans" should get to keep his ill-gotten gains.[25]

For the war-damaged, the old German distinction between productive and rapacious capital, stripped of its explicit—but not its implicit—anti-Semitic associations, still resonated. Many war-damaged justified their demands simply by asserting that they were not speculators. They contrasted themselves, "the solid [individuals], those who through physical or mental activity . . . stood positively in life, the savers, and those who used their strength and health honorably, laboriously, and true to their personal, communal, and general life principles," with the "speculators, racketeers, and economic hyenas." They distinguished sharply between their own "solidly earned property" secured through "work and frugality" and the "easily earned rearmament profits or wartime capital gains" that profiteers had secured "in a dishonorable way."[26]

Some Germans went so far as to assert that the undamaged would have to earn back their property. The SPD was the major proponent of this notion, arguing in mid-1948 for levies sufficient "that the propertied must in practice obtain anew by their labor the greater part of that which they, unlike the damaged, were able to save through the war and postwar." Yet both a writer in the business journal *Handelsblatt* and the officials of the Administration for Finances of the Bizone implicitly embraced this view.[27]

In proposing to confiscate some property to relegitimate the property system, the war-damaged did not neglect pragmatic arguments. They asserted that private property could only survive if West Germany was not divided into a few (lucky and often morally questionable) large property owners and a mass of impoverished propertyless. Lukaschek, citing papal encyclicals, asserted that "the full propertylessness of the broad masses next to the piling up of property [by a few] . . . must in the long run endanger the institution of private property." The undamaged, the war-damaged pointed out, must recognize that without a Lastenausgleich the size and strength of the "proletarianized" with no stake in private property would grow so large that private property would end. They should look on a Lastenausgleich, Nöll von der Nahmer said, as "properly considered an insurance premium for the property that had been preserved."[28]

The war-damaged echoed widespread postwar concerns about "leveling" and "massification." They reiterated eighteenth- and nineteenth-century arguments that property ownership was the basis of an independent, potentially responsible existence; they then deplored the loss of economic strength, political stability, and cultural values Germany would suffer unless it reversed the leveling effects of war damages through a Lastenausgleich. The German Federation of Rentiers warned that, without a Lastenausgleich, "the economically independent strata would be condemned to die out; without the backing of secure property, economic independence and with it the bases of economic and personal freedom would be undermined. The free cultural sphere would also no longer be able to survive." Massification, the war-damaged warned, contributed to what Karl Böttcher called the "wider and wider spreading decay of the Western cultural heritage."[29]

The war-damaged also called on a centuries-old tradition of the social obligations of property. They pointed to Article 153 of the Weimar Constitution, which stated, "The ownership of property entails obligations. Its use must at the same time serve the common good." Such obligations, the bomb-damaged asserted, constituted a "social mortgage" on all property. More important, especially in war-damaged attempts to influence the CDU/CSU, traditional Christian moral teaching supported the notion that property rights were not absolute but that in an emergency all had a claim against property.[30]

The war-damaged were asserting that one had to deserve property. Mere possession was insufficient. The ZvF, for example, justified confiscating wartime capital gains outright because their possessors had "no moral claim" to that wealth. It wanted a "careful sifting out . . . of those who from the standpoint of justice really have a claim to compensation," and this could be done only by excluding those whose claims were from "easily earned rearmament profits and wartime capital gains."[31] The war-damaged particularly abhorred the fact that the capricious operation of material forces, as opposed to individual virtue, had decided which individuals would suffer war damages. As Bauser complained, "I would like to say, from the deepest conviction, that it is impossible and unbearable to demand of someone that he should have to do without all that he possessed, while others get to keep all they had, indeed could increase their wealth, without any blame having rested on the former or any merit having characterized the latter." For the war-damaged, outcomes had to depend on individual character and agency, not happenstance, and moral equals had to enjoy equal outcomes. Moreover, individuals were entitled to state intervention to assure those equal outcomes.[32]

The vision of social justice that the war-damaged were promoting reflected a powerful tradition. In the seventeenth and eighteenth centuries, German craftsmen and retailers had believed that they were entitled to a *bürgerliche Nahrung*, a modest but assured livelihood commensurate with their superior honor, social status, and worth. Each individual had to have demonstrated upright character to be accepted into a guild as a master. Yet once he had attained membership, and so long as he demonstrated superior virtue by upholding the honor of the trade, the master could expect the guild to regulate the larger economy to ensure that he would secure that modest livelihood. The war-damaged presumably derived their expectations at least partly from this older moral vision, to which they occasionally alluded with references to "the honor of their estate."[33]

The war-damaged's perception of their particular virtue also echoed nineteenth-century notions of middle-class (*bürgerliche*) virtue. The canon of middle-class virtues included characteristics such as orderliness and cleanliness, but thrift, diligence, and self-renunciation had been central as well. These virtues were also often seen as particularly German.[34]

Another way to conceptualize the war-damaged's view of their rights is in terms of what E. P. Thompson, in discussing eighteenth-century England, called a moral economy, a "consistent traditional view of social norms and obligations, of the proper economic functions of several parties within the community." The war-damaged's moral economy legitimated the prewar German social order by asserting that the unequal distributions of wealth and status had reflected accurately the social contributions various more or less virtuous individuals had made. It thereby reassured middle-class Germans that their privileges were morally sanctioned and promised that future effort would be rewarded. It implied that members of the lower social orders deserved their less-privileged positions because of their relative lack of virtue. Moreover, it suggested that great wealth often resulted from questionable or even immoral profiteering or speculation, affirming the moral superiority of the middle classes over their economic superiors. Against the claims of the social-market economy, it legitimated, indeed made morally imperative, far-reaching government intervention whenever the amoral play of material forces deprived the virtuous of their property. As Schäffer complained in May 1950, the war-damaged were demanding that "the state guarantee to its citizens in general a right to the preservation of their wealth."[35]

The desire for status and moral order helps explain the failure of efforts by some war-damaged leaders to shift the basis of war-damaged compensation claims. Having invested five years in demanding a Lastenausgleich among members of the German community of risk, some bomb-damaged and ex-pellees flirted with abandoning entirely the notion of a Lastenausgleich among members of the German community in favor of an obligation by the state to recompense individual citizens for damages suffered. A (West) German state reappeared in late 1949 and declared itself the legal successor to the predefeat German state. In April 1950, in a front-page article, *Selbsthilfe* announced that "the bomb-damaged and currency-damaged have never ceased to consider the state their debtor. . . . [N]o doubt could have arisen that all these obligations were to be fulfilled by the German central power as the representative of the totality of the German people if the German central power had not been abolished at war's end . . . [so that] one sought an expedient that would make possible compensation when and for as long as the central power was lacking. . . . Now that a unified federal power exists once again in West Germany, every reason for solving the compensation problem without the state has fallen away." Mattes (ZvF) had been quietly repeating such arguments since late 1948, to anchor his members' compensation claim legally and to legitimate a demand to tap general government revenues to increase compensation beyond what a capital levy could finance.[36]

Meanwhile, the expellees were having their own problems with demands for a "Lastenausgleich." Among the strongest supporters of expellees groups were expelled civil servants, who had also lost "property" in the form of their tenured positions. Securing restitution for these people was the ZvD's highest priority. Kather demanded programs of preferential hiring to channel the employable among them back into jobs. He also proposed an "internal balancing of burdens among the civil servants," through a special levy on currently employed, overwhelmingly nonexpellee, civil servants to provide adequate pensions or unemployment benefits for expelled civil servants. By mid-1950, though, policy makers, under enormous pressure from currently employed civil servants opposed to any special levies, had abandoned the idea of any Lastenausgleich among civil servants (though the government would later meet most expellee civil servant demands from other sources).[37]

Perhaps not coincidentally, expellee organizations then shifted—partially and temporarily—to demanding compensation from the state. For example, the ZvD declared on 2 November 1950, "The compensation claim of the damaged is directed primarily not against the undamaged but against the state. Only when the state has exhausted all its possibilities of satisfying the claim does it have the moral right and the duty to obtain the funds for the compensation of war losses through levies from its propertied citizens." The expellee leadership, though, quickly shifted back to a Lastenausgleich, leaving Mattes and his ZvF as the major proponents of the compensation argument.[38]

Virtually all of Mattes's members possessed a state-guaranteed legal claim to payment, under either the War-Damages Decree or the Civil Code. If Mattes could compel the West German state to accept legal responsibility for such claims, the bomb-damaged and savers would be in a much stronger bargaining position. The expellees, though, seldom had any convincing legal claim under pre-1945 legislation. They, arguably, could not afford to abandon the concept of a Lastenausgleich because only the Lastenausgleich legitimated their compensation claims against German taxpayers.[39]

One could interpret this curious development as proof that the Lastenausgleich was nothing but an expedient, created out of whole cloth to dress up a self-interested desire for payment at someone else's expense. War-damaged Germans had every reason in 1945 to cast about for an alternative to the no-longer-extant German state to pick up the tab for the burdens of defeat. The undamaged fit the bill because they were the only ones with assets to be tapped in a devastated economy producing less than half of its prewar output. The war-damaged would then need to develop a compelling theory to explain why those alternative obligors should face confiscatory levies to make good losses for which they bore no direct responsibility. Telling in this regard is the fact that (except for Finland) only West Germany, where the state disappeared for four years, posited a claim by the war-damaged against undamaged property holders.[40]

If the Lastenausgleich had been a mere expedient, though, one would expect the war-damaged to drop it completely the moment a more attractive alternative, the West German state and its taxing power, came along. Yet Mattes's proposal to shift to compensation based on a prior legal claim had surprisingly little resonance among individual war-damaged. Virtually all of them persisted in arguing for a Lastenausgleich, and most of the very few who embraced a compensation approach continued to assert their claims under the Lastenausgleich as well.[41]

In the flood of letters and petitions the Lastenausgleich evoked, the war-damaged were strikingly—and convincingly—vehement in denouncing the unfairness of the way that war had distributed its burdens among the German people. The postwar property distribution was wildly fortuitous. Not surprisingly, Germans who had suffered disproportionate losses, often for the second time in a generation, bitterly resented their misfortune and, especially, the unmerited good fortune of so many others. (Notably in this regard, Mattes was himself *not* war-damaged but had come into the bomb-damaged movement as a financial expert.) Human beings do often seem to want to believe that people ultimately get what they deserve. The legal formalism of Mattes's assertions of individual rights under decade-old legislation apparently held less appeal for war-damaged Germans than did the emphasis in their Lastenausgleich theory on their superior status and on a larger moral order, an inherent balance, that the state must restore.

SUBJECTS, NOT OBJECTS

The formerly propertied war-damaged insisted that the society honor their individual agency. Their property could only be an expression of their putatively superior virtue if they had been able to affect the world by exercising that virtue. Moreover, they could be sure that they had some control over their lives and that the universe rewarded virtue only if they could continue to act efficaciously in the future. This desire to establish agency for themselves — to be subjects, not objects — expressed itself in their claim that they had a right to a Lastenausgleich and in their resistance to being considered victims.

The formerly propertied war-damaged emphasized repeatedly, and even more vehemently than the proponents of a social Lastenausgleich, that they had a *Rechtsanspruch,* a legal claim or entitlement, to recompense for their lost property. They hoped a legal claim would provide the most secure basis for their demands and might maximize their compensation. The war-damaged, though, also sought the increased social status that a legal claim would offer.[42]

In addition, though, as long as war-damaged individuals had no legal claim, they were objects of forces beyond their control. The war-damaged clearly wanted to reassert control over their own lives. To do so, they usually insisted they had an entitlement to state assistance that was inherent in their virtue and their right to a Lastenausgleich. As one local group asserted, amazingly enough, its members "are of the view that in the first place one must create a framing law that secures the legal claim of the expellees. As against this legal guarantee, the question of the amount of compensation and the form of compensation is in the end of secondary importance." In this statement these expellees were acknowledging the need for legislation, but only to secure a legal claim that already existed, and they were doing so to reclaim agency, not to secure any specific amount or form of compensation.[43]

The war-damaged often explicitly tied their insistence on a legal claim to a rejection of the dependent status of welfare recipient. German law granted the welfare authorities broad (potentially capricious) discretion in determining who deserved what kind of assistance. Creditors who had lost their retirement savings in the 1920s had secured a claim to an "elevated welfare" from the national government. The local welfare officers who administered this system, though, had simply refused to acknowledge any entitlement for this privileged assistance; they had insisted on subjecting these formerly independent individuals to the same humiliating investigations of their personal circumstances as other would-be welfare recipients. The former creditors had bitterly resented this procedure. Their post-1945 counterparts feared being subjected to the same fate and demanded an entitlement to an individual Lastenausgleich to avoid it. One expellee wrote in 1948, for example, that the expellees rejected any social Lastenausgleich because "thereby, however, every objective basis for calculation would be lost, so that the amount of the compensation would in the end depend on the subjective discretion of the Welfare Office." Such dependence on the assessments and power, the whims, of others was both dangerous and humiliating.[44]

The war-damaged hence asserted their agency as protectors of their own rights. Campaign literature for the expellee political party, the BHE, frequently emphasized the party's significance as an expression of the expellees taking charge of their lives and fighting for their rights. As BHE leader Kraft wrote, "The expellees are not supplicants and are not willing to be charity recipients. They are creditors and demand their rights, and their elected leaders are the guarantors that the struggle for [their] rights will be conducted unyieldingly and without compromise." Kather argued that, through the entitlement to a genuine Lastenausgleich, the war-damaged individual "shall master his existence out of his own strength and not be dependent on welfare, public assistance, or benefits." The war-damaged were not asking the state to bestow a gift but were fighting to compel it to acknowledge a preexisting entitlement.[45]

The efforts of the war-damaged to reassert their autonomy were part of a larger West German effort to come to terms with the negative potentials of modernity. The rationalizing, normalizing, and disciplining aspects of post-Enlightenment societies threatened the autonomy and security of individuals. Any dependence on means-tested state assistance made one particularly vulnerable to such efforts. By founding their security, even in adversity, on entitlements independent of bureaucratic discretion, the war-damaged, and other West Germans, would evade becoming objects of external discipline, would be subjects once again.[46]

The subjects in question, though, were male. When the war-damaged referred to themselves in the singular, it was the masculine singular, particularly in reference to individuals who were to use Lastenausgleich funds to reintegrate themselves actively in the economy. The war-damaged leadership was virtually entirely male, and the handful of women who wrote letters demanding a Lastenausgleich did so as wives or widows. The Basic Law guaranteed equal rights for women, but implementing that guarantee would take decades. In view of the gender distribution of the ownership and control of property in mid-twentieth-century Germany, to re-create lost wealth in a Lastenausgleich was to re-create patrimony and male property and to contribute to reestablishing patriarchy.[47]

Because organized war-damaged emphasized their autonomy and moral superiority, they resisted identification as victims. *Kriegsgeschädigte* (war-damaged) does denote almost the same as the primary recent meaning of *Opfer* (victim): someone who has suffered an injury or an evil. Yet victimization rests on the assertion that at least for a time the person has been the object of forces beyond his or her control, that is, has been an ineffectual loser — hardly a status to be cherished, especially by those touting their own superior virtue and efficacy. Postwar Germans initially used *Opfer,* in the sense of victim, to describe the killed and wounded or the politically and racially persecuted. They referred to those who had suffered material losses as the bomb-damaged, refugees, expellees, or (more broadly) the damaged or the war-damaged. In 1946 and 1947, in articles in *Selbsthilfe* and in letters from individuals, the bomb-damaged called themselves either the damaged or "those (most heavily/seriously) affected." [48]

Yet the war-damaged did — grudgingly — refer to themselves as victims after 1947. They would have to justify their compensation claims in competition with other Germans who faced disproportionate burdens: disabled veterans, war widows and orphans, civilian casualties, among others. Greg Eghigian has argued that already in the 1920s a "politics of victimization" characterized Germany. As human control over the natural world and the ability to finance assistance grew in the nineteenth century, people increasingly perceived unmerited suffering as a basis for demands for redress by society. By the 1920s the notion of victims as specially deserving had become widespread, and a competition developed among different groups for a share of the limited social resources available for redress. The more victimized one was, the better one's case. Victim status became "a kind of cultural capital," one that the war-damaged could not ignore.[49]

Unfortunately for the war-damaged, other "victims" had strong bargaining positions in the politics of victimization. The politically and racially persecuted, under Allied sponsorship, had gotten in an early claim to recompense. War widows and orphans and disabled veterans had a recognized claim on the society that was rooted in past battles over recompense and resources (especially after World War I) and in the need to give meaning to the suffering World War II had brought.[50]

Further, formerly propertied war-damaged could undercut their claim to privileged recompense if they identified themselves as victims. If justice meant equal treatment for equals, then Germans must presumably structure any aid to victims so that all would be treated equally. Soldiers' survivors and disabled veterans, though, received social assistance on the basis of current need, not prewar social status. Supporters of a social Lastenausgleich hence objected to an individual Lastenausgleich because it would provide better recompense to those who had suffered material losses than West Germany was providing to those who had suffered disability or the loss of a breadwinner.[51]

Hence, even while playing the victim game after mid-1948, the war-damaged continued to emphasize their entitlement and efficacy. Expellee Erich Dederra, for example, characterized the expellees as "victims," but he also emphasized their previous self-reliance, their noble efforts thus far in overcoming despair, and their desire to be "active again in the interests of the whole people as they once were." Moreover, Albrecht Lehmann notes of 1980s expellee memories of the postwar years, "In the stories, the opposing patterns 'fate' and 'personal skillfulness' usually do not express themselves separately: There is scarcely a longer story of flight in which the two schema do not unfold after one another and next to one another." The war-damaged were trying to have it both ways.[52]

Significantly, postwar West Germans did not accept every claim to victim status or to compensation. They were disinclined to accept Jews and political persecutees as victims, and they refused recognition and recompense to various other groups who suffered because of Nazi persecution or war, for example, Sinti and Roma, homosexuals, and so-called asocials. In each case, West Germans did not see these people as fellow members of a mutually obligated moral community. They also denied restitution to people who had lost their jobs because of the war. Moreover, women who had been raped at war's end might have a claim to recompense in principle, but the social stigma against rape was so great that virtually no women applied for compensation. And whereas West Germans deployed the experience of these women as a group as a political weapon in the battle against Communism, they refused to recognize the experience of individual women as victimization, virtually obliterating it in a conspiracy of silence. Workers and women might be members of the community, but they still were not fully entitled members.[53]

Hence, the war-damaged could not simply assert victim status and a claim to recompense but would have to construct a convincing case that they were in fact deserving victims. Paradoxically, efforts by the war-damaged to construct that case compelled them to downplay their own agency. They had to distance themselves from responsibility for the Nazi regime and its policies, from any political effectiveness, 1930–45.

Societies like their victims innocent. People are generally unwilling to help those who brought misery on themselves. Self-inflicted suffering seems a matter of individual fault, to be overcome by the individual. If a society does assist the culpably miserable, it is with socially disdained welfare or charity. Further, in the case of Germany, tort law has long recognized the principle of coresponsibility: one's claim to recompense can be reduced or nullified if one had contributed to one's own injury or losses. The War-Damages Decree included this principle, limiting compensation where individuals contributed to their damages (e.g., by failing to have fire-fighting materials available), and even the war-damaged could acknowledge it as a consideration in establishing the degree of compensation.[54]

A few postwar Germans, though, sought to use the principle of coresponsibility to block any war-damages compensation. For example, according to one unhappy expellee, western Germans were whispering that the Germans expelled from the Sudetenland were all either German-speaking Czechs who had become fanatical Nazis or Reich Germans who had gone there after 1938 to exploit the Nazi conquest. The expulsion of both groups, these western Germans were saying, "had thereby happened only justly, as they had fully deserved their — even if harsh — fate through their behavior." The expellee author sought to prove that the Sudeten Germans had not been rabid Nazis or carpetbaggers, but he accepted that individuals deserved no recompense if their actions had helped cause their losses. Proposals to exclude "Nazis" from war-damages compensation also rested, sometimes explicitly, on the same principle. Any suggestion that individual war-damaged shared responsibility for their losses undermined their demands for recompense — as victims or as legal claimants.[55]

Although some war-damaged had been innocent of any responsibility for the Nazi regime and its crimes, most war-damaged had voted for Hitler or supported his regime and its war, as long as things were going well. Almost none of them actually claimed not to have supported Hitler, and the Nazis could not have conducted their war so long — or so brutally — without significant popular support. Germans would not have had to pursue martyrdom to undercut Nazi barbarity but merely to have shown the kind of passive resistance to Nazi delusions that Italians showed toward Fascist fantasies. Some relationship did exist between the willingness of many or most war-damaged to support Hitler and carry out his brutal policies and the fact that bombs fell on their property or Eastern Europeans expelled them from their former homes. The degree of misery suffered was frequently, and often egregiously, disproportionate to culpability, and Germans are justified in complaining that carpet bombing and mass expulsions of the innocent and the culpable alike were unjust. Nonetheless, most war-damaged could well be seen as having contributed to their own losses.[56]

Whether support for Nazism implied culpability for Nazi crimes is a *historical,* as well as a moral, problem. To assert such culpability is to posit a causal relationship between individual action and historical consequence. One could argue (as, for example, a materialist or postmodernist) that no individual could be a cause of Nazi crimes — and hence culpable — because no individual could have any autonomous, meaningful impact on historical process.

Or one could argue that it was the sum of individual decisions by Germans to support Hitler and his war, even if within a particular historical context, that produced the historical outcome.

Whatever one's theory of historical causality, the war-damaged based their justification for privileged recompense on an assertion of individual historical agency. They insisted that they deserved to have their prewar wealth and status restored because that wealth and status resulted from their earlier virtuous, historically efficacious choices. Yet if they were effective agents when they secured that property, then presumably they were also effective agents when they voted for Hitler or supported German aggression. If they wanted to take credit for morally admirable choices, they would presumably need to accept responsibility for morally reprehensible choices.

A few Germans did acknowledge some German responsibility for the misery Nazi Germany had caused. Expellees from outside the 1933 Reich occasionally argued they were innocent of any responsibility for Hitler's rise to power but that "the overwhelming proportion of Germans from within the old Reich" were "the actual ones obligated to pay through [their role in] transferring power to Hitler." A few Germans, often with strong Christian or socialist beliefs, argued that any demand for "justice" for German war victims or war-damaged had to include an acknowledgment of German responsibility, in light of the fact that Germans had brought Hitler to power and tolerated his crimes.[57]

The war-damaged had good reason to avoid any discussion of the relationship between pre-1945 political actions and postwar rights to a Lastenausgleich. They could have argued that they were deserving victims even if they had voted for Hitler or supported the war, either because as individuals they had not been able substantively to affect political developments (even if they had affected their economic circumstances) or because their degree of complicity was incommensurate with their current misery. Either assertion, though, would have been a subtle, messy case to make, especially for a group claiming that their earlier historical efficacy entitled them to privileged recompense.

A few Germans, remarkably insensitive to the suffering Germans had imposed on others, openly identified the misery of the war-damaged with that of Nazism's direct victims. One CDU Lastenausgleich expert commented in 1948 that "through their unsocial policies the Allies are driving needy Germans not into the gas chambers of the concentration camps but to the gas chamber, namely the gas tap in their own houses." One local group of bomb-damaged contended in 1951, "All those who opposed the regime and were incarcerated for years in the concentration camp have long since been fully compensated for this incarceration. Not so those who opposed the Nazi regime with an inner resistance and avoided incarceration in the concentration camp." One may well doubt how much "inner resistance" to the regime most bomb-damaged mustered before things began to go very badly indeed in 1944 and 1945, but the concentration camp inmates had certainly not been "fully compensated" for their suffering by 1951 — or in most cases ever.[58]

Most war-damaged, though, chose to present themselves, in varying forms, simply as innocent, and hence politically inefficacious, victims. Some insisted on total innocence. For example, the expellee businessman Fritz Seiler insisted, in the space of seven lines, that the state had to guarantee the property of a war-damaged individual who "bore no sort of guilt [Schuld]," was "in no way culpable [schuldig]," and was a "totally innocent [schuldlosen] property owner, who acted totally blamelessly." More typically, though, the war-damaged merely insisted that they had suffered their losses "without any personal culpability [ohne eigene Schuld or unverschuldet]." They also emphasized the fortuitousness of war damages. References to the damages as Zufall or Glück or Willkür are ubiquitous. Thus, a saver asserted, "It is not merit but mere luck that one has not been bombed or expropriated."[59]

In another characteristic gesture, the war-damaged repeatedly referred to their losses as the product of fate. The totalitarian demands of the Nazi regime and the exigencies of war had drastically reduced the amount of control individual Germans had been able to exercise over their lives. Nonetheless, the ascription of events to fate also served to distance the war-damaged from moral responsibility. The rhetoric of fate suggested that the war-damaged had been purely, if temporarily, victims, mere objects, lacking any control over, and hence any responsibility for, what had befallen them. One ZvD leader asserted that the expellees "who had once worked actively on the structuring of the life of the nation, have been torn abruptly out of their field of action and have been tumbled at first, without being able to exercise their will, into the maelstrom of events, so that their ability to act has been paralyzed for a certain time." They had proven to be ineffectual losers, indeed demanded to be considered ineffectual losers — albeit only "for a certain time."[60]

The intermingling of accident and activism in the rhetoric of the war-damaged was rooted in a paradox in demands for victim status. Modern Europeans, including war-damaged Germans, value autonomy and self-reliance yet must recognize that people often are not in control. When the war-damaged asserted their innocent victimhood, they talked of accident and fate, of circumstances beyond rational understanding or control. When they demanded a Lastenausgleich, however, they acted as modern Europeans who assumed every problem, including war damages, could and should be rationally analyzed and addressed through human action. Further, they cast their claim not as a gift to ineffectual losers but as an entitlement, based on past efficacy, which the society had to recognize. Moreover, they threatened to become radicalized, to take efficacious but negative political action, if they failed to get what they wanted. The war-damaged were engaged in a double game of simultaneously asserting victimhood and self-reliance.

Despite the complexities of the politics of victimization and the radicalism of their claims, formerly propertied war-damaged were strongly placed to demand privileged, individual compensation because their concept of social justice had deep historical roots and reflected social values widely shared among (propertied) mid-twentieth-century Germans. Other Germans had made analogous arguments in the past. More important, undamaged postwar Germans proved willing to accept that concept, even though doing so increased the likelihood they would have to pay substantial Lastenausgleich levies.

The war-damaged were not the first Germans to demand privileged assistance for the putatively virtuous. To demonstrate superior virtue, relative to the indigent, lower-middle- and middle-class Germans had struggled for generations to secure enough capital to ensure that they would not fall prey to the humiliation of having to accept charity or welfare. Scarcely a generation before, the impact of World War I and inflation had, though, immiserated a million formerly self-sufficient Germans (e.g., disabled veterans, inflation-battered savers), leaving them dependent on charity or welfare. Like post–World War II war-damaged, these individuals had protested bitterly, "We rentiers, who have a life of toil behind us, [in which we] secured through diligence and thrift enough that we would be supported in old age and would fall as a burden on no one, have been betrayed in an unheard of fashion." They, too, had insisted that they were not "typical" welfare recipients and did not deserve to be treated as such; they had demanded and secured (at least in principle) an "elevated welfare," that granted them marginally higher benefits and, more important, validated their moral and social superiority.[61]

Significantly, most 1940s undamaged proved willing to accept the war-damaged's discourse on virtue. All of the major political parties acknowledged the lack of culpability of the war-damaged and supported their demand for a Lastenausgleich. Some local groups representing undamaged individuals would attack the use of capital levies to finance a Lastenausgleich. Remarkably, though, no national-level economic interest group ever attacked the war-damaged's claims to virtue or to some Lastenausgleich, including those representing property owners who would pay any capital levies.[62]

By the early 1950s, West Germans were simply unwilling to talk about Nazi crimes and responsibility for them—except to pardon all but the most compromised. Too many Germans had been implicated in the Nazi regime and its crimes, so any discussion was likely to produce embarrassment or even the risk of criminal prosecution. Moreover, West Germany could not afford to alienate the millions of usually middle- and upper-middle-class Germans whom de-Nazification had touched. Even Germans who had not been complicit and who believed Germans needed to accept responsibility soon discovered that saying so led to social isolation and the loss of close elections. The new Federal Republic even passed legislation between 1949 and 1953 offering effective amnesty to all but the most compromised Nazis and war criminals. Telling here are comments by Eugen Gerstenmaier (CDU), who had been active in the anti-Hitler resistance. In 1946, he urged Germans to recognize "our great guilt" for having given Hitler the chance to commit his crimes. By 1950 he supported the law the Bundestag passed ending de-Nazification because, he said, one should not punish political views as such and because West Germany needed the millions of the "seduced" (i.e., former Nazi supporters) to reconstruct the fatherland and to build a "genuine national solidarity" through a "genuine reconciliation." Such arguments, as problematic as they were, did allow millions of compromised West Germans to participate in the new democracy. They also allowed the war-damaged to demand compensation without having to answer embarrassing questions about the degree of their responsibility for their own losses.[63]

On a practical level, denying war-damaged claims about the fortuitousness of damages and the arbitrariness of the current distribution of property was difficult and potentially dangerous. Once the bombs had started falling and formerly oppressed neighbors had started expelling Germans, chance did determine which particular German lost his or her property. Moreover, to virtually all postwar Germans, war and black-market profits were burdened with an undeniable moral opprobrium. Luck and profiteering were shaky bases for legitimating the postwar distribution of property, especially in the face of Communist expansion. Even *Handelsblatt* commented, "Without a Lastenausgleich the idea of private property would lose its justification among us because it rests only on chance who today can still call any real property his own." A government official reported that the undamaged generally recognized that only a Lastenausgleich would confer on their property the validity it needed to protect it against any future arbitrary grabs.[64]

Demands by the war-damaged to redistribute property could draw on a long tradition that saw a broad property distribution as crucial to social and political stability and, especially, to the preservation of private property. "A relatively equal distribution of property," the CDU asserted in 1946, "is an essential security for a democratic state." Even the SPD based its support for a Lastenausgleich on "the dangers of propertylessness. We must not have a nation of have-nothings within the nation." Many Germans agreed that property had social obligations that could legitimate redistribution. The Conference of Catholic Bishops, in a 1948 pastoral letter, noted that "God ordained the goods of this world not to the benefit of any individual person . . . but only to the benefit of all people," so a Lastenausgleich to make whole the social order "would not infringe upon the principle of private property." Indeed, from the mid-1950s, under CDU auspices, West Germans would actively debate the implementation of policies to broaden wealth distribution.[65]

The undamaged also shared the fear that massification posed a threat to the whole traditional social order, especially in the context of the Cold War with Soviet Communism. As the major German charitable organizations jointly commented, in reference to the Lastenausgleich, Germany must find its way "out of massification to the well-ordered society. . . . The situation of Germany — spiritual middle between West and East — makes the decisive and upright intertwining of currency reform [including a Lastenausgleich] and social reform a pressing command of good sense. . . . It is the last moment [in which] to reestablish in Germany the bases of freedom of the person and of the society." Postwar Christian ethical teaching, while emphasizing private property's social obligations, also emphasized, as had Kant and Hegel, its crucial role in human development: "a sensibly structured private property is necessary in order to guarantee the freedom of the person and personal development." As Wilhelm Röpke argued, "Mass society is simply a sand-heap of individuals who are more dependent than ever, . . . more isolated, uprooted, abandoned, and socially disintegrated than ever." Most middle- and upper-class Germans, damaged and undamaged, believed that the hierarchical, ordered society with broad property ownership was the stable, prosperous, free, cultured society. A Lastenausgleich could contribute to reestablishing such a society.[66]

In addition, the undamaged appeared quite willing to acknowledge that property ownership did reflect the inherent virtue of the owner and that the formerly propertied war-damaged were notably virtuous. The chemical-industry interest group, for example, whose members would have to contribute to any Lastenausgleich, agreed that an at least partially quotal Lastenausgleich was just because "in the majority of cases property and wealth rest on virtue." Finance Ministry officials agreed that one must at least partially restore the prewar property distribution, even if at a lower level, because otherwise one would be treating the virtuous worse than the unvirtuous. The undamaged could also agree that outcomes should reflect individual agency, not mere chance. As Erhard wrote, "If one part of the German people has lost all through no fault of their own, it cannot be countenanced that other favored individuals, without having merited it, should preserve perhaps their whole capital through the war."[67]

The undamaged and policy makers generally accepted the war-damaged's rejection of welfare as a humiliation — and a dangerous dependency — inappropriate to those who had fallen into misery "through no fault of their own." As the conservative Protestant journal *Christ und Welt* explained, the war had shattered "the natural course of things." This massive disruption meant to the formerly self-reliant "that he could no longer pluck up his courage and make his way with his own strength. For every clever, aspiring, and diligent person it means a deep humiliation to have to recognize this fact. For he must out of necessity now grant the state rights where until now he knew how to help himself; he must submit to communal regulation where earlier he decided alone and was also ready to bear the responsibility." Even a SPD publication could state, "The expellees are not objects of general welfare provisions but subjects in the construction of the necessary reordering of social relations in Germany." Implicitly, for the party of social equality, welfare recipients were objects, not subjects, were qualitatively different from and implicitly inferior to the war-damaged.[68]

This general acceptance of the war-damaged's self-characterization reflected the widely shared conviction that the society had an interest in convincing the mass of Germans that playing by the rules—working hard, saving, being self-reliant—would be rewarded, not punished. *Christ und Welt,* for example, rejected consigning the war-damaged to welfare, because "the Lastenausgleich would be the highest injustice if it should once again make the provident, clever, and diligent into the simpletons, and the careless, stupid, and lazy once again into the winners." The probusiness journal *Industrie-Kurier* printed an article whose author, in attacking SPD calls for a social Lastenausgleich, celebrated the socially virtuous property owners, arguing, "People are different. The one prefers to spend his income and enjoy the day; the other squirrels his money away, through self-denial, dime for dime, to become propertied and not to be dependent on the state in his old age. Such civil virtues are unfortunately never properly honored by the state, although without their cultivation it can scarcely survive."[69]

The organized war-damaged had articulated a potentially powerful social philosophy. Not only did it offer legitimacy for their claim for privileged recompense, but it appealed to influential currents among policy makers and the undamaged. Nevertheless, supporters of a social Lastenausgleich continued to propound an alternative ideal, and supporters of a productive Lastenausgleich were making themselves increasingly heard.

Chapter 6

ECONOMIC EXIGENCIES

Accumulating or preserving assets in a competitive, temptation-filled world generally does require some degree of virtue, but moral philosophers have been loathe to legitimate private property by appealing to the property holder's putative virtue. Too many morally dubious individuals can be seen to own often vast amounts of property. Moreover, if the moral basis of property is the exercise of virtue necessary to obtain it, then any property obtained through unearned fortune (e.g., through inheritance, speculation, gambling) would presumably be illegitimate. The wealthy are sometimes lucky, but undeserving. The poor are sometimes simply unfortunate, though honorable.[1]

More important in the context of the Lastenausgleich, those whose character we most admire might not be those able to use valuable economic resources most efficiently. The virtues that the formerly propertied claimed for themselves seem admirable enough, but in the rough-and-tumble of the marketplace they may pale beside other "virtues" such as rationality, practical competence, entrepreneurship — even greed and ruthlessness. The community may be better served if the nasty but economically efficient hold property rather than the nice but ineffective. Moreover, in a free market, success is its own justification. The society is to assume that the market correctly rewards the most efficient user of society's resources, regardless of his or her putative personal virtue.[2]

The war-damaged were well aware that they could not simply ignore such arguments from economic expediency. That alternative discourse of efficiency was especially powerful in postwar West Germany because the scope of destruction convinced most Germans that production would have to take precedence to meet Germans' pressing needs. After 1948, though, the rising influence of neoliberalism, growing support for what came to be called an "achievement society," and West Germans' decision to participate in the American-sponsored world trade order also undercut demands for an individual Lastenausgleich. Increasing numbers of Germans began to argue that economic necessity compelled West Germany to organize any Lastenausgleich productively, so that property fell to those who could use it most efficiently in the future—not to those who were currently in need or had once possessed property.

WAR-DAMAGED ECONOMICS

The organized war-damaged wanted, above all, an individual Lastenausgleich that would recompense damaged individuals for specific property losses. They actively opposed any social or productive Lastenausgleich that would assist the war-damaged solely by eliminating the worst need and by providing opportunities for them to reenter the economy as employees and as tenants instead of as independent businessmen and home owners. Yet to secure such an individual Lastenausgleich, the war-damaged had to demonstrate its economic efficacy— or at least its feasibility.[3]

Unlike the war-damaged elsewhere in Europe, the organized war-damaged in Germany insisted that Lastenausgleich levies had to force obligors actually to transfer real capital—in substantial amounts—to the individual war-damaged. If one allowed levy payment in cash, one would have to allow the obligors to pay in installments over years, while they accumulated that cash. Only the immediate transfer of real property could ensure that war-damaged individuals would obtain quickly the real productive assets necessary to reestablish an independent livelihood. Immediate capital transfers would also reduce significantly the net worth of the undamaged, imposing a meaningful share of the war's burdens on those thus far spared. Only thus could one reestablish, on a lower level, the prewar distribution of wealth and status. The war-damaged took quite seriously the notion of ensuring that every German shared proportionally in war's burdens. Varying mixtures of envy, calculation, and injured amour propre drove this demand.[4]

To defend this drastic proposal, the war-damaged often simply asserted that a Lastenausgleich would be advantageous to the economy as a whole. They occasionally tried to strengthen such assertions by invoking metaphors of organic interconnection or health. *Selbsthilfe*, for example, contended that "a state organism can only remain healthy when all parts are healthy. If one lets the damaged go to ruin economically, one has, willingly or unwillingly, planted the seed of corruption." As long as West Germany's economic recovery looked shaky, the war-damaged could hope simply to trumpet a Lastenausgleich as a sovereign remedy for that economy's ills, but in the longer term they would need to show that a Lastenausgleich would positively assist the West German economy.[5]

The war-damaged often insisted that an individual Lastenausgleich would be better for the economy because it would enable people with proven talents to be put back to work in the most appropriate economic slot. Millions of expellees and evacuees had fetched up in isolated villages with no job opportunities except as agricultural laborers, while hundreds of thousands of war-damaged small businessmen lacked the capital necessary to reestablish their old businesses. The war-damaged argued that the government should secure reconstruction by restoring the productive assets of the war-damaged, who would then reopen their old enterprises and put their fellow Germans back to work. As Wackerzapp noted, "What is at issue is to make useful once again, in the right place and the right way, the valuable treasure of diligence, knowledge, and skill that is so richly present among the expellees and that currently lies, for the most part, idle. Then the Lastenausgleich will not, as its opponents fear, damage the German economy, but rather *promote and increase it in its productivity,* while simultaneously disarming the ever more alarming social conflicts and tensions."[6]

This argument had some merit, as the undamaged could recognize. Human capital would be a major element in West Germany's economic boom. Allowing a skilled and diligent individual to sit idle in an isolated village or to work as an unskilled laborer was an enormous waste for both the individual and the economy. Yet the most vocal political proponent of ensuring employment for talented war-damaged, the SPD, favored a productive Lastenausgleich because it wanted to ensure that funds went to individuals and firms that currently had the resources, abilities, and contacts to create jobs and promote economic growth, not to people who had once had such elements but might not any longer.[7]

The war-damaged also argued that a just Lastenausgleich would promote their willingness to work. They were playing two cards here. On the one hand, they asserted that their poverty made them willing now to work harder than any undamaged individual so that, if given the opportunity, they would exploit more fully the society's resources. On the other hand, they suggested that unfair treatment, an unjust Lastenausgleich, would reduce their willingness to work—and destroy their virtue.[8]

Closely related to this argument, and much more frequent, was the argument that one could reestablish in Germany a willingness to save only if one offered a just Lastenausgleich. The willingness to save is economically crucial for providing funds both to invest and to help individuals weather life's uncertainties without recourse to social assistance. German governments, though, had twice connived, through inflationary policies and unsocial currency reform, at the de facto expropriation of their citizens' savings. The war-damaged insisted that no one would save in Germany again unless the state demonstrated through a just Lastenausgleich that paper-asset holders (including compensation-claim holders) would end up being rewarded, not punished.[9]

The undamaged agreed that a just Lastenausgleich was necessary to promote a willingness to work and to save. The Working Group for the Chemical Industry, for example, asserted, "Germany needs for its recovery also and especially private initiative, and this must be stimulated. A failure to consider individual damages would be the exact opposite. It would once again have a chilling effect on the natural urge to private accumulation." Government officials also recognized the force of these arguments.[10]

The war-damaged even asserted that an individual Lastenausgleich would positively affect the actions of those who would have to pay a levy. Rejecting assertions that a high capital levy would overburden the economy, the war-damaged insisted that, as one bomb-damaged put it, "The national economic science has long since proven that *a high burden does not interfere with production,* but to the contrary is a spur to more intensive work and increased performance, that it works as a powerful incentive to increased effort, to most thrifty management, to technical and organizational progress."[11]

This argument had much less resonance among the undamaged than did other arguments for the economic advantages of a Lastenausgleich. Heinrich Troeger (SPD) did promote this argument, asserting that an 80 percent levy would force property owners to work and would also force a "sifting out of the virtuous" from among current property holders. One CDU economic advisory group extolled the virtues of a Lastenausgleich burden for promoting economic efficiency, but only when demanding that publicly owned enterprises pay Lastenausgleich levies, not in discussing a capital levy on private assets. Ironically enough, this argument was deployed regularly in the 1980s — by those seeking to legitimate the junk bond–fueled leveraged buyouts that regularly left companies with enormous debt burdens.[12]

The war-damaged also promised macroeconomic benefits from an individual Lastenausgleich. On the consumption side, they argued that a substantial Lastenausgleich would spur economic growth by providing additional purchasing power. The transfer of funds to impoverished war-damaged with an enormous backlog of needs, they believed, would translate into a surge of expenditures for goods and services, spurring economic recovery. The war-damaged also foresaw a substantial boost to the economy through a Lastenausgleich's effects on credit. They argued that legally recognizing each individual's war-damages claim would provide people with the collateral necessary to get loans to finance reconstruction and thereby economic growth. Some asserted that one could rely on the banks to make to the war-damaged only loans that would lead to a new livelihood (and hence be "productive").[13]

Some war-damaged proposed increases in net credit and in the money supply to satisfy Lastenausgleich claims. They rejected fears of the inflationary consequences of such increases. Calling on the experience of the depression of the 1930s and occasionally on the writings of John Maynard Keynes and others, they asserted that as long as the German economy had idle resources available, of labor, plant, and raw materials, an expansion of purchasing power or credit would automatically create the economic basis for the increase in the money supply by putting those idle resources to work. Indeed, unemployment in the early 1950s was high, and Germany had come out of the war with unused plant and some stocks of raw materials.[14]

Most war-damaged counted on government intervention to solve any problems their policy preferences might entail. The organized war-damaged were not neoliberals. The free play of material forces, military and economic, had led to the losses they sought to reverse. Believing firmly in the primacy of moral over material considerations, they opposed giving free rein to market forces. Instead, they proposed government controls to ensure justice. Proponents of compensating the war-damaged immediately with certificates, for example, often proposed that such certificates should be realizable only if the individual war-damaged could convince the authorities that the funds, as W. von Rheinbaben put it, "would provably go for the reconstruction of his old livelihood or for reconstruction in another area." Such governmental supervision would ensure that Lastenausgleich funds were not frittered away on consumption, but it was incompatible with the neoliberalism that the CDU/CSU and FDP were increasingly embracing.[15]

As the economy slowly recovered, the war-damaged also pointed to evidence that obligors could easily afford real transfers of capital or substantial levies. Economic growth, the high level of investment, and substantial public and private expenditure on new office buildings all suggested untapped — and increasing — resources that should justly go the war-damaged. The war-damaged, still often impoverished, were angry, and more than a bit envious, that increasing numbers of Germans could now afford (often imported) luxuries; they frequently argued that substantial capital levies would be easily payable because obligors could economize on such frivolous expenditures. They also believed that obligors, especially farmers, had often made enormous profits from 1933 to 1948, which they could draw down to cover a Lastenausgleich. Millions of war-damaged, forced to share housing with West German farmers, could see the "local yokels" doing (relatively) well, perhaps for the first time in their lives, while formerly prosperous war-damaged Germans vegetated in misery and resentment.[16]

The Deutsche Mark balance sheets companies created in 1948–49 were a particular sore point. West German companies usually valued their assets on the high side, to justify substantial depreciation allowances against taxes. The war-damaged argued that these balance sheets showed companies had not suffered as badly as they claimed, making them well able to afford capital levies. To some extent the war-damaged were right, because companies' real assets generally were higher in 1948 than in 1938. The companies were, however, gambling that long-term Lastenausgleich levy rates would not be so high as to obviate the medium-term advantage from tax write-offs.[17]

The war-damaged never developed a full-blown economic theory. They believed they had a moral and legal claim to a Lastenausgleich and simply wanted the society to recognize that claim and allow them to get on with their lives. Because any meaningful Lastenausgleich would obviously have far-reaching economic consequences, they did sketch out the economic advantages of a Lastenausgleich as they saw them. They had made some good points, but the weight of expert economic opinion and of the business community would soon be brought to bear — against them.

LEVYING CAPITAL

One of the most amazing things about the Lastenausgleich debate was the almost universal willingness of Germans, damaged and undamaged, to contemplate substantial, in some cases draconian, levies on capital. Despite the potentially serious economic problems that direct intervention in the ownership and control of capital might provoke, virtually no one opposed capital levies or (at least initially) capital-gains levies as sources of funds for the Lastenausgleich.

Although German elites in the 1920s had rejected capital levies to finance debt revaluation, their 1940s counterparts quite willingly contemplated such levies for the Lastenausgleich. An exemplary figure here is Hans Luther, who was finance minister and chancellor from 1923 to 1926. In the 1920s debate over financing a revaluation, which he dominated, he vehemently and unreservedly rejected capital levies as impossible to assess, an inducement to tax evasion, and an obstacle to the effective collection of other taxes. Yet in his 1946 currency reform plan, he took it for granted that Germans would impose a "capital levy" as part of a general reorganization of finances. The Special Agency for Money and Credit experts, too, took it as a given in spring 1948 that a capital levy on real property would be part of any currency reform and Lastenausgleich package. They rejected "excessive" levies and were quite conscious of the difficulties of formulating, assessing, and collecting a levy. Nonetheless, the political situation had changed. Driven by popular revulsion at 1920s inflation and revaluation policies, West German politicians insisted that real and money wealth must be treated "equally" in any currency reform and Lastenausgleich, whatever the technical difficulties. Concerns about how one could implement a capital levy would assume growing importance. Yet *no one* in the documents I have seen openly rejected it — and most accepted or even welcomed it. Only Finland implemented any similar capital levy to finance war-damages compensation.[18]

One can scarcely exaggerate the degree of popular revulsion in Germany at war and postwar profiteering or the determination to seize those profits for the common weal. The war had supposedly been a communal enterprise defined by shared sacrifice, but "war profits" made up a substantial share of West Germany's early 1948 capital (11 percent of productive real capital and well over 50 percent of paper capital). Such profits for any German seemed to call into question all the sacrifices — of life, health, loved ones, wealth — that other Germans had made. As one veteran complained, he had lost all his possessions while away serving his country, while others escaped service and piled up money and goods. Crucial here was the war-damaged's determination to restore a moral order in which property ownership reflected virtue. Only if unvirtuous property, including property based on war and speculative profits, was somehow eliminated would that moral order be restored. Capital-gains levies thus promised to do double duty, both punishing "immoral profiteering" and providing additional funds. Special Agency experts agreed in 1948 that a capital-gains levy would be part of any currency reform and Lastenausgleich, and the parties, including the FDP, supported capital-gains levies into 1950.[19]

Assessing a capital-gains levy would be a daunting task. To calculate capital gains while minimizing cheating, one had to possess or reconstruct some official record of two assessments of each individual's capital: as of some starting date before World War II and as of a valuation date in 1948 or later. Moreover, a Deutsche Mark was not equal in purchasing power to a Reichsmark, raising questions of fairness unless the difference could somehow be adjusted in the assessment process. Finally, not all capital gains, 1935–48, had necessarily reflected dishonorable war or postwar profiteering.[20]

These arguments involved a delicate ambiguity. Germans hoped to sweep up inequitable war profits with capital-gains levies, yet part of the increased paper assets reflected the foregone consumption of working- and lower-middle-class Germans (as savings). For millions of Germans, tight wartime labor markets had provided the only opportunity in their lives to secure full-time employment at decent wages and to set aside some savings. Workers had thus "profiteered" from the war compared to their peacetime income opportunities. Some war-damaged — and Finance Minister Schäffer — were hence willing to exclude post-1939 savings from any Lastenausgleich; they were implicitly or explicitly identifying wartime savings as not legitimate because they represented not "genuine voluntary renunciation of consumption" but rather forced savings (compelled by wartime rationing) out of "inflated money." Most Germans, though, wanted to believe that capital-gains levies, with some reasonable personal exemption, would catch out only nefarious war and black-market profiteers. Very few wanted to get into the messy details of establishing just what constituted profiteering.[21]

Strikingly, financial experts generally ignored all these problems before 1949–50. Special Agency experts had alluded to these problems in 1948. Moreover, they had never expected the capital-gains levy to produce much revenue, because they had believed, rightly, that the currency reform would obliterate most paper assets and, wrongly, that few firms or individuals had increased their net real assets during the war. They had nonetheless included a capital-gains levy in their Homburg Plan. As late as mid-1949, Bizone finance officials assumed that records of each German's 1 January 1940 net worth were available or could be reconstructed and that a Lastenausgleich would include a capital-gains levy. These financial experts accepted popular demands for the levy not because they thought it was a good idea economically or fiscally but because they saw no way to avoid it politically. If Germans had promulgated Lasten-ausgleich legislation in 1949 or earlier, they probably would have included a capital-gains levy, with a perceptible impact on wealth distribution.[22]

In late 1949 and early 1950, though, the financial experts turned against a capital-gains levy. They now concluded that the disadvantages of such a levy made it a bad idea. They highlighted the amount of capital destroyed or dismantled, 1940–49, and hence the likely low yield. The inadequacy of 1940 financial records now loomed larger in their eyes, or at least in their public statements. The difficulties firms would face in paying the levy, now that currency reform had wiped out much of their liquidity, began to seem dangerously high. By January 1950 one subcommittee of the Finance Ministry's Academic Advisory Committee supported only a carefully limited gains levy; by March 1950 another subcommittee rejected any capital-gains levy as too costly, time-consuming, and problematic.[23] The environment was worsening for the war-damaged.

A NEW WORLD ORDER

The rejection of a capital-gains levy was symptomatic of a sea change in West German attitudes toward the economy and toward economic policy. The relative success of the German economy under neoliberal policies, though shadowed by high unemployment and foreign-exchange problems through early 1951, was swinging support away from the interventionist attitudes of the immediate postwar period and toward a more market-oriented approach. The ongoing conflict with Communism and West German dependence on the economically liberal United States only strengthened this tendency. Simultaneously, the business community was able to increase its influence.

After 1945, the United States succeeded in establishing a more liberal world trade order. Using pressure and economic assistance tied to movement toward free trade, the United States was able to convince its Western European partners to join the General Agreement on Tariffs and Trade and to reduce gradually the trade barriers that had risen since World War I. With the aid of international institutions such as the European Payments Union, the United States was also able to cajole European governments into gradually reducing foreign-exchange controls and other policies that had distorted trade in the 1930s. Free trade within Europe and between Europe and the rest of the world was increasing significantly.[24]

West German elites chose to fit themselves into that world trade order. One of the main impetuses behind twentieth-century German expansionism had been a desire to secure access to markets and resources (e.g., iron ore, foodstuffs) unavailable (at competitive prices) within the boundaries of the German nation-state. Defeat in two world wars showed that Germany was not going to be able to secure those resources by conquest. Economic elites began to realize even before World War II's end that in the future they would have to cooperate with the United States if they were to secure necessary imports (though not all businessmen were initially inclined to do so). By founding a West German state integrated into the American trade order, West German political elites showed that they too accepted that only free trade could secure for (West) Germany the resources it needed.[25]

Opting for the American world trade order did limit one's policy options somewhat, but it did not mean cookie-cutter policies among the European countries. For example, Britain, France, and Italy nationalized substantial chunks of industry and banking in the immediate postwar period, much to the horror of American officials. France pursued a dirigiste economic policy into the 1980s and beyond, and Italy used national control of many industries and of banking for purposes of economic intervention. France and Italy also ran much looser monetary policies than did the Federal Republic. Moreover, all industrialized European countries gradually introduced extensive social-welfare programs.[26]

West Germany turned toward economic policies at least nominally more in the spirit of the American-sponsored free trade order. Under Erhard's leadership as Bizone economics director and later as West German economics minister, West Germany moved quickly but incrementally to reduce controls on its economy, to free up individual initiative and maximize production. This choice reflected a mistrust of controls, an emphasis on struggle and individual achievement as a means of promoting the best, an obsession with production in the aftermath of war's massive destruction, and a long-standing but newly heightened fear of Communism. Furthermore, the economic successes West Germany began enjoying under neoliberal policies strengthened the position of the neoliberals substantially.[27]

The Nazis had promoted an increased emphasis on performance or achievement (*Leistung*) as the key criterion for judging individual worth. Their Social Darwinism focused on a "racial" conflict for survival in which individuals had to subordinate their particular interests to the communal imperatives necessary for group survival. Yet that Social Darwinism also required that the different individuals in the society contribute according to their varying individual abilities. Significantly, the Nazis emphasized that the community should honor contributions to the communal good that resulted from superior achievement. For example, their policy toward small business tended to privilege and reward the efficient rather than to protect all small businessmen from competition, as the latter had often expected. Besides, the imperatives of survival in a global war with industrially more powerful enemies gave an added impetus to efforts to realize superior efficiency and achievement, including performance-based wages.[28]

West Germans accepted and expanded this emphasis on achievement, eventually touting their "achievement society." Dictatorship and war had destroyed most institutions and ties above the family, and postwar Germans turned inward, to their families or to themselves, as sources of identity and support. Traditional markers of status (noble birth, university education, the honor of a particular social order, virtues such as thrift) gave way to a new emphasis on current individual achievement, defined in terms of instrumental rationality and (especially economic) efficiency, as the measure of individual value. This kind of achievement was seemingly perfect for a society that increasingly extolled individual success in the competitive struggle among different firms or individuals in a large, technically advanced, free-market economy. It accorded with the emphasis on hard work and increased production to make good the enormous destruction that Germany had suffered. Last but not least, it helped to shift attention away from the Third Reich's crimes and individual Germans' responsibility for them, away from past errors and toward the present and future successes.[29]

The emphasis on achievement constituted a significant shift in social values. The war-damaged had acknowledged that achievement mattered, as they legitimated their property as a reflection of their successful exercise of certain traditional virtues. Nonetheless, their emphasis, and their claim to legitimacy, rested far more on the possession of virtue than on its exercise. For them, character counted. For 1950s West Germans, though, the focus increasingly became neither traditional virtues (e.g., foresight and thrift) nor some essential and permanent identity (e.g., a child of the *Mittelstand*, a virtuous person). Instead, one's status lay in one's practical efficiency and ongoing contribution. Past contribution might be admirable, but it was more or less irrelevant to an achievement-based distribution of rewards. Furthermore, prestige rested less on accumulated property than on a high income (which was assumed, in a social-market economy, to reflect accurately one's competence) and the increased consumption that such income allowed. The war-damaged were pursuing their compensation claims in a society that was coming to define achievement and entitlement differently.[30]

During and after World War I Germany had suffered substantial losses of national wealth, but these losses had not been immediately obvious to most Germans. The running down of plant and equipment during the war, in the name of maximizing wartime production, had significantly reduced Germany's economic strength, but this deterioration was not visible to the average citizen. Allied confiscation of German assets abroad, the growing barriers to international trade, and even reparations were also not immediately tangible within the Reich. Hence, post–World War I creditors could insist that German debtors could afford substantial revaluation because the country's real productive assets were visibly intact.[31]

After World War II, no one who saw a bombed German city could deny the enormous destruction Germany had suffered. Indeed, the average observer would tend to overestimate Germany's losses because the preservation of productive capital was hidden behind the shattered walls of Germany's factories. In fact, the worst losses and the most pressing needs were the ones most obvious to the average citizen: shelter, food, and personal possessions. Further, occupation and Allied interventions in German life made obvious the degree to which foreign interference was disrupting the vital interconnections on which the German economy depended. Even optimistic estimates of German losses were large enough to make it obvious that financing a Lastenausgleich and all the other burdens postwar Germans faced would not be easy.[32]

Most postwar Germans hence sought to maximize work and production. Economic experts and industrialists focused on the need for investment in enterprises to make good the losses, especially in bottleneck areas, that war and defeat had brought. Neoliberals promised that the social-market economy would promote efficient and rapid recovery. Crucially, for all their deep concern for the less fortunate in society, trade unionists and Social Democrats agreed on the need to maximize production, given Germany's parlous postwar situation. Social Democrats and some trade unionists did demand modest nationalization and planning, or at least guidance, of the economy as the key to recovery. Nonetheless, they were conscious that, as long as such policy prescriptions were ignored, the imperative to maximize production within the structures of a market economy did set limits on the kinds of policies one could implement.[33]

The fear of Communism helped to weaken support for governmental intervention in the economy. Proposals for a Third Way between Communism and capitalism seemed less convincing in the us-versus-them mentality of the Cold War. The subtleties of calling for guidance but not planning, as the Left did to distinguish itself from the Communist enemy, were lost on most Germans. Moreover, Soviet treatment of German POWs and continued incarceration of hundreds of thousands as forced labor embittered millions of Germans against the Soviet government and Communism. Finally, the vicious brutality and oppression associated with the Red Army and Communist East Germany discredited not only the German Communist Party but also democratic socialists such as the SPD.[34]

Soviet-sponsored, Communist North Korea's invasion of American-sponsored, anti-Communist South Korea, on 26 June 1950, sent a special tremor of fear through West Germans. They were almost all convinced that Soviet leader Joseph Stalin was implementing the first step in a calculated plan of world conquest, with a Soviet-sponsored invasion of West Germany as the next logical step. Such fears were not unreasonable under the circumstances, and they persisted, as the Korean War dragged on and American and European leaders debated the best ways to defend Western Europe, including West Germany, against the Soviet threat. By aggravating fears of Communism, the Korean War further strengthened the hand of neoliberals, with their opposition to governmental controls on the economy.[35]

A mixture of successes and problems characterized West Germany's economy between 1948 and 1951. Industrial production rose almost continuously, from 50 percent of its 1938 level at the end of 1947 to 146 percent of its 1938 level at the end of 1951, and the end of all food rationing in May 1950 was a clear sign of improvement. Yet employment stagnated until late 1950, and returning POWs and a continuing flow of refugees kept unemployment high. Meanwhile, the cost of living rose more quickly than did hourly wages until 1951. Already in July 1948, business circles were complaining about excessively strict credit policies. Rising deflationary pressures from late 1949 led to increasingly strident demands for a more interventionist economic policy. This clamor became a roar when the Korean War added new problems. This mixed picture meant that the fundamental economic order for West Germany was still in dispute into early 1951, even among those on the Center and Right.[36]

The reasons for West Germany's postwar economic growth were numerous and complex. The economy certainly benefited from the large productive plant it inherited from previous generations. West Germany also enjoyed a large, highly skilled workforce that was willing to work hard for low pay, to make good the obvious losses individual Germans and the economy had suffered. The flow of willing, educated labor from the east, from 1945 through 1961, provided a subsidy to the Federal Republic far in excess of Marshall Plan aid. Further, after a generation of disruptions from two wars and a serious depression, the economy faced an enormous backlog of demand from its citizens for goods and services and an enormous backlog of innovations that industry could introduce. The American-sponsored free-trade order provided the necessary access to raw materials and markets, especially when spurred in the 1950s by a slightly undervalued Deutsche Mark. Moreover, the terms of trade shifted after 1945 to the benefit of industrial European nations. Indeed, despite widely varying economic policies, almost all of America's Western European clients experienced substantial growth from 1945 through 1973, in some cases greater than West Germany's.[37]

Yet the signs of economic recovery in West Germany had become obvious only since the currency reform and decontrol of mid-1948, and they became undeniable after mid-1951, under neoliberal policies, as real wages began to rise, unemployment to fall (if slowly), and exports to exceed imports. While the SPD and many in the trade unions still believed that the interwar depression had shown capitalism to be a failure, that position had after 1948, and especially after 1951, less and less resonance among German voters. West Germans continued to debate the exact economic policies and degree of government intervention that was appropriate, with even Center and Right parties favoring some government intervention, but by early 1952, the neoliberal emphasis on minimizing such intervention had the upper hand. Barring an SPD victory in some future election, West Germany was going to have a primarily free-market economy based on private ownership of the means of production. The currently propertied could insist that any Lastenausgleich had to ensure that they could continue to invest and to prosper, to the benefit of all West Germans.[38]

QUESTIONING THE FEASIBILITY OF A LASTENAUSGLEICH

Although few West Germans directly challenged the idea of a Lastenausgleich, the scope and nature of that Lastenausgleich were debatable. As World War II receded into memory, as neoliberal ideas became more popular, and as the moment to legislate approached, West Germans, especially potential obligors, increasingly began to raise objections to the dramatic and potentially deleterious shifts of capital and to the kinds of expenditures that formerly propertied war-damaged were demanding.

The passage of time was translating into a declining willingness among undamaged Germans to sacrifice for war-damaged fellow citizens. The war was more than five years in the past, dimming the memories of the undamaged, even if not of the war-damaged. The former found it difficult to recall just how lucky they had felt in 1945 to escape with their property more or less intact. Moreover, though no one said so explicitly, the postwar property distribution was becoming less fortuitous: West Germans were in practice relegitimizing their property claims by their performance, by preserving and expanding their property in difficult postwar economic conditions. Finally, as journalist Fritz Brühl noted, "The halo of martyrdom around the expellees and bomb-damaged" was eroding as their necessary efforts to organize made them appear just another interest seeking funds from the public purse.[39]

Those few who openly rejected a Lastenausgleich were private individuals or local economic interest groups. *All* the national-level economic interest groups that represented the potential obligors in any Lastenausgleich (e.g., the

German Chambers of Industry and Commerce, the Union of Building and Property Owners) acknowledged the need for some generous Lastenausgleich. However, individuals and local groups had less responsibility for the political stability of a fragile new state full of impoverished war victims; they could be quite vehement in denouncing what they saw as the inflated demands of greedy war-damaged. These Lastenausgleich opponents dismissed it as impossible, risky, or immoral. When currently propertied citizens in the small city of Coburg staged a protest meeting against a Lastenausgleich, the local paper reported it, sympathetically, under the title "Blood Donor Dead — Patient Lives," a neat summation of how some obligors within the small-business community viewed the Lastenausgleich.[40]

A particularly nasty aspect of the opposition that did develop toward a Lastenausgleich was an undercurrent of occasionally vicious prejudice against German expellees from the East. One local group of home and building owners responded to expellee demands, "We have in our woods enough oaken staves and clubs with which we know how to lay about, if only a nail or a handful of the mother earth of our property were to be unjustly stolen. We West Germans are hewn from somewhat harder wood and won't let ourselves be threatened by an alien [sic] politician." West German elites and the political system moved quickly to accept the expellees into society as formal equals, a process that was crucial for the Federal Republic's political and social stability. Nonetheless, many West Germans were not initially willing to be so receptive.[41]

The war-damaged asserted that such open opposition was just the tip of the iceberg. They complained that the undamaged were coordinating a deceitful whispering campaign to call into question the feasibility of any capital levy and to convince the war-damaged that a Lastenausgleich was hopeless. The war-damaged also believed that economic leaders were supporting a Lastenausgleich publicly and then returning privately to party leaders to tell them "No."[42]

Although 90 percent of West Germans (in a November 1951 poll) still favored aid to the war-damaged, the undamaged did not welcome the individual Lastenausgleich the organized war-damaged favored. A Lastenausgleich could mean a good faith effort, within the constraints set by economic rationality in a private property–based, market economy, to redistribute more fairly the burdens of war and defeat. If so, then a substantial majority of Germans were willing, though not necessarily happy, to support a Lastenausgleich — even if that would mean some sacrifice on their part. Yet a Lastenausgleich could mean, as the organized war-damaged insisted, an immediate transfer from the undamaged to the war-damaged of sufficient real and paper capital to reestablish on a lower level the prewar distribution of wealth. If so, the undamaged overwhelmingly opposed a Lastenausgleich. They were willing to make only modest sacrifices and take only moderate risks for fellow members of the German community; increasingly fearful of the potential personal and national-economic costs of an individual Lastenausgleich, they began systematically deploying economic arguments against any massive, short-term transfers of capital.[43]

The easiest argument for opponents of a substantial levy to make was that Germany lacked sufficient resources to afford a generous Lastenausgleich. The very scope of destruction that so burdened war-damaged individuals had also arguably so damaged the German economy that it could not finance a restoration of the prewar distribution of wealth and power, even at a lower level. Further, Germany's defeat had left a plethora of other burdens that the shrunken social product had to finance.[44]

Partly in reaction to the economy's overall weakness, the central issue in this debate quickly became whether the levy would come through some immediate transfer to war-damaged citizens of real assets, or through a transfer in installments over many years of part of the property's yield. The war-damaged wanted real assets, part of the substance of an obligor's property, now, to begin rebuilding their lives. They also argued that transferring real assets would obviate concerns about larger economic weakness by simply transferring ownership without affecting production or productivity.[45] Obligors, and other Germans, were not convinced.

The main objection that opponents of a transfer of real assets raised was that the different enterprises within the German economy constituted "organic" wholes that could not be broken up without seriously damaging, and perhaps destroying, them, with potentially disastrous consequences for the German economy and all Germans. The West German Institute for Economic Research complained sarcastically in 1948, "Just as four hundred years ago there were iconoclasts who believed they could serve their faith by destroying works of art, and just as about one hundred years ago there were machine breakers who imagined they could improve workers' social situation by smashing machines, by all appearances there are today people of the opinion that one can achieve 'an increased exploitation of the enterprise's capacity' by smashing the enterprise. . . . It is self-evident that an enterprise is to be considered as an organic whole from which one cannot cut out individual parts at will without decreasing its efficiency disproportionately." Crucially, even people on the Left, in the trade unions and the SPD, shared this view.[46]

This argument was deeply threatening to the organized war-damaged's position. One could scarcely dispute that forcing a factory to sell half its machinery would almost certainly paralyze its operations. A craftsman, to husband his capital, would normally own only the tools necessary for his trade—with few spares. Taking half his tools would usually make it impossible for him to carry on the trade. A farmstead might be able to cover its overhead with the yield from eight hectares but would often not be viable at four hectares. Because the war-damaged desperately wanted to secure a transfer of real capital, they proposed various expedients to address such concerns.

Some war-damaged proposed that the Lastenausgleich provide them with certificates as immediate compensation. They would use the certificates to "buy" real assets from the undamaged, who could then pay their levies with the certificates. The undamaged would be able to choose which of their (presumably productive) assets were surplus and available for sale. The war-damaged would then have access to productive assets and an opportunity to rebuild a livelihood, while the undamaged would avoid tearing the heart out of their enterprises. The war-damaged were assuming that large numbers of firms had surplus productive assets and that they would exploit the real assets they received as efficiently as the former owners.[47]

Policy makers, though, were increasingly dubious about issuing such certificates. As maintaining a stable currency assumed increasing importance, the danger that certificates might function as money (because they could be used to purchase real assets) loomed larger. The central bank and other observers began warning of the inflationary risks of such an indirect increase in the money supply. Many Germans had long worried that the certificates would divert resources from productive to wasteful purposes (to consumption or to inefficient uses of productive assets by unsuitable war-damaged). Crucially, as neoliberal ideas gradually took hold, proposals to rely on government supervision to ensure that the certificates were used in an economically rational manner came to be unacceptable. By mid-1950, government officials and the political parties had quietly abandoned such certificates as a means to implement a Lastenausgleich.[48]

The war-damaged also proposed that the Lastenausgleich transfer some claim on real capital through some sort of "participation" in an enterprise. They suggested that corporations could be required to issue to war-damaged Germans a number of shares equal to those already outstanding, which would be equivalent to a 50 percent capital levy and would provide at least some war-damaged with a revenue-yielding capital asset. Other firms could be required to take on silent partners, with a claim to half the firm's annual (net) revenues, or small firms could be required to take on a war-damaged small businessmen as an active partner.[49]

The notion of participation also ran into difficulties. Doubling the number of a corporation's shares and halving the dividend per share would, business circles complained, devastate the firm's credit. Smaller enterprises could seldom afford to take on an additional partner, silent or active. Further, making a war-damaged person a silent partner might simply tempt the undamaged, active partner to cook the books to minimize (net) revenues. Moreover, forcing businessmen to accept unknown individuals as active partners would often provoke animosities that could undermine the viability of thousands of small businesses and produce only bitterness on all sides.[50]

In a major, but ultimately unsuccessful, concession, the war-damaged organizations agreed to limit their demand for a transfer of capital to fortunes greater than 35,000 DM. They argued that the undamaged with substantial property would have a more differentiated set of assets, so they could transfer ownership or control of some real assets, particularly subsidiaries or branches, without damaging their enterprises. Larger firms might also be able to issue more shares or take on partners more easily than could small firms. Bigger businesses resisted this proposal as well.[51]

War-damaged Germans had good reasons for demanding a transfer of capital. A capital levy paid out of the yield over thirty years could not provide the immediate aid that they often desperately needed. Indeed, the war-damaged feared that without immediate restitution many of them would die before they received compensation. They also feared, given Germany's recent history, that over the course of thirty years some economic or political disaster could deprive them of compensation. Further, the amount of any levies from the yield would depend on what the impoverished West German economy could afford for them. That amount threatened to be far less than the war-damaged hoped to receive, especially because they would be competing directly with other war victims for the limited funds the economy could provide to deal with war's burdens.[52]

More important, the formerly propertied war-damaged desperately wanted to regain their prewar social status. To the extent that their status had been based on their *relative* wealth in the community, they could only regain it by reducing the wealth of the undamaged and raising their own wealth so that each ended up preserving the identical percentage — 25 percent or 40 percent or whatever — of their prewar wealth. Moreover, only a capital transfer could spare the unemployable from a government transfer payment that might be interpreted as charity or welfare.[53]

By mid-1950, policy makers had decided that they could not, on economic and political grounds, demand from the undamaged a levy that forced the immediate transfer of real capital. Firmly rejecting compulsion, they would struggle to find ways to promote voluntary transfers of real capital. The war-damaged now found themselves fighting over the rate at which Germans could afford to levy the yield of capital.[54]

Not surprisingly, potential obligors wanted to limit their individual Lastenausgleich liability as much as possible. They generally accepted that some sacrifice by the undamaged was necessary as a matter of social policy. Nonetheless, despite occasional demands from the war-damaged or church circles that the undamaged should give voluntarily and generously from a spirit of social solidarity or Christian charity, most Germans were unwilling to give any more personally than they absolutely had to and were willing to argue—perhaps sincerely—that their personal ability to pay was limited.[55]

The undamaged sought to move the discussion of Lastenausgleich levies from the realm of individual recompense (i.e., equity or entitlement) to the realm of national economic viability (i.e., efficiency). They supported the principle of an individual Lastenausgleich, in the name of preserving private property. Nonetheless, they emphasized that their ability to pay levies depended on the strength of the national economy in which their capital earned its yields, so that only future economic growth could ensure an economy that was thriving enough to finance a Lastenausgleich.[56]

In a private property–based economy, which is what the war-damaged wanted, anything that threatens the viability of private firms threatens the functioning of the economy as a whole. German businessmen and their supporters were not shy about emphasizing this fact. Indeed, they occasionally repeated the traditional practice of speaking about "the economy" as though that meant only (still-existing) private businesses, with workers, savers, consumers, and the government (and the war-damaged) implicitly having no role—and no rights.[57]

Business circles then strove to secure a capital-levy rate that was "bearable" for the economy, in other words, that did not "overburden" individual firms. After two inflations in a generation, German capital markets were extremely weak. Firms depended primarily on self-financing for necessary investment. Potential obligors complained that high levy rates would siphon substantial sums from the firms, undercutting investment and the future viability of the firms and the German economy. Indeed, if the levies were high enough, hundreds of thousands of firms might become insolvent. Moreover, West Germany had to be able to sell its products in world markets to finance necessary imports. Yet increased costs from capital levies would, business claimed, have to be shifted onto prices and could make West German goods uncompetitive. These problems were aggravated, business circles warned, by the already high burdens firms faced from taxes and social contributions to deal with all those other problems plaguing postwar Germany. As the war-damaged had feared, shifting the debate from transferring real capital to levying yields did bring them into competition with investment and with other war victims for scarce resources.[58]

Crucially, in opposing "excessive" burdens, the currently propertied could look for support to at least some trade unionists and Social Democrats. Trade unionists had to worry about the competitiveness and viability of the firms for which their members worked. Yet even SPD Lastenausgleich spokesman Herbert Kriedemann, for example, denounced demands by the war-damaged that any levies paid in installments be subject to market rates of interest as "fully infeasible and indeed economically destructive."[59]

Many on the Left feared that the burden of any capital levy from the yield would simply be shifted to consumers and workers—including the war-damaged themselves!—in higher prices and lower wages. As the trade unionist Lorenz Wolkersdorf argued, "As the greatest part of the social product consists of buying claims of the productive population (earned income), [a generous Lastenausgleich] can only be implemented by having employees renounce a part of their wages and salaries either through lower wages (because of higher taxes) or higher prices—in order to restore to the propertied 50 percent of their wealth. You'll excuse me if I have trouble getting excited about that kind of Lastenausgleich." Numerous undamaged and some (presumably usually unpropertied) war-damaged shared Wolkersdorf's fears.[60]

The degree to which obligors would be able to transfer the levy to consumers or workers depended on their differing competitive situations. Landlords were initially in the weakest position, because rent control made it virtually impossible to shift the burden. Agriculture's competitive situation made it difficult for farmers to raise prices. In commerce and industry, the situation was more varied. If a firm faced little competition, it could transfer a substantial share of the burden to consumers. Moreover, high unemployment gave firms some leverage to hold down wages to maintain profits in the face of any increased burdens. On the other hand, neoliberal policies were making West Germany a more competitive economy, which in turn made it harder for firms to shift the levy burden. We can never know how successful firms were in shifting the costs of the Lastenausgleich, but it was a factor in the overall distribution of postwar burdens.

The desire to maximize production also affected opinions about Lastenausgleich expenditures. Organized war-damaged had generally owned real, productive capital; they wanted real, productive capital in recompense. Many West German undamaged, though, were more or less explicitly dubious that the war-damaged could use the capital they received productively.[61]

Crucially, many observers feared that the talents of expellees and the bomb-damaged were not always suitable for postwar West Germany's different economic structure. A remarkable consensus existed across party lines that Lastenausgleich expenditures must not promote "cigar stores and ice cream stands," as Seuffert put it, but productive, viable enterprises. The organized war-damaged sought primarily to re-create the German middling classes. Their proposals would often have diverted funds from large concerns (which promised stable jobs in an export-oriented industrial economy) to formerly propertied war-damaged who sought to reestablish small or medium-sized businesses (which might prove unable to survive in the competitive American-sponsored world trade order). The moral economy of the war-damaged, with its rejection of the consequences of the free play of material forces, was deeply conservative, yet the SPD, as the party of workers and socioeconomic progress, was no more interested in re-creating the cozy, traditional world of small enterprises protected from competition than were West German economic and political elites. The business community, the SPD, many in the unions, and key policy makers such as Schäffer, Johannes Kunze, and Erhard all favored a productionist Lastenausgleich that would turn its back not only on past property ownership as a basis for compensation but on past economic structures as a pattern for the new Federal Republic.[62]

Similarly, the undamaged and even some war-damaged warned repeatedly that Lastenausgleich expenditures must be structured so as not to reduce, indeed preferably to increase, net capital accumulation and investment. Many, many war-damaged (at least 1.25 million as of 1950) had come out of their experiences too old or disabled to reestablish an independent livelihood. They would receive their Lastenausgleich as social support that they would devote almost entirely to consumption. Moreover, even economically active war-damaged wanted and often needed speedy recompense to provide themselves with such basic necessities as a bed or kitchenware. That, too, would be consumption. The future productivity of any economy, however, rests on adequate investment. People have to be willing to, or compelled to, forego some consumption now to free resources for investment to maintain or increase future production and consumption. Not only business and the political Right, but the Left, "laid particular worth thereon," as Kriedemann said, "that that, which will be diverted from productive capital for the Lastenausgleich, will also be applied again productively." Even organized war-damaged, who usually wanted primarily to reestablish their own productive independence, agreed that any substantial shift of funds from investment to consumption was inappropriate.[63]

A more general suspicion of consumption also played a role. Many commentators feared that, unless Lastenausgleich expenditures were carefully focused, they could erode incentives to work by providing an unearned income for perhaps only nominally disabled war-damaged. The central bank saw consumption expenditures as potentially inflationary, a view shared by others. Further, despite the growing importance of consumption in West Germany's social-market economy, West Germans often revealed an implicit disdain for, an emotional rejection of, the weakness of consumers and consumption as against the strength of producers and production. They often associated production with active, masculine virtues such as efficiency and rebuilding, while characterizing consumption as a merely passive (implicitly feminine) activity —unless they referred to it in terms of "eating up" resources.[64]

HARD REALITIES?

Unfortunately for war-damaged Germans, the exigencies of a private property-based market economy threatened their hopes and expectations. By 1950 they were losing control of the debate over an individual Lastenausgleich to those who emphasized its potential dangers.[65]

Most enterprises in postwar West Germany, as in any economy, did constitute coherent, if not necessarily "organic," wholes. Owners and managers would seldom have accumulated unnecessary stocks of tools, supplies, and buildings, but only the capital actually necessary to provide their good or service. Even when factors of production were in surplus, very few profitable enterprises would have had twice as many factors as necessary for their operation. Compelling firms to surrender half their assets to the war-damaged would have at least temporarily paralyzed most enterprises without providing war-damaged Germans with the right mix of assets to start up new businesses, to the serious detriment of the West German economy. Even in those relatively rare cases where an enterprise consisted of self-contained units, division would often have been difficult. In the abstract, an expelled or bombed-out business-man might have been as efficient a manager for a subsidiary or branch of an existing enterprise as was the current owner or manager. Nonetheless, finding the right person to whom to transfer control or ownership would have been a chancy proposition. Such problems might have worked out in the long run, but the West German people would have suffered in the meantime.

Compelling enterprises to take on partners does seem particularly problematic. Partners who have voluntarily set up a partnership can fall out, but imposing on an unwilling obligor a partner who would bring nothing to the enterprise would often have proved a recipe for disaster. Silent partners would always face the risk that creative bookkeeping would deprive them of their just return. Even unusually sympathetic obligors, willing to make sacrifices for the community of risk, might well have balked at surrendering substantial control over an enterprise they had built up to an active partner they had never met.

Making the capital levy due immediately (at least for larger fortunes), while allowing obligors to sue to pay in installments, had potential advantages as well as potential problems. In principle it would allow those who knew an enterprise best, its owners, to decide which was more economically rational, immediate payment or payment in installments at market rates of interest. Besides, the need to pay off the levies could spur firms to a more efficient use of their resources. Even so, large numbers of enterprises would probably have sued to pay in installments, overwhelming whatever agency had to adjudicate such claims. In addition, West German market interest rates were so high (after two inflations in a generation) that paying them might have proven to be as, or nearly as, financially debilitating as immediate transfer of half the firm's capital.

Once policy makers had decided for payment in installments, they had to set amortization and interest at rates bearable for the economy, but asserting that one must not "overburden" the economy begged the question. Absent perfect information about current and future economic conditions, no one could establish just what rate of interest and amortization would be too great a burden for the economy or particular firms. Policy makers would have to guess. The higher they set the rate, the more marginal firms would become insolvent. Some of those firms were presumably tying up resources that could be used more efficiently elsewhere. Driving them into bankruptcy, though, would cut output and employment immediately, whereas it might be years before the freed-up resources could find more efficient uses. Moreover, the owners of and workers at those firms were voters who would resist bankruptcy and unemployment. Hence, policy makers felt compelled to set the levy rate low enough to protect all but the most marginal firms, substantially reducing Lastenausgleich revenues.

The Lastenausgleich was about protecting private property—but not all property is created equal. To its owner(s), each piece of property may be sacred, but to the economy and society as a whole, productive real assets are more valuable than unproductive real or paper assets, including compensation claims. Only existing productive real assets can in the future directly generate new goods and services. Unproductive real assets cannot do so at all. Paper assets can contribute indirectly to future production, but they can more easily be replaced, through the effects of monetary and fiscal policy, than can real assets. Opponents of a substantial, individual Lastenausgleich were demanding that the society, in the name of the broader economic and social good, privilege "capitalists," that is, owner/managers of privately held but socially vital productive real assets. How successful the war-damaged would be in securing an individual Lastenausgleich would depend substantially on how policy makers responded to such arguments.

Chapter 7

THE POLITICS OF A LASTENAUSGLEICH

Within the context of a fragile new democracy, the political parties struggled to develop consistent Lastenausgleich policies. Narrow economic and fiscal constraints, conflicting conceptions of social justice, and divergent political calculations made it impossible to generate unanimity among, or even within, the parties. Meanwhile, many Germans found problematic the predominance in postwar West German democratic politics of men and a few women who had been active in, and were seen as symbolic of, the failed Weimar Republic. These men and women, including the early leaders of the war-damaged, did bring liabilities to the renewal of political life, but they also brought experience with democratic politics and a commitment to making the system work. The Lastenausgleich illuminates how policy makers and interest-group leaders in the early Federal Republic proved able to work together to address the society's problems and to build a stable democracy—unlike the politically active in the Weimar Republic.

AMBIVALENCE ON THE RIGHT

As the war-damaged realized, Adenauer's right-of-center governing coalition was not going to accept all of their demands. The coalition parties had to answer to the practical needs of a still-weak, market economy. Supporters of those parties included hundreds of thousands of currently propertied undamaged who were willing to accept some Lastenausgleich but who saw much narrower limits to it than did the war-damaged. Moreover, the CDU, which nominally favored private property, had joined the SPD to promulgate the primarily social Lastenausgleich of the First Lastenausgleich Law.

Johannes Kunze (CDU), chairman of the Bundestag Lastenausgleich Com-

mittee, was the most powerful single individual in the Lastenausgleich conflict. He had lost half his personal possessions to Allied bombing, but, as a
white-collar worker, his major asset was the human capital he embodied. As
long as he stayed employed, he lacked the personal stake of those who had
lost a livelihood and identified themselves as war-damaged. Deeply rooted
in Christian social thought, and with connections to moderates in the SPD,
Kunze represented the Left CDU and its preference for a social and productive
Lastenausgleich. Schillinger sees Schäffer as using Kunze to promote a Lastenausgleich on Schäffer's productionist principles. Kunze, though, had long emphasized the priority of economic considerations, rejected Schäffer's extreme
fiscalism, and would succeed in blocking many of Schäffer's "unsocial" proposals. The CDU/CSU Bundestag delegation announced they had chosen him
to lead the Bundestag Lastenausgleich Committee because, as the longtime
manager of a major Protestant charitable institution, "he is a guarantor for
the preservation of social interests and simultaneously as one knowledgeable
about economy and agriculture would have the confidence of their organizations." The focus in this pronouncement on social and economic factors did
not bode well for the organized war-damaged's preference for legal claims and
individual recompense.[1]

Over time, Kunze would adjust his ideas about what was economically feasible in the Lastenausgleich, but national economic considerations would remain preeminent for him — as for the CDU. Like many Germans (including
some war-damaged), he was concerned with the economic risks of "excessive"
capital levies and inappropriate Lastenausgleich expenditures. The CDU had
long placed economic constraints at the forefront of its Lastenausgleich discussions. Already in 1946 the party had supported land transfers to expellees only
if they could be implemented "without endangering the amount of production." Even CDU politicians sympathetic to a Lastenausgleich usually emphasized that one must first establish what burden surviving capital could bear before trying to determine what Lastenausgleich one could offer. Once the Allies
had imposed currency reform, CDU politicians increasingly emphasized that
any capital levy must come from the yield, not the substance, of the economy.[2]

Kunze favored a primarily social Lastenausgleich. As a devout Protestant,
he was committed to the principle of private property in the abstract. Nonetheless, he rejected proposals to restore each piece of lost property. Instead, he
asserted, "To put it simply, the decisive task is to integrate the expellees and
bomb-damaged economically into the total life of the populace of the Federal
Republic, to give them the basis for building up a new livelihood." He therefore
rejected any purely quotal Lastenausgleich because virtually none of the war-
damaged could ever hope to establish a new livelihood with the 5–15 percent
compensation a quotal Lastenausgleich would permit.[3]

Within the CDU/CSU, Kunze was not alone in preferring a social Lastenausgleich. In some ways the word "social" was trumps in postwar West Germany. West Germany was a "social state" with a "social-market economy." Socially oriented Christian Democrats, though, were much more responsible than were neoliberals for pushing through the policies that made the social-market economy social. Christian social teaching (which has always emphasized each Christian's social responsibility and the obligations as well as rights of private property) had experienced a revival in the late nineteenth and early twentieth centuries in the face of the problems accompanying economic and social transformation. Further, Germany's bitter experiences since 1914 made West German politicians sensitive to the risks of political instability that unrestrained market forces could engender. Christian Democrats were generally more committed to ensuring that each war-damaged citizen had a humanly worthy existence than they were to restoring lost private property.[4]

Social and electoral demographics also played a key role, one that the war-damaged leadership would rather have ignored. As Kunze noted, and as the war-damaged acknowledged, some 70 percent of war-damaged Germans had been employees living in rental property and had owned no productive capital. These people's war damages consisted of the loss of jobs, dwellings, and household goods and clothing. They had no interest in a Lastenausgleich focused on restoring the lost productive assets of a minority of the war-damaged and, unless they were unemployable, relatively little interest in a Lastenausgleich at all compared to other issues. The fact that in a mid-1949 opinion poll only 9.5 percent of workers and 11.4 percent of agricultural workers listed the Lastenausgleich as the most pressing national problem is indicative of their priorities.[5]

Moreover, even among those 30 percent who had had some productive assets, the overwhelming majority had been small farmers, artisans, or shopkeepers with modest to very modest assets. On one 1951 estimate, 80 percent of the war-damaged had had before the war less than 20,000 RM (less than $5,000 at prewar exchange rates), and 50 percent had had less than 6,000 RM (less than $1,500). A quotal Lastenausgleich, with its necessarily small percentage compensation rates, would give these smallholders only meager payments, insufficient to reestablish themselves in business or to live on. These formerly small propertied stood to gain much more, economically, from a social and productive Lastenausgleich than from any feasible quotal Lastenausgleich.[6]

These crucial facts about the social structure of the war-damaged were the deep, dark secret of the war-damaged groups, which were dominated by the formerly propertied minority; they are also central to understanding the failure of the war-damaged groups to secure their goals. The groups spoke, in fact, for a relatively small minority. On economic grounds, as the SPD periodically noted, at most 25 percent of war-damaged citizens, perhaps 8 percent of the electorate, had an economic interest in the quotal Lastenausgleich that war-damaged groups were promoting. For ideological and political reasons the FDP and the CDU/CSU barely mentioned this reality—but they could not ignore it. To placate the mass of the war-damaged they feared might become radicalized, the parties would have to disburse Lastenausgleich funds primarily on the basis of current need, not past wealth.[7]

Personal ties seem, on balance, to have played little role in the Lastenausgleich. Such ties gave both undamaged property owners and war-damaged former property owners direct access to CDU politicians. Nevertheless, because the CDU was committing West Germany to a private property–based economy, the current national-economic importance of surviving business enterprises, of current property, was more important in deciding CDU policy than were personal ties. The CDU/CSU was choosing to privilege current over former property holders on national-economic grounds and to emphasize a social Lastenausgleich on ideological and electoral grounds.[8]

Nonetheless, the CDU/CSU and its liberal coalition partner, the FDP, had to pay some attention to the (formerly) propertied. Christian social teaching and liberalism had always emphasized that property ownership was a natural right. The German Center and Right had for nearly a century been defending private property against the rise of socialism. Germany's recent experience with National Socialism and the creation of a Communist East Germany had sharpened the sense of dire threat from collectivist tendencies. By 1949 the CDU/CSU and the FDP were championing private ownership of the means of production as a distinguishing characteristic of democratic, Western, Christian, and German culture. Many West Germans feared not only some Communist takeover, but also a "creeping socialism" that would insidiously erode the bases of private property and Western values. In particular, some Germans feared a social Lastenausgleich would advance collectivist tendencies by taking private property away from currently propertied individuals through capital levies without necessarily creating corresponding private property among the war-damaged. The formerly propertied war-damaged played on these concerns. They warned that they might become radicalized absent a generous Lastenausgleich, and they vigorously promoted an individual Lastenausgleich as crucial for securing property rights generally against collectivist tendencies.[9]

The FDP quite probably did play a significant role in forcing the CDU/CSU to grant a more individual Lastenausgleich than the latter initially seemed inclined to allow. The FDP, with its roots in nineteenth-century liberalism, was strongly committed to private property. Its members complained privately that the CDU had chosen to send to the Bundestag Lastenausgleich Committee primarily people who stood on the party's Left wing. Nöll von der Nahmer regaled his party colleagues with tales of how he and the FDP had stood up for the restoration of private property to the war-damaged against the "stiff opposition of the SPD and the left wing of the CDU." The FDP's central role in the coalition did give it leverage to strengthen the quotal elements in coalition

Lastenausgleich policy, even as its ties to business pushed it to help limit the levy burden on surviving property.[10]

The Left CDU remained committed to a productive and social Lastenausgleich, but pressure from the war-damaged, the Right CDU, and the FDP forced it to accept some individual Lastenausgleich measures. For example, in defending the CDU against accusations it had adopted a "collectivist" Lastenausgleich policy on housing assistance, Kunze insisted that he and his colleagues believed that "for the securing of the bases of our people it is 100 times more important as a goal that over the long run the most private property possible is created as that private ownership in this area should decline to the benefit of public ownership." The question remained, though, how much private property would be possible in the Lastenausgleich Law—and how long the long run would be.[11]

THE WAR-DAMAGED FIGHT BACK

From early on, leaders of the war-damaged focused on building strong organizations to carry on a vigorous fight for their rights. The war-damaged faced a daunting struggle, in the context of limited resources, to convince their fellow citizens and the political system to hearken to their demands for a generous and individual Lastenausgleich. They might have preferred to rely on the justice of their cause, but their leaders knew that the more numerous and better organized they could show themselves to be, the better their chance of getting the ear of politicians.[12]

Contemporaries and historians have generally emphasized the political apathy of postwar (West) Germans, but that judgment seems oversimplified. Postwar opinion polls revealed a disinclination to participate in politics, and Germans often articulated their doubts about political activity. Moreover, younger Germans had no experience with autonomous political activity. Yet many older Germans could draw on a pre-1933 socialization to and experience in interest-group and political activity, and enough of them, and their younger colleagues, did participate to provide an adequate base for West German politics. Indeed, by the late 1950s, West Germans were more likely to participate in political activity than the citizens of at least some other "democratic" countries.[13]

Organizing the war-damaged did prove difficult, but not impossible. The ZvF had little competition as spokesman for the bomb-damaged and the savers (though it emphasized the interests of the former). It organized nearly 5 percent of bomb-damaged (250,000 of 4.6 million). The expellees remained divided between the ZvD, which represented their economic and social interests, and the *Landsmannschaften,* one for each region from which the expellees had come, which represented their regional-cultural interests. Even the union of expellee groups into the Federation of Expelled Germans (Bund der vertriebenen Deutschen, BVD) in November 1951 could not erase all differences. The ZvD organized nearly 17 percent of the expellees (1.5 million of 9 million). By late 1949, despite having organized only a minority of each subgroup, the war-damaged had built up a formidable array of organizations that could claim to speak for most war-damaged.[14]

The war-damaged recognized that their success would depend at least partly on how well their subgroups cooperated. The bomb-damaged, expellees, and savers were all "war-damaged," but they had had different experiences and potentially different needs. They might end up fighting among themselves, weakening their position as against the potential obligors. Leaders of all the war-damaged groups continuously promoted the idea of cooperation, even preparing a joint statement of demands in early 1949. Whether such cooperation would continue was another matter.[15]

Crucially, the war-damaged recognized that whatever the putative justice of their claims, they could win only if they engaged in political struggle. Mattes pointed out, "The number of undamaged reaches into the millions, and they can with their majority suppress the upstanding fighter for his rights, under the rules of democracy. And they will if we do not defend ourselves." Indeed, *Selbsthilfe* quoted Pascal that "Right without power is powerless. . . . Hence one must bind right and power together and take care that what is right is powerful and that what is powerful is right." It then identified Pascal's idea as "*the* basic idea of our struggle." Expellees shared this view.[16]

In the 1920s, creditors organized to secure their political ends but never came to terms with the need for political struggle in a democracy. Bolstered by a favorable court decision, they counted on the justice of their cause to ensure their complete victory. Moreover, they reacted with outrage when debtors strove to defend their interests through political action. Having researched both the revaluation and Lastenausgleich conflicts, I am struck by how much more pragmatic the war-damaged were. The latter were just as convinced of the justice of their cause as creditors had been. Nonetheless, the war-damaged were under no illusions that right would automatically triumph over might, making them more politically effective than their 1920s counterparts in the creditor movement.[17] Although direct evidence is lacking, this greater willingness to accept the role of power in politics presumably derived both from knowledge of 1920s creditor failures and from the Nazis' constant emphasis on "struggle" as central to politics.

In deploying their power, the war-damaged emphasized their numbers and the vehemence with which they would defend their rights. Those who had suffered minor losses never perceived themselves in any politically influential sense as being war-damaged, but those who had lost significant amounts of personal, residential, or productive property made up a substantial plurality of the electorate, perhaps 30 percent. Moreover, those war-damaged who had lost their livelihoods, property, and social status had an incentive to invest considerable energy in political struggle to regain their earlier possessions and positions. War-damaged leaders repeatedly asserted, with some justice, that the Lastenausgleich was a determining issue for millions of the war-damaged and that an inadequate Lastenausgleich would radicalize them and lead them to reject democracy, capitalism, and private property. This vehemence made the war-damaged a power the rulers of the new republic could not ignore.[18]

Waldemar Kraft and other expellees created an expellee political party in January 1950, the Block of Expellees and Disenfranchised (the BHE), in addition to the expellee interest groups. Citing in particular the failure of the revaluation parties in the 1920s, expellee members of the major parties (e.g., Kather and Lukaschek [CDU]) had argued that any expellee party would only waste expellee votes. It could never secure even a significant minority because its pool of potential voters was relatively small and would be reduced by splits over broader constitutional, economic, and social issues. Nonetheless, many expellees (up to half in 1950/51) were convinced that the major parties were tools of the locals, who all too often despised and feared the expellees and their demands for aid. Only an expellee party, they believed, could adequately represent their interests.[19]

The BHE described itself as a "non-Marxist social party" and rejected "both the lash of Marxist compulsory planning and liberal avarice." In a long tradition of German lower-middle-class parties, it sought to protect (primarily small) property holders battered by material (including free-market) forces. That meant defending property rights: "Justly acquired property is sacrosanct." Yet it also meant promoting interventionist government to protect individuals against the full impact of competitive forces because "the economy must serve the people." The BHE firmly rejected class conflict. It claimed to represent all Germans who had been deprived of their rights as a result of war, defeat, and currency reform, but it remained overwhelmingly an expellee party.[20]

The BHE was committed to a fully quotal Lastenausgleich. It demanded a confiscatory capital-gains levy and a capital levy that transferred substantial amounts of real capital to the war-damaged. It wanted the levy implemented in "an economically rational manner" but warned that a levy from the yield would be transferred to consumers in higher prices and insisted that a levy from the substance was feasible. Members of the party also insisted that a legal claim to appropriate compensation existed for all war-damaged, proportional to individual losses. Party leaders vociferously rejected any form of compensation that might be construed as welfare. The BHE did demand a "consideration of social viewpoints" and characterized the reestablishment of a livelihood for individual war-damaged as the first task of a Lastenausgleich, but this language could not mask the party's relative indifference to the mass of unpropertied war-damaged.[21]

The party represented a potentially radical force in West German politics. Its leaders reminded other Germans of that potential, not least to bolster demands for a generous Lastenausgleich. In a widely reported speech, for example, Kraft warned of the risks to the currently propertied of the growth of a second anti–private property movement, alongside Bolshevism, if the private property of the war-damaged was not honored through a just Lastenausgleich. Also frightening were the many threads that connected the BHE to the Nazis. The party openly courted former Nazis embittered at their treatment in the de-Nazification process, suggesting that their only crime had been "having committed the mistake of having believed uncritically in Germany's future." The party also paired these former Nazis with the war-damaged as fellow war victims. The BHE's major early leaders, Kraft and Theodor Oberländer, had been politically active under the Nazis. The Allies had interned Kraft, 1945–47, for his wartime activities in occupied Poland, and Oberländer would subsequently face (still unresolved) war-crimes accusations.[22]

Initially at least, the party leadership flirted with fanning that radicalism. For example, according to a local SPD paper, the BHE organized hecklers to disrupt a January 1950 speech by Lukaschek, to "terrorize" the CDU into allowing Kraft and Alfred Gille to speak. In any event, once Lukaschek agreed that Kraft and Gille could speak, the latter quieted the hecklers with a few words. For the SPD paper, this event brought back disquieting memories of Nazi campaign tactics from the early 1930s. The SPD paper did report, though, that Kraft and Gille praised Lukaschek when they spoke and that they also had a private meeting with Lukaschek in which a purely objective discussion took place.[23]

The BHE threw the political system into turmoil. It quickly secured representation in a number of state legislatures and governments in 1950 and 1951. It seemed set to enter the Bundestag at the next election. Having promised that the war-damaged would get more through mainstream parties than through a special-interest party, the government parties could lose votes if they failed to deliver. Moreover, the BHE might form coalitions with the opposition SPD. Such coalitions could drive the CDU/CSU and FDP from state governments and perhaps eventually from the federal government — if the BHE and the SPD could learn to cooperate.[24]

AMBIVALENCE ON THE LEFT

Despite FDP fears of a ruthlessly "collectivist" SPD, the Left had mixed feelings about the Lastenausgleich (and about West German capitalism). Most Social Democrats and some trade unionists were socialists and did not particularly want to re-create private property in the means of production. Others could accept private property but found the postwar property distribution problematic. Still others wanted to expand the definition of war losses to cover loss of a job. In spite of these differences, all were concerned that the burden of a Lastenausgleich not undercut economic recovery and not be shifted to average citizens in higher prices and taxes. These multiple concerns produced disagreement about Lastenausgleich policy—and a flirtation with the BHE.

The unions divided sharply on the Lastenausgleich. The conflict seems to have played itself out as a battle between two individuals, Lorenz Wolkersdorf, of the Economic Institute of the Trade Unions, and Ulrich Grote-Mißmahl, a regional union official, neither of whom was a friend of private property in the abstract.[25]

Wolkersdorf's proposals would have protected postwar property owners at the expense of formerly propertied war-damaged. He believed that a capital levy from the substance of the economy would be deleterious. As long as West Germany remained a capitalist economy, any attempt to divide privately owned enterprises for partial transfer to war-damaged individuals would seriously disrupt the economy. The major victims of such disruption would be the workers who would be laid off and those among the elderly and disabled whom the society could no longer afford to support. The only sensible capital levy, he argued, was a payment in installments from the yield of productive capital. He vehemently opposed tying compensation to prewar property ownership. However fortuitous and illegitimate the postwar property distribution, he held no brief for the prewar distribution either. Moreover, he saw the loss of a job as just as much of an unjustified blow to the individual as the loss of real or paper assets. The decisive problem for expellees, he argued, was their successful economic integration into West Germany—and that meant targeting the modest Lastenausgleich funds to provide livelihoods, housing, and, where necessary, support payments for needy war-damaged.[26]

Grote-Mißmahl's proposals would have burdened postwar owners sharply to the benefit of war-damaged property owners. He was convinced that a levy from the substance of the capital was feasible and necessary. He rejected any levy from the yield because many companies could pass on the costs to consumers in the form of higher prices (an issue that concerned Wolkersdorf as well). Implicitly acknowledging the deleterious consequences of any forced breakup of productive units, he proposed to give the war-damaged certificates with which to "buy" assets from undamaged individuals, who could thereby decide voluntarily which assets to transfer to obtain the certificates to pay their levies. The government was to supervise the realization of the certificates to ensure their economically rational use. He emphasized that formerly propertied individuals had a legal claim to their property that the state had to recognize, though he too saw the loss of a job as a recompensable loss. The Lastenausgleich was initially to be based on social need but would eventually provide individual recompense based on past property holdings. He did seem much more interested in ensuring a capital levy from the substance than in exactly how the resulting revenues would be expended. His primary motive, indeed, seemed to be a moral revulsion at the capriciousness of war and defeat.[27]

The German Federation of Trade Unions, in March 1951, came down somewhat closer to Grote-Mißmahl's position. The Federation did support a levy from the yield to finance aid for the unemployable, but they also insisted that the postwar property distribution was so unjust that only a levy on the substance, due in principle immediately, could relegitimate property. Expenditures for socially necessary purposes (support for elderly and disabled, replacement of household goods, housing construction, and job creation) were to have absolute priority over any balancing of capital losses and were to go to war-damaged Germans independent of earlier losses. Nonetheless, the government was eventually to disburse funds from the capital levy as individual compensation, graduated so that higher losses got lower compensation rates.[28]

The SPD split internally over how to create the most equitable Lastenausgleich, with the sharpest conflicts over the same issues, levy from the substance or the yield and payment according to need or to amount of losses, that plagued the unions. It was also under pressure from the demands of political reality and political expediency.

The SPD initially promoted a social Lastenausgleich. The party saw itself as the paladin for any who were defenseless—including the often desperately impoverished war-damaged. Suspicious of private ownership of the means of production, it preferred a Lastenausgleich that focused not on past property but on current human need. Its first priority was always some nonwelfare support payment that would ensure a humanly worthy existence for all elderly and disabled war-damaged. Its next priorities were replacing lost household goods, building new housing, and integrating the war-damaged economically, either as small businessmen or workers. Like Wolkersdorf, many party members feared that focusing on property losses would mean that all Lastenausgleich funds would go to recompensing a few rich folks, with nothing left for the 70 percent of the war-damaged who had lost only a job and their household goods.[29]

The SPD split sharply on whether to acknowledge an individual (legal) claim to a Lastenausgleich. Heinrich Troeger (SPD), finance minister of Hesse, argued that the party should have the courage of its convictions on private property and should implement a "collective Lastenausgleich" in which all funds were expended to help the needy and to integrate the war-damaged into the West German economy, irrespective of an individual's particular war losses. However, "collective" was a dirty word in postwar West Germany; the term was associated with the hated Communists. More pragmatic Social Democrats argued that one had to accept the desire of many war-damaged Germans, including many workers, for some legal claim that would confirm their past status and differentiate them from welfare recipients. Despite Troeger's efforts, the party early on accepted that any Lastenausgleich law would have to recognize past losses, and SPD Lastenausgleich spokesman Seuffert was at pains to deny that the SPD supported a "collective" Lastenausgleich. The party did, though, emphasize that all war-damaged, not just the formerly propertied, were entitled to a legal claim to some Lastenausgleich.[30]

The SPD was deeply ambivalent about the type of capital levy West Germany could implement. The party shared union fears that a levy from the yield would be shifted to the average citizen, so it favored in principle a levy paid out of the substance. Nevertheless, as early as mid-1948, SPD economic expert Gerhard Weisser was warning party leaders that any levy could come only from the yield, not the substance. From 1950 the party's two Lastenausgleich experts, Seuffert and Kriedemann, were calling in principle for a levy on the substance but were discussing in practice payment in installments from the yield with a modest interest rate. By December 1950 a party position paper contended, "Insofar as such a transfer of capital can succeed, it shall be striven for. In most cases, however, the capital levy must be paid in installments."[31]

Politics, though, intervened. Many longtime Social Democrats had suffered war damages, and perhaps half the war-damaged had voted SPD in the late 1940s—and might again. In March 1951, the party leadership prepared a Lastenausgleich resolution announcing SPD support for a levy from the substance, priority for social measures, and recognition of a legal claim to individual recompense payable to the degree funds were available after satisfaction of social needs. The resolution provoked a sharp debate in the SPD Executive Committee. Fritz Henßler "considered it unworthy that we should hypocritically propose concessions to a quotal Lastenausgleich when we know the funds for it are simply not there." Wenzel Jaksch (an expellee from the Sudetenland) asserted the party had to do this because 50 percent of the workers from the Sudetenland had had some modest assets. Erich Ollenhauer pointed out that the refugees "have not yet politically decided. Here lay new fields for the party. The talk is of a quotal Lastenausgleich only *after* the implementation of social measures." It then came out that the resolution had already been published and could not be amended. Even so, the party Executive Committee approved it only narrowly, 12-10.[32]

When the BHE began winning seats in state legislatures in 1951, Schumacher saw an opportunity to realize his postwar dream that the experience of war damages would detach the middling classes from their traditional deference to the wealthy. He hoped to win a portion of the expellees from the CDU/CSU, especially as a SPD-BHE coalition in Lower Saxony would be able to form a government that excluded the CDU. He and Kraft personally negotiated a coalition agreement for a Lower Saxony government. Without consulting Kriedemann or Seuffert, Schumacher promised SPD support for "a real levying of the substance of the capital through immediate falling due of the levy," social and quotal Lastenausgleich, an individual legal claim, and a certification of the losses.[33]

The Schumacher-Kraft agreement apparently shocked Kriedemann and Seuffert. An obviously angry Kriedemann complained that the SPD-BHE agreement directly contradicted recent SPD policy pronouncements on a quotal Lastenausgleich, on making the levy due immediately, and on whether to certify each individual's damages. Because he and his colleagues were going to have to debate such issues in Bundestag committees, he demanded that the party decide how to reconcile its past statements and the realities of any Lastenausgleich with its recent agreement with the BHE.[34]

The SPD soon backpedaled, at least in practice. The coalition parties remained committed to a levy from the yield, not the substance, and the SPD tacitly rejoined them. CDU/CSU and SPD delegates in the Bundestag Lastenausgleich Committee continued to work together to craft a primarily social and productive Lastenausgleich. Kurt Klotzbach sees the SPD as supporting the unpropertied in the Lastenausgleich, but it was not that simple. Economic exigency in a capitalist economy pushed the SPD to defend unpropertied war-damaged and current property holders against the demands of formerly propertied war-damaged. Meanwhile, the BHE and the SPD, content with their coalition in Lower Saxony, tacitly ignored their differences on the Lastenausgleich.[35]

Schumacher had bigger fish to fry than the Lastenausgleich: he hoped to create a coalition of disadvantaged Germans, establish an SPD-dominated government, and introduce democratic socialism to Germany. As a socialist, he held no brief for the existing property distribution and may have believed that one could safely compel a transfer of significant amounts of real capital. He would have favored the latter to ensure the burden of a Lastenausgleich would not be shifted to average citizens. He presumably could support some quotal Lastenausgleich and a certification of individual damages because these were supposed to be subordinate to the social and productive measures the party had long touted. Finally, the BHE shared the SPD's opposition to the Adenauer government's neoliberal policies and favored its own version of state intervention to manage the economy for the social good. Schumacher was right to see some areas of agreement between the SPD and some of the organized expellees. On the other hand, in reporting the initial SPD-BHE agreement, the SPD Press Service called it a "marriage of convenience." Marriages of convenience don't always last.[36]

CONFLICT AND COOPERATION

Despite the often deep suspicion of the SPD among coalition party delegates, Kunze strove successfully to secure crucial SPD cooperation in preparing

Lastenausgleich legislation. As they had with the Immediate Aid Law, he and others in the CDU hoped to get SPD support for the final Lastenausgleich Law, to legitimate the government's Lastenausgleich policy and to prevent the SPD from using the issue against the CDU/CSU in the next election. Kunze soon recognized that the SPD would vote against any coalition Lastenausgleich bill, but, as he later reported, he could not have gotten the bill written up without SPD assistance in the back-breaking committee work the enormously complicated law required. Indeed, when Adenauer warned him darkly that the SPD intended to sabotage the bill, Kunze replied that he faced greater obstacles from certain coalition-party delegates than from the Social Democrats.[37]

This day-to-day cooperation rested on substantial underlying agreement — and even friendship. At a public "disputation" in early 1951 between Kunze and Seuffert, Gille (BHE) complained from the audience that "it is extraordinarily difficult to conduct this disputation to a successful conclusion and indeed because — and this will become ever clearer as the discussion progresses — the disputants are not of opposing opinions on the central issues." Kunze and Seuffert spent the rest of the evening trying to highlight their differences, but Gille was right. Neither Kunze nor Seuffert favored the individual Lastenausgleich, financed by levies from the substance of the capital, that the organized war-damaged wanted. Although their differences (e.g., on exempting publicly owned assets from the capital levies and disbursing Lastenausgleich housing funds) were not trivial, they paled beside their agreement on basic principles.[38]

The cooperation the major parties displayed on the Lastenausgleich and other key issues was crucial for the new Federal Republic. For all of Adenauer's and Schumacher's determination to present voters with a clear choice between government and opposition, both government and opposition delegates realized that a parliamentary system cannot function without some cooperation and compromise among even opposing parliamentary factions. The Social Democrats saw parliamentary democracy as the only feasible route for attaining democratic socialism. Most of them had lived through the collapse of Germany's first parliamentary democracy, a collapse brought on in part by the inability of (relatively) moderate political forces to cooperate. Hence, in the Lastenausgleich, as in other bills, they avoided positions that would undercut the parliamentary ground on which they themselves stood. Indeed, the SPD voted for fully 83.9 percent of the laws the first Bundestag promulgated.[39]

Gille's annoyance at the Kunze-Seuffert road show was mild compared to that of at least some other expellees. For example, in an article entitled "The Masks Fall before the Microphone," an expellee newspaper bitterly denounced the cooperation and friendliness Kunze and Seuffert demonstrated in a radio interview. It accused them of cutting a deal at the expense of the war-damaged in which, supposedly, the SPD would spare West German property from high levies and the CDU would support a social Lastenausgleich. Such attacks on Kunze and Seuffert's chumminess were symptomatic of a deeper anger among many war-damaged at apparently cavalier treatment at the hands of the undamaged majority and the new political system.[40]

The increased prosperity, or at least comfort, that many West Germans were beginning to enjoy aggravated the anger of the war-damaged. Economic growth was slowly allowing many Germans to improve their living standards and was quickly allowing a lucky minority to live in luxury. The latter especially provoked envy and annoyance among war-damaged who were still impoverished. The generous recompense for government officials and Bundestag delegates and the "palatial" office buildings the government was constructing in Bonn were a source of real outrage, given the widespread misery in postwar West Germany. The government did pass relatively generous legislation for expelled civil servants in April 1951, but currently employed and retired civil servants from western Germany received even more generous treatment. Moreover, the legislature was gradually promulgating legislation to assist the many groups in German society who had suffered because of Nazi oppression, war, or defeat. Even though the war-damaged could not overtly begrudge most of these people some assistance, they often did feel slighted that they had not yet received recompense.[41]

The organized war-damaged were convinced the government was deliberately dragging its feet. In truth, West German politicians did want to put this issue behind them quickly, but they faced substantial difficulties.[42]

For starters, coalition members had difficulty constructing a mutually acceptable Lastenausgleich bill. Schäffer (whose Finance Ministry had jurisdiction) was concerned primarily with West Germany's economic and fiscal health. He sought to limit the Lastenausgleich burden below what the Unkeler Circle (of coalition-party Lastenausgleich experts) had already agreed was politically necessary. He rejected the Unkeler guidelines on the levy's scope and nature and refused to consider tapping other government revenues to help finance the Lastenausgleich. He also sought to put elderly and disabled war-damaged back on welfare, with a modest supplement in recognition that they were not "typical" welfare recipients—a de facto reintroduction of the "elevated welfare" that 1920s war victims had so bitterly resented. Leaked reports of his views sparked outrage among war-damaged Germans and consternation among members of the Unkeler Circle. These fundamental conflicts delayed the introduction of a government Lastenausgleich bill for more than a year.[43]

Moreover, the Lastenausgleich Law's staggering complexity imposed delays. Even though the expellees would threaten to introduce their own Lastenausgleich bill, in practice only the government, with its access to the resources of the civil service, could effectively draft such far-reaching legislation. And even after legislators had received the government's bill, they would require 200 committee sessions and unnumbered subcommittee and informal sessions to master this material and produce a law of 375 paragraphs whose text ran to more than 100 pages in book form.[44]

One reason the government could get away with delaying for almost three years was that the Lastenausgleich, while indispensable in the long run, had a relatively low immediate priority for most Germans, war-damaged and undamaged alike. According to a mid-1949 opinion survey, the important issues for West Germans were housing, the status of refugees, unemployment, the Lastenausgleich, and tax reform. Rentiers were most interested in the Lastenausgleich, and urban and rural workers were least interested. The free professions and businessmen were almost as interested in the Lastenausgleich as rentiers, but some would have been potential recipients and others potential obligors. Given the disastrous housing shortage and the high unemployment, the Lastenausgleich's relatively low importance is not surprising. It took on central importance for the majority of the war-damaged only after other legislation began to address more immediate problems, such as equal rights for refugees, housing, and jobs.[45]

Schäffer's equivocations and these painful and occasionally insensitive delays could have driven the war-damaged to seek radical solutions. Millions of war-damaged Germans still lived in abject misery, often "vegetating" in some isolated village far from home, relatives, friends, and any hope of work. Fortunately, economic elites, policy makers, and the war-damaged all proved to be moderate, pragmatic, and open to compromise.

Economic elites were surprisingly responsive to the concerns of the war-damaged, much more so than their 1920s counterparts had been to the creditors. In the 1920s, businessmen and government officials had cavalierly rejected any meaningful revaluation and had expressed virtually no compassion for impoverished creditors. Post-1945 businessmen and officials, on the other hand, took it for granted that war-damaged citizens had a right to demand recompense. They made it clear that they accepted some Lastenausgleich as just and inevitable.[46]

Business groups wanted to limit their own burdens as much as possible, but they sought to do so in a way that did not rub salt into the wounds of the war-damaged. In November 1948, CDU politician Paul Binder had warned his brother Odilo, who was prominent in business circles, that "it is in my view tactically false to get into a position that would be able to characterize the Lastenausgleich with the words 'abandon the balancing out [*Lasst den Ausgleich*].'" Industry, Paul warned, must instead accept the inevitable Lastenausgleich and work to structure it as reasonably as possible. The business community did seek to do so. In September 1950, for example, officials from the Finance and Expellee Ministries met with obligor representatives to get their input on Schäffer's efforts to limit the Lastenausgleich levies sharply. Two representatives applauded Schäffer's proposal because it would be cheaper for business. Yet according to Dr. Hinz (Expellee Ministry), another (unnamed) business representative chimed in: "This issue cannot be considered only from a purely accounting viewpoint, with the wish to hold the levy as low as possible; rather, tactical political considerations should be decisive in addressing the issue. He considers it out of the question that the [Finance Ministry] draft will prove politically feasible. . . . Before one runs the risk that, by supporting the [Finance Ministry] draft against Unkel, one should lose the feasible Unkel compromise and call up significantly costlier proposals and amendments, one should support the Unkel proposal." Hinz, no friend of business, added, "It is obvious here that the business community is relatively clear about the seriousness of the situation."[47]

Schillinger ascribes such attitudes to a certain complacency among businessmen, but I would argue they reflect a recognition that past insensitivity to popular opinion had proved deleterious. Business did count on having friends in high places to help it prevent Lastenausgleich levies from getting out of hand, yet businessmen were also conscious, as S. Jonathan Wiesen has argued, of the need "to recapture *moral* legitimacy" after twelve years of cooperation with Nazism. Business representatives also remembered the anticapitalism that business attitudes toward revaluation had provoked and realized that similar callousness toward impoverished war-damaged could well produce disastrous electoral consequences. Moreover, businessmen had seen their property destroyed by Allied bombs and had often been imprisoned by the Allies for their Nazi ties. They recognized that relying on dictatorship to crush their opponents, as they had in 1933, had not worked out too terribly well and that the Western Allies would not allow them to try it again anyway. The neoliberals were only one expression of a new awareness among supporters of a market economy of the threat of antibusiness protest and politics and of the need for sensitive policies to reduce that threat.[48]

Business did not win over the war-damaged, but it made its position and the government's task easier. The war-damaged recognized that business's proposal to pay the capital levy in installments would reduce Lastenausgleich income and their recompense considerably. The ZvF in particular could occasionally be quite vituperative about greedy big business. Nonetheless, individual war-damaged almost never expressed the virulent anticapitalism that had characterized 1920s creditors. The fear of appearing pro-Communist in the context of Germany's postwar division into free-market West and Communist East may have played a role. Nonetheless, business's willingness to accept in principle a 50 percent capital levy, while otherwise keeping a low profile, almost certainly played a role as well.[49]

While not exactly thrilled at having to listen to the war-damaged, officials in the Federal Republic, unlike their 1920s counterparts, recognized that, in a parliamentary democracy, they had no real choice. After ignoring war-damaged groups initially, the Finance Ministry quickly added them to its list of those who would receive reports on its Lastenausgleich preparations. Its officials were careful thereafter to consult regularly with those groups. The war-damaged would have liked more input, but they became more contented as they had more meetings with government officials.[50]

West German politicians were also extremely responsive to broader demands by the war-damaged to be taken seriously. Where 1920s politicians had virtually ignored the creditors, 1950s politicians reached out to the war-damaged repeatedly. By 1951 numerous politicians, including various federal ministers and Chancellor Adenauer, were accepting invitations to attend and speak at assemblies called by the war-damaged groups. The war-damaged seem to have been quite pleased that important politicians took them so seriously. These visits appear to have had a generally very positive effect on war-damaged attitudes toward the political system, even when politicians did not say what war-damaged Germans wanted to hear.[51]

War-damaged citizens and their leaders showed no doubt about their right to speak for themselves and their cohort—and to expect policy makers to listen. The war-damaged groups repeatedly urged their members to talk to, write, and petition their elected representatives. In letters, petitions, and newspaper articles war-damaged Germans reiterated their rights as citizens of a democratic state to petition for redress of grievances. Meanwhile, their central organizations lobbied government officials directly and organized letter-writing and petition campaigns from their regional and local organizations, which also generated their own petitions.[52]

Such self-assertiveness is arguably both indispensable for a functioning democracy and inadequate to assure one. If a democracy is to retain its legitimacy, its citizens must be willing to undertake the lobbying activities that will inform their representatives of, and press them to respond to, popular opinion. Yet such assertiveness had in the early 1930s contributed not to democracy but to the rise of Nazism. The Nazi Party had relied on political agitation to increase its electoral support. Moreover, the Weimar Republic's policies had angered many politically active Germans, disillusioning them with parliamentary democracy and opening them to Nazism as a populist alternative. Political stability for the Federal Republic would depend not just on citizen activism but on official responses to that activism and on broader popular attitudes toward parliamentary democracy.[53]

The war-damaged used effectively the democratic technique of the mass demonstration. Unlike the creditors in the 1920s, both the bomb-damaged and expellees held numerous mass demonstrations in small and large cities, to bring their views to public attention and to pressure the Bundestag to meet their demands. They also held in Bonn two mass demonstrations of the war-damaged from all across West Germany, in February 1951 and May 1952. These demonstrations served their purpose, forcing the coalition parties to address the demands of the war-damaged.[54]

The 1951 demonstration and its aftermath reflected ambivalence about democratic expression in the early Federal Republic. Dissatisfied with the Lastenausgleich bill that the government finally introduced, the expellee leadership called a mass demonstration in Bonn for 18 February 1951 — in midwinter. Perhaps 50,000 people, from one of the most impoverished strata in German society, attended. Extremely fearful of violence, the government called out hundreds of riot police and kept the demonstrators far away from the parliament building, which was closed anyway because it was Sunday. This hostile response angered many demonstrators. Some even held signs saying "Lastenausgleich with Adenauer — or by Stalin," an implicit threat to acquiesce in or support a Soviet invasion if the Lastenausgleich proved unsatisfactory. Kather, though generally conciliatory in his speech, did comment that the undamaged could only expect the expellees to respect private property for as long as the latter could hope to see their demands fulfilled.[55]

The appearance of masses of demonstrators in the streets called up frightening memories of Nazi and Communist rallies in early 1930s Germany and post-1945 Eastern Europe. The conservative *Tages-Anzeiger* of Regensburg, for example, considered the demonstration to be scarcely different from what the "Reds" did: putting "pressure from the street" on the parliament and pushing for the redistribution of wealth. Social Democrats saw echoes of the 1930s in the uniformed "East German Youth," which reminded them of the Hitler Youth and whose participation in the demonstration supposedly culminated in the quasi-Nazi chant, "Kather commands — we obey." Such anxieties echoed postwar discussions, provoked by prewar Nazi successes, of the dangers of "mass democracy," discussions that tended to ignore both Hitler's inability to break the 40 percent barrier in free elections and the role of an elite conspiracy in bringing him to power.[56]

Some within the political elite sought to punish the expellees. The government was subsidizing interest groups, including the ZvD (140,000 DM per year, more than half of its central-office budget) and the ZvF (around 36,000 DM per year, about one-third of its income). Because representatives of expellee organizations at the demonstration had attacked the government and "slandered" several ministers, some officials proposed cutting off the subsidies. At a Bundestag committee meeting, Hans Schütz (CSU), an expellee, led the charge: "It just was not acceptable," he thundered, "to accept money from German taxpayers that was granted for the support of the Central Association [of Expellees] through the accommodating attitude of the federal minister for finances and simultaneously in all openness and in the press to attack this minister as especially hostile to refugees." A Finance Ministry official who attended the meeting noted that all committee members except Kather "unanimously and very forcefully declared themselves in agreement with Schütz's words." The official said that Paul Stech (SPD) added that "even in conceding a broad-minded possibility of criticism and in the frame of a democratic freedom of opinion, it was no longer justifiable to make money available from the public purse without the strictest supervision of the public activities of such organizations."[57]

The expellees, not surprisingly, reacted negatively to these proposals. Kather said in the committee meeting that he should be entitled to make healthy criticisms despite the fact that his organization received money from the government. If necessary, the ZvD would do without the money, though its withdrawal would only further antagonize expellees. Clemens Neumann (ZvD) argued, "The withdrawal or reduction in state subsidies to expellee organizations with the goal of strangling any criticism of the government would merely throw an odd light on the democratic demeanor of the young Federal Republic." Neumann also warned that cutting the subsidies would be counterproductive: "The government would thereby only alienate the expellees all the more and drive [them] into opposition. The profit from such deplorable maneuvers would in any case fall to the 'others': all those on this side or that side [of the Iron Curtain] who would like to profit from division and destruction, from the ruin of the current political structure."[58]

The government apparently thought better of Schütz's threats, but politicians had placed leaders of the war-damaged on notice that they might lose their comfortable subsidies if they made their attacks too radical. What effect this admonition had on war-damaged-group policies is impossible to tell from the Lastenausgleich documentation, but it may well have been a moderating influence, as Rupert Breitling suggested in 1955.[59]

Overall, the CDU/CSU proved more circumspect than did the SPD about criticizing the expellees and their demonstration. Memories of 1930s Germany and of postwar Eastern European countries driven into Communism, and general fears of pressure from the street, did contribute to a cautious, in some ways authoritarian attitude among political elites toward popular protest. Despite these feelings, forcing Kather to resign from the CDU or actually cutting the subsidies would have alienated the frustrated expellees whom the CDU sought to recruit. The CDU contented itself with discussing the issue more in sorrow than in anger. Its press service did quote the Catholic Church's agent for refugee affairs that "the expellees need to recognize their task with a clear-headed view to the public and common good and to beware of great mass assemblies, which can only work them up and lead them into false paths." In practice, though, CDU politicians found themselves acquiescing in the right of citizens not only to petition but to assemble peaceably and to criticize vigorously in order to influence policy.[60]

If political elites were proving occasionally ambivalent about popular expressions of opinion, the situation was forcing war-damaged Germans to become active proponents of the democratic rights of freedom of assembly and of speech. Neumann celebrated the peaceful conduct of the demonstrators as a sign of the "high *moral-political quality of the expellees*" and as evidence that the expellee leadership could be trusted to call such demonstrations because they had chosen not to misuse their position with demagogy. He was taking an implicitly conservative view of who could be trusted to demonstrate, but he ended by promoting the right of (all) citizens to use all legal means. Shortly thereafter, his *Vertriebenen-Korrespondenz* printed an unsigned article attacking those who criticized the demonstrations, saying, "When in addition the rubber truncheon is recommended as the best means against the 'noisy totalitarians,' that seems ill considered coming from a newspaper that otherwise proclaims itself proudly as 'guardian' of democratic freedoms. Have they given sufficient thought to the fact that with such methods they simultaneously defame the freedom of opinion and of assembly according to Articles 5 and 6 of the Basic Law and thereby agree with totalitarian suppression of opinion and conscience?"[61]

War-damaged leaders and some followers demanded a right to direct participation (*Mitwirkung*) by war-damaged groups, as representatives of an important social constituency, in preparing and implementing any Lastenausgleich. In part, they simply did not trust the undamaged to understand their situation and make policy justly, but they also sought to reassert control for themselves, even if mediated through an interest-group leadership. Here they were echoing the demands of numerous groups in German society, including war victims from both wars, for a kind of direct democratic supervision of administration. Even though the war-damaged never explicitly used the terminology of corporatism, war-damaged leaders and most of their followers clearly would have preferred a quasi-corporatist system in which recognized social groups would participate in governance through the representation of their leaders in policy-making and policy-implementing bodies. That demand implied a right to popular input, but the focus on group participation through leaders also implied a structured, hierarchical view of democratic government, one arguably at odds with their call for mass demonstrations.[62]

The parliament responded to these concerns by amending the Lastenausgleich bill to include representatives of the war-damaged in key committees charged with supervising the implementation of the Lastenausgleich. These committees would hear appeals of decisions by the authorities and would provide expert advice on administrative choices. By recognizing the war-damaged groups as positive social forces, policy makers had strengthened the value of such organizations and their leadership positions.[63]

These formerly middle- to upper-middle-class, but now partially marginalized, war-damaged group leaders, national and often local, proved to be remarkably moderate in their demands on the political system. They certainly proclaimed their moderation, especially with reference to the dangers of Communism. Kather, for example, asserted, "I'm no radikalinski!" A group of bomb-damaged emphasized that "we have thus far . . . troubled ourselves to engage in measured speech and objective discussion. We have always and repeatedly admonished [our members] to calm and objectivity." As Hans-Peter Schwarz and Hans Braun have argued, a fear of renewed catastrophe dominated most Germans' attitudes after the disastrous decades of 1914–48, so stability was the primary desideratum.[64]

Crucially, the war-damaged were willing to contemplate compromise. Because clear majorities for any single policy prescription are virtually never attainable on complex issues, compromise is indispensable if a democracy is to function. However, 1920s creditors had considered compromise anathema. They believed they had a right, recognized by the German Supreme Court, to a full or nearly full revaluation. As one of their number wrote angrily, there is no such thing as "25 percent justice." War-damaged leaders, though, recognized that the undamaged had a majority and that compromise was unavoidable. Kather even warned the demonstrators at the February 1951 mass meeting, "Certainly, we know that in politics as in life it is only very seldom possible to achieve a 100 percent solution and that in raw reality one cannot come through without compromise. And we are also ready for rational compromise." The ZvF was not willing in 1950 and 1951 to proclaim the necessity of compromise, but it repeatedly approved of compromise in practice.[65]

War-damaged leaders could look for cooperation from the political system up to the highest levels, reflecting a deep-seated change in German political culture that would gradually become permanent. In the 1920s, Chancellor Hans Luther had been a former municipal civil servant who was deeply convinced that voters should simply defer to his expertise on such issues as the revaluation; he had to be dragged by the parliament, kicking and screaming, into even modest compromise. In the 1950s, Chancellor Konrad Adenauer was a former municipal civil servant who certainly had no doubts about his own brilliance and who sought to isolate defense and foreign policy from popular and parliamentary interference. Nonetheless, he recognized that on domestic policy issues such as the Lastenausgleich he had to pay attention to popular feeling and parliamentary demands. As the Lastenausgleich reached a stalemate in autumn 1950, he warned Schäffer, "It's really pointless for us to introduce as a cabinet a proposal that we most certainly know will not be approved in decisive points by the coalition parties." He then urged Schäffer to meet him to work out a compromise. Schäffer had in 1945 obviously hoped to create a government in which neutral experts, insulated from "politics," would develop and implement policy. Nevertheless, in a striking sign of the growing influence of democratic values, Schäffer grudgingly noted in December 1950 that in a democracy it was better "to consult with the political forces of the legislative bodies in good time" so that bills "would go into the legislative bodies with some prospect of success and acceptance."[66]

A political and social base for democracy existed in West Germany in the late 1940s and early 1950s. Some base for democracy had developed in pre-1914 Germany, with an elected parliament and the increasing willingness of German citizens to speak out and to organize to influence public affairs. That base was in place in 1919, or Germans could not have created the Weimar Republic and run it as a democracy for eleven years. Democratic values of self-assertion and protest had, paradoxically, played a key role in undermining the Weimar Republic and preparing the way for the Nazi seizure of power. Many Germans with democratic attitudes and skills survived the Third Reich (e.g., Bauser of the ZvF, Adenauer, Schumacher). Moreover, the events of 1930–45 had strengthened democracy substantially. Antidemocratic elites had been discredited by their actions, and West Germans could see how certain attitudes undermined parliamentary democracy and how a dictatorial alternative had proven disastrous. Successful democratization was not inevitable in 1945. We can never know if (West) Germans could have built a stable parliamentary democracy absent American, British, and French prodding and assistance. Nonetheless, the Federal Republic grew on German soil. It was not, as Richard L. Merritt has asserted, "democracy imposed."[67]

The government, the opposition, and the war-damaged wanted to do a deal, but they were far apart in January 1951. The bill that the government submitted to parliament in December 1950 reflected a compromise between those (such as the Unkeler Circle and Adenauer) who sought a politically viable solution and those (such as all the ministers except Lukaschek) who sought a fiscally and economically modest solution. Many war-damaged, however, rejected the bill as fully inadequate because it failed to transfer real capital or guarantee substantial individual recompense. Moreover, the SPD-dominated state governments had a majority in the Bundesrat and shared the SPD's preference for a social Lastenausgleich. When the Bundesrat issued its preliminary assessment of the bill in January 1951, it demanded a social and productive Lastenausgleich with no individual compensation. It also demanded measures to spare state and municipal finances. The organized war-damaged were outraged—but they also had to recognize that they faced opposition on different fronts to their vision of an individual Lastenausgleich. Getting what they wanted would not be easy, as the Bundestag Lastenausgleich Committee met throughout 1951 to hammer out a Lastenausgleich bill.[68]

Chapter 8

MAKING POLICY

As politicians, government officials, the war-damaged, and the undamaged struggled in 1951 and 1952 to craft a viable Lastenausgleich compromise, they debated a series of proposals that would determine the type and scope of Lastenausgleich West Germans would implement. Reinhold Schillinger has recounted those struggles in some detail in a fine study on decision making in the Lastenausgleich. Yet certain key issues need to be explored here to clarify the Lastenausgleich's development.[1]

REVENUES

The government chose to take as its starting point the level of capital levies that (it supposed) the economy could afford, not the amount of recompense war-damaged citizens might deserve. This choice reflected the predominance of the state's national-economic responsibilities over the war-damaged's preference for an individual Lastenausgleich. On the basis of the 1949 gross domestic product and of a priori assumptions about what would overburden the economy, two independent analyses had in early 1950 concluded that the economy could afford about 1.5 billion DM a year for levies. The government and the ruling political parties chose a capital levy rate of 50 percent to suggest that burdens were being divided evenly between the damaged and the undamaged. They then picked a thirty-year amortization period and established amortization and interest rates that would cost the economy 1.5 billion DM a year. Raising the levy rate would be pointless because the government would only adjust the amortization and interest to produce the same annual revenue of 1.5 billion DM. The government also varied the combined annual amortization and interest rates for different types of property to take account of their differing ability to pay: 4 percent for agricultural and forest land, 5 percent for urban real estate, and 6 percent for industrial and commercial assets. Finally, in a concession to the business community, the bill allowed businesses to credit their inventory levies against any capital levy they owed, effectively expunging the inventory levy.[2]

The war-damaged were not stupid. They could easily see that a capital levy with substantial exemptions paid over thirty years with low interest rates was merely a modest property tax, not worth anywhere near its nominal rate. The personal exemptions alone could reduce the levy on a farmer with 30,000 DM in assets from a nominal 15,000 DM to an actual 6,147 DM. If one added in the changes in the value of currency since 1948, the undervaluation of properties in the official assessments, and the below-market interest rates, the present value of a 50 percent levy even on assets above 35,000 DM that could deduct no exemptions would be as low as 12–33 percent of 1948 capital.[3]

The expellees insisted that the capital levy must be due immediately. Only immediate payment could secure some transfer of capital from the surviving substance to individual war-damaged and a genuine redistribution of burdens. Further, levies paid over thirty years could neither bring the timely assistance most war-damaged needed nor ensure recompense before millions of the war-damaged would have died. Moreover, the war-damaged had lived through a forty-year period in which Germany had suffered two wars, two inflations, a great depression, and three changes of regime; they had a reasonable (though in the event unfounded) fear that some future catastrophe would prevent the continued payment of the levies or make the installments worthless in real terms.[4]

Nonetheless, in deference to claims that forcing the transfer of real capital would break up productive units, with economically disastrous consequences, the expellees offered two concessions. They would agree that any obligor would be entitled to sue to pay in installments—albeit only if the obligor paid interest on the levy principal at market rates. Such substantial interest charges would presumably induce some significant proportion of the undamaged to sell off or transfer real assets quickly to clear their levy obligation. For political and social reasons, expellees also conceded that only those with more than 30,000 (later 35,000) DM in assets should be required to pay immediately.[5]

The organized bomb-damaged left the expellees in the lurch on this issue. Mattes insisted that the state, not private capital holders, was liable for war damages and must guarantee Lastenausgleich payments out of its whole revenues. Such a compensation-based argument, if accepted, promised to maximize recompense to war-damaged persons with viable claims under the 1940s War-Damages Decree. Moreover, the bomb-damaged, unlike the expellees, might themselves be subject to a capital levy on surviving property or have West German relatives and friends who would be subject to a levy. Hence, the bomb-damaged may have been more sensitive to the possibly deleterious consequences of demanding immediate payment.[6]

Opponents of immediate payment mounted a forceful and successful resistance. Schäffer, while warning of the economic risks that immediate payment or market-interest rates could pose, also emphasized the chaos that would ensue if civil servants had to grapple with the hundreds of thousands of petitions for relief any requirement for immediate payment would provoke. Both CDU and SPD Lastenausgleich experts came to agree that immediate payment was impossible. As Kriedemann (SPD) commented, "We have until now also rejected this suggestion [immediate payment] as fully infeasible and indeed as economically destructive. Despite our repeated requests, no representative of the other side has brought forward an even only partially useful formulation of principles according to which a decision could be made, whether and to what degree an individual obligor could be required to pay immediately."[7]

One way to increase the early revenues available would be to induce some obligors voluntarily to pay off their levies early. The government and Bundestag Lastenausgleich Committee included positive inducements for early repayment, but any inducement generous enough to evoke a significant degree of early repayment was likely to reduce total Lastenausgleich revenues excessively. As everyone recognized, Germany's recent history would suggest to any rational obligor that it would be foolish to pay off the levy any sooner than necessary, absent some very generous reduction, because some catastrophe was likely to intervene that would substantially and perhaps completely erode the value of the levies.[8]

A number of the war-damaged, especially expellees, demanded that *all* surviving real capital, no matter how modest, be subject to the capital levy. Often, the war-damaged had lost all of their property in a war all Germans had, supposedly, fought in common. Hence, some war-damaged argued, undamaged Germans, however poor, must contribute to recompensing war losses. The goal here clearly was a radical redistribution of goods to produce a "genuine" balancing out of burdens. Moreover, eliminating any exemption for smaller assets could nominally double the funds available for compensation.[9]

This proposal was a nonstarter. Imposing a capital levy on an elderly widow with a tiny house and a subsistence income seemed heartless and unfair. Moreover, one could extract only minimal revenues from such modest fortunes, at high administrative costs. Further, it would be unwise to burden onerously millions of lower- and middle-class voters who were generally positively disposed toward war-damaged citizens and their needs. The government parties and the opposition agreed to an exemption of 5,000 DM for levyable assets up to 25,000 DM, with a gradual decline in the exemption to 0 DM for assets over 35,000 DM. The bill also allowed reductions for dependents.[10]

West Germans had to decide to what extent individuals who had suffered war losses but still possessed some real assets would be able to credit those losses against their capital levy. So many West German capital holders had suffered war losses that if obligors were allowed to reduce their levy obligations by the amount of their losses, scarcely any money would flow into a Lastenausgleich. Nonetheless, the Lastenausgleich Committee quickly recognized that politically it could not compel seriously damaged individuals with modest assets to pay capital levies (in full). It therefore included a complicated point system allowing socially graduated reductions in the levy owed on levyable assets up to 150,000 DM. (In the booming West German economy, most of those with levyable assets over 150,000 DM had recovered from their war losses with the aid of post–currency reform credits and a favorable tax code.) Many war-damaged who had preserved modest assets were outraged because they were subject to a capital levy starting in 1952 whereas their compensation might not come until 1979. Nonetheless, even strong supporters of the war-damaged recognized that the government had no choice.[11]

Both the bomb-damaged and expellees demanded that policy makers impose some levy on household goods. They admitted that substantial exemptions would be necessary to allow each undamaged citizen the household goods for a "modest standard of living," but they insisted that those with more than modest assets or a comfortable income must pay such a levy. Initially, they wanted to assess the market value of every surviving household good in West Germany. When opponents of such a procedure complained that it would require police searches of millions of households, the war-damaged grudgingly proposed estimating each individual's household goods on the basis of dwelling size or income. Many members of the Bundestag Lastenausgleich Committee were initially sympathetic, but the coalition and opposition parties came to oppose this proposal, arguing that a household-goods levy would be impossible to administer efficiently and fairly, would be too expensive relative to the revenue generated, and would provoke too much resistance.[12]

The amount of energy the war-damaged expended on fighting for a household-goods levy reflects its importance, substantive and symbolic. Even five years after the war, millions of war-damaged still lacked the most basic necessities of life. Expellees in particular, but also many bomb-damaged, found themselves without a bed to sleep in, a pot to cook in, or an untattered sweater to wear. Replacing such necessities had to be a high priority, and a significant share of Lastenausgleich funds was going to go into such compensation. The organized war-damaged, who generally focused on securing the restitution of lost productive assets, disliked this distribution of Lastenausgleich funds. They hoped to increase Lastenausgleich funds by tapping those undamaged who had kept their household goods. Further, though, almost all war-damaged believed that justice demanded a real redistribution of war's burdens, including the burden of having lost most of one's personal possessions. Moreover, they resented the smug arrogance of those undamaged neighbors, often from a lower social background, who now lorded it over them as "have-nothings."[13]

The government did concede that it had to impose special levies on currency-reform profits. It had in 1950 rejected a general levy on capital gains, arguing that the available documentation was insufficient to establish 1940–48 capital gains accurately. This decision outraged most war-damaged, who were morally offended that they had lost all while others had "profiteered" during the German people's misery. To assuage that outrage, and to increase revenues, the government folded the 1948 levy on mortgagors' currency-reform profits into the final Lastenausgleich Law and added levies on profits from the conversion into Deutsche Mark of Reichsmark corporate bonds and commercial credits. Ironically, the German government had after the 1920s currency stabilization rejected proposals for such levies as too complicated. The war-damaged complained—possibly correctly—that this system of currency-profits levies would be even more complicated to administer than a comprehensive levy on paper and real capital gains would have been. The central issue for the government was not complexity, however, but limiting burdens on the real capital of productive enterprises.[14]

In a break with the logic of a Lastenausgleich as a onetime shift between private capital holders and capital losers, the government parties decided to require certain "sacrifices" from federal, state, and municipal budgets to benefit the Lastenausgleich Fund. Despite vehement resistance from the SPD and the unions, the Lastenausgleich bill provided that public assets that competed with private assets (e.g., public utilities) would be subject to the capital levy. The Immediate Aid Law had established the 21 June 1948 capital stock as the basis for any Lastenausgleich capital levy, but that stock and the resulting income would inevitably decline over the years as individuals and companies faced bankruptcy and other problems. Fortunately, the states currently received the revenue from a running capital tax on old and new capital, so the Bundestag Lastenausgleich Committee decided to divert part of that revenue temporarily to the Lastenausgleich Fund. The bill also reduced governmental revenues and eased obligor burdens substantially by allowing the latter to deduct the interest on the capital levies from their income taxes. Further, the bill provided that state and municipal governments must transfer to the Lastenausgleich Fund any savings they made because Lastenausgleich revenues were now supporting former welfare recipients. Finally, any cost-of-living increases for the Support Aid were to come out of the federal budget.[15]

EXPENDITURES

The Lastenausgleich bill both granted and denied legal claims to war-damaged Germans. It did specifically acknowledge that the expellees, bomb-damaged, and Reichsmark savers had certain legal claims, varying among the three groups, to compensation and assistance (e.g., to the Primary Compensation, household-goods compensation, and the War-Damages Benefit), but it explicitly offered other forms of compensation (such as loans for economic reintegration or training) as voluntary grants to which no legal claim existed. Only natural persons, not legal persons such as corporations, were entitled to recompense. Moreover, it implicitly denied that any legal claims had existed before the law was passed and explicitly repealed the 1940 War-Damages Decree, preventing future appeal to it.[16]

The Lastenausgleich Law did designate compensation for property losses as the "Primary Compensation," but social concerns actually had the highest priority. Kunze referred to "the fundamental social idea that runs like a red thread through the whole law." The single greatest expenditure under the Lastenausgleich Law would be for Support Aid, and Kunze summarized the bill's expenditures: "Certain social necessities were recognized as preeminent, the [economic] integration through loans was not absolutely limited to the circle of capital damaged, but beyond that the principle of an entitlement to a Primary Compensation was anchored in the law."[17]

Organized war-damaged disliked both the Immediate Aid Bill and Schäffer's initial proposal on Support Aid. They disliked the Immediate Aid Bill because it provided payments to all needy "war-damaged" who had lost their livelihood because of their war damages, including hundreds of thousands of unemployed expellees who had never been self-supporting. (The latter were assumed to have lost their livelihood through expulsion and the accompanying loss of employment and social and family ties.) Schäffer proposed to abandon the Support Aid and relegate all needy war-damaged to the welfare system, albeit with supplements to those with property losses greater than 150,000 RM, an enormous sum. He sought to reserve Lastenausgleich revenues, which would theoretically come from investment capital, for investment purposes such as housing construction or the formation of new businesses, rather than have them frittered away in consumption. This proposal sparked a flood of outrage because, as an expellee wrote in an SPD newspaper, "People who never in their lives had laid claim to public assistance would, through the will of the Federal government, then be degraded to welfare recipients."[18]

The Lastenausgleich Committee sought to square a social and individual Lastenausgleich by establishing a two-tier War-Damages Benefit, which the organized war-damaged grudgingly accepted. Too many expellees, while suffering no substantial property losses, had fetched up in West Germany broken by their experiences and deprived of the familial and social contacts that might have enabled them to reestablish themselves. Such people needed help, and West Germans seemed nearly unanimous that these expellees deserved a "humanly worthy existence" without being "degraded" to the status of welfare recipients. The Lastenausgleich Committee provided that all currently elderly and unemployable war-damaged (including expellee but excluding bomb-damaged former employees) would get privileged, nonwelfare Support Aid of 70 DM a month (with supplements for each dependent). In a concession to the formerly propertied, though, those who had had substantial property would get an additional Compensation Benefit proportional to their individual losses, to mark their putative superiority to those who had not accumulated or inherited substantial assets. Legislators assumed that Support-Aid payments would dwindle rapidly as those eligible died off.[19]

The bill provided modestly graduated compensation for the loss of more than 50 percent of one's household goods. Most members of the Lastenausgleich Committee were convinced on social and political grounds that they had to offer even those who had owned meager household goods enough compensation to purchase some significant amount of replacement goods. Nonetheless, committee members were unwilling to ignore differences in earlier wealth. As Kunze explained, "I represent the view that we simply cannot engage in total leveling in the household goods compensation and give the smallest tenant [Kötter] on a noble estate the same compensation for his household goods as the estate owner himself, who had perhaps 2 millions. Yet there cannot be any doubt that we cannot simply proceed quotally." The committee also wanted to be sure the war-damaged spent most of the money on consumer durables rather than squandering minimal payments on daily consumption. It hence decided to offer the claimants fixed compensation amounts, paid out in lump sums over twelve years: 800 DM for those with up to 4,000 DM in current income, 1,200 DM for those with 4,000–6,500 DM, and 1,400 DM for those with 6,500–10,000 DM. The committee included supplements for spouses and children. This system recognized not past assets and virtue but present income and achievement.[20]

Many war-damaged bitterly resented this system, particularly women, whose identity and responsibilities were still focused primarily on the home. Many war-damaged were unhappy that some one-third of the war-damaged, who had lost 49 percent or less of their household goods, would get nothing. Most war-damaged needed household goods immediately and despised the twelve-year pay-out period. Moreover, the bill privileged the neediest, giving those with incomes under 1,000 DM a year first priority and denying compensation to those with annual incomes greater than 10,000 DM. (The maximum income requirement would not save much money, but Kunze hoped it would make a positive impression on the 80 percent of recipients who would get the meager 800 DM.) Most formerly affluent war-damaged (including those who currently earned more than 10,000 DM a year) remained committed to a quotal Lastenausgleich here: an individual household-goods compensation that would help restore a level of household goods appropriate to each individual's status-based "honor."[21]

The provisions on economic integration of the war-damaged reflected the productionist proclivities of the government and government parties—and the opposition. The bill did provide assistance to war-damaged persons who wished to establish a business. Against the wishes of some delegates, all SPD and most CDU members of the Lastenausgleich Committee determined that the assistance should take the form of loans and that the amount of the loan should not depend on the amount of losses suffered. The ZvD objected to the maximum loan amount of 15,000 DM, especially because it was insufficient to enable expellee farmers to reestablish themselves as independent farmers in West Germany. Those war-damaged who had compensation claims would be able to deduct the loan from their claim, rather than repaying it. Crucially, the government and the Lastenausgleich Committee insisted on allowing loans of Lastenausgleich funds to undamaged firms that created long-term jobs for war-damaged individuals, with a maximum of 3,000 DM per job and 75,000 DM per firm. All war-damaged groups vehemently, but unsuccessfully, rejected such loans because Lastenausgleich funds would thereby be alienated from what the organized war-damaged viewed as the Lastenausgleich's essential purpose: creating new property for individuals who had lost their earlier wealth.[22]

Kather publicly declared that the provision of land for expelled farmers was the most important issue in the Lastenausgleich, once 1951 legislation had assured new jobs or suitable retirements for expelled civil servants—a telling comment on the social priorities of Kather and other war-damaged leaders. Underlying this declaration were three special issues—all with a restorationist thrust. One was a certain nostalgia for and superior valuation of rural over urban life. Further, some Germans believed that people had an inherent right not only to their social and economic status but to their traditional occupation as well. Finally, the organized war-damaged repeatedly asserted that Germany needed to reestablish expelled farmers in West Germany to preserve their agricultural skills so that they could reclaim "German" lands in the east, should the opportunity to do so arise. The tide of economic development had been running against small farmers for generations, and prospects of the expellees' regaining their lost land were by 1950 minimal anyway. Not surprisingly, the CDU/CSU was not willing to alienate its West German agricultural supporters by compelling the latter to give up sufficient land to resettle a significant number of expelled farmers.[23]

The organized war-damaged rejected the Lastenausgleich Committee's plans to continue using Lastenausgleich funds for social housing construction, as the Immediate Aid Bill had provided. Organized war-damaged, almost all Free Democrats, and many Christian Democrats wanted such funds to go only or primarily to former home or building owners, to help them regain their previous property and social standing. They feared that, as one war-damaged argued, "The *collective ownership of housing* is indeed nothing more than a precursor of collectivism in general."[24]

Housing construction did have important economic implications. West German territory had more productive capital in 1949 than it did in 1938. The single most important step in securing adequate labor to utilize that capital was to build housing quickly for workers within commuting distance of existing factories. Moreover, as the Bizone's Administration for Finances had noted, "For many damaged, probably the great majority, the primary precondition for reestablishing a livelihood is not the securing of some modest capital but, for example, the provision of a dwelling in the right place or the provision of a job." The mass of the bombed-out and expellees, most of whom had formerly lived in rental housing, were indifferent to who owned any new housing complexes — they just wanted a decent place to live. Consequently, even Federal Housing Minister Eberhard Wildermuth (of the vociferously pro–private property FDP) successfully insisted that the housing crisis was so great and private housing construction so inadequate that Lastenausgleich funds must continue to flow to social-housing agencies, who could build many inexpensive housing units quickly. Even the business community showed no interest in opposing this social use of funds extracted from private capital. Economic and social considerations were pushing the Federal Republic to pursue a housing policy similar to that of Communist East Germany.[25]

Nonetheless, the commitment of the government parties to private property was too strong for them to ignore the complaints of the war-damaged. As Kunze acknowledged, simply channeling Lastenausgleich funds to social-housing construction was unacceptable because thereby "hundreds of millions [of Deutsche Mark] are in fact socialized annually, in order to be diverted from the damaged." The Lastenausgleich Committee hence provided that the war-damaged had first claim on housing-construction funds, if they could use them efficiently. Any housing built with Lastenausgleich funds could only be rented to war-damaged. Also, housing funds provided to the undamaged would be as interest-bearing loans repayable in later years to the Lastenausgleich Fund to finance compensation to the war-damaged. The government parties could defend this compromise as consistent with their commitment to private property, although the housing minister would still direct most Lastenausgleich housing funds to undamaged builders in the first years.[26]

Among the potentially most restorationist elements in the Lastenausgleich were the efforts to ensure that the children of the war-damaged would get an education appropriate to their parents' social status. This issue was extremely important to the war-damaged — and to many undamaged. As Kunze argued, in mid-1949, "We all want unreservedly the advancement of talented children even of parents without means. . . . We do also desire that the children of damaged families, insofar as they are correspondingly talented, are not deprived through inadequate financial resources of an education and training corresponding at least somewhat to that of their parents. Thereto belongs under certain conditions the provision of funds for [postsecondary education]." Implicitly, all children were equally entitled to an education, but the children of formerly socially superior parents were entitled to extra Lastenausgleich funds to ensure access to a superior education. Significantly, some Social Democrats supported such discriminatory policies. Interior Minister Gustav Heinemann (CDU, though he eventually joined the SPD) even argued that this educational aid should be available *only* to those whose parents had formerly been propertied and should be granted "when the earlier social conditions would have made possible a superior [*gehobene*] education of the child or youth." If West Germany could not restore the preexisting social hierarchy in the current generation, widespread support was present for recreating it in the next generation through privileged access to educational opportunities. This development is yet another illustration of how widely and deeply rooted was the assumption that those who had, deserved what they had — and their children after them.[27]

In spite of this deep-seated feeling, making special provision for the children of the formerly propertied was too obviously discriminatory to succeed. The Immediate Aid Law had allowed all war-damaged to apply for educational assistance: retraining for adults or occupational or professional training for children. The SPD insisted on educational assistance for all war-damaged Germans, including children, who needed it to secure a livelihood. Even the organized expellees ultimately agreed to make an exception and accept Lastenausgleich payments to expellees who had lost no capital but whose education had suffered because of expulsion. Notably, civil servants and white-collar workers, who might have owned no productive assets, would want to ensure that their children could inherit the parent's class status. Moreover, in a competitive world, West Germans could not easily afford to discriminate against talented youth from disadvantaged backgrounds. The Lastenausgleich Law hence provided that all damaged and their dependents, including those who had lost only "occupational or other bases of subsistence," could apply for educational assistance. Nonetheless, those provisions were open to bureaucratic discretion, so a detailed study would be necessary to determine just how equally Lastenausgleich officials in fact granted funds as between children of formerly propertied and unpropertied.[28]

As Schillinger and Rudolf Fritz have noted, the demand by the war-damaged for a Certification [of Damages] Law (*Feststellungsgesetz*) was an important effort to prejudice the final Lastenausgleich Law in the direction of an individual Lastenausgleich. Rejecting any formal certification of damages would promote a social/productive Lastenausgleich: Absent data on individual losses, one would have to base compensation on some current social or productive consideration. Conversely, leaders of the war-damaged hoped that if they could provide each person with a record of all losses, those individuals would put irresistible pressure on the government to recompense each individual loss. Kather and the expellee delegates in the Bundestag, along with the FDP, therefore introduced identical bills for a full certification of losses, even though they recognized that most war-damaged had had no productive capital and were uninterested in any certification of damages.[29]

Opponents of any certification law questioned its practicality and cost. Government officials had already certified bomb damages, 1939–45. The expellees though, lacking any records of their former wealth, would have to construct estimates of their own losses. A large bureaucracy, assisted by committees of expellees from each neighborhood, would then have to vet these estimates. The expellees would have a mutual interest in backing up one another's perhaps inflated assertions. (As western Germans later joked bitterly, Hitler didn't need to start a war for *Lebensraum* [living space] in the East because, according to expellee claims, Germans must already have owned all the land between the Oder and the Urals.) Any certification procedure would also be costly, and opponents argued it was criminal to squander funds to certify losses that West Germany could never afford to compensate. Moreover, the SPD in particular accused expellee organizations of demanding a role in the certification process simply to secure jobs for themselves as quasi-civil servants and to drum up new members for their groups. Indeed, some expellee groups did fraudulently suggest that group membership (including payment of dues) would be a precondition for certification of damages. Both CDU/CSU and SPD Lastenausgleich experts opposed any general certification.[30]

The organized war-damaged offered various reasons to justify a certification law. Many formerly middle- to upper-class war-damaged wanted to demonstrate their putative superiority. As Gille contended, it was a matter of millions of expellees "who came into the West Zones, as circumstances drove them, lacerated and tattered, and who have a right to have things as they were in the past somehow certified, whether something material comes out of it or not." War-damaged Germans also suggested that the country would benefit in any future negotiations over a peace treaty or reparations by having a record of the losses German expellees had suffered. Further, they argued that their putative legal claim to a Lastenausgleich, the principle of private property, and the need to avoid arbitrariness in providing compensation all demanded certification of each individual property loss. Ultimately, though, they demanded a certification to provide the basis for an individual Lastenausgleich.[31]

Helped by confusion in the ranks of the war-damaged, by the fundamental complexity of the material, and by tacit support from Kriedemann and Seuffert, Kunze managed to postpone action on the certification legislation until the Lastenausgleich Committee had established the basic outlines of the Lastenausgleich Law. He was then able to structure the Certification Law, which came into effect on 24 April 1952, so that it covered primarily those losses subject to recompense under the Lastenausgleich—not all material losses, as the war-damaged had hoped. The law also stipulated that damages totaling less than 500 RM would not be certified because the individual could be expected to absorb them, saving considerable administrative and some compensation costs while leaving many of the poorest war-damaged with nothing. The law only marginally strengthened the principle of an individual Lastenausgleich, but it provided that committees of expellees, recruited from the *Landsmannschaften*, would play a major role in implementing the certification process. Moreover, the Bundestag, as the SPD complained, virtually had to rewrite this law in the Lastenausgleich Law.[32]

To certify damages, one needed some method for valuing the property whose loss was to be certified. This proved to be devilishly complicated. In a market economy, something is worth what it can command in the marketplace—a valuation that fluctuates more or less continuously as price levels, economic circumstances, and individual demands change. Yet most assets do not come on the market very frequently and so have no recent market valuation.[33] The government hence concluded that it would have to use, on the levy and expenditure sides, the balance sheet values of most business assets and the assessed value for tax purposes (*Einheitswerte*) of real estate—provoking a storm of protest from the war-damaged. The assessed values dated from 1935–36 (1940 for the Sudetenland) and did not record an asset's value at the moment of loss in the 1940s or its replacement cost in the 1950s. More distressing, the assessed values systematically and substantially understated the market value of assets, particularly in agriculture. They had just been artificial constructs for establishing the relative tax burden among individuals. Besides, policy makers had adjusted the assessed values to reflect the differing returns on different types of assets. Some people wanted to reassess both losses and levyable capital, but Kunze and others successfully argued that this would just open a Pandora's box of confusion, conflict, and delay.[34]

The clearest victory for the organized war-damaged was in securing the inclusion in the Lastenausgleich Law of the Primary Compensation for individual losses. Most Social Democrats, and even many Christian Democrats such as Kunze, would have preferred a Lastenausgleich based on current social and economic needs. Nonetheless, the Lastenausgleich Committee followed the government in making compensation for individual losses "primary," at least in principle. The bill set a preliminary Basic Amount of compensation for each level of estimated losses, with a 10 percent supplement added for expellees and for evacuees who had been able neither to return to their home towns nor to secure a "suitable" livelihood in their evacuation location. Because other expenditures were more urgent and because certifying individual losses would take some years, the final amount of the Primary Compensation would not be fixed and its expenditure would not begin until 31 March 1957. The Lastenausgleich fund would pay interest on the Basic Amount at 1 percent per quarter from 1 January 1953.[35]

The CDU/CSU and SPD argued that compensation rates must be graduated, with lesser amounts for those with greater losses and with a maximum for compensation. Even supporters of individual compensation often believed it unjust to compensate millionaires at the same rate as those with modest fortunes, because the higher the compensation for larger fortunes, the more likely it was that the compensation rate for the less affluent would be so low as to be meaningless. The SPD especially resisted efforts to raise or eliminate the maximum, arguing that to do so would divert substantial funds to re-creating a few large fortunes at the expense of millions of individuals from the middling and working classes.[36]

After initially accepting graduated compensation and a maximum as inevitable, the organized war-damaged fought vociferously and successfully against any maximum. Kather denounced the finance minister's proposed maximum of 15,000 DM as "an uncompensated expropriation not only of all larger, but indeed of all medium fortunes [that] means in practice the annihilation of the eastern German middling classes." With strong FDP support, he managed to compel the government and Lastenausgleich Committee to raise and then eliminate the maximum compensation, although the war-damaged did have to agree to a graduated compensation, culminating in a 2 percent rate for losses greater than 2 million RM. Kunze was not thrilled at this development because it reserved more than 1 billion DM in Lastenausgleich funds to the benefit of perhaps 52,000 of the 9 million expellees. The logic of an individual, private property–based Lastenausgleich and the traditional power of the (formerly) rich had, though, proved stronger than the social inclinations of CDU/CSU delegates such as Kunze.[37]

The government and the Lastenausgleich Committee agreed to exclude from the Lastenausgleich Law compensation for currency-reform losses. Various individuals mentioned various reasons for this decision. Most important, most currency-damaged savers had not lost a livelihood because of currency reform, unless they were elderly or disabled, and had not lost a dwelling or all personal possessions. Unemployable savers would receive Support Aid anyway. Any additional compensation for savers within the Lastenausgleich Law would come at the expense of other war-damaged, whom most Germans agreed had been "harder hit" by fate. Moreover, most observers agreed that legislating a coherent compensation system for the varying financial instruments would be complicated, possibly delaying unconscionably the crucial Lastenausgleich.[38]

The currency-damaged put up remarkably little resistance to the decision to separate their compensation from the Lastenausgleich Law. They showed much less enthusiasm for organization and activism than had their 1920s counterparts or their fellow post-1945 war-damaged. The ZvF claimed to represent the savers, but its organizational heart and policy focus clearly lay with the bomb-damaged. The German Federation of Rentiers did begin lobbying on this issue — but only from 1951. The currency-damaged obviously felt relatively little inclination to act, presumably because, for all except the unemployable (who received Support Aid anyway), their losses were relatively minor compared to the losses of other war-damaged. The upshot was that the government could get away with separating — and delaying until 1953 — action on compensation for currency-reform damaged.[39]

Chapter 9

TOWARD LIBERAL DEMOCRATIC STABILITY

The Lastenausgleich contributed to and illuminates the Federal Republic's success in securing a degree of stability that had escaped other twentieth-century German regimes. Like other social interests, the war-damaged had to fight for their preferences — and then compromise, accepting a Lastenausgleich compatible with the social-market economy. Nonetheless, their concept of a Lastenausgleich as a recognition of the virtuous proved sufficiently influential to enable them to squeeze from the society and the government significant concessions that reaffirmed social hierarchy. Surprisingly clear-headed about their political limitations, they accepted this outcome and the Federal Republic, with decisive consequences for the establishment of liberal democracy in West Germany.

THE WAR-DAMAGED RECOGNIZE THEIR LIMITS

The organized war-damaged faced real constraints on their ability to argue for an individual Lastenausgleich — from larger political, economic, and fiscal forces and from their own internal differences. Recognizing these constraints, war-damaged leaders focused on securing concrete gains in the Lastenausgleich Law.

For the war-damaged, fear of Communism remained compelling. The stream of refugees fleeing Communist oppression in East Germany kept vivid the memory of Red Army and Communist brutality, while the ongoing Korean War stoked fears of a Soviet invasion of West Germany. Communism called into question the whole worldview of most propertied Germans. Emphasizing the inherent equality of all human beings, it proposed a radical leveling of society that would eliminate the differences in status that the organized

165

war-damaged were fighting to restore. Communist East Germany had already repudiated the preferences of the war-damaged by refusing to implement any Lastenausgleich and was steadily eliminating private property in the means of production.[1]

War-damaged leaders also perceived a direct threat to their organizations from Communist subversion. The ZvF warned its members periodically against the Communist-dominated Unified Association of War-Damaged, emphasizing that the latter did not stand on the basis of private property, as the ZvF did. Expellee leaders worried about the West German Refugee Congress, whose petitions have a Leninist flavor and which the BVD and the CDU denounced as a Communist front. Expellee leaders also feared that the Communists were seeking to infiltrate, and presumably later to subvert, BVD locals and demonstrations.[2]

Concerns about the dangers of Communism limited the war-damaged's options. Anti-Communism functioned as a powerful legitimating force, but it also became, as Christoph Kleßmann argues, "a social means of disciplining [citizens] of considerable social importance." By successfully casting postwar West German politics as an either-or proposition, as Western "freedom, social security, and economic stability" or Eastern "suppression of freedom, poverty, and forced collectivism," Adenauer gave West Germans little room to maneuver. The war-damaged especially stood to lose so much from any communization of West Germany that they feared to contribute to any radicalization of West German society or politics.[3]

The war-damaged could not turn to the radical Right, either. Although West Germans were loath to denounce Nazism and its supporters, Nazism had brought about the most catastrophic defeat in German history and the very destruction for which war-damaged Germans sought a Lastenausgleich. At no point in the Lastenausgleich debate were the war-damaged willing to risk another disaster like World War II by supporting neo-Nazis in search of a more generous Lastenausgleich. In particular, the Cold War further undercut the radical Right by making West Germany dependent on the protection of Western countries that reacted allergically to any hint of neo-Nazism.[4]

The apparent logic of capitalism also narrowed Lastenausgleich options. Economic developments called into question, but then seemed to confirm, the neoliberal discourse that militated against the economically interventionist policies an individual Lastenausgleich would have required.

Economic developments in 1951 at first threatened the social-market economy. The Korean War brought dangerous inflationary pressures, a balance-of-payments crisis, and debilitating shortages. Adenauer, though opposed to Marxian socialism, had no objection in principle to government intervention in the economy and feared sitting idle in the face of West Germany's serious economic difficulties. Nevertheless, he also feared to abandon Erhard, which would have weakened his ties to the FDP and strengthened those members of the CDU who preferred a coalition with the SPD. The U.S. government was also pressing Adenauer to introduce economic controls to ensure that West Germany's resources could be directed as necessary to support Western rearmament against the Soviet threat. Hence, under extreme pressure, the German government in early 1951 scaled back foreign-trade liberalization, reintroduced indirectly some economic controls, and directed investment to bottlenecks. Erhard, though, did prevent any rhetorical abandonment of neoliberalism, and tight-money advocates at the BdL used the balance-of-payments crisis to push through what turned out to be a permanent West German central-bank commitment to monetary rigor.[5]

Whether because or in spite of these interventionist policies, West Germany won through to prosperity, strengthening support for the social-market economy. West German exports had been rising before the Korean War, and they continued to rise. By the second half of 1951, West Germany's balance of payments turned positive — and has remained so. Industrial production increased more than 50 percent from March 1950 to November 1951, and real wages were at last rising, with a 6 percent increase just in 1951. West Germans began in early 1952 to speak of an economic miracle. As the officially reigning social philosophy, the social-market economy seemed to be the cause of West Germany's growing prosperity.[6] Not surprisingly, war-damaged demands for extensive government intervention to manage the economy — and to ameliorate any negative consequences of an individual Lastenausgleich — simply tailed off after 1950.

A shift in the Catholic Church's position on the Lastenausgleich shows strikingly the decline of an interventionist-moralistic attitude toward property and economy, the increasing influence of neoliberal economics within German Catholicism, and growing support for a West German contribution to defense against the threat of godless Communism. In the late 1940s, church pronouncements had emphasized the "moral-legally based claim" of the war-damaged, the social obligations of private property, and the personal obligation of the undamaged to accept capital levies. The church decided in late 1951 to revise its position. Catholic moral theologians began to argue that carrying the principle of a legal claim to a Lastenausgleich to its logical conclusion would imply a complete expropriation of property; they therefore called for a replacement of the "legal obligation" with a vaguer "moral obligation" based on need. Expellee leader Clemens Neumann complained bitterly, "That means, in plain German, *Not a Lastenausgleich, but charity, not a legal claim to compensation, but welfare!*" Under vehement pressure from Catholic refugees, the Catholic Refugee Committee ultimately pronounced for the creation of private property as the primary focus of a Lastenausgleich — but only "in the frame of the economically possible." Neumann warned that even this statement would strengthen those in the CDU/CSU who preferred a "charitable-welfare 'balancing out.'" The committee's document also noted that a Lastenausgleich would be "the most effective contribution to [national] defense."[7]

The West German economy was successful enough to legitimate the social-market economy and finance a meaningful Lastenausgleich—but weak enough to justify limits on any Lastenausgleich. Life had improved dramatically for most employed Germans, with disposable incomes beginning to increase enough that more and more workers could think about buying more than just the barest necessities. The economy had grown sufficiently by 1952 that the capital levies, which Schäffer had in 1949 set at the putative limits of the economically bearable, were now quite bearable for the economy and most obligors. Yet, as much as the economy had grown since 1945, it still faced serious problems. Most obvious was the 10 percent unemployment rate, but most employed Germans had still not replaced all the things they had had to do without since 1939. Moreover, West Germans had to wonder if recent economic improvements would prove to be temporary, as such advances had after World War I. The war-damaged were hence unable to argue convincingly that the economy could risk higher levies.[8]

West Germany faced real fiscal problems as well. Tax rates were still relatively high, but balancing the budget remained difficult. The war-damaged were in sharp competition for scarce resources with the needs of the economy, the needs of other Germans (including other war victims), and the Cold War demands of national defense. Federal budget expenditures doubled between 1950 and 1953, and by 1953 more than 25 percent of the West German population would be receiving some monthly benefit, a widespread dependence on state handouts that disturbed many Germans. In addition, debates over restitution for Jewish victims of Nazi brutality, resumption of payments on Germany's prewar foreign debt, and rearmament shadowed the Lastenausgleich debate.[9]

West Germans grudgingly offered restitution for Nazi atrocities. The Allies had compelled Germans to begin the process of restitution in the immediate postwar years. Subsequent West German efforts to distance most Germans from responsibility for Nazi crimes included trivializing or denying any compensation claims by the politically and racially persecuted. Adenauer, though, believed that moral and expedient foreign-policy considerations required that West Germans respond positively to foreign demands, especially by the international Jewish community and the state of Israel, for additional compensation. Adenauer faced stiff resistance within his own cabinet, particularly from Schäffer. Difficult negotiations over substantial sums of money for restitution extended through and beyond the debate over the Lastenausgleich Law. Only Adenauer's vaunted political skills succeeded in pushing his government into agreeing to a generous restitution settlement in August 1953. Even then, restitution legislation more effectively recompensed losses of property than of freedom or health (perhaps not surprisingly, given the capitalist and bureaucratic nature of twentieth-century Germany), and its implementation was marked by what Christian Pross has called a "guerilla war" against the victims by unsympathetic German officials.[10]

The West German government was also negotiating in 1952 a resumption of payments on Germany's prewar foreign debt, which the Weimar and Nazi governments had suspended in the 1930s. Adenauer sought to reestablish (West) Germany's moral and financial credit by settling foreign claims. Germany's failure to continue payment on its old debts was a political sore point with its current allies and a serious economic problem because it interfered with international commercial transactions by West German businesses. After painstaking negotiations, concluded only in February 1953, West Germany and its creditors settled on West German recognition of prewar debts of 7.3 billion DM (instead of the nominal 13.5 billion), plus interest at two-thirds of the contractual amount, payable in installments. This agreement restored West German credit but laid another substantial burden on the federal budget.[11]

One of the major burdens Nazism bequeathed was the need for an expensive program of West German rearmament. Having engineered a catastrophic German defeat, Hitler had left Russian troops occupying eastern Germany and positioned to dominate all Europe. The Western Allies had allowed the Federal Republic's creation to secure West German resources for their side against the Russian menace, but they initially limited its sovereignty because of widespread mistrust of Germany after two world wars. The outbreak of the Korean War, however, strengthened decisively those who insisted on rearming West Germany to help defend Western Europe against any Soviet attack. Despite vigorous resistance from some of West Germany's neighbors, especially France, the United States was adamant that such rearmament was necessary.[12]

The war-damaged quickly realized that military spending could sharply limit the funds available to compensate them. They were particularly angry that the government announced it had 2.7 billion DM a year for rearmament only months after it had claimed it could come up with only 1.5 billion a year for a Lastenausgleich. That anger deepened as the proposed defense bill soared above 10 billion DM a year (albeit, part of this would replace the occupation costs West Germans had been paying for the Allied armies). The government argued that it could afford new defense expenditures because the growing economy was generating more tax revenue. War-damaged Germans, though, insisted that their claim to those additional revenues was preeminent—and certainly superior to rearming for World War III when Germany had not yet recompensed the deserving victims of World War II.[13]

If broader economic and fiscal concerns threatened the hopes of the war-damaged, so did divisions among the war-damaged themselves. Such divisions occurred both within and between the two main subgroups, the expellees and the bomb-damaged.

The bomb-damaged faced debilitating organizational weaknesses. The ZvF did secure government recognition of its claim to speak for all bomb-damaged and did organize 5 percent of the bomb-damaged—but primarily the economically and politically weakest. The most active portion of the bomb-damaged were the most likely to reintegrate themselves economically and the least likely to join the ZvF. Even bomb-damaged who still had some property might well consider themselves more as potential obligors than as potential Lastenausgleich recipients. The complex social realities behind the global term "bomb-damaged" undercut the ZvF's effectiveness.[14]

The expellees succeeded in organizing a greater portion of their greater numbers, but three separate sorts of expellee organizations competed bitterly. For example, BHE leaders sniped constantly at the ZvD, which claimed to speak objectively for expellee social and economic interests but whose leader was a CDU politician. In the squabble over who would enjoy the enormous funds the government would disburse to help in administering the Certification of Damages Law, one *Landsmannschaften* head unleashed a vicious attack on the ZvD: he accused it of having a materialist base that could only divide the German people by adding a new class rather than bringing them together on the basis of *Landsmannschaften* communal ideals.[15]

Despite efforts to cooperate, leaders of the bomb-damaged and of the expellees faced powerful centripetal forces. The expellees proved unable to resist the temptation to expand their share of the limited pie at the expense of the bomb-damaged. Organized expellees were more numerous and, having generally lost everything, more committed to a Lastenausgleich than were their bomb-damaged counterparts. They were convinced that they had suffered more than the bomb-damaged and were entitled to privileged treatment. Moreover, they lacked the moderating influence of undamaged relatives and friends, which restrained the bomb-damaged. Fearing potential expellee radicalism, the government and the political parties tended to privilege the expellees over the bomb-damaged. Expellee self-righteousness and governmental discrimination, though, outraged the bomb-damaged, who were too conscious of their own sufferings to accept unequal treatment. No bomb-damaged leader could do anything but demand the kind of equal rights for all war-damaged that the expellees could never accept.[16]

The formerly propertied war-damaged also had to recognize that they could not ignore the needs of the great mass of formerly unpropertied who had lost only household goods and a dwelling. They could not forestall the creation of competing interest groups touting the needs of formerly unpropertied war-damaged if they opposed social measures the government had to pass to guarantee all Germans a "humanly worthy existence." As Kather admitted of the Lastenausgleich Committee's bill, "From the beginning, a 'no' to this law was, despite its deficiencies, not unproblematic. . . . The War Damages Benefit offered a substantial improvement over the Support Aid, and the Household Goods Compensation would also provide significantly greater payments."[17]

Relative weakness and diverging interests were pushing war-damaged groups to compromise. Absent total victory, they could best justify their existences by securing concrete improvements for their members. The ZvF had been doing this since 1948, touting various policy developments, including the passage of the Immediate Aid Law, as the result of the group's pressure and as evidence that the bomb-damaged should continue to support the group and its leadership. Extracting more concessions from the government over the Lastenausgleich Law would be a further sign of the group's value. Notably, in a front-page article in the *Vertriebenen-Korrespondenz* in late February 1952, Neumann announced, "The Federation of Expelled Germans must now throw its whole weight into the balance for the attainment of a bearable compromise."[18]

Once war-damaged groups recognized that this parliament was not going to legislate an immediate transfer of capital, they could best help their members by focusing on securing more funds in the short run. For social reasons, the government bill reserved virtually all Lastenausgleich revenues for the first years for support payments, loans for housing construction, and household-goods compensation, which would begin meeting the most immediate needs of the poorest war-damaged, formerly unpropertied or propertied. Yet formerly self-supporting war-damaged individuals also demanded Lastenausgleich payments quickly—as recompense or loans—to finance reestablishing their businesses while they were still young enough to make a go of it. Already in July 1950, expellee representatives had alluded to securing loans ("advance financing") for the Lastenausgleich Fund so it could meet the immediate "capital needs" of war-damaged persons. By October 1951, Kather was asserting that "the most important issue [was] how one could solve the liquidity problem of the first years."[19]

Consequently, the expellees' only nonnegotiable demand in spring 1952 was that the government commit itself to substantial advance financing. They demanded 3 billion DM in such financing over the first three years, to ensure minimally adequate funds to integrate war-damaged Germans economically. Otherwise, they threatened to repudiate the government's Lastenausgleich policy, with serious political consequences. After assessing the primarily social thrust of the Lastenausgleich Committee's bill and analyzing the political situation, the expellees had drawn a line in the sand. They had drawn it not over the principle of a truly individual Lastenausgleich or of a genuine levy from the substance but over an adequate economic integration of the war-damaged, albeit, primarily the formerly propertied.[20]

The government resisted the demands of the war-damaged for more money. Nonetheless, the war-damaged had several powerful cards to play—most visibly, but not necessarily most importantly, their support for or opposition to rearmament.

Allied demands for rearmament gave Adenauer the powerful lever he sought to attain his highest priority: securing sovereignty for the Federal Republic. After two catastrophic defeats in a generation, most Germans were fed up with war. Significant opposition to any rearmament swept West Germany in the 1950s, with strong support in the SPD and among some Germans in the Center and on the Right. Adenauer would have to pay a price politically if he accepted Western demands for West German rearmament. In return, though, the Western Allies would have to help Adenauer by making political concessions if they wanted West German troops to help defend Western Europe.[21]

The war-damaged knew that the best way to get Adenauer's attention was to threaten his plans to use rearmament to regain (West) German sovereignty. They pressed repeatedly on that neuralgic point. A hefty defense expenditure at the expense of the Lastenausgleich would be counterproductive, they argued, because war-damaged citizens would be little inclined to defend a state that ignored their rights. One widowed expellee, for example, wrote the finance minister, "If it's a matter of defending the country, then the government should take the youth of those who still have their property and not the youth who were robbed by enemy and friend, for this [latter] youth has nothing more to defend, not even a just German fatherland." The war-damaged argued that the best defense contribution Germany could make was to ensure social peace by satisfying the victims of the last war. The message was clear: no Lastenausgleich, no rearmament.[22]

Adenauer, other politicians, and the press agreed that an adequate Lastenausgleich was a precondition for war-damaged support for rearmament. Speaking off the record with journalists in July 1951 Adenauer said, "If we cannot fulfill our social obligations, the domestic front will collapse," so that social expenditures would be a kind of defense contribution. The final Bundestag debate on the Lastenausgleich bill took place amid a vigorous public debate about the treaties Adenauer had negotiated reestablishing (still partially limited) West German sovereignty in return for West German rearmament. The head of the CDU Bundestag delegation, Heinrich von Brentano, warned Adenauer that passage of the Lastenausgleich Law was "an unconditional precondition" for passage of those treaties in the Bundestag. Adenauer even emphasized this connection in seeking to secure more Lastenausgleich funding from Schäffer.[23]

The coalition parties also recognized that their hold on expellee voters, and hence their political futures, hung in the balance. The CDU had recovered from its mid-1951 low point in the polls, and more respondents approved than disapproved of Adenauer's policies from early 1952. Yet in the spring of 1952 the SPD was still eight percentage points more popular than the CDU/CSU. The coalition and its parties were under stress from divisive issues such as codetermination for workers in industry as well as from the Lastenausgleich. Adenauer had to fear not only future electoral losses but, as FDP leader and vice chancellor Franz Blücher warned, the possible collapse of his government if Kather made good his threat that an inadequate Lastenausgleich would drive him to take the other CDU expellee delegates with him into the BHE. Adenauer hence met personally with Kather in early May, clear evidence of his continuing dependence on popular acquiescence in the new democracy.[24]

Adenauer and the CDU/CSU faced a delicate balancing act. They could not promote too much government intervention without risking their coalition with the market-oriented FDP or too loose a fiscal policy without risking economic problems. Nevertheless, they had to pursue social policies sufficiently generous that the SPD could not tar them as agents of capitalist elites. Adenauer and other CDU leaders, though, were influenced by Catholic social teaching and were suspicious of neoliberal materialism, so they could accept generous social policies as the price necessary for securing private property and social hierarchy against materialist Marxism. Adenauer was also convinced that West Germany had to integrate all major groups, including expellees, not segment the society as Bismarck had done. The CDU was therefore positioned to negotiate with the war-damaged and other war victims over suitable forms of state-sponsored assistance.[25]

West German politicians also recognized that the long-term stability of Germany's second liberal democracy was on the line. The war-damaged were reiterating their long-standing warnings of radicalization if the Federal Republic, like the Weimar Republic, failed to provide a just distribution of war's burdens. Politicians of all parliamentary parties and the war-damaged leadership had, though, staked their careers (and perhaps even their lives) on making interest-group representation in a parliamentary democracy work. Everyone involved had a strong incentive to come to some compromise to secure the support of a substantial constituency for the new (liberal-democratic) Federal Republic of Germany. As Kunze commented in his closing remarks at a "Disputation" on the Lastenausgleich before university staff and students, "By all the seriousness of this task and by all willingness to take ultimate responsibility in this task, I see in addition a much greater responsibility that befalls us here: to make democracy credible to you, gentlemen, especially those studying, who are the bearers of the future Germany."[26] Absent the rearmament issue, war-damaged citizens would probably have had to settle for a bit less, but they and the government parties would have come to terms.

Some government officials feared that the SPD would sabotage the whole process by refusing to provide votes for the two-thirds Bundestag majority needed for two technical constitutional amendments to enable the states to administer Lastenausgleich funds. The SPD had been denouncing the Lastenausgleich Law as fundamentally flawed because its burdens were likely to be shifted to average citizens in the form of higher prices and taxes and because it devoted too much money to recreating the fortunes of a small group of the very wealthiest war-damaged. Moreover, the party was angry that its Bundestag delegates were speaking to defend the government bill against amendments put forward by the war-damaged, while government-party delegates sat silent, fearful of antagonizing war-damaged voters. The SPD, though, was committed to making the new democracy work. As Seuffert told the Bundestag, "It would certainly be easy for Social Democracy to apply this blocking majority, which it possesses, against a law about which it has very significant objections and which it must characterize as fully unsatisfactory. We will not do that. We will vote for the constitutional amendments, and we ask you to see that as proof that we allow ourselves, on this point as in all our motions and decisions, to be guided only by a purely objective view." Although pompously phrased, this statement did reflect a recognition that the Lastenausgleich Law was too important to sabotage. Moreover, by voting against the final bill, the SPD could reap the political advantages of opposing a deeply disputed law.[27]

The Lastenausgleich bill's provisions were so complexly interrelated that the coalition parties sought to use party discipline to block all amendments, a policy reminiscent of the 1925 parliamentary government's use of party discipline to force through revaluation legislation. The government majority then systematically voted down Kather's efforts to expand the quotal elements in the Lastenausgleich Law. Increasingly angry, Kather seemed on the verge of shifting to the BHE, taking his expellee allies in the coalition with him.[28]

Fearful of the political consequences if Kather did so, CDU leaders Gerd Bucerius and Robert Pferdemenges hammered out a deal with Kather, in the presence of Adenauer and Blücher, during a dramatic break in the floor debate on 15 May; they then pressured Schäffer into accepting it. The package guaranteed at least an additional 850 million DM a year for three years for economic integration programs for the war-damaged, especially the formerly propertied. The funds were to come from the .75 percent capital tax (for eight years), governmental housing-construction funds, and general government revenues. The governing parties also promised to entertain proposals for amending the Lastenausgleich Law in the future, and the CDU/CSU loudly proclaimed that it was freeing its deputies from party discipline on this bill. This compromise fell within the BVD's original (secret) resolution to accept the Lastenausgleich Law if Kather could secure at least 800 million to 1 billion DM a year for integration for the first three years. These concessions were enough to get Kather to rise in the Bundestag "in the name of expellee delegates of the coalition" to announce, "Under these circumstances, a No to this law is no longer justifiable. . . . We will therefore give the law our approval."[29]

The government's decision to rely on fiscal largesse to secure the support of the war-damaged was risky. Well aware of the ballooning burdens the Federal Republic faced, Schäffer only grudgingly acquiesced. Hermann Abs, Adenauer's negotiator on the foreign debt settlement, later admitted that he and Adenauer had gambled in those negotiations that the West Germany economy would grow enough to cover the substantial bills they were signing. Adenauer had in the 1920s, as mayor of Cologne, sought to solve social problems not by welfare measures but by state-financed investment to expand the economy and provide jobs. That effort had failed. The Lastenausgleich Law, too, was a gamble on state investment financing itself through economic growth.[30]

At a meeting of the BVD's General Board, Kather managed to secure a vote of confidence. As unsatisfactory as the Lastenausgleich Law was, he argued, it represented so great an improvement over the Immediate Aid Bill and offered so much additional aid to hard-pressed (although mostly formerly unpropertied) war-damaged that rejecting it was not justifiable. Months would pass, while millions of war-damaged continued to vegetate, before any new — and not necessarily better — bill could come up for a vote. Moreover, the compromise did exceed the minimum additional funds the board had demanded. The representatives of most state organizations of expellees agreed that their membership could be brought to accept Kather's decision, especially because he had secured governmental acknowledgment that an amending law would be necessary. Even Gille (BHE), Kather's main opponent at the meeting, said, "Dr. Kather's position in the parliamentary debate should not be criticized; he had in the given circumstances attained the best possible." Gille added that while the BHE would vote "No" in the Bundestag (where its votes were unnecessary to secure the bill's passage), it would help ensure that the Bundesrat passed the bill. The board issued a resolution explaining the situation and "unanimously approving" Kather's actions in the Bundestag.[31]

Yet all was not sweetness and light within the expellee movement. At the BVD board meeting, a few representatives said their state groups would have to reject the bill. Gille emphasized how unsatisfactory the Lastenausgleich Law was because it provided neither a transfer of real assets nor ironclad promises of advance financing. In particular, though, he denounced the unwillingness of Kather (CDU) to countenance any criticism of Adenauer or the CDU in the BVD resolution. Gille soon made his concerns public, and various expellee groups also issued resolutions deploring or even rejecting the Lastenausgleich Law.[32]

Despite these complaints, the BVD touted the Lastenausgleich Law as a success for its efforts and hence a proof of its efficacy and importance, and other expellee observers concurred. Neumann headlined his *Vertriebenen-Korrespondenz* article on the bill's passage "Success" and described the law as "the virtually complete approval by the government and government parties of the main demands of the expellees." The *Ostdeutsche Zeitung* commented that the expellee delegates around Kather "have as a tiny minority . . . ultimately pushed through essential demands of their fellow sufferers." Horst von Zitzewitz, writing in another expellee paper, contended, "Even the BHE will not be able to justify to its—meaning our—people allowing this bird to escape over the roof of the waiting [recipients]. Innumerable among them simply lack the strength to wait two more years."[33]

The bomb-damaged leaders had been left on the sidelines, as Kather and the government negotiated the compromise, but they, too, declared the Lastenausgleich Law a success. Already in early 1952 the ZvF had trumpeted its achievements in winning improvements for the bomb-damaged in the Lastenausgleich Committee bill. When the Bundestag passed the bill, *Selbsthilfe* described its provisions, especially increased advance financing, as "partially positive results" often secured at ZvF instigation. Although the ZvF complained that the Lastenausgleich Law sacrificed the bomb-damaged to the interests of the expellees, it blamed this not on the government or the Federal Republic but on "the bomb-damaged themselves"—for their failure to organize as effectively as the expellees. A month later, the group praised itself for resisting calls to make up for its smaller numbers with louder cries. Its leaders bragged that they stuck to the "basis of objectivity" and won "successes" on the basis of expert knowledge.[34]

Crucially, this willingness to claim partial successes helped legitimate the new Federal Republic of Germany. It stood in marked contrast to the 1920s creditor leadership's response to the revaluation laws. Instead of taking credit for the substantial increases in revaluation they had wrung from the parliamentary system by democratic means, creditor leaders had denounced that system as hopelessly corrupt for its failure to provide everything the creditors had demanded. Their vehemently antidemocratic and anticapitalist rhetoric had substantially weakened the Weimar Republic. The war-damaged leadership, though, by speaking of the Lastenausgleich Law as a (partial) success and avoiding antidemocratic and anticapitalist rhetoric, underwrote the Federal Republic as a responsive and effective system and bolstered support among war-damaged citizens for West German liberal democracy.

The SPD, with a majority in the Bundesrat, had one more chance to push for its Lastenausgleich priorities, but too much was at stake for it to block the Lastenausgleich Law. After much huffing and puffing on both sides, the Bundesrat and Bundestag reached a compromise, culminating in the promulgation of the Lastenausgleich Law on 14 August 1952, more than seven years after the war's end. The Bundestag accepted revised wording on loans for job creation that increased the likelihood the loans would go to undamaged firms to create jobs for (often formerly unpropertied) war-damaged persons, though the repaid loans would ultimately be available for individual recompense to formerly propertied war-damaged who lived long enough. The states agreed to transfer all capital-tax revenues to the Lastenausgleich Fund for five years. The states and the federal government also agreed to pay 410 million DM a year into the fund, to cover their savings on welfare costs from the War Damages Benefit and to cover cost-of-living increases for that benefit. The fund was to repay most state- and federal-government subsidies after five years from the levies on (mostly private) capital. Nonetheless, as the SPD complained, some one-third of early Lastenausgleich revenues would come not from capital levies but rather from the taxpayers in general, so war-damaged Germans would help pay for their own compensation.[35]

Both the Immediate Aid Law and the Lastenausgleich Law had granted a legal claim to monthly benefits to savers who had lost their livelihoods through the currency reform, but not to other savers. Under vehement pressure from the ZvF and the savers, however, the government stipulated in the Lasten-ausgleich Law that the parliament would promulgate by 31 March 1953 a law regulating recompense for "old savers."[36]

Old savers were those who had accumulated savings before 1 January 1940, before the rise of significant, if suppressed, inflation. Wartime limits on consumption had increased the savings rate enormously. Limiting recompense to savings accumulated before 1940 would reduce the government's compensation costs substantially and would increase the compensation rate for old savers. Moreover, Germans often considered wartime savings morally suspect because they resulted from earnings in inflated currency and the lack of products to buy, not from voluntary renunciation of consumption for the purpose of putting hard-earned income aside against disability or old age. This policy discriminated against workers, who had often been so poorly paid that they had been able to accumulate savings only under wartime conditions of full employment and overtime. Some savers, the credit institutions, the German Federation of Rentiers, and the ZvF did unsuccessfully oppose this limit, arguing that all savings were legally the same.[37]

A desire to spur savings in West Germany contributed substantially to the government's grudging willingness to compensate savers. After inflation had destroyed their life savings twice in a generation, Germans were saving at an abysmally low rate, limiting drastically the ability of private enterprises and the government to secure loans. As banker Rudolf Zorn complained, "Today, savers and savings banks sometimes have the not completely unrealistic impression that the state treats them like bees in the beehive, which one is quite happy to allow to collect, so that one can as needed take away the honey-filled combs." One could only increase the savings rate if one offered Reichsmark savers some recompense that would reassure West Germans that future saving would not — once again — be in vain.[38]

Instead of having a "revaluation," as after World War I, the government insisted on offering the currency-damaged "compensation." A revaluation might endanger the currency by tampering with the currency-conversion legislation. Also, a revaluation would have applied in principle to all savings instruments, while one could more easily limit compensation to natural persons and pre-1940 savings. The government was determined to derive the necessary revenues solely from Lastenausgleich funds, lest financial institutions pressure the Federal Republic to issue more debt to refund at higher rates the savings deposits formerly backed by Reich debt.[39]

Compensation was modest. Schäffer had originally proposed compensation of 3.5 percent for old savers, on top of the 6.5 percent conversion of their Reichsmark savings into Deutsche Mark that they had received under the Allied currency reform. Savers and their representatives denounced this bitterly, and the Lastenausgleich Committee increased the compensation to 13.5 percent. Old savers would hence secure in Deutsche Mark 20 percent of their Reichsmark savings, in effect restoring the blocked account and shadow quota amounts the Allies had canceled in October 1948. Most old savers, though, would receive payment only after the Lastenausgleich Fund had met more urgent needs of the expellees, bomb-damaged, and impoverished savers.[40]

The Lastenausgleich and Old Saver Laws were significant steps in the creation of a West German national community. They incorporated almost all West Germans into a community of shared interests and responsibilities: war-damaged and undamaged; rich and poor; propertied and unpropertied; expellee and local. Crucially, undamaged West Germans had shown themselves willing to make some sacrifices for war-damaged fellow citizens in the name of that community, "for," as Mary Douglas notes, "solidarity is only gesturing when it involves no sacrifice." In the process, they had taken a major step toward social stability and legitimacy for the new Federal Republic. At the same time, however, by denying Lastenausgleich compensation (except for minimal "hardship" payments) for refugees from and war damages in the territory of the German Democratic Republic, West Germans had written East Germans out of their community of risk. That choice would return to haunt them in the 1990s, when many East Germans in the newly unified Germany pled unsuccessfully for a "second Lastenausgleich" to their benefit.[41]

THE WAR-DAMAGED REASSESS THEIR PRIORITIES

In 1952, most Germans expected the Lastenausgleich struggle to continue, perhaps longer and more bitterly than it had until then. The Federal Republic had gotten a breathing space by passing a Lastenausgleich law that even many of its opponents saw as a partial success, but the organized war-damaged still demanded a more individual Lastenausgleich financed through transfers of real capital. Even some members of the coalition parties had described the Lastenausgleich Law as a "bad compromise," and the government had conceded that an amending law would be necessary. Moreover, the West German political system was still very much in flux. No one could know how the new republic's institutions would develop, what political values its citizens would adopt, or how a new party system would evolve. Only time would tell if war-damaged citizens would become reconciled to the government's Lastenausgleich — and to liberal democracy.[42]

Despite the BHE's stunning victories in state elections, 1950–52, it came out of the 1953 Bundestag election much weakened, receiving only 5.9 percent of the vote. BHE leaders, and even many undamaged Germans, had believed that a substantial majority of the expellees and at least some other Germans would vote for the party, giving it enough leverage in the Second Bundestag to force the replacement of the Lastenausgleich Law with an individual Lastenausgleich. Yet only about one-third of the expellees, and scarcely any other Germans, voted for the party, and in several states it secured only half the vote it had in recent state elections. The election was widely seen as a referendum on Adenauer and his policies — and to the degree it was, Adenauer won. His party and its allies secured enough seats to form a government without the BHE, thwarting the latter's hopes of determining the next government and its expellee policies. Adenauer nonetheless offered the BHE cabinet seats. Determined to win respectability and credit for any successes in expellee policies, BHE leaders accepted, tying the party to Adenauer's policies.[43]

Adenauer's success in the 1953 election suggests strongly that a substantial majority of war-damaged Germans were already coming to terms with the Federal Republic and its policies. The mass of the war-damaged would be best helped by the kind of social and productive Lastenausgleich the Adenauer government had promulgated. Despite the preference of the war-damaged leadership for an individual Lastenausgleich, it could not ignore the desires of most war-damaged without undermining its own legitimacy and prospects. By their votes, the mass of the war-damaged were pushing their leaders away from an individual Lastenausgleich.

In debates over amending the Lastenausgleich Law, war-damaged groups placed a high priority on increasing the still-meager Support Aid for unemployable war-damaged, notably in the important Fourth (1954) and Eighth (1957) Lastenausgleich Amending Laws. (Other such amending laws dealt with technical and administrative details.) Many war-damaged depended on the payments to survive — and to keep off the despised welfare. Their relatives, often hard hit by war-damages themselves, recognized that, absent those payments, unemployable relatives could become a burden on them. Significantly, in September 1956, a Finance Ministry official commented that the parties, who would be sensitive to public opinion in the run-up to the 1957 elections, were primarily interested in increasing Support Aid payments.[44]

Most war-damaged had lost only household goods, and millions of them suffered real misery from the absence of such goods. All the war-damaged groups hence listed increasing the speed and amount of household-goods compensation as among their top two or three demands for the Fourth and Eighth Amending Laws. One state association of the ZvF even described it as "our main demand under the Lastenausgleich." More than half of those who applied under the Lastenausgleich Law requested only household-goods compensation. The Federal Lastenausgleich Bureau approved such payments for almost 6 million families, a considerable burden on the Lastenausgleich Fund. Nonetheless, the amount per family was still scarcely enough to buy two beds with bedclothes, leaving the war-damaged with massive bills for replacing other lost household goods.[45]

Significantly, even the formerly propertied war-damaged were often less interested in the Primary Compensation—payable sometime between 1957 and 1979—than in more immediate concerns, such as jobs. For example, Paul Ittner, an expelled white-collar worker, wrote to the Federal Lastenausgleich Bureau to reiterate his offer to renounce his damage claim of 68,000 RM (minimum Primary Compensation of 9,800 DM) in return for a job as a white-collar worker (not even as a tenured civil servant) with the bureau. "Only with a job placement," he wrote, "can I be perceptibly helped." A job in hand was surely worth far more to most war-damaged individuals than often modest compensation at some unspecified future date. War-damaged group membership and voting habits strongly suggest that most war-damaged, once integrated into the economy, were not sufficiently upset about the modesty of their compensation to abandon the mainstream parties.[46]

The experience of war damages seems to have provoked fundamental shifts in attitudes toward personal economic security, particularly among the expellees. Security for the middling classes had traditionally rested on possession of private property. War, inflation, depression, and war had destroyed savings (often twice) and real property, impoverishing one-third of West Germans and shattering faith in property as a guarantor of security. The desire for security still remained, as efforts to secure a Lastenausgleich from society showed, yet expellees also became more focused on education. As one East Prussian couple of noble heritage told their children, "Don't depend on earthly possessions! Learn something. That's the main thing today. What you have in your head, that no one can take from you!"[47]

Nonetheless, many formerly propertied war-damaged did remain angry supporters of a more individual Lastenausgleich to restore property. Leaders of the war-damaged had every incentive to contend that they were holding the lid on a superheated pot that could boil over unless the government made concessions, but their warnings of widespread anger do ring true. Most convincing in this regard are the somewhat desperate articles in the war-damaged press that were aimed at convincing volatile elements among the war-damaged that their leaders were doing all that was humanly possible, under the circumstances, to advance the Lastenausgleich, so that radicalization was inappropriate. Also telling are the effusive letters war-damaged leaders wrote to government officials apologizing for occasional vitriolic attacks by war-damaged individuals.[48]

In fact, one of the most striking aspects of the Lastenausgleich conflict is how the war-damaged leadership sought to be accepted into, not to overthrow, the Federal Republic. Unlike the leadership of the 1920s creditor movement, these men accepted the legitimacy and usefulness of Germany's second parliamentary republic.

War-damaged leaders continued after 1952 to be at great pains to emphasize their moderation, strongly suggesting that neither they nor their followers ever perceived in political extremism a viable alternative to the Federal Republic of Germany. The GB/BHE, for example, asserted, "We are however above all else not an extreme party. The 'All-German Block/BHE' rejects political radicalism, as it is expressed in the activity of extreme political parties and groups, because this activity tends to disturb perceptibly the image of the German Federal Republic abroad and its democratic development at home. Every responsible German should be conscious of this fateful consequence for the whole of our people and hence let his attitude be determined solely by political rationality." The war-damaged also sought to associate themselves with mainstream politicians by drawing the latter into their interest groups as advisory members, as the ZvF did with Kunze. This policy both reflected their moderation and tended to reinforce it.[49]

Pragmatic and material concerns reinforced such moderation. The leaders of the 1920s creditors had had civil service jobs or civil service pensions. The usually impoverished 1950s war-damaged leadership, whom war and defeat had torn from their previous livelihoods, wanted primarily to regain their footing, perhaps to secure employment helping to implement the Lastenausgleich Law, not to exacerbate their insecurity by conducting a vendetta against the new republic. Gille noted bitterly of the BVD board's debate over approving the Lastenausgleich Law, "My comment that one should say explicitly how many well-paid positions one wanted was passed over without protest." One does not have to be quite so cynical about motives here to recognize that expellees in particular would feel a certain pressure to take what they could get. The Federal Republic's willingness to subsidize war-damaged groups may also have played a role. The groups faced ongoing financial difficulties that made such subsidies extremely attractive, indeed necessary when membership stagnated and then fell from the mid-1950s. As Ruud Koopmans notes of interest groups generally, "To profit from the opportunities offered by institutional channels, contenders have to be willing to compromise, to accept incremental gains, and to define their goals in a narrow way." War-damaged leaders moved from extreme demands in 1949–51 to compromise in 1952 and to incremental and narrowly defined goals from 1954/55 onward.[50]

The war-damaged still feared a Bolshevik triumph in West Germany. The country's exposed position opposite Communist East Germany, on the front lines in a still frightening Cold War, exacerbated traditional fears of Communist or socialist expropriation of private property. It also stoked war-damaged leaders' anxieties that Communist agents might subvert their movement.[51]

Crucially, though, war-damaged leaders also explicitly attacked the radical Right. These attacks reflected longer-standing concerns—but also West German and Allied efforts to nip neo-Nazi activities in the bud. The Third Reich's irresponsible collapse had already disillusioned the overwhelming majority of Germans, including war-damaged Germans and their leaders, with Nazism. In October 1952, though, the Federal Republic banned the neo-Nazi Socialist Reich Party (and the Communist Party) under the constitutional prohibition of antidemocratic groups. In February 1953, British occupation authorities arrested a circle of ex-Nazi leaders, although the British soon released most of them. The Federal Republic and the occupying powers had demonstrated unmistakably that limits existed to their willingness to tolerate neo-Nazi activity. The GB/BHE, perhaps in part because so many of its leaders had held responsible positions in the Third Reich, had already been rejecting right-wing radicalism. In late February 1953, though, it denounced the Left revolution of Lenin and Stalin but also warned that "the Right Revolution of Hitler/Mussolini has brought Germany and Europe to the very edge of the abyss." The failure of radical Right parties to get more than 1 percent of the vote in the 1953 federal elections then confirmed the marginalization of political extremism. With extreme solutions of Right and Left not viable, the Federal Republic became a reality with which one would have to come to terms.[52]

War-damaged leaders continued to display a pragmatic willingness to compromise, to seek those incremental improvements and worthwhile if less than (and often far from) perfect deals that parliamentary democracy offers. BVD leaders recognized the value of postponing larger goals to accelerate passage of more pressing demands and of supporting bills they found inadequate in order not to delay the improvements they did offer. The ZvF also promoted incrementalism. For example, in a series of columns in Selbsthilfe called "Mrs. Müller Knows What's What," the sober, knowledgeable Mrs. Müller would calm and inform the excitable Mrs. Schulze. In a 1953 column, after Mrs. Schulze attacked the upcoming Bundestag elections as a sham, Mrs. Müller told her that things weren't that bad; that while the Lastenausgleich legislation was imperfect, it was a start that the next Bundestag would improve; and that one had to vote to have influence.[53]

Moreover, circumstances were conducive to reform but not to fundamental revision of the Lastenausgleich Law. The Federal Republic's development was favorable enough that it could defend its fundamentally neoliberal order while offering substantial payoffs to various groups to purchase their acquiescence in the new dispensation.

Perhaps the Federal Republic's most important characteristic in the 1950s was its economic success. From 1952, Germans and others began to speak of West Germany's "economic miracle": its enormous economic growth, its rapidly increasing employment (which enabled it to integrate a stream of expellees and refugees from the East, 1945–61), and its stable prices. As the war-damaged pointed out, from 1951 to 1956 the social product grew by 58 percent, investment rose 65 percent, and tax revenue increased 61 percent. Increases since 1945 and since 1948 were even more striking.[54]

Nonetheless, uncertainty remained, making stability seem desirable and experimentation risky. The war and postwar chaos and insecurity had been terrifying. Despite the improvements since 1945, about one-third of West Germans still lived in poverty in the early to mid-1950s. Moreover, West Germans still feared that the Federal Republic could face the soap bubble economics that had plagued the Weimar Republic, and most could remember vividly how the extravagant promises of the Nazis had ended in disaster. Adenauer would famously run — and win — the 1957 election on the slogan: "No Experiments!"[55]

In terms of foreign policy, the Federal Republic was also a success in the eyes of most West Germans. Germany in 1945 had been an occupied, divided, and despised nation. Most West Germans saw themselves presented with a Manichean choice between Soviet dictatorship and Western freedom. They hence accepted the creation of the semisovereign but Western-oriented Federal Republic in 1949 as unavoidable. Although they seldom shared Adenauer's near obsession with foreign policy, most could welcome his success in negotiating substantial West German sovereignty as an achievement — all the more because it offered some security against a possible (if unlikely) Soviet invasion.[56]

The Federal Republic's domestic political success was also striking. The first Bundestag generated a remarkable volume of social legislation that helped to reconcile millions of West Germans to their new democracy. The Codetermination Law, benefits for war widows and orphans and disabled veterans, the law to reintegrate dismissed civil servants, aid for returning POWs, legislation placing the massive social-insurance system back on a sound fiscal footing, various legislation promoting the integration of expellees and refugees, and (not least) the Lastenausgleich Law: all offered positive benefits to virtually all West Germans or their relatives. Along with the benefits of economic growth, this blizzard of legislation gave most West Germans good reason to consider the new Federal Republic a system beneficial to (West) Germany and to them individually.[57]

West Germany found itself in a virtuous cycle. Inclusion in the postwar American-sponsored world trade order spurred economic growth. Economic growth increased both support for the Republic, strengthening it politically, and tax revenues, allowing the state to further increase its popularity by passing generous social legislation. Increasing domestic political stability made investment attractive, leading to further economic growth and still greater political stability.

War-damaged leaders recognized from 1954 that growing support for West German liberal democracy made the introduction of an individual Lastenausgleich extremely unlikely. Telling here is Gille's attitude. In 1952, he deplored BVD acquiescence in the Lastenausgleich Law, even though he had acknowledged that the war-damaged could not secure any better legislation at that time, given the balance of power in the first Bundestag. In 1954, he recognized the logic of his own 1952 position when he commented at the BHE Party Convention, "The problematic of the Lastenausgleich in the current moment lies less in that one should develop new constructive ideas but rather lies solely in establishing in what degree it is politically feasible to push through this or that. . . . We may not forget that the election results of 6 September [the elections for the second Bundestag] allow no possibility that we could take up the Lastenausgleich problem, which we consider unsolved, from the ground up again." In mid-1956, moreover, *Selbsthilfe* admonished its readers, "Naturally it would be utopian, even if one wished it, to demand at this moment an increase in the [capital] levies. A year before the parliamentary elections every political party would be overtaxed by it. With an eye to the elections, not a single party would dare it." [58]

Crucially, war-damaged citizens seemed to realize that their real opposition came not from a particular political system or politicians but from the millions of undamaged Germans who were being asked to take on a more equitable but onerous share of war's burdens. Where 1920s creditors imagined that their opponents were a minority of greedy (capitalist) debtors and a corrupt political system, 1950s war-damaged recognized that the Federal Republic's Lastenausgleich policy represented a significant concession to their needs in the face of considerable, if sub rosa, resistance from the majority. Their realization after the 1953 elections that they lacked the political leverage to force through an individual Lastenausgleich left them a choice between impotent kvetching and a struggle for incremental improvements from a generous social state.[59]

The earlier dreams of a "genuine" Lastenausgleich having proved unattainable, the war-damaged leadership now chose to squeeze the maximum in assistance, incrementally if necessary, from the larger society. In the process, they moved both rhetorically and programmatically away from their earlier moral economy and toward the social-market economy—but in ways that affirmed the right to a Lastenausgleich and the moral superiority of the formerly propertied war-damaged.

The war-damaged focused their efforts on the Eighth Amending Law (1 April 1957), which constituted a kind of closure for the Lastenausgleich debate. The law was originally intended to be the Lastenausgleich Finalization Law, which would set the Primary Compensation whose final calculation the Lastenausgleich Law had postponed to 31 March 1957. It represented the last chance for fundamental change in the Lastenausgleich, and the structure it gave the Lastenausgleich remained substantially unchanged thereafter, despite many more amending laws.[60]

The war-damaged continued to insist on their entitlement to a Lastenausgleich. They sometimes argued that the Federal Republic's claim to be the pre-1945 German Reich's legal successor compelled it to recognize their rights under the 1940 War-Damages Decree. Alternatively, though, they continued to insist on the existence of a community of risk and the fortuitousness of their losses as the bases of an entitlement to privileged recompense.[61]

The organized war-damaged never abandoned the demand for an individual Lastenausgleich that would reestablish a prewar socioeconomic order perceived as inherently just. ZvF and brief ZvD efforts in the early 1950s to emphasize the rhetoric of compensation over that of a Lastenausgleich had failed to strike any chord among the mass of war-damaged. The post-1952 absence in government files of letters from individuals and petitions from local and regional groups makes it difficult to assess the views of the mass of war-damaged individuals. Many war-damaged Germans, though, apparently still believed passionately that a shift of real capital was the only just policy for redressing the fortuitous postwar distribution of losses and gains. Moreover, propertied war-damaged reiterated that, as morally superior individuals, they deserved some restitution of their lost property and status. Finally, the continued recourse to the notion of a community of risk and a Lastenausgleich suggests that most war-damaged still had a more communitarian and less liberal idea of the relationship among Germans than the notion of compensation implied and the social-market economy required.[62]

The war-damaged hence continued to insist that they should in principle come off no worse than the undamaged. As the ZvF announced, "Following a suggestion of the BVD, one expects a compensation of 100 percent for losses up to 5,000 RM. As capital up to 5,000 DM is spared from the levies, that is a demand of parity and equity. The undamaged have to pay in the frame of the Lastenausgleich a levy of 50 percent (at least theoretically) from capital above 5,000 DM. Correspondingly, a compensation of in principle 50 percent must be demanded for damages over 5,000 RM." (The damaged groups did recognize that limited Lastenausgleich funds compelled in practice a degression in the compensation rate for larger fortunes.)[63]

Despite these efforts, developments after 1952 compelled the war-damaged leadership to refocus their arguments. They could more easily argue from the entitlements the legislature had granted in the Lastenausgleich Law than from arguments for a "genuine" Lastenausgleich that the legislature and the electorate had already rejected. The growing emphasis in West Germany on current performance undercut the force of their arguments from past virtue. Furthermore, to maximize their share of the increasing national income, they had to situate themselves favorably relative to other claimants in German society, especially other victim groups.

Strikingly, after 1953 the war-damaged organizations virtually abandoned demands to restructure the capital levy to actually shift real capital from undamaged to war-damaged citizens. Mattes's ZvF had scarcely supported that demand earlier. The BHE had campaigned in the 1953 election on that policy, but by 1956 it no longer demanded any transfer of capital. In 1957, the BVD attacked the "fire-red [Communist]" *Flüchtlingsstimme* for implying Kather had called the Eighth Amending Law a fraud because it failed to include a transfer of real capital. Kather had said no such thing, the BVD contended, and this assertion was just another Communist trick to confuse the expellees and undercut their support for defense expenditures.[64]

In a fundamental shift, the expellee leadership was primarily, though never entirely, replacing the original notion of a Lastenausgleich as a balancing out among members of a community with a demand for compensation against a state obligated to protect its citizens' property and status. The ZvF leadership had long been demanding compensation based on the state's "debt" to its war-damaged citizens. The expellee leadership, though, also began using this rhetoric. The BHE's Lastenausgleich spokesman, Dr. Klötzer, argued in July 1956, "the debtor in the Lastenausgleich . . . is not the undamaged fellow citizens but solely and alone the state." Reiterating that recompense should be based not on what was currently affordable but on what the damaged could justly demand, the war-damaged now asserted that the state must seek the necessary revenues by increasing general taxes or decreasing non-Lastenausgleich expenditures.[65]

Central to this shift of rhetoric was the effort to tap the Federal Republic's economic success by diverting much of the government's swelling tax revenue to Lastenausgleich compensation. In the dire aftermath of war, transfers of surviving capital had seemed the best source of Lastenausgleich funds because no one could imagine how much growth (West) Germany would enjoy in the 1950s. Once that growth had occurred, however, the war-damaged believed they had a right to a share of it to finance their just claims to recompense.[66]

With other war victims securing more favorable compensation rates than the Lastenausgleich Law offered, the war-damaged were driven to define their fair share of that economic growth by comparing themselves to other victims in German society. They abandoned after 1955 their earlier resistance to a victim identity and began demanding treatment — and compensation rates — equal to those received by fellow war victims. The war-damaged leadership recognized that the society could never offer them the generous recompense that some much smaller victim groups had secured; however, they wanted the minimum Lastenausgleich compensation to be no less than the minimum offered to other war victims. In the Lastenausgleich Law, the minimum had been 2 percent (for very high losses), but war-damaged groups argued that the 20 percent compensation offered to old savers should also be the minimum Primary Compensation for war-damaged real-property holders.[67]

The Eighth Amending Law finalized the structure of the Primary Compensation. The Finance Ministry had dawdled in implementing the Certification Law. The government still did not know how much in damages would be recompensable under the Lastenausgleich Law, though it was clear it had overestimated the damages in 1952. Against Schäffer's protests, the legislature set the Primary Compensation at an average 70 percent above the minimums that the Lastenausgleich Law had promised, assuming it could cover any compensation in excess of Lastenausgleich revenues from rising general government revenues. The law provided 100 percent compensation for losses up to 4,600 RM and offered increases in the graduated compensation rates for higher amounts, leading to a minimum of 2.4 percent compensation for the largest fortunes. Interest on the Primary Compensation would accrue at 4 percent a year. Payment would take place over twenty-two years (as levy payments and loan repayments flowed in) and in lump sums (to increase the likelihood recipients would invest, rather than consume, it). Despite the Primary Compensation's quotal nature, the government chose to use social criteria (age and disability) to determine the order in which recipients would receive it. Elderly and disabled war-damaged could then support themselves in a humanly worthy, more socially honored fashion and might enjoy some compensation before they joined the 12 percent of entitled recipients who had already died.[68]

Harsh economic realities compelled legislators to continue economic-integration grants. In 1956/57, many war-damaged, especially expellees, were still not integrated into their old social positions, but most war-damaged Germans would not receive compensation payments for years, and that compensation would usually be too little to enable them to reestablish themselves economically anyway. Despite vigorous resistance from Schäffer, the legislature had to finance integration aid from general revenues because post-1957 Lastenausgleich funds were already earmarked for other purposes.[69]

Increasing the Primary Compensation rates and continuing the integration loans would cater to widespread desires to spread the distribution of property as widely as possible. Self-financing by firms, favored by the Federal Republic's tax policy, had underwritten enormous growth, but it had made property distribution in the Federal Republic even more unequal than it had traditionally been. In the contest with the Communists, though, West German elites had counted on a broad distribution of property ownership to bolster support for private property and a market economy. West German officials were increasingly concerned to introduce policies that would promote capital accumulation among broad strata of the population. In one of the first expressions of this concern, the CDU Expellee Committee played this card in pushing the party to end the expenditure of Lastenausgleich funds to those (already propertied) undamaged who promised to provide jobs to the damaged. Such funds would then be available to spur property accumulation among the (currently unpropertied) war-damaged.[70]

The continued prominence of household-goods compensation in the Eighth Amending Law reflected its central importance for most war-damaged. Unexpectedly high revenues had allowed the Lastenausgleich Fund to disburse money for this purpose more quickly than expected, but the war-damaged clamored for more. Against Schäffer's vigorous resistance, the government provided an additional 400 DM in household-goods compensation, with increased supplements for dependents. The government resisted demands to make the compensation more purely quotal, but it eliminated the ban on household-goods compensation to those with incomes greater than 10,000 DM, reflecting its ideological commitment to rewarding achievement, not, in this case, past property ownership.[71]

Economic growth had increased living standards for most West Germans, and the varying categories of war victims insisted on sharing in those improvements. They argued that their meager benefits were a consequence of the war fought and lost in common and that it was unjust for them to remain impoverished as the rest of the society recovered from defeat. Adenauer, for electoral but also for moral reasons, was open to these arguments. The most important result of these desires was the reform of the social-insurance system in February 1957, which established that social-insurance benefits would in the future rise in concert with increases in employees' average real wages.[72]

War-damaged groups also argued that the war-damaged were entitled to share in the society's growing prosperity and, indeed, deserved in principle at least 20 percent higher benefits than welfare recipients. That desire, while understandable, contradicted the Lastenausgleich's original logic as restitution for wartime losses. Nonetheless, the Eighth Amending Law provided a 20 percent increase in the War-Damages Benefit, the first of many under twenty-one additional amending laws. The Lastenausgleich Law had granted the benefit only to men born before 1 January 1890 and women born before 1 January 1895. Many younger war-damaged, though, had not been able to reestablish themselves successfully enough to make the payments necessary to get themselves and their spouses vested in the social-insurance system. The war-damaged groups now demanded that those individuals be allowed to avoid the stigma of welfare by "aging into" a right to the benefit. The Eighth Amending Law allowed formerly self-supporting individuals who had had at least 3,600 RM in capital (albeit, all expellees) to age into the benefit if they lacked pensions.[73]

The Eighth Amending Law, in closely modeling the social-market economy, both negated and confirmed the original idea of a Lastenausgleich. West German Lastenausgleich legislation would neither redistribute capital from the undamaged to formerly propertied war-damaged nor reestablish the prewar distribution of wealth and status. Instead, it promoted production and offered entitlements to support benefits and socially structured compensation financed by a mixture of capital levy, capital taxes, and regular government revenues. As the legislation has developed, 80 percent of funds have gone to productive and social expenditures. Nonetheless, by establishing entitlements to support for war-damaged Germans, that legislation separated the war-damaged from "typical" welfare recipients and restored their autonomy; by establishing a separate compensation program partially tied to former property ownership, it also officially recognized the claim to privileged status of the formerly propertied and partially reestablished their moral order. Like the social-market economy in general, the Lastenausgleich gave a sense of entitlement and security to virtually all West Germans while maintaining a hierarchical structure that catered to individual feelings of social superiority.

CONCLUSION

In the 1940s, some 18 million West Germans, the so-called war-damaged, lost all or most of their property because of bombing, expulsion from their original homes in Eastern Europe, or currency reform. Germany risked disastrous instability if it did not somehow economically reintegrate or recompense these immiserated people. Other European countries assisted their war-damaged citizens with limited compensation, from general governmental revenues. Communist East Germany offered its war-damaged social assistance comparable to what it offered all needy citizens. Only West Germans, who were trying to rebuild a market economy, debated and partially implemented an extensive Lastenausgleich, a "balancing out of burdens," in which massive capital levies to redistribute surviving property would finance individual restitution for war-related (property) losses.

The war-damaged enjoyed broad support for restitution among their fellow Germans. Post–World War I German governments had allowed inflation to shift the costs of war one-sidedly to the holders of paper assets (while sparing real-asset holders) and to erode compensation payments for other war victims; they had also consigned impoverished war and inflation victims to the mercies of often imperious welfare officials. These policies had eroded support for democracy and capitalism, and postwar Germans were determined that society not distribute the second war's costs so unfairly. Meanwhile, the Nazis had proclaimed relentlessly that Germans constituted a racial community in which none must suffer or profiteer disproportionately. Hence, virtually no postwar German was willing to deny that Germans constituted a "community of risk" whose members had to bear war's burdens, and perhaps life's other uncertainties, more or less proportionally. Indeed, many Germans could contemplate even radical policies to address any disproportion.

Initially, most Germans hoped to distribute war burdens fairly through a "social" currency reform. To buy support, the Nazis had guaranteed monetary claims, including war-damage compensation claims, far in excess of Germany's resources; they had expected their defeated enemies to foot the bill. A defeated, impoverished Germany, though, was going to have to annul some paper claims — to expropriate some citizens' property — in order to reestablish a stable currency. To ensure that rich and poor and real- and paper-asset holders would share war's burdens, Germans wanted favorable currency-conversion rates for poor and modest savers, confiscatory levies on real capital, and far-reaching Lastenausgleich policies.

Despite German preferences, American-sponsored currency reform in 1948 shifted most of the war's costs to the holders of paper assets. To ensure monetary stability and economic recovery, that reform canceled more than 90 percent of West German paper assets, including all war-damage claims. Frightened by the radical implications of capital levies, American officials implemented currency reform without a Lastenausgleich. They also backed German supporters of neoliberal economic policies and tight money at a time (1948/49) when most Germans preferred government intervention in the economy and easy credit. Currency reform and Lastenausgleich offer a striking example of American influence on West German development wherever its policy choices could build on the desires of powerful, even if initially minority, segments of German society.

Like other post-1945 Germans and Europeans, war-damaged Germans struggled to secure social recognition of individual entitlements, to reassert individual autonomy and security. Germans and other Europeans had come to expect a certain degree of economic security, but postwar Germans found themselves trapped between the inadequacy of individual rights and the risks of social dependence. Formal rights to private property had proved unable to protect even the most virtuous of individuals from immiseration by powerful material forces such as inflation, depression, and total war. Many Germans, including many war-damaged, concluded that private property was an oxymoron, that property and security depended ultimately on *society's* willingness and ability to protect individual property and other rights. Nevertheless, most Germans could not reestablish security for themselves on their own. Despite society's earlier failures, they had no choice but to turn to it again for some new form of security. To reassert autonomy, though, they would insist that they had an entitlement to a certain degree of wealth and status that the state must recognize, independent of their formal property rights.

In spite of a shared experience of material loss due to war, the war-damaged held varying attitudes toward a Lastenausgleich. Most who had suffered minor damages did not perceive themselves as war-damaged or strive for a Lasten-ausgleich. Moreover, even those who demanded a Lastenausgleich had differ-ing priorities and could conceptualize the Lastenausgleich in varying ways, depending on the nature of their losses, their social and political values, and their economic options and needs.

Most Germans and most war-damaged favored a social Lastenausgleich, in which assistance (support for the unemployable, job creation, replacement of housing and vital household goods) would be based on current need, not pre-vious property ownership. A social Lastenausgleich would concentrate limited Lastenausgleich funds on the neediest citizens. Its supporters defined justice as treating equals equally; they argued that all Germans were equally entitled to "an existence worthy of a human being" but that war-damaged persons were less responsible for their misery than welfare recipients and were entitled to a less humiliating program of assistance.

War-damaged organizations, dominated by former property owners, de-manded an individual Lastenausgleich, in which compensation would be pro-portional to individual property losses. Such compensation would restore their lost property and thereby their security and status. These formerly proper-tied individuals wanted equals treated equally, too, but they saw themselves as equal to the still-propertied undamaged and superior to the formerly unprop-ertied war-damaged because their lost property had been the result of their superior virtue (e.g., diligence, thrift). They argued that the existing property distribution did not deserve social protection, because it reflected immoral profiteering or the operation of amoral forces (military action, expulsion, cur-rency reform) rather than individual virtue. To restore a morally legitimate property distribution, they maintained, Germans had to restore at least part of the fortuitously lost property of war-damaged citizens. The war-damaged were able to make this argument because it reflected a view of property and virtue widely shared in early and mid-twentieth-century Germany.

Both formerly propertied and unpropertied war-damaged also struggled to assert their autonomy. They rejected welfare in part because it subjected them to the whims of the bureaucracy, a dangerous helplessness that 1920s war and inflation victims had experienced and denounced. The war-damaged — like other Germans — preferred to believe they possessed certain rights to con-trol their lives that society must recognize. The obverse of their desire for au-tonomy was their disinclination to accept a status as (implicitly incompetent) victim. Innocent victimhood, however, had become a powerful tool for maxi-mizing one's share of the limited pool of assistance society could afford. The war-damaged hence grudgingly acknowledged their temporary victimization while asserting their past and current efficacy.

Many West Germans, concerned about a still fragile economy, favored a productive Lastenausgleich, which would structure the Lastenausgleich primarily to promote economic recovery. They argued that West Germany must not weaken investment by "overburdening" the economy with excessive levies or by favoring consumption. Lastenausgleich funds must go to those enterprises that could most efficiently provide jobs and housing for war-damaged individuals, regardless of whether the enterprise or its owners had suffered war losses. In view of the economy's postwar devastation, most citizens (Right or Left, employer or employee, undamaged or war-damaged) agreed that economic considerations, especially increasing production, must predominate.

West Germans were committing themselves (if gradually and imperfectly) to a social-market economy, making an individual Lastenausgleich problematic. In the social-market economy, government was to limit its intervention in the productive economy to the minimum necessary to establish efficient, competitive markets. To implement an individual Lastenausgleich, however, the government would have to intervene in the economy to ameliorate the potentially disruptive effects of shifts of real capital. Long accustomed to an interventionist state, the war-damaged initially had no trouble promoting such intervention. Only the growing success of West Germany's social-market economy and the contest with Communist East Germany compelled the war-damaged (and most other West Germans) gradually to abandon calls for substantial government intervention after 1950.

Meanwhile, a new definition of virtue as achievement was becoming predominant in the Federal Republic. The market had long privileged competitiveness, competency, and efficiency. Germans had often disdained these "virtues," associating them with a pushy selfishness, but the Nazis had lauded them if exercised for the community. The chaos of war and defeat then made practical efficiency seem indispensable and admirable. Thereafter, the centrality of economic success in legitimating the Federal Republic, against its Nazi past and its East German competitor, confirmed the importance of achievement for West Germans. They did not denigrate traditional ideals of good character that the war-damaged cherished, but they implicitly subordinated them to achievement.

The social-market economy did reflect reality in important ways. Its postulate that one must not "overburden" the economy begs the question of what constitutes overburdening in any particular case. Also, German economists could declare a capital levy in a market economy to be counterproductive in the mid-1920s, fully feasible in the late 1940s, only partially feasible in the early 1950s, and inconceivable in the 1990s. Yet, just as formerly propertied war-damaged were correct in asserting a need for consumption as well as investment and some connection between character and property accumulation, so obligors were right to assert that one could not shift capital about willy nilly without consequences. Those who manage real productive assets (no matter what the economic system) usually have a practical expertise that gives them a vital economic role. Productive assets are almost always brought together in cohesive operating units that cannot be divided arbitrarily. Society does need to ensure adequate investment, and individuals must have the incentive to perform efficiently. The war-damaged had enough leverage to secure some recompense, but the need to maximize production in the context of a social-market, export-oriented economy limited policy makers' Lastenausgleich options.

Multiple forces compelled the government to legislate meaningful assistance for war-damaged citizens — and other war victims. On electoral grounds, the parties needed to offer a Lastenausgleich law that was acceptable to most war-damaged, who constituted a significant share of the electorate and whose support the government needed for its legislative priorities. More broadly, virtually all West German policy makers were deeply fearful that war and inflation victims could again become antidemocratic and anticapitalist if the society did not offer some just solution to their problems. Moreover, West German elites, competing with Communist East Germany, needed to legitimate a free-market, private property–based system that gave control of most of the society's wealth to a minority. That need and the powerful, deep-rooted ideological claims of the formerly propertied militated in favor of an individual Lastenausgleich that would re-create as much lost private property as possible.

The Lastenausgleich Law of August 1952 was a hard-won compromise. It reflected electoral demographics, the imperatives of the social-market economy, and, crucially, differing conceptions of social justice and of a Lastenausgleich. It also reflected the powerful support for a social and productive Lastenausgleich among the ruling Christian Democrats, despite pressure for an individual Lastenausgleich from some Christian Democrats and from the Free Democrats in the governing right-of-center coalition. Indeed, as usual, the social element in West Germany's 1950s social-market economy came here at the behest not of neoliberals but of Christian Democrats with roots in Christian social teaching or the trade unions. Legislators directed about 50 percent of Lastenausgleich Law expenditures — and a greater share of its early expenditures — to social and productive assistance that would promote economic recovery, meet the most urgent needs for subsistence, and help primarily the 70 percent of war-damaged who had owned no productive assets before the war. Nonetheless, they also provided substantial, privileged recompense to the formerly propertied, which they called the "Primary Compensation."

In the mid-1950s, a striking transformation occurred in the attitudes of war-damaged leaders, underlining the increasing preeminence of the social-market-economy ideology. Faced with a worse-than-expected vote for war-damaged candidates in the 1953 parliamentary elections, war-damaged leaders tacitly abandoned the original idea of a Lastenausgleich as a shift of real capital. Instead, they began arguing for improved Lastenausgleich benefits on the grounds that all war victims, including the war-damaged, should receive comparable recompense from the booming economy. The influence of these efforts and of social ideals on the amending laws to the Lastenausgleich Law shifted the weight of the program so that, by its completion in the twenty-first century, 80 percent of expenditures will have gone for productive and, especially, social assistance. War-damaged leaders did, though, reiterate the special virtue of formerly propertied war-damaged, as they secured relatively modest increases in the Primary Compensation.

The success of war-damaged Germans in getting compensation came even though not every German disadvantaged by war and defeat could convince West Germans to recognize him or her as deserving victim. West Germans of the 1950s resisted offering restitution to the politically and racially persecuted and to German women who had been raped at war's end; they refused to identify as war victims a range of traditionally despised social groups (e.g., Sinti and Roma, Communists, homosexuals). The Nazis had admitted "nationally" minded workers into the national community. West Germans did accept Social Democrats, but, in compensating the various victims of World War II, they continued to discriminate against most of the "outsiders" that their forbears — and the Nazis — had.

In the 1950s the Federal Republic revealed its priorities in its decisions about government spending in response to the plethora of war-related problems. Economic recovery from war's devastation had the highest priority, and West German policies tended to privilege (private) productive enterprises. Housing construction also had a very high priority, both economically (to bring labor to surviving productive capital) and socially. Substantial rearmament spending reflected fear of domination by a Russia now positioned in Central Europe. The renegotiation of Germany's prewar debt reflected both economic and international-political concerns. The new state also emphasized reintegration of expelled and dismissed civil servants in ways that would not burden still-employed officials, a policy that reflected civil servants' importance and the need to tie these traditionally conservative individuals to Germany's second liberal democracy. Nonetheless, the society still spent greater sums on social programs, including the Lastenausgleich, than on rearmament and foreign debt. These social programs seemed necessary to meet human needs and to buy legitimacy for the new Federal Republic. The Lastenausgleich had particularly high priority because it affected so many West Germans, rested on widely accepted social values, and represented the fulfillment of a solemn (even if Nazi-issued) social promise. Finally, most 1950s West Germans did not want to acknowledge the crimes of the Nazis and their own possible culpability, so only foreign pressure motivated them to implement limited recompense for some of those whom Nazi Germany had persecuted.

Observers have often perceived postwar West Germans as being more comfortable recompensing property losses than providing social assistance because of the society's bias in favor of property. West Germans did implement economic liberalization, government-financed credits for business, and probusiness tax policies that promoted economic recovery, business, and private property. Further, the Lastenausgleich's Primary Compensation did reflect efforts to bolster private property. Nevertheless, organizing compensation around property losses was advantageous bureaucratically, as well as "capitalistically," because property provided an objective measure to define—and limit—recompense. More important, West Germans had to establish a *social*-market economy. They did, overall, structure compensation for war's consequences (e.g., the Lastenausgleich, housing construction, provision for war-injured) not to restore lost property but to aid the needy and to legitimate an inegalitarian order.

Crucially, by offering West Germans various entitlements to nonwelfare assistance in the event of "undeserved" immiseration, the republic won their support. European society since the Enlightenment has promised honor, security, and control to those who succeed in the competitive struggle, but it has imposed dishonor and dependence on bureaucratic whim on those who do not. In practice, however, even virtue and competence have not always guaranteed success, as war-damaged Germans discovered. Modernity had proved to be a two-edged sword, and between 1914 and 1945 it cut painfully for most Germans. By providing entitlements for broad categories of "innocent" victims of life's uncertainties, the post-1945 social state has restored to them honor and some sense of control and has bolstered the emancipatory and security-enhancing aspects of modernity. It has thereby contributed substantially to the popular support the socioeconomic order has enjoyed since World War II.

War-damaged Germans sought to secure some just Lastenausgleich within a new, fragile parliamentary democracy. Most Germans were initially suspicious of parliamentary democracy, despite its century-old roots in late-1940s Germany. Germany's first such democracy had collapsed ignominiously, and many Germans disliked the open conflict that characterizes this brand of politics. West Germans ended up with a parliamentary democracy in part because its supporters were among those most likely in the late 1940s to be politically active and because Allied decisions favored those German supporters. Moreover, widespread unwillingness to confront the country's brutal recent past prevented a thorough purge of authoritarian elements, although it allowed millions of compromised individuals to participate in the new system instead of opposing it from the outside. Finally, the numerous problems the new republic faced would have tested even a long-established state. Anchoring democratic values in West Germany would therefore take time.

Nonetheless, already in the early 1950s, West Germans were becoming committed to important elements of a democratic political culture. Drawing on pre-Nazi experience with activism in a democracy, the war-damaged—like many other interest groups — drew enough West Germans into political action to create effective organizations. They recognized that, as a minority, they could not count on the righteousness of their cause but would have to fight with all legal means to convince the political system to address their needs. Yet in carrying on that fight, the war-damaged, but especially their leaders, were remarkably moderate, with much more realistic expectations than had characterized their 1920s counterparts. After their recent experiences, they, like almost all West Germans, rejected left- or right-wing extremism and were coming to accept compromise as a necessary part of democratic politics. Christian and Social Democratic leaders also recognized that a parliamentary system could not function without some cooperation between government and opposition. Furthermore, policy makers accepted democratic rights of popular protest and petition and recognized that they must actively consult the war-damaged and other interest groups.

The war-damaged, like most West Germans, came to acknowledge the legitimacy, efficacy, and justness of the new Federal Republic. The republic's economic and political success had been sufficiently great, its social programs offered sufficient security and recognition of status pretensions, and Germany's recent experiences had left war-damaged leaders sufficiently moderate that those leaders chose to accept the existing social order and to strive to convince their followers to do so. Most formerly propertied war-damaged were apparently slower than their leadership to abandon both antidemocratic attitudes and the desire to restore the prewar socioeconomic order. Nonetheless, already in the early 1950s those war-damaged individuals were also gradually shifting toward support for the social-market economy, the achievement society, and West German democracy.

This narrative, by focusing on West Germans' success in crafting an acceptable Lastenausgleich and a stable liberal democracy, reads as a tale of triumph. The Lastenausgleich offered innumerable individual successes for impoverished war-damaged who wanted a job or some honorable form of social assistance and some restitution of lost property. The Federal Republic, whatever its shortcomings, is undoubtedly an improvement over its Nazi predecessor. The social-market economy and liberal democracy did win out over alternatives in the Federal Republic. The republic itself has "triumphed," by securing prosperity and stability for almost two generations and by absorbing its major competitor, Communist East Germany.

This triumph, however, was neither complete nor inevitable. Within the Lastenausgleich, the formerly unpropertied war-damaged did not get the level of assistance they desired, and the formerly propertied did not get the individual Lastenausgleich they demanded. The Federal Republic could not possibly meet the aspirations of all its citizens. It remained a status society, with widely varying life chances and, especially recently, occasionally sharp social divisions. Moreover, most (West) Germans did not favor parliamentary democracy and free markets in 1948, and their long refusal to come to terms with the Nazi past could have provided the basis for a more authoritarian politics. The Federal Republic had to build support for liberal democracy, and it might have failed to do so had circumstances been less favorable. Finally, West Germans' refused in 1990 to grant the "second Lastenausgleich" that East Germans demanded, offering instead only social and productive aid that East Germans often find humiliating; that decision has contributed to the alienation many East Germans feel against their new country, the Federal Republic of Germany. German history was open and heterogeneous after 1945 — and it still is.

NOTES

INTRODUCTION

1. For quote: Hitler comments of 6 May 1942 in Picker, *Hitlers Tischgespräche*, 270; M. Bormann, reporting Hitler's comments of 25 Mar. 1942, in ibid., 140–41; "Hitler vor Leitern der Rüstungsindustrie auf dem Obersalzberg Anfang Juli 1944," in Hitler, *Es spricht der Führer*, 344–45; Dr. Heinrich Heimerich, "Einige allgemeine Betrachtungen zum ersten Lastenausgleichsgesetz," *Zehntagedienst für Wirtschafts-, Steuer- und Sozialrecht* 3, no. 27 (30 Nov. 1948), in BAK, NL Holzapfel, no. 111.

2. For executions for defeatism, see, e.g., Müller, *Hitler's Justice*, 188–91; T. Eschenburg, "Zur Kurzfassung der Denkschrift 1943/44," in Erhard, *Kriegsfinanzierung*, vii–xxii. A few economic experts, protected by the economics minister or the SS, were discussing these problems: Brackmann, *Vom totalen Krieg*, 75–125.

3. "Vier Forderungen zum Lastenausgleich," *Christ und Welt* 1, no. 7 (17 July 1948), in BAK, B 126/5691.

4. Dr. Hans von Neuhoff, "Entschädigungsregelungen in fremden Staaten," and "Entschädigungsregelungen für Vertreibungsschäden," Oct. 1961; and Dr. H. A. O. Schröder, "Das Kriegsschadenrecht in der Gesetzgebung Deutschlands und des Auslands," all in BmVt, ed., *Lastenausgleichsgesetze*, 4/1:400–402, 431, 435–77; Cahn, *Kriegsschadenrecht*.

5. Hughes, *Paying for Inflation*.

CHAPTER 1

1. Keegan, *Second World War*, 590–91.

2. Botting, *Ruins of Reich*, 104–6; Boelcke, *Kosten von Hitlers Krieg*, 7–8, passim. In this work billion will mean 1,000 million.

3. "Die Personenkreise der Berechtigten," in BmI, ed., *Lastenausgleichsgesetze*, 2/1:121.

4. BmVt, *Dokumente Kriegsschäden*, 2/1:509, passim; Amato, *Victims and Values*.

5. See, e.g., Hazard, *European Thought in the Eighteenth Century*, 18–25, 113, 156–57; Manuel and Manuel, *Utopian Thought in the Western World*, 463–86, 492–518; Brooks, *Melodramatic Imagination*, 15, passim. For approximately 1,800 proposals on war losses, see BmVt, *Dokumente Kriegsschäden*, 2/1:509, 512–14; Cahn, *Kriegsschadenrecht*, 105–6, 112, 124.

6. Cahn, *Kriegsschadenrecht*, 118–24. For quotation, H.A., "Vorwärts statt Rückwärts," *Wirtschaftszeitung* (20 Aug. 1948), in BAK, B 126/5759; for similar attitudes toward war victims, Geyer, "Vorbote des Wohlfahrtsstaates," 234; cf., though, Dr. Artur Moser, "Tun wie neugeboren," *Wirtschaftszeitung* (8 Oct. 1948), in BAK, B 126/5759.

7. Cahn, *Kriegsschadenrecht*, 100; BmVt, *Dokumente Kriegsschäden*, 2/1:509, 514.

8. G. Weisser mit Assistent Schayer, "Vergleich der Leistungen . . . Bundesversorgungsgesetz/Lastenausgleichsgesetz" (summer 1954), ASD, NL Weisser, no. 1220; Sachße and Tennstedt, *Armenfürsorge in Deutschland*, 49–56, 88–94, 213; Geyer, "Vorbote des Wohlfahrtsstaates," 236; Whalen, *Bitter Wounds*.

9. BmVt, *Dokumente Kriegsschäden*, 2/1:509–10, 527–49; [Verwaltung für Finanzen], "Die Regelung der Entschädigungsfrage nach dem 1. Weltkrieg," BAK, NL Blücher, no. 338.

10. Danckelmann, "Einleitung," *Kriegssachschädenrecht*, 6; "Sachschädensfeststellungsverordnung," in ibid., A3a, 1–7; Boelcke, *Kriegspropaganda*, 389; see also BmVt, *Dokumente Kriegsschäden*, 2/1:550–51; "Kriegssachschäden und Versicherungswirtschaft," *Der deutsche Volkswirt*, no. 52 (27 Sept. 1940), in ibid., 575–76.

11. Krause, *Flucht vor Bombenkrieg*, 38–39.

12. Kriegssachschädenverordnung and various implementation decrees, in Danckelmann, *Kriegssachschädenrecht*; "Einleitung," ibid., 7–13.

13. [Disputation between W. Seuffert and J. Kunze], [spring 1951], P-A, I-332, B 9; see also [draft by Dr. Fauser for] BmF Schäffer to Staatssek. des Innern, Bundeskanzleramt, 8 May 1950, BAK, B 126/5682. See, similarly, Schäffer on military-pension legislation: Diehl, *Thanks of the Fatherland*, 160.

14. "Kriegssachschädenverordnung" and various implementation decrees, in Danckelmann, *Kriegssachschädenrecht;* cf. Cahn, *Kriegsschadenrecht*, 129–30; for broader discussion of liberal content in Nazi-era jurisprudence, see Stolleis, "Gemeinschaft und Volksgemeinschaft," 101.

15. "*Opfer,*" *Meyers Lexikon*, 8 (1940); Goebbels, "Kundgebung des Gaues Berlin," 18 Feb. 1943, in Goebbels, *Reden,* 2:187 (his emphasis); for churches, Kitchen, *Nazi Germany at War,* 224; for revenge, see, e.g., "Die Schlacht um die Reichshauptstadt," *Völkischer Beobachter* 56, no. 330 (26 Nov. 1943).

16. Goebbels, "Rundfunkansprache am Vorabend von Hitlers 52. Geburtstag," 19 Apr. 1941, in Goebbels, *Reden,* 2:55 (his emphasis); Goebbels "Rundfunkrede," 26 July 1944, in ibid., 2:354; Danckelmann, "Einleitung," *Kriegssachschädenrecht,* 4; "Ersatz von Fliegerschäden," *Völkischer Beobachter* 56, no. 90 (31 Mar. 1943).

17. Dr. Reinhold Zenz, "Im Bereich der Terrorbomber," *Völkischer Beobachter* 56, no. 234 (22 Aug. 1943); Goebbels, "Kundgebung der NSDAP," 5 June 1943, in Goebbels, *Reden,* 2:228 (his emphasis); Herbst, *Der totale Krieg,* 314–16, 327–39.

18. Holtfrerich, *German Inflation,* esp. 102–8, 115–19; Brackmann, *Vom totalen Krieg,* 7.

19. Holtfrerich, *German Inflation,* 108–81, 275–78; Feldman, *Great Disorder,* 25–51, passim.

20. Hughes, *Paying for German Inflation,* 17–70.

21. Ibid., 71–158.

22. Ibid., 159–67; for post-1945 developments, see below, chap. 2.

23. Hero Moeller, "Geldabschöpfung und Geldüberhang," *Zeitschrift der Akademie für deutsches Recht* 10, no. 11 (10 Aug. 1943): 1–3; Schwerin von Krosigk, *Staatsbankrott,* 298–303; Hansemeyer and Caesar, "Kriegswirtschaft und Inflation," 370–417; Brackmann, *Vom totalen Krieg,* 24–33.

24. For recent overviews of these developments, see Brackmann, *Vom totalen Krieg,* 18–33; Hansemeyer and Caesar, "Kriegswirtschaft und Inflation," 404–14; for lack of things to buy, see, e.g., diary entry for 9 March 1943 by Charlotte G. in Breloer, *Mein Tagebuch,* 460; Wolf, "Geld- und Finanzprobleme der deutschen Nachkriegswirtschaft," 198.

25. See reports in Boelcke, *Kriegspropaganda,* e.g., 232, 258, and in Boberach, *Meldungen aus dem Reich,* e.g., 178–79, 304–5; see diary entries in Breloer, *Mein Tagebuch,* 63, 460, 467, and in Hammer and zur Nieden, *Sehr selten habe ich geweint,* 285, 351, 354, 356–57; "Schulden, Clearingsverkehr und Kriegsanforderungen," *Völkischer Beobachter* 55, no. 79 (20 Mar. 1942); "Nie wieder Inflation oder Deflation!" ibid. 55, no. 114 (24 Apr. 1942); "Gerechte Preis- und Währungsrelation," ibid. 56, no. 314 (10 Nov. 1943); Brackmann, *Vom totalen Krieg,* 64–74; Scott, "Money Talks," 30, 33–36; Schwerin von Krosigk, *Staatsbankrott,* 297–98.

26. For Hugenberg, see Kitchen, *Germany at War,* 285; for average citizens, see, e.g., the savings bank clerk Charlotte G. in Breloer, *Mein Tagebuch,* 460.

27. See, e.g., Brackmann, *Vom totalen Krieg,* 75–119, 126–78; Scott, "Money Talks," 40–67.

28. Overy, *Air War,* 24, 30–39, 73–74, 78, 105–8, 117–18, 123–25; Diefendorf, *Wake of War,* 5–7.

29. Schroeder, "Long Road Home"; Krause, *Flucht vor Bombenkrieg;* BmVt, *Dokumente Kriegsschäden,* 1:69–370; Schulze, *Unruhige Zeiten.*

30. Breloer, *Mein Tagebuch;* Rumpf, *Bombing of Germany,* 123–29, 148–49, passim; for poll results, Krause, *Flucht vor Bombenkrieg,* 13; Yeager, *Yeager,* 63–64; Diefendorf, *Wake of War,* 9–13.

31. Diefendorf, *Wake of War*, 9–13; BmVt, *Dokumente Kriegsschäden*, 1:51–62, and vol. 2.

32. BmVt, *Dokumente Kriegsschäden*, 2/1:551–52, 553, 559, passim; for range of reactions to the different experiences of bombing, see the diary entries from various people in Breloer, *Mein Tagebuch*, 44–45, 47, 158, 163–64, 208, 211, 229, and in Hammer and zur Neiden, *Sehr selten habe ich geweint*, 106–7, 157–63, 183–84, 196–97, 206, 211, 283, 286–87, 291, 340, 349–53.

33. Rumpf, *Bombing of Germany*, 191, 199–206; Werner, "Belastungen der deutschen Arbeiterschaft," 37, 40, 42; Trommler, " 'Deutschlands Sieg oder Untergang,' " 215–25; Henke, *Die amerikanische Besetzung*, 89–90, 264–66, 809, passim.

34. First quotation: cited in Kitchen, *Nazi Germany at War*, 233–34; second quotation: in BmVt, *Dokumente Kriegsschäden*, 1:76; more generally: Bankier, *Germans and Final Solution*, 147.

35. Wurm quotation cited in Gerhard Beiser, "Zwischen Neuanfang und Restauration. Die evangelischen Kirchen in Deutschland nach dem Zweiten Weltkrieg," in Volkmann, *Ende des dritten Reiches*, 740, n. 101. For contemporary German reactions, see innumerable references in the diary entries in Breloer, *Mein Tagebuch*, and Hammer and zur Neiden, *Sehr selten habe ich geweint*; Matthias Simon, "Bericht des Evangelisch-Lutherischen Pfarramtes St. Matthäus in Augsburg an das Dekanat Augsburg," 25 May 1945, in Gelberg, ed., *Kriegsende und Neuanfang in Augsburg*, 166.

36. Manfred Messerschmidt, "Die Wehrmacht: Vom Realitätsverlust zum Selbstbetrug," in Volkmann, *Ende des Dritten Reiches*, 223–58; Henke, *Die amerikanische Besetzung*, 87, 157, 163–71, 255, 341, 355, 389–90, 795–861.

37. Henke, *Die amerikanische Besetzung*, 813–61, passim; Hammer and zur Nieden, *Sehr selten habe ich geweint*, 308, 381–82, 459–62; Breloer, *Mein Tagebuch*, 49, 78, 81, 84–85, 146, 178, 181, 182, 213, 230; "Weil der Nazikreisleiter die Flucht vereitelte," in Nahm, *Sich selbst geholfen*, 37.

38. Nicholls, *Bonn Republic*, 2–3.

39. Marrus, *Unwanted*, 40–50, 96–106; Skran, *Refugees in Interwar Europe*, 13–48.

40. Marrus, *Unwanted*, 129–30, 166–70, 220–27; Lemberg and Edding, *Die Vertriebenen*, 1:28–33.

41. de Zayas, *Nemesis at Potsdam*, 1–14, 17, 35–37; Birke, *Nation ohne Haus*, 16.

42. Birke, *Nation ohne Haus*, 14, 35–36; Bartov, "Savage War" and *Hitler's Army*.

43. Bankier, *Germans and Final Solution*, 148, passim; de Zayas, *Nemesis at Potsdam*, 61–69.

44. Thorwald, *Die große Flucht*, 60–63, 87–90, 182–83, passim; Schieder, *Vertreibung der deutschen Bevölkerung*, 1/1.

45. Schieder, *Vertreibung der deutschen Bevölkerung*, 1/1; de Zayas, *Nemesis at Potsdam*, 105–7, passim.

46. de Zayas, *Nemesis at Potsdam*, 80–89; Marrus, *Unwanted*, 327; Wolfgang Krieger, "Die amerikanische Deutschlandplanung. Hypotheken und Chancen für einen Neuanfang," in Volkmann, ed., *Ende des dritten Reiches*, 45; Nawratil, *Die deutschen Nachkriegsverluste*, 34–35.

47. J. Foschepoth, "Potsdam und danach: Die Westmächte, Adenauer und die Vertriebenen," in Benz, ed., *Vertreibung der Deutschen*, 70–90; de Zayas, *Nemesis at Potsdam*, 108–30; Schieder, *Vertreibung der deutschen Bevölkerung*, 1/2:653–896; for the experience of one town, see Schmidt, *Graslitz*, 106–16; Nawratil, *Die deutschen Nachkriegsverluste*, 29–32; Ther, "Expellees in Germany and Poland," 785, n. 30.

48. For the variety of refugee experiences, see Schulze, *Unruhige Zeiten*, 83–84, 98–99, 129, 131–32, 162–63, 171–75, 184–85, 193, 198–202, 218–21; Schieder, *Vertreibung der deutschen Bevölkerung*; Lehmann, *Im Fremden ungewollt*, 20, 28–29, passim; Niethammer, "Privat-Wirtschaft," 43.

49. Martin Broszat et al., "Einleitung," in Broszat, Henke, and Woller, eds., *Von Stalingrad*

zur *Währungsreform,* xxv–xxix; Woller, "Germany in Transition," esp. 23–28; Niethammer, "Privat-Wirtschaft," esp. 52–53.

CHAPTER 2

1. For contemporary assertion of *Stunde Null* by war-damaged, see "Um das 'moralische Prinzip' in der politischen Welt," *Archiv* hvp-Kommentare 39/51 (27 Sept. 1951): 1–2; for continuities, see Niethammer, "Zum Wandel der Kontinuitätsdiskussion," in Herbst, ed., *Westdeutschland,* 65–84; for options, see Mintzel, "Der akzeptierte Parteienstaat," and Herf, "Multiple Restorations."

2. Kleßmann, *Die doppelte Staatsgründung,* 28, passim; Benz, *Von der Besatzungsherrschaft,* 19–26.

3. Naimark, *Russians in Germany,* 141–204; Deighton, *Impossible Peace,* 5–7, 11–16, 23–28, passim; Mastny, *Cold War,* 23–24, passim; Soutou, "Frankreich und die Deutschlandfrage," 75–112; Fisch, *Reparationen,* esp. 41–80, 92–109; Eisenberg, *Drawing the Line,* 8–10, 99–101, 202–3, 210–12.

4. Leffler, *Struggle for Germany,* 14–15, 24–25, 29; Loth, "Historiker und deutsche Frage," 17.

5. See, e.g., Dahrendorf, *Democracy and Society in Germany;* Jill Stephenson, "Widerstand gegen soziale Modernisierung am Beispiel Württembergs 1939–1945," in Prinz and Zitelmann, eds., *Nationalsozialismus und Modernisierung,* esp. 96, 102–3, 108–9, 115–16; Michael Prinz, "Die soziale Funktion moderner Elemente in der Gesellschaftspolitik des Nationalsozialismus," in ibid., 301–3, 306–8, 319–21; Kershaw, *Nazi Dictatorship,* 131–49; Naimark, *Russians in Germany,* 141–54.

6. See, e.g., Schornstheimer, *Bombenstimmung und Katzenjammer,* esp. 42–44.

7. See, e.g., the articles in *Frankfurter Hefte,* 1946–48; von der Gablentz, *Über Marx hinaus.*

8. For the SPD, see, e.g., Herbert Kriedemann to sozialdemokratische Mitglieder des Bundesrates, 2 Jan. 1951, 3, ASD, NL Seuffert, no. 53; Westdeutsches Institut für Wirtschaftsforschung, *Der Lastenausgleich wirtschaftlich gesehen!* 5–6; Katholische Volksarbeit, "Leitsätze zum Lastenausgleich," 21 Aug. 1948, ACDP, NL Theiss, 005/II; Albertz in Karrenberg, "Lastenausgleich," *Die Stimme der Gemeinde* 2, no. 12 (Dec. 1950): 8, in BAK, B 126/10444.

9. Gessner, "Politische Apathie," in Gessner, *Kommentare,* 1:7, 11; Arendt, "Aftermath of Nazi Rule," 248–52; Koebner, "Schuldfrage," 314–15, in Koebner, Sautermeister, and Schneider-Grube, eds., *Deutschland nach Hitler;* Güstrow, *In jenen Jahren,* 42–43, 54–55; Mitscherlich and Mitscherlich, *Inability to Mourn;* Moeller, "War Stories," 1008–34. See chap. 5 below.

10. Güstrow, *In jenen Jahren,* 53–54; Henke, "Trennung vom Nationalsozialismus," 29–32.

11. Henke, "Trennung vom Nationalsozialismus," 33–34, 63, 70–71; Herbert, "Rückkehr in die Bürgerlichkeit?" 162–63.

12. See, e.g., Mommsen, "Von Weimar nach Bonn," and "Der lange Schatten der untergehenden Republik," 380–99; Prowe, "Democratization as Restabilization"; Boehling, *Question of Priorities,* 72–155; Benz, "Konzeptionen für die Nachkriegszeit," 211–12; Herf, "Late Victory of Lost Causes," 388–89; Rogers, "Transforming the Party System."

13. Nicholls, *Freedom with Responsibility,* 15–29, 131, 139, passim; Gessner, "Wirtschaftlicher Neuaufbau Deutschlands," in Gessner, *Kommentare,* 1:99, 101–2; Werner Bührer, "Die Unternehmerverbände nach den beiden Weltkriegen," in Niedhart and Riesenberger, eds., *Lernen aus dem Krieg?* 148; Berghahn, *Americanisation of West German Industry,* 101–5, passim; Werner Abelshauser, "Die ordnungspolitische Epochenbedeutung der Weltwirtschaftskrise in

Deutschland," in Petzina, ed., *Ordnungspolitische Weichenstellungen*, 20–28; Ott, *Wirtschafts-konzeptionen der SPD;* CDU, "Ahlener Programm," 157; von der Gablentz, *Über Marx hinaus*, esp. 12, 19, 36, 38.

14. For a striking example of this dream of a Third Way, see Berghahn, "Resisting the Pax Americana?"; see also Vaubel, *Zusammenbruch und Wiederaufbau*, 63–64, 108; Mitchell, "Materialism and Secularism"; Cary, *Path to Christian Democracy;* Ambrosius, *Durchsetzung der Sozialen Marktwirtschaft*, 21–28; "Flüchtlingsprogramm der FDP," [pre-1948], THA, FDP, no. 8; Boehling, "Symbols of Continuity and Change," 364–65.

15. For neoliberals, see, most recently, Nicholls, *Freedom with Responsibility*, 4–5, passim; Berghahn, "West German Reconstruction," 71–72; Ambrosius, *Durchsetzung der Sozialen Marktwirtschaft*, here esp. 29–37; Abelshauser, "Erhard oder Bismarck?" 376–78.

16. Bomb-damaged quotes in A. Bauser, "Notgemeinschaft der Fliegergeschädigten," *Selbsthilfe* 20, no. 4 (15 May 1946): 1, and "Was wir wollen," ibid. 20, no. 7 (1 July 1946): 1; "Wirtschaft in der Entscheidung," ibid. 23, no. 14 (2. Juli Ausg. 1949): 2; "Soforthilfe und Preisbildung," ibid. 22, no. 24 (2. Dez. Ausg. 1948): 2; Bund der Fliegergeschädigten und Ver-triebenen in Baden, Kreisverband Hochschwarzwald, to Bundestagsabgeordneter, 20 Jan. 1951, P-A, I 332/B 7; for policy makers, see, e.g., Verwaltung für Finanzen, "Volkswirtschaftliche Überlegungen zum endgültigen Lastenausgleich," 1 June 1949, 20, BAK, B 126/5686.

17. Nicholls, *Freedom with Responsibility;* Abelshauser, *Wirtschaftsgeschichte*, 65–84; for alternative Western European models, see Eichengreen, *Europe's Postwar Recovery.*

18. Kramer, *West German Economy*, 7–16; Abelshauser, *Wirtschaftsgeschichte*, 13–20, 33.

19. Abelshauser, *Wirtschaftsgeschichte*, 27–31; Kramer, *West German Economy*, 105–10.

20. Boelcke, *Der Schwarzmarkt;* Nicholls, *Freedom with Responsibility*, 126–27.

21. Eduard Wolf, "Geld- und Finanzprobleme der Nachkriegswirtschaft," esp. 232; Abelshauser, *Wirtschaftsgeschichte*, 46–47; Brackmann, *Vom totalen Krieg*, 38–39, passim.

22. Kimball, *Swords or Ploughshares?;* Abelshauser, *Wirtschaftsgeschichte*, 24–27; Kramer, *West German Economy*, 58–60; Fisch, *Reparationen*, 94–96.

23. Schelsky, *Wandlungen der deutschen Familie*, 75–92, passim; Tenbruck, "Alltagsnormen und Lebensgefühle," 290–91; Peukert, *Improvisierter Neubeginn*, esp. 14.

24. Enssle, "Theses on German Everyday Life"; Wildt, *Traum vom Sattwerden* and *Beginn der "Konsumgesellschaft."* For emphasis on performance, see Siegel, *Leistung und Lohn*, 20, 43, 65–66, 122–23, passim.

25. Abelshauser, *Wirtschaftsgeschichte*, 20–24; Kramer, *West German Economy*, 11, 17–24; Wiesemann and Kleinert, "Flüchtlinge und wirtschaftlicher Wiederaufbau," 307–9, 311.

26. Henke, *Die amerikanische Besetzung*, 177, 184–85, 447–48, 987–91; Eisenberg, *Drawing the Line*, 80–81, 130, 143–51, 176–86, passim.

27. Braun, "Streben nach 'Sicherheit,' " esp. 283–87; Dietrich, *Eigentum für Jeden*, 135.

28. Erhard, *Kriegsfinanzierung*, 7–8, 34, 149, passim; "Professoren-Kriegsfinanzierungs-gutachten," 9 Dec. 1939, in Möller, ed., *Vorgeschichte der Mark*, 35–36. For early stages of this process, see Richard Overy, "Guns or Butter? Living Standards, Finance, and Labour in Germany, 1939–1942," in Overy, *War and Economy in the Third Reich.*

29. See, e.g., Erhard, *Kriegsfinanzierung*, 34, 149. Foreign debt to finance a war effort creates more complex problems but was a negligible factor in Nazi war finance. To the extent the debt financed net investment, it *increased* the wealth of future generations.

30. See, e.g., Erhard, *Kriegsfinanzierung*, 34, 146–47, passim; various memoranda in Möller, ed., *Vorgeschichte der Mark*, 58, 64–65, 74–75, 89–90, 104, 126–27.

31. For the post–World War I period, see Führer, "Für das Wirtschaftsleben 'mehr oder weniger wertlose Personen,' " 179; for 1945 recognition, see, e.g., "Abschrift. Wortlaut des Hamburger Senatsgutachtens zur Währungsfrage," [15 Sept. 1945], in BAK, Z 32/36; Huber,

Die Ordnung der finanzwirtschaftlichen und sozialen Verhältnisse, 4; Erich Kuby, "Randbemer-
kungen zur Währungsreform," in Friedrich, *Mein Kopfgeld,* 94–95; see numerous articles in
the newspaper of the bomb-damaged, *Selbsthilfe,* for 1946–48.

32. "Hilfe für die Fliegergeschädigten," and "Bund der Sparer und Fliegergeschädigten,"
Selbsthilfe 20, no. 2 (15 Apr. 1946): 1; "Fliegergeschädigte gründen Zentralverband," ibid. 21,
no. 15 (15 Sept. 1947): 1.

33. Among numerous examples, Adolf Bauser, "Gerechtigkeit: Gerechte Lastenverteilung!"
Selbsthilfe 20, no. 1 (1 Apr. 1946): 1; Wilhelm Mattes, *Wir fordern Gerechtigkeit!* (Stuttgart,
1948): 3; and Oskar Wackerzapp, "Lastenausgleich," *Das Blatt der Ostvertriebenen* 1948:1, 1,
both in BAK, B 126/5680.

34. "Vertriebenenprogramm der Freien Demokratischen Partei," [later 1948], THA, FDP,
no. 8; for economic experts, see the extended discussion in Brackmann, *Vom totalen Krieg,*
17–188; Erhard, *Kriegsfinanzierung,* 70, 191–94; Dr. Hermann Heimerich, "Einige allgemeine
Betrachtungen zum ersten Lastenausgleichsgesetz," *Zehntagedienst für Wirtschaft-, Steuer- und
Sozialrecht* 3, no. 27 (30 Nov. 1948). Note here the development of poor relief and social insurance in nineteenth-century Germany in response to similar fears of popular radicalization:
Steinmetz, *Regulating the Social,* esp. 44–48, 50–51, 57–63.

35. See, e.g., Diehl, *Thanks of the Fatherland,* 144–45.

36. See *Selbsthilfe,* 1946–48.

37. For first quote: U.S. Senate Committee on Foreign Relations, *Documents on Germany, 1944–1959,* 13; for legal discussion, see Walter Schwengler, "Das Ende des 'Dritten
Reiches'—auch das Ende des Deutschen Reiches?" in Volkmann, ed., *Ende des Dritten Reiches,*
175–88; Diestelkamp, "Rechtsgeschichte als Zeitgeschichte"; Stolleis, "Rechtsordnung und
Justizpolitik," 251–54, 270; Vertretung der Ostdeutschen Betriebe, "Forderungen zum Lastenausgleich," 18 Aug. 1948, BAK, Z 26/187; for war-damaged acknowledgment, implicitly, that
the disappearance of the German state created problems for their legal claim, see "19. August
1952," *Selbsthilfe* 27, no. 16 (2. Aug. Ausg. 1953): 1; for the annoyance of war-damaged with
the Federal Republic's selective claims to status as legal successor, see, e.g., "Der Topf des
Lastenausgleichs," ibid. 30, nos. 15/16 (Aug. Ausg. 1956): 1.

38. For first quote: Schäffer in 103. Sitzung (29 Sept. 1955), *VerhBT, Sten. Ber.,* 26:5687; for
government refusal to acknowledge any preexisting legal claim to a Lastenausgleich, see the
carefully crafted language of the Lastenausgleich Law, Preamble and § 373; for second quote:
Dr. Fauser, "Grundlagen des endgültigen Lastenausgleichs," [early 1950], BAK, B 126/5678;
for Constitutional Court, "Urteil des Bundesverfassungsgericht, 1BvR 987/58," in BmI, ed.,
Lastenausgleichsgesetze, 4/1:371–84; see also Diehl, *Thanks of the Fatherland,* 145–46.

39. BmVt, *Dokumente Kriegsschäden,* 2/1:587–604; Finanzminister a. D. Dr. Mattes, *Wir
fordern Gerechtigkeit!* July 1948, 3, in BAK, B 126/5680.

40. Prof. Dr. Scheuner, "Äußerung zu dem Rechtsgutachten RA Danckelmann über
Rechtsansprüche aus dem Kriegsschadenrecht für Sowjetzonenflüchtlinge," 3 Mar. 1952,
B 126/10473; Kurt Blaum, "Der Lastenausgleich als soziales Problem," *Nachrichtendienst
des Deutschen Vereins für öffentliche und private Fürsorge,* Apr./May 1950, in BmVt, ed.,
Lastenausgleichsgesetze, 1/2:249; de Zayas, *Nemesis at Potsdam,* 78–91.

41. Fischer and Budczies, "Erster Entwurf, Gesetz zur Neuordnung des Geldwesens,
Begründung," 35, IfZ, Sammlung Möller; Dr. Fauser, "Grundlagen des endgültigen Lastenausgleichs," [early 1950], 3, BAK, B 126/5678; Seuffert in "[Disputation]," 7, P-A, I 332/B 9.

42. Dr. Fauser, "Grundlagen des endgültigen Lastenausgleichs," [early 1950], 1, BAK,
B 126/5678; Dr. Artur Moser, "Tun wie neugeboren," *Wirtschaftszeitung* (8 Oct. 1948), both in
BAK, B 126/5759.

43. See, e.g., Dr. Fauser, "Grundlagen des endgültigen Lastenausgleichs," [early 1950], 1,

BAK, B 126/5678; Leitsätze der Arbeitsgemeinschaft der Industrie und Handelskammern des Vereinigten Wirtschaftsgebietes zum Lastenausgleich, 4 Oct. 1948, 1, ACDP, NL Binder, 043 C II 3A; "Lastenausgleich — Idee und Fiktion," *Pressedienst für undoktrinäre [sic] Politik,* [Aug. or Sept. 1948], in ASD, NL Weisser, no. 1086.I. Even in the 1990s, Americans of the World War II generation often bristle at the notion that Germans might demand recompense, even from other Germans, for war damages incurred in a war Germany started and conducted so brutally.

44. Dr. Fauser, "Grundlagen des endgültigen Lastenausgleichs," [early 1950], 1, BAK, B 126/5678; Kurt Schumacher, "Konsequenzen deutscher Politik," summer 1945, in Schumacher, *Reden und Schriften,* 33; "Was wir wollen," *Selbsthilfe* 20, no. 7 (1 July 1946): 1; O. Lautenbach, Walker, and Hochstetter, "Sofortprogramm zur . . . Überwindung der Kriegsschäden," 30 Jan. 1946 [Oct. 1944], BAK, Z 1/311; for quote Anton Prothmann to Gerhard Weisser, 17 July 1948, ASD, NL Weisser, no. 1086.II.

45. Friedhelm Rostock, "Berechtigte, Verpflichtete und Grenzen im Lastenausgleich," *National-Zeitung* (1 Sept. 1948), in BAK, B 126/5691; for double punishment, see, e.g., Dr. R. Herrmann, "Amerikanischer Vorschlag zur Währungsreform," *Selbsthilfe* 20, no. 14 (15 Oct. 1946); Hanns von Breunig "Vorschläge für eine Währungs-Reform," [mid-1947], BAK, Z 32/30.

46. Clemens Vollnhals, "Entnazifizierung. Politische Säuberung unter alliierter Herrschaft," in Volkmann, ed., *Ende des dritten Reiches,* esp. 386–87; Klaus-Dietmar Henke, "Die Grenzen der politischen Säuberung in Deutschland nach 1945," in Herbst, ed., *Westdeutschland,* 127–33; Herf, *Divided Memory,* esp. 201–66.

47. Kogon, "Recht auf Irrtum," 655; Herf, *Divided Memory,* 202–3.

48. Hughes, *Paying for Inflation,* 32–42, 50, passim; A. Bauser, "Gerechtigkeit: Gerechte Lastenverteilung!" *Selbsthilfe* 20, no. 1 (1 Apr. 1946): 1; cf. A. Bauser, "Auf ihre Verantwortung, Herr General Clay!" ibid. 22, no. 20 (2. Okt. Ausg. 1948): 1, where Bauser appeals to *Recht* but does not mention the *Rechtsstaat.*

49. Finanzminister a. D. Dr. Wilhelm Mattes, "Ein Finanzprogramm für das neue Deutschland," [ca. Sept. 1945], BAK, Z 32/37; for Nöll von der Nahmer, see Brackmann, *Vom totalen Krieg,* 109, passim, and Robert Nöll von der Nahmer, "Denkschrift über Umfang und Rückzahlungsmöglichkeit der Reichsschuld," 9.II.46, 13, BAK, Z 32/44.

50. For liability community, see, e.g., Giersch, *Der Ausgleich der Kriegslasten,* 14, 17; for risk community, Förderungsverband zur Eingliederung der Flüchtlinge Schwabmünchen, "Entschließung," 29 Sept. 1948, BAK, B 126/5680; for war and defeat in common, BvD — Pfalz, "Resolution," 11 Mar. 1951, BAK, B 126/5696.

51. For assertions of postwar coinage, see, e.g., Staatsminister Heinrich Albertz (SPD), "Das falsche 'Entweder-Oder,'" *VK* 2, no. 6 (17 Feb. 1951); for Nazis, see above, chap. 1; Erhard, *Kriegsfinanzierung,* 15, 70, 82, 83, 184–85, passim; for early postwar use of "Lastenausgleich," see the earliest issues of *Selbsthilfe,* which shifted immediately from "just distribution of burdens" (20, no. 1 [1 Apr. 1946]: 1) to "Lastenausgleich" (20, no. 2 [15 Apr. 1946]: 1).

52. For prewar roots of communalism, see, e.g., Walker, *German Home Towns;* Baranowski, *Sanctity of Rural Life,* 51–52, 64–67, 71–76, passim; Mommsen, "Nationalität im Zeichen der Weltpolitik," 131, 133, 138; Brubaker, *Citizenship and Nationhood;* for an overview of the "national idea" in German history, see, e.g., the articles in Breuilly, *State of Germany;* Stolleis, "Gemeinschaft und Volksgemeinschaft," 97–98; for World War I, see Sombart, *Händler und Helden,* 66–71, 75–76, 87, passim; for interwar, see "German National People's Party (DNVP), Program," in Kaes, Jay, and Dimendberg, eds., *Weimar Republic,* 348–49.

53. Josef Goebbels, "Rundfunkrede," 26 July 1944, in Goebbels, *Reden,* 2:354; "Ersatz von Fliegerschäden," *Völkischer Beobachter* 56, no. 90 (31 Mar. 1943); Stolleis, "Gemeinschaft und

Volksgemeinschaft"; the general discussion in Welch, *Third Reich,* 52–65; and the striking communal imagery in Leni Riefenstahl's 1936 film *The Triumph of the Will.*

54. Broszat, Henke, and Woller, *Von Stalingrad zur Währungsreform,* xxv–xxix; Irinia Korschunow, "Damals am Rosenwall," in Friedrich, *Mein Kopfgeld,* 75; Dr. Ehlers, "Die Opfer mahnen," 16 Aug. 1952, in BmVt, ed., *Dokumente Kriegsschäden,* 1:63; Jünger, *Jahre der Okkupation,* 63; Erhard, *Kriegsfinanzierung,* 15–16, 85–86; Lehmann, *Im Fremden ungewollt,* 188, 190.

55. "Letzte Hoffnung der Ostvertriebenen," *Ostvertriebenen-Korrespondenz* 1, no. 5 (5 Sept. 1948): 1; "Kirche und Lastenausgleich," *Stimme* (11 Mar. 1951), P-A, D 515/3; "Vom Lastenausgleich zur Teilentschädigung," *Archiv,* hvp kommentare 18:52 (1 May 1952): 1.

56. Dr. Konrad Theiss, "Entschädigung oder Versorgung?" [summer 1948], in ACDP, NL Theiss, 005/II; Kriedemann in 13. Sitzung des Zonenbeirates der britisch-besetzten Zone, 8./9. July 1947, in Plum, ed., *Akten zur Vorgeschichte,* 3:241; "Lastenausgleich," *Deutsche Wirtschaft* (24 Sept. 1948), in BAK, B 126/5685.

57. "Report no. 169, German Appraisals of Lastenausgleich," 6 May 1949, IfZ, OMGUS, DK 110.001.

58. Connelly, "The Uses of *Volksgemeinschaft,*" esp. 901–4, 928–29; see also Stolleis, "Gemeinschaft und Volksgemeinschaft," 101.

59. Schröder, "Kriegsschadenrecht in Gesetzgebung," in BmI, ed., *Lastenausgleichsgesetze,* 4/1:435–79.

60. Dr. Ulrich Leffson, "Im Dienst sozialen Ausgleichs," *Deutsche Zeitung und Wirtschafts-zeitung,* 12 Apr. 1950, in BAK, B 102/8227-1; Kather to Holzapfel, 26 Nov. 1948, BAK, NL Holzapfel, no. 187; "Was bedeutet Lastenausgleich?" *Nachrichtendienst des deutschen Vereins für öffentliche und private Fürsorge* 1948, no. 12 (Dec. 1948): 222, in BAK, B 126/5691.

61. See below, chaps. 5 and 9.

62. For Basic Law, see Benz, *Von der Besatzungsherrschaft,* 233–35; Schwarz, "Modernisie-rung oder Restauration?"

63. R. Nöll von der Nahmer, "Vermögensausgleich," *Allgemeine Zeitung,* 17 Oct. 1947, in Z 32/52; F. Blücher (FDP) in *Wörtliche Berichte, Wirtschaftsrat,* 2:241; Kurt Schumacher, "Von der Freiheit zur sozialen Gerechtigkeit," 23 June 1947, in Schumacher, *Reden und Schriften,* 117; A. Bauser, "Abwertung oder Blockierung?" *Selbsthilfe* 22, no. 3 (1 Feb. 1948): 1; Entschließung des Bayerischen Gewerkschaftsbundes zum Lastenausgleich, BAK, NL Blücher, no. 325.

CHAPTER 3

1. Eisenberg, *Drawing the Line,* esp. 9–10; Mastny, *Cold War;* Leffler, *Struggle for Germany,* 13–14, passim.

2. Paterson, *Meeting the Communist Threat,* 18–34; Eisenberg, *Drawing the Line,* 16–20, passim; Yergin, "Shattered Peace," 113–14, 119–21.

3. LaFeber, *America, Russia, and the Cold War,* 35–37, 44; Deighton, *Impossible Peace,* 49, 209; Mastny, *Cold War,* 23–24; Soutou, "Frankreich und die Deutschlandfrage," 100–106, 111–12.

4. Schwarz, *Adenauer;* Wilfried Loth, "Adenauers Ort in der deutschen Geschichte," in Foschepoth, ed., *Adenauer und deutsche Frage,* 273–77.

5. Gimbel, *Origins of Marshall Plan;* Eisenberg, *Drawing the Line,* 234–40; Bennett signed Clay to AGWAR, Personal for Echols, 31 July 1946, NA RG 260, Box 74.

6. Hughes, "Lastenausgleich unter Sozialismusverdacht," 38–39; Clay to War Department, 23 May 1946, NA RG 200, Box 1.

7. Colm, Dodge, and Goldsmith, "Plan for Liquidation of War Finance," esp. 209–14, 218, 221–22, 224.

8. Ibid., 206 (quote), 211–14; Krohn, *Intellectuals in Exile,* 169.

9. Colm, Dodge, and Goldsmith, "Plan for Liquidation of War Finance," 208, 230; "Niederschrift über die Besprechung von Mr. Dodge mit den Ministerpräsidenten," 8 May 1946, 3, BAK, Z 1/311, Bl. 241.

10. Krohn, *Intellectuals in Exile,* 53–54, 127–29; A. Bauser and Dr. Kaufmann, "Denkschrift zur Währungs- und Finanzreform," Apr. 1947, BAK, Z 1/311; Hans Luther, "Entwurf einer Zwischenlösung," Mid-Feb. 1946, BAK, Z 1/311.

11. Clay, *Decision in Germany,* 210; Clay to Echols, 23 May 1946, and Bennett (signed Clay) to Echols, 8 July 1946, NA RG 260, Box 74, File AG 100.

12. Haraldson to Kindleberger, 12 July 1946, NA RG 59, Box 6575; OMGUS (Clay) to WDSCA, 20 Aug. 1946, Laird to Rusk, 20 Aug. 1946, and Dean Rusk, "Memorandum for the Asst. Secretary of War," 4 Sept. 1946, all in NA RG 107, Box 8 (ASW 091 Germany). For a more detailed discussion of American concerns, see Hughes, "Lastenausgleich unter Sozialismusverdacht."

13. For American attitudes, Cunliffe, *Right to Property,* esp. 16, 18–19; Bennett, *Demagogues in Depression,* esp. 60, 117, 120–23; *Wall Street Journal,* 1946–49. For German attitudes, see below, chap. 5; for Clay et al., see, e.g., Clay to Echols, 8 July 1946, and Clay to AGWAR, 3 Aug. 1946, NA RG 260, Box 74, AG 100.

14. "Extract from Minutes of 2d Special Meeting," 18 Sept. 1946, NA RG 260, Box 24, File 1; Jack Bennett, "Memorandum for General Clay," 19 Sept. 1946, NA RG 260, Box 119, File 7; Gottlieb, *German Peace Settlement,* 103–22, esp. 103–5, 112, 115–16; Mai, *Alliierte Kontrollrat,* 257–60, 279–95; Laufer, "UdSSR und deutsche Währungsfrage," 467–68, 474–75.

15. Schillinger, *Entscheidungsprozeß beim Lastenausgleich,* 69–70; "Amerikanischer Vorschlag zur Währungsreform," *Selbsthilfe* 20, no. 14 (15 Oct. 1946): 1; A. Bauser and Dr. Kaufmann, "Zur Währungs- und Finanzreform," ibid. 21, no. 5 (15 Apr. 1947): 1.

16. Möller, *Zur Vorgeschichte der Mark;* BAK, Z 32.

17. Benz, *Von der Besatzungsherrschaft,* 37–41, 43–48, 51–53, 58–64, 108–16.

18. Brackmann, *Vom totalen Krieg,* 244–45.

19. For a fuller discussion of these issues, see Hughes, "Hard Heads, Soft Money?"

20. Brackmann, *Vom totalen Krieg,* 254–58; Schillinger, *Entscheidungsprozeß beim Lasten-ausgleich,* 94; Paul Binder, "Das deutsche Währungsproblem: Vortrag Binder," [early 1948], ACDP, NL Binder 007 A I/14; Lorenz Wolkersdorf, "Sozial gerechte Währungsreform," *Der Bund,* no. 1 (3 Jan. 1948), in ASD, K 291/1947, 1948 I.

21. For quote: Sonderstelle Geld und Kredit, "Kurzgefaßte Darstellung des Währungs-plans," 12 Jan. 1948, IfZ, Sammlung Möller, SGK II; also, e.g., 18. Sitzung, 20 Nov. 1947, 10–13, and 44. Sitzung, 26 Feb. 1948, 3, both in IfZ, Sammlung Möller, Protokolle der Sonderstelle Geld und Kredit.

22. See, e.g., 18. Sitzung, 20 Nov. 1947, 10–13, IfZ, Sammlung Möller, Protokolle der Sonderstelle Geld und Kredit; § 8 of "Entwurf eines Gesetzes zur Neuordnung des Geld-wesens," in Möller, ed., *Zur Vorgeschichte der Mark,* 479–80, 482–83.

23. "Erstes Ergebnis der Währungsbesprechungen der Sonderstelle Geld und Kredit," IfZ, Sammlung Möller, Geld Neuordnung; 16. Sitzung, 13 Nov. 1947, 4–7, IfZ, Sammlung Möller, Protokolle der Sonderstelle Geld und Kredit; C. Fischer and W. Budczies, "Erster Entwurf, Begründung," IfZ, Sammlung Möller, Begründung zum Gesetz zur Neuordnung des Geldwesens, 23–24, 61, 63–64.

24. See, e.g., 42. Sitzung, 19 Feb. 1948, IfZ, Sammlung Möller, Protokolle der Sonderstelle

Geld und Kredit; C. Fischer and W. Budczies, "Erster Entwurf, Begründung," 35; "Entwurf eines Gesetzes zur Neuordnung des Geldwesens," in Möller, ed., *Zur Vorgeschichte der Mark,* 492.

25. "Entwurf eines Gesetzes zur Neuordnung des Geldwesens," in Möller, ed., *Zur Vorgeschichte der Mark,* 495.

26. First quote: C. Fischer and W. Budczies, "Erster Entwurf, Begründung," 59, IfZ, Sammlung Möller, Begründung zum Gesetz zur Neuordnung des Geldwesens; Erhard quote: 8. Sitzung, 8 Jan. 1948, 13–14, IfZ, Sammlung Möller, Protokolle der Sonderstelle Geld und Kredit.

27. Brackmann, *Vom totalen Krieg,* 254–58; 31. Sitzung, 10 Jan. 1948, 32. Sitzung, 11 Jan. 1948, 33. Sitzung, 13 Jan. 1948, 38. Sitzung, 4 Feb. 1948 (Erhard quote, 8), all in IfZ, Sammlung Möller, Protokolle der Sonderstelle Geld und Kredit. For arguments against capital levies, see below, chap. 6.

28. Brackmann, *Vom totalen Krieg,* 254–58; see the scathing critique by OMGUS finance expert Jack Bennett: "Memorandum To: General Lucius D. Clay," 5 Mar. 1948, NA RG 260, Box 93, File 13; Dr. E. Wolf, "Zum Problem der Vermögensabgabe und des Lastenausgleichs," 25 Mar. 1948, IfZ, Sammlung Möller, Materialien Vermögensabgabe.

29. "Besprechung mit den Generälen Clay und Robertson," 14 Apr. 1948, BAK, Z 3 — Anhang/1; W. Budczies, "Vermerk," IfZ, Sammlung Möller, Materialien Vermögensabgabe; "Entwurf eines Gesetzes zur Neuordnung des Geldwesens," in Möller, ed., *Zur Vorgeschichte der Mark,* 493–95. Curt Fischer, in "Entwurf zur Neuordnung des Geldwesens," 99, 102, in BAK, NL Blücher, no. 354.

30. Francke and Nitsch, "Beitrag der Währungsumstellung"; Kitterer, "Rechtfertigung und Risiken."

31. Möller, "Die westdeutsche Währungsreform von 1948," 447; Länderrat des Vereinigten Wirtschaftsgebietes to General Clay, 28 May 1948, NA RG 260, Box 365; "Konferenz der Minister Präsidenten der amerikanischen, britischen und französischen Besatzungszonen," 28 May 1948, in Weisz, ed., *Akten zur Vorgeschichte,* 4:533; Holtfrerich, "Die Deutsche Bank, 1945–1957," 439.

32. Eisenberg, *Drawing the Line,* esp. 280–81, 289–91; Manfred Knapp, "Das Deutschlandproblem und die Ursprünge des europäischen Wiederaufbauprogramms," 22–31, and "Deutschland und der Marshallplan," 35–59.

33. Mastny, *Cold War,* 27–29; LaFeber, *America, Russia, and the Cold War,* 61.

34. Knapp, "Deutschland und der Marshallplan," 52–54; Eisenberg, *Drawing the Line,* 319, 322–27, passim; H. Berger and A. Ritschl, "Germany and the Political Economy of the Marshall Plan, 1947–1952: A Re-revisionist View," in Eichengreen, ed., *Europe's Postwar Recovery,* 211–14; Memorandum of Conversation by the Under Secretary of State, 21 May 1948, in U.S. Department of State, *Foreign Relations of the United States, 1948,* 2:271–72.

35. Chambers, "Post-War German Finances," 371; Brackmann, *Vom totalen Krieg,* 236; Buchheim, "Die Währungsreform 1948," 207–8.

36. Buchheim, "Die Währungsreform 1948," 208–9; for German openness to separate currency reforms, see, e.g., Paul Binder to Prof. Gerhard Colm, 1 Apr. 1946, ACDP, NL Binder, I 105/039; Memorandum of Conversation by the Political Adviser for Germany (Murphy), 18 Dec. 1947, in U.S. Department of State, *Foreign Relations of the United States, 1947,* 2:827; see also ibid., 819–20, 830; Mai, *Alliierte Kontrollrat,* 297–99.

37. Jack Bennett to Sir Eric Coates, 23 Dec. 1947, NA RG 59, Box 3764A; General Clay's Statement at the First Meeting, [Jan. 1948], NA RG 260, Box 102, File 4; Brackmann, *Vom totalen Krieg,* 240; Mai, *Der alliierte Kontrollrat,* 299–301; Laufer, "UdSSR und deutsche Währungsfrage," 478–79, 484–85.

38. LaFeber, *America, Russia, and the Cold War,* 73; Eisenberg, *Drawing the Line,* 369; Niethammer, "Structural Reform," 231–32.

39. Frank Wisner to [Robert] Lovett, w/Tab A, 10 Mar. 1948, NA RG 59, Box 3769.

40. Eisenberg, *Drawing the Line,* 390–92; Mai, *Der alliierte Kontrollrat,* 303; Buchheim, "Die Währungsreform 1948," 210–11.

41. Brackmann, *Vom totalen Krieg,* 241–42; Mai, *Der alliierte Kontrollrat;* Teleconference, Clay, Draper, and Gray, 12 Mar. 1948, in Smith, ed., *Papers of General Clay,* 2:574–75; Clay to Draper, 6 June 1948, in ibid., 669–70.

42. For Germans, see Hielscher, *Jahrhundert der Inflation,* 40; J. C. deWilde to Mr. Saltzman, 22 Jan. 1948, NA RG 59, Box 6576; Turner, "Great Britain and German Currency Reform," 702–7; for Clay, see, e.g., Clay for Royall, 20 Mar. 1948 [marked "Not sent"], in Smith, ed., *Papers of General Clay,* 2:589–90.

43. J. C. deWilde to Mr. Saltzman, 22 Jan. 1948, NA RG 59, Box 6576; Hamby, *Beyond New Deal,* 82–84, passim; Teleconference, Draper and Clay, 13 Sept. 1947, in Smith, ed., *Papers of General Clay,* 1:427; Clay personal for Royall, [Mar. 1948], ("Not Sent"), in ibid., 2:589–95.

44. See Buchheim, "Die Währungsreform 1948," 205–6; Hielscher, *Leidensweg der Währungsreform,* 14, 26–27, 38, and 39, though Hielscher wanted the sharp shock to be followed by "flexible" credit for *business;* Jack Bennett to General Lucius D. Clay, 5 Mar. 1948, NA RG 260, Box 93; see also the comments of Tennenbaum in, e.g., 18. Sitzung, 20 Nov. 1947, in IfZ, Sammlung Möller, Protokolle der Sonderstelle Geld und Kredit.

45. For quote: "Zonenbeirats-Rahmengutachten," Aug./Sept. 1946, in Möller, ed., *Zur Vorgeschichte der Mark,* 289; also "Mindener Gutachten," in ibid., 346; "Abschrift. Wortlaut des Hamburger Senatgutachtens zur Währungsfrage," [Sept. 1945], 12, BAK, Z 32/36.

46. Turner, "Great Britain and German Currency Reform," 698, 702–4; Buchheim, "Marshall Plan and Currency Reform," 70; see also the British representative to the Special Agency for Money and Credit, Mr. Knoblock, in 18. Sitzung, 20 Nov. 1947, in IfZ, Sammlung Möller, Protokolle der Sonderstelle Geld und Kredit.

47. For Erhard, see Carter, *How German Is She?* 46; Wünsche, *Ludwig Erhards,* 123.

48. Brackmann, *Vom totalen Krieg,* 260–61; Wandel, *Entstehung der Bank deutscher Länder,* 106–18.

49. Hielscher, *Leidensweg der Währungsreform,* 27, 19, passim; "Mittwoch, 12. Mai 1948," IfZ, Sammlung Möller, Protokolle der Plenarsitzungen [Rothwesten]; "Dienstag 11. Mai," ibid.; Wrede, "Eigene Haltung bei der gemeinsamen Aussprache zw. den Vertretern der Militärregierung, den Mitgliedern der deutschen Währungsausschusses und den Sachverständigen im Konklave," 11 May 1948, IfZ, Sammlung Möller, Schlußverhandlungen; Buchheim, "Die Währungsreform 1948," 214–15.

50. Buchheim, "Die Währungsreform 1948," 214–15; Turner, "Great Britain and German Currency Reform," 704–5.

51. "Die Regelung der privaten Schuldverhältnisse," 10 May 1948, IfZ, Sammlung Möller, Protokolle der Plenarsitzungen in Konklave; von Wrede, "Eigene Haltung . . . Behandlung der privaten Schuldverhältnisse," 12 May 1948, IfZ, Sammlung Möller, Schlußverhandlungen; Buchheim, "Die Währungsreform 1948," 214. Cf. Brackmann, *Vom totalen Krieg,* 266.

52. Hielscher, *Jahrhundert der Inflation,* 34.

53. Dickhaus, "Bank deutscher Länder," 168–69.

54. Wandel, *Entstehung Bank deutscher Länder,* 76–77; "Unsoziale Währungsreform Sozialer Lastenausgleich," *Selbsthilfe* 23, no. 13 (5 July 1948): 1.

55. "Wieder ehrliches Geld für ehrliche Arbeit," *Stuttgarter Zeitung* (19 June 1948), in BmVt, ed., *Dokumente Kriegsschäden,* 2/1:713–14; Brackmann, *Vom totalen Krieg,* 262–68; Buchheim, "Die Währungsreform 1948," 215.

56. Clay, *Decision in Germany,* 212–13; Buchheim, "Die Währungsreform 1948," 216–17; Eisenberg, *Drawing the Line,* 394–404.

57. Wandel, *Entstehung Bank deutscher Länder,* 122, 129–30.

58. Military Government—Germany, *Laws no. 61–63;* Winkel, *Wirtschaft im geteilten Deutschland,* 56–57.

59. § 14, Law no. 63, Military Government—Germany, *Laws no. 61–63;* Scott, "Money Talks," 319–20; "Entwurf, Kriegsfolgelastengesetz," *VerhBT, Anlage,* Drucksache 1659, 43; "Urteil des Bundesverfassungsgerichts, 1 BvR 987/58," 14 Nov. 1962, in BmI, ed., *Lasten-ausgleichsgesetze,* 4/1:378, passim.

60. Der Chef des Büros für Währungsfragen, "Kurzinfo über Tagesnachrichten," 7 July 1948, and Junius, "Anrechnung der Kopfquote," *Süddeutsche Zeitung* (26 June 1948), both in BAK, Z 26/372/373; Arbeitsgemeinschaft deutscher Sparkassen und Giroverbände, "Berück-sichtigung der Sparer innerhalb des Sofortprogramms des Lastenausgleichs," [Oct. 1948], ACDP, NL Binder, I 105/043; "Besprechung der Militärgouveneure mit bizonalen Vertretern," 15 July 1948, in Weisz, ed., *Akten zur Vorgeschichte,* 4:682–83.

61. Buchheim, "Die Währungsreform 1948," 217–18; Brackmann, *Vom totalen Krieg,* 271; Kramer, *West German Economy,* 134–35; "Auf ihre Verantwortung, Herr General Clay!" *Selbsthilfe* 22, no. 20 (2. Okt. Ausg. 1948): 1; Dr. F. Sarow, "Der zweite Geldschnitt im Westen," *Telegraf* (9 Oct. 1948), in BAK, Z 26/372/373.

62. Schillinger, *Entscheidungsprozeß beim Lastenausgleich,* 107; Brackmann, *Vom totalen Krieg,* 275, 286; Buchheim, "Die Währungsreform 1948," 228; Niethammer, "Privat-Wirtschaft," 82, 85–86.

63. For a contemporary recognition that pensions and social insurance payments consti-tuted capital, see, e.g., [ehemalige Wehrmachtsangehörige] to Wirtschaftsrat, 22 Aug. 1949, BAK, B 126/5704; Military Govt. Law No. 61, Article II, Military Government—Germany, *Laws no. 61–63;* Arbeitsgemeinschaft für betriebliche Altersfürsorge to Harmening, 17 July 1948, BAK, Z 26/484.

64. "Rundfunksprache von Franz Blücher," 20 June 1948, *Kurze Nachrichten,* THA, D 2-1; Niethammer, "Privat-Wirtschaft," 82–87; "Unsoziale Währungsreform Sozialer Lasten-ausgleich," *Selbsthilfe* 22, no. 13 (5 July 1948): 1; Karl Albrecht, "Nicht Lastenausgleich—: Gerechte Sozialhilfe!" 3 Nov. 1948, ACDP, NL Binder, 013 B I.1; Frau Catharine Oechsner to Direktoren des Bizonalen Amtes, 10 Apr. 1949, BAK, B 126/5704; for quote: Major a. D. F. Keller to Verwaltung für Finanzen, 8 Jan. 1949, BAK, B 126/5681.

CHAPTER 4

1. Overesch, "Einheit oder Teilung?"; Eisenberg, *Drawing the Line,* esp. 489–90.

2. Davison, *Berlin Blockade,* 100–102, 139–41, 168–69, 281–89; Eisenberg, *Drawing the Line,* esp. 427, 435–36; Benz, *Von der Besatzungsherrschaft,* 144–45, 156; Klotzbach, *Weg zur Staats-partei,* 160–64; entries for mid-1948 and following in Troeger [SPD], *Interregnum. Tagebuch, 1947–1949;* Hans Apel, "Noch einmal davongekommen?" in Friedrich, *Mein Kopfgeld,* 145.

3. Clay, *Decision in Germany,* 409–11; Benz, *Von der Besatzungsherrschaft,* 156–75.

4. See, e.g., Plumpe, *Vom Plan zum Markt;* Ambrosius, *Durchsetzung der Sozialen Marktwirtschaft;* Klotzbach, *Weg zur Staatspartei,* esp. 80–81, 122, 147, 149–50, 153–54; for bureaucratic arbitrariness, see, e.g., G. Weisser [SPD], "Auszug aus meinem Schreiben an den Allgemeinen Deutschen Gewerkschaftsbund Rheinland-Pfalz," 28 Aug. 1948, ASD, NL Weisser, no. 1244; Niethammer, "Privat-Wirtschaft," esp. 60–61, 64, 94; Nicholls, *Freedom with Responsibility,* 215.

5. Nicholls, *Freedom with Responsibility*, 212–17; Erhard, *Kriegsfinanzierung* and other writings; Abelshauser, *Wirtschaftsgeschichte*, 52–53.

6. Nicholls, *Freedom with Responsibility*, 214–18; Benz, *Von der Besatzungsherrschaft*, 145–49.

7. Abelshauser, *Wirtschaftsgeschichte*, 72–75; Wallich, *Mainsprings*, 16, 18–19, 78–79; Dietrich, *Eigentum für Jeden*.

8. Buchheim, "Die Währungsreform 1948," 224–25; Kramer, *West German Economy*, 144–48, 163, 166. See the brief memoirs in Friedrich, *Mein Kopfgeld*.

9. Erhard, *Kriegsfinanzierung*, 167–69; Möller, "Die westdeutsche Währungsreform," 462, 466–71; Turner, "Great Britain and German Currency Reform," 705; Drexler, *Planwirtschaft in Westdeutschland*, 170–71.

10. Kramer, *West German Economy*, 146; Nicholls, *Freedom with Responsibility*, 221–22, 224–25.

11. Quote cited in Dickhaus, "Bank deutscher Länder," 168, and see also 173–74; Buchheim, "Die Währungsreform 1948," 227–30; Hardach, *Marshallplan*, 254–55.

12. Vertretung der Ostdeutschen Betriebe to Verwaltung für Finanzen, 13 Oct. 1948, BAK, B 102/8215/1; Heimatvertriebene des Kreises Hanau am Main, "Resolution!" 25 July 1948, BAK, B 126/5760; "Arbeitsschutz für Ostvertriebene!" *Ostvertriebenen-Korrespondenz* 1, no. 4 (25 Aug. 1948); Nahm, *Sich selbst geholfen*, e.g., 23–24, 26, 51; Connor, "Refugees and Currency Reform," 305–16.

13. For traditional state role, see, e.g., Henderson, *Rise of German Industrial Power*, esp. 71–79, 207–33; for postwar West Germany, see, e.g., Berghahn, *Americanisation*, 20–21, 111–16, 124–27, 155–81, passim; Kollmer von Oheimb-Loup, "Die Wirtschaftspolitik Erhards," esp. 467–68, 474–76; "Gutachten," esp. 27 Feb. 1949, 8 May 1949, in Der wissenschaftliche Beirat, *Gutachten*, 51–60.

14. "Letzte Hoffnung der Ostvertriebenen," *Ostvertriebenen-Korrespondenz* 1, no. 5 (5 Sept. 1948): 1; "200,000 demonstrieren," *Selbsthilfe* 22, no. 19 (1. Okt. Ausg. 1948): 1; Arbeitsgemeinschaft der IHK des Vereinigten Wirtschaftsgebietes, "Leitsätze . . . zum Lastenausgleich," 4 Oct. 1948, ACDP, NL Binder, 043 C II/3A; "Tagung über Fragen des Lastenausgleichs, Karlshöhe," 13–15 Aug. 1948, ACDP, NL Binder, 044 C II/3B.

15. "Tagung über Fragen des Lastenausgleichs, Karlshöhe," 13–15 Aug. 1948, ACDP, NL Binder, 044 C II/3B, 5; for communalist logic, see chap. 2 below; "Nicht Lastenausgleich, aber Hilfe," *Christ und Welt* (21 Aug. 1948), in BAK, B 126/5759.

16. Aristotle, *Politics*, book 3, chap. 9; Kamenka and Tay, *Justice*; for quote: "Vorschläge des Zentralverbandes der Fliegergeschädigten und Währungsgeschädigten zum Entwurf eines Gesetzes über einen Allgemeinen Lastenausgleich," [17 Mar. 1951], 1 BAK, B 126/5699; see also, e.g., Diehl, *Thanks of the Fatherland*, 144, 147, 149; Geyer, "Vorbote des Wohlfahrtsstaates," 250.

17. "Währungsreform und Besitzlose," *Der Neubürger* 2, no. 7 (July 1948), in ACDP, NL Theiss, 015/III; "Unsere Forderungen zur Innenpolitik," *Selbsthilfe* 23, no. 16 (2. Sept. Ausg. 1949).

18. Seraphim, *Heimatvertriebenen in Sowjetzone*, 32–38; Wille, "Zentralverwaltung, Umsiedler," 49–50; Ther, "Expellees in Germany and Poland," 793–94, 799.

19. "Lastenausgleich! Gründe und Gegengründe der Sozialdemokratie," [ca. Dec. 1950], 4–5, in ASD, NL Weisser, no. 1080; Anton Wopperer, "Das wohlbestellte Haus," 21 Aug. 1948, 3, in ACDP, NL Binder, 044 C II 3B; "Gerechte Verteilung der Lasten," *Badische Zeitung*, 9 Sept. 1948, in BAK, B 126/5691; businessman Karl Albrecht, "Nicht Lastenausgleich — Gerechte Sozialhilfe!" 3 Nov. 1948, ACDP, NL Binder 013 B I.1.

20. Burleigh and Wippermann, *Racial State;* Bartov, *Hitler's Army,* esp. 71, 85, 87, 111–12, 154–55; § 1 of Basic Law in Hildebrandt, *Quellen,* 32.

21. For quote: Dr. Anton Moser, "Tun wie neugeboren," *Wirtschaftszeitung,* 8 Oct. 1948, in BAK, B 126/5759; "Sozialdemokratische Grundsätze zum Lastenausgleich," [summer 1948], BAK, NL Blücher, no. 325; "Stellungnahme der Industrie- und Handelskammer Braunschweig zum Lastenausgleich," 27 Aug. 1948, BAK, B 126/5680; "Gespräch über den Lastenausgleichsentwurf . . . Dr. Kunze (CSU [*sic*])—Seufert [*sic*] (SPD)," 24 Jan. 1951, 5, BAK, B 150/3293.

22. R. Gerstung, "Der Lastenausgleich ist kein Konkursverfahren," *Sozialdemokratischer Pressedienst* 3, no. 85 (19 July 1948): 2; [Lorenz] Wolkersdorf, "Stellungnahme zum Gesetzentwurf des Allgemeinen Gerwerkschaftsbundes Rheinland-Pfalz über den Lastenausgleich," 30 Nov. 1949, 7, BAK, B 126/5759.

23. Brandes, "Das Lastenausgleichsproblem," [July 1948], 8, ASD, NL Weisser, no. 1086.II; Kunze, "Erste Aufgabe für den Bundestag," *Freie Presse,* [July 1949], in ASD, NL Weisser, no. 1080.

24. Ludwig Vaubel, "Einführung," in Walter-Raymond-Stiftung, ed., *Eigentum und Eigentümer,* 15; Soyka, *Währung,* 3–5; Schelsky, *Wandlungen der deutschen Familie,* 178–80, 187.

25. Rettet die Menschen, *Geldwirtschaftliche Neuordnung unter Anerkennung aller Schäden und Erhaltung des Sparkapitals,* 1947, in BAK, Z 32/39; Elisabeth von Behr, in "Schreiben der Rentenempfänger an ihr Versicherungsunternehmen," [July 1948], in BAK, NL Holzapfel, no. 112 (her emphasis).

26. Gerhard Brandes, "Das Lastenausgleichsproblem," [July 1948], ASD, K 291/I; "Vermögensausgleich aus dem Steueraufkommen," *Handelsblatt* no. 2 (8 Jan. 1948), in BAK, Z 32/52; for the expellees and their children, see chap. 9 below.

27. A. Bauser, "Unsoziale Währungsreform Sozialer Lastenausgleich," *Selbsthilfe* 22, no. 13 (5 July 1948): 1, and "Kleiner Mann—was nun?" ibid. 22, no. 14 (2. Juli Ausg. 1948): 2; Haussleiter in "Tagung über Fragen des Lastenausgleichs, Karlshöhe," 13–15 Aug. 1948, 5, ACDP, NL Binder 044 C II 3B.

28. Hermann Pünder in "24. Vollversammlung," 9–10 Nov. 1948, *Wörtliche Berichte, Wirtschaftsrat,* 2:1080; Bund der Fliegergeschädigten, Landesverband Nordrhein-Westfalen, "Berücksichtigung der Fliegergeschädigten," [Oct. 1948], ASD, NL Weisser, no. 457; Kather to Pünder, 16 Sept. 1948, BAK, NL Holzapfel, no. 187; A. Bauser, "Ringen um den Lastenausgleich," *Selbsthilfe* 22, no. 17 (1. Sept. Ausg. 1948): 1.

29. See chap. 2 above for precurrency reform discussions; "Gemeinsame Sitzung der Finanzausschüsse des Wirtschaftsrates und des Landrates," 16 July 1948, BAK, Z 4/552; Drucksachen 397, 412, and 479, *Wörtliche Berichte, Wirtschaftsrat,* vol. 4; "18. Vollversammlung," 17 and 18 June 1948, ibid., 2:622–23; "19. Vollversammlung," 8 and 9 July 1948, ibid., 2:723–25, 738–42; "20. Vollversammlung," 17, 18, and 19 Aug. 1948, ibid., 2:841–43.

30. "Der große Gedanke der Einheit," *Ostvertriebenen-Korrespondenz* 1, no. 4 (25 Aug. 1948); A. Bauser, "Revision der Währungsreform?" *Selbsthilfe* 22, no. 16 (2. Aug. Ausg. 1948): 1.

31. See chap. 3 above.

32. See the debates in *Wörtliche Berichte, Wirtschaftsrat,* 2:1079–93, 1135–49, 1160–97, and 1265–67.

33. "SPD Ansichten haben sich durchgesetzt," *Frankfurter Rundschau* (1 Dec. 1948), in ASD, K 291/II; Mattes, "Verfälschter Lastenausgleich," *Selbsthilfe* 23, no. 1 (1. Jan. Ausg. 1949): 1.

34. Erhard, Wirtschaftsrat speech, 21 Apr. 1948, in Erhard, *Economics of Success,* 33–

34; Brackmann, *Vom totalen Krieg,* 251–52; for popular revulsion, see also Niethammer, "Privat-Wirtschaft," 81–82, 85–86.

35. For Erhard warning, Wirtschaftsrat speech, 21 Apr. 1948, in Erhard, *Economics of Success,* 34; for early recognition of economic advantages of such a levy, see, e.g., E. Hielscher to F. Blücher, 16 Apr. 1948, IfZ, Sammlung Möller, SGK IV/7–9, Materialien zur Geldreform; for Erhard quote, see "1. Sitzung des Ausschusses für den Lastenausgleich," 5 Nov. 1948, BAK, Z 3/85; Paul Binder, "Vortrag," 9 May 1948, ACDP, NL Binder, 007 A1/14.

36. For subsequent observers, see, e.g., Schillinger, *Entscheidungsprozeß beim Lasten-ausgleich,* 127–28, 132; Erhard, *Kriegsfinanzierung,* and *Prosperity through Competition,* esp. 100–140, 181–97.

37. For a sample of the flood of petitions from businesses, see, e.g., BAK, Z 13/858; "Kurz-bericht über die Sitzung der Finanzminister der 3 Westzonen am 25. Nov. 1948," BAK, NL Blücher, no. 327.

38. Blücher in "24. Vollversammlung," 9–10 Nov. 1948, *Wörtliche Berichte, Wirtschaftsrat,* 2:1086; Schillinger, *Entscheidungsprozeß beim Lastenausgleich,* 28; for Erhard quote: "Nieder-schrift, 7. Plenarsitzung, Gutachterkommission für den Lastenausgleich," 25 Oct. 1948, ACDP, NL Binder, 041 C II 1A.

39. See "26. Vollversammlung," 30 Nov.–1 Dec. 1948, *Wörtliche Berichte, Wirtschaftsrat,* 2:1173–76; "31. Vollversammlung," 19 Jan. 1949, ibid., 1379–80; Drucksache 777, ibid., vol. 5.

40. Arbeitsgemeinschaft der Industrie- und Handelskammern des Vereinigten Wirt-schaftsgebietes, "Entschließung, Hauptausschuß zum Lastenausgleich," 24 Nov. 1948, BAK, B102/8215-1; "Stellungnahme, industrielle Wirtschaftsverbände zum Sofortprogramm-Lastenausgleich," [Oct. 1948], ACDP, NL Binder 043 C II 3A.

41. "25. Vollversammlung," 19–20 Nov. 1948, *Wörtliche Berichte, Wirtschaftsrat,* 2:1136–37, 1139; "26. Vollversammlung," 30 Nov.–1 Dec. 1948, ibid., 2:1161, 1167–69, 1188; Mattes, "Verfälschter Lastenausgleich," *Selbsthilfe* 23, no. 1 (1. Jan. Ausg. 1949): 1–2; Haus- und Grundbesitzerverein Regensburg und Umgebung to Pünder, 25 Mar. 1949, BAK, Z 13/858.

42. "Begründung, Entwurf, des ersten Gesetzes zum Ausgleich der Lasten," 10 Nov. 1948, *Wörtliche Berichte, Wirtschaftsrat,* 4:1046–51; for Würzburg: Krause, *Flucht vor Bombenkrieg,* 231; for interwar efforts to get relatives to support indigents, see Crew, " 'Wohlfahrtsbrot ist bitteres Brot,' " 222–23; Mattes, "Verfälschter Lastenausgleich," *Selbsthilfe* 23, no. 1 (1. Jan. Ausg. 1949): 1; "Tagung über Fragen des Lastenausgleichs, Karlshöhe," 13–15 Aug. 1948, ACDP, NL Binder, 04 C II 3 B.

43. Haus- und Grundbesitzerverein Regensburg, "Entschließung," 13 Mar. 1949, BAK, Z13/858; "Stenographische Aufnahme [of Mattes speech]," 4 June [1950], BAK, B 126/5682; Weisser to Schäffer, 26 Feb. 1950, ASD, NL Weisser, no. 1079; "Stellungnahme des Deutschen Gewerkschaftsbundes . . . zum Allgemeinen Lastenausgleich," [10 Mar. 1951], P-A, I 332/B 7.

44. Franz Blücher, "Lasten-Ausgleich," *Kurze Nachrichten* 28 (1948), THA, NL Blücher, D 2-1; "Begründung zum zweiten und dritten Teil des Entwurfes des 1. Lastenausgleichs-gesetzes," 50, BAK, NL Blücher, no. 327; "24. Vollversammlung," 9–10 Nov. 1948, *Wörtliche Berichte, Wirtschaftsrat,* 2:1081 (Hartmann quote: 1083).

45. "24. Vollversammlung," 9–10 Nov. 1948, *Wörtliche Berichte, Wirtschaftsrat,* 2:1081, 1084–85; for alternative dates, see, e.g., W. Mattes, "Bedenkliche Tendenzen," *Selbsthilfe* 24, no. 3 (1. Feb. Ausg. 1950): 1; for business concern, Arbeitsgemeinschaft der Industrie- und Handelskammern des Vereinigten Wirtschaftsgebietes, "Leitsätze . . . zum Lastenausgleich," 4 Oct. 1948, ACDP, NL Binder, 043 C II 3A.

46. "24. Vollversammlung," 9–10 Nov. 1948, *Wörtliche Berichte, Wirtschaftsrat,* 2:1081, and "Begründung z. . . . ersten Gesetz zum Ausgleich von Kriegs- und Kriegsfolgeschäden," Drucksache 687, ibid., 5:1031.

47. Kather, *Die entscheidenden Jahre*, 131.

48. Johannes Dieter Steinert, "Organisierte Flüchtlingsinteressen und parlamentarische Demokratie: Westdeutschland 1945–1949," in Bade, *Neue Heimat im Westen*, esp. 62, 65–67, 69–70.

49. Günther Ziehm, "BHE im Kampf!" [1953], BAK, Zsg 1-54/15; for expellee faith up to 1948 in return, see, e.g., Neumann, *Block der Heimatvertriebenen*, 10; for neglect of Lastenausgleich in early discussions of refugee affairs, see, e.g., "Konferenz der deutschen Ministerpräsidenten, Zweiter Tag," 7 June 1947, IfZ, NL Staatssek. Dr. W. Strauß, 75:1–17; [Kanzlei des Ostkirchenausschusses], "Wort des Ostkirchenausschusses zum Lastenausgleich!" [Sept. 1948], ASD, NL Weisser, no. 1079; Karl Kaps, Georg Graf von Brühl, and Oskar Wacker-zapp, *Notwendiges Vertriebenenrecht* (1948): 3–4, in BAK, Z 2/100; Goebel quoted by P. P. Nahm in "Bericht über die Arbeitstagung der deutschen Flüchtlingsverwaltungen, 13./14. Sept. 1948," 1, BAK, B 126/5693.

50. See the articles in *Ostvertriebenen-Korrespondenz* 1, no. 4 (25 Aug. 1948): 1; Wambach, *Verbändestaat und Parteienoligopol*, 42, 71–72.

51. Blücher and Oellers in "24. Vollversammlung," 9–10 Nov. 1948, *Wörtliche Berichte, Wirtschaftsrat*, 2:1086–87; "25. Vollversammlung," 19–20 Nov. 1948, ibid., 1144–45; "26. Vollversammlung," 30 Nov.–1 Dec. 1948, ibid., 1171–72, 1180, 1189–90; "37. Vollversammlung," 23–25 May 1949, ibid., 1715; Dr. Oellers, "Erstes Lastenausgleichs-Gesetz und Vertriebene," *Kurze Nachrichten* 35 (3 Dec. 1948), in THA, NL Blücher, D 2-1.

52. Schillinger, *Entscheidungsprozeß beim Lastenausgleich*, 133–34; Hockerts, *Sozialpoli-tische Entscheidungen*, 90; Weisser to Erich [Ollenhauer?], 16 Aug. 1948, ASD, NL Weisser, no. 466.

53. For a detailed study of American attitudes, see Hughes, "Lastenausgleich unter Sozia-lismusverdacht" and sources cited there; "German Relief Tax Endorsed by West," *New York Times* (30 Apr. 1949): 2:5.

54. On levies on UN property, see the extended exchange of cables in NA RG 165, Box 505; "Lastenausgleich mit Hindernissen," *DUD* 3, no. 15 (21 Jan. 1949): 2.

55. "Fragen, die aufgrund der Entscheidung des Bipartite Board zu klären sind," 1 May 1949, BAK, B 126/5763; "Alliierte Vorbehalte zum Lastenausgleich," *SPD Pressepolitik* 4, no. 51 (2 May 1949), ASD, K 291, 1949/I (blau); "37. Vollversammlung," 23–25 May 1949, *Wörtliche Berichte, Wirtschaftsrat*, 2:1711–21, and Drucksache 1267, ibid., vol. 6.

56. Nahm, "Lastenausgleich und Integration der Vertriebenen und Geflüchteten," 820.

57. Dudek to Blücher, 1 Mar. 1949, BAK, NL Blücher, no. 336; Verwaltung für Finanzen to Vorsitzender [Dudek] der Gutachterkommission, 6 May 1949, BAK, B 126/5686; "Weiterarbeit am Lastenausgleich," *Handelsblatt* (15 July 1949), in BAK, B 126/5691.

CHAPTER 5

1. Mommsen, "Der lange Schatten der untergehenden Republik," 388–89, 392–96; Prowe, "Democratization as Restabilization"; Benz, *Von der Besatzungsherrschaft*, 177–235; Benz, "Die Diskussion um deutsche demokratische Traditionen," and "Verfassungspläne und Demo-kratiekonzepte in Widerstand, Exil und unter alliierter Herrschaft," both in Benz, *Zwischen Hitler und Adenauer*.

2. See the comments in Pohl, *Adenauers Verhältnisse*, 66, 69; Koerfer, *Kampf ums Kanzler-amt*, 53–54, 56, 59; "Wirtschaftspolitische Leitsätze der CDU," in Heck, ed., *CDU und ihr Programm*, 26–38.

3. For election results, Ritter and Niehuss, *Wahlen in der Bundesrepublik*, 74; Adenauer, *Erinnerungen 1945–1953*, 223–30; the introduction and documents in Wengst, ed., *Auftakt zur*

Ära Adenauer, esp. "Aufzeichnung Gebhard Müller," 21 Aug. 1949, 33–41; Schulz, "Konrad Adenauers gesellschaftspolitische Vorstellungen," 168; Birke, *Nation ohne Haus*, 245–49.

4. Adenauer in *VerhBT, Sten. Ber.*, 5. Sitzung (20 Sept. 1949): 22; Morsey, "Adenauer und Bundestag," 24–27; Edinger, *Schumacher*, 88–89; Mommsen, "Der lange Schatten der untergehenden Republik," 396–97.

5. Adenauer in *VerhBT, Sten. Ber.*, 5. Sitzung (20 Sept. 1949): 23 (his emphasis), 25; Adenauer, "Rede vor Studenten im Chemischen Institut der Universität Bonn, 21. Juli 1948," in Adenauer, *Reden*, 108–9; Schillinger, *Entscheidungsprozeß beim Lastenausgleich*, 154–55; "Die Kriegsgeschädigten zur Bonner Regierungserklärung," *Selbsthilfe* 23, no. 20 (2. Okt. Ausg. 1949): 1.

6. Lemberg and Edding, *Die Vertriebenen*, 1:534; Kather, *Die entscheidenden Jahre*, 186–87; for Lukaschek isolation in the cabinet, see, e.g., 70. Kabinettssitzung (31 May 1950) in Enders and Reiser, eds., *Kabinettsprotokolle der Bundesregierung*, 2:417.

7. [Karl-Ulrich Gelberg], "Einleitung," in Gelberg, ed., *Kabinett Schäffer*, 25–26; Henzler, *Fritz Schäffer*, 50–80, 93–186, 229–62; Niethammer, "Die amerikanische Besatzungsmacht," 186–87.

8. For Schäffer comments, see, e.g., M.-G. Giesel, "Unfähigkeit," *Ost-West Kurier* 3, no. 5 (4–10 Feb. 1950); Kather to Bundeskanzler, 9 June 1950, BAK, B 136/644; "Wir fordern Schäffers Rücktritt," *Selbsthilfe* 24, no. 14 (2. Juli Ausg. 1950): 1; for Schäffer reservations about Lastenausgleich, [BmF] to ZvF, May 1950, BAK, B 126/5699.

9. For Schäffer's general tight-fistedness, see, e.g., Hockerts, *Sozialpolitische Entscheidungen*, 115 (quote), 119–21; Henzler, *Fritz Schäffer*, 71, 128–32, 307–10, 435, 501, passim; Wengst, *Beamtentum*, 89, 155, passim; 21. Kabinettssitzung (11 Nov. 1949) in Enders and Reiser, eds., *Kabinettsprotokolle der Bundesregierung*, 1:195.

10. Henzler, *Fritz Schäffer*, 229–30, 253–54, 457, passim; [Schäffer], "Dem Herrn Bundeskanzler vorzulegen," 4 Dec. 1950, BAK, B 136/644.

11. Diehl, *Thanks of the Fatherland*, 93–107, 116–40; Schulz, "Eigenheimpolitik," 415–16.

12. Arbeitsgemeinschaft der Kriegsgeschädigten Sitz Köln, "Einladung zu unserer II. Öffentlichen Protest-Kundgebung am Sonntag, den 4. Mai 1952," ACDP, NL Kuntscher, 008/1; Kather, "Die Mindestförderungen," 4 May 1952, in Kather, *Eingliederung durch Lastenausgleich*, 8, in BAK, B 150/4791-2; O. Blaß, "Christentum und Lastenausgleich," *Selbsthilfe* 22, no. 8 (15 Apr. 1948): 2.

13. Aristotle, *Politics*, book 3, chap. 9; Cupit, *Justice as Fittingness*, esp. 2–4; Kather, *Gerechter Lastenausgleich!* 3; von Plato, "Fremde Heimat," 210–11. For lowering wealth of the undamaged to raise wealth of the war-damaged proportionally, ZvD/ZvF, *Forderungen . . . zum Lastenausgleich*, Jan. 1949, BAK, B 126/5681.

14. Oskar Wackerzapp, "Lastenausgleich," *Das Blatt der Ostvertriebenen* Jhrg. 1948, no. 1, in BAK, B 126/5680; Dr. Hans Fülster, "Wirkt der Lasten-Ausgleich produktionshemmend?" *Deutscher Kurier*, no. 34 (30 Sept. 1951), in BAK, B 126/5714.

15. First quote: A. Liebisch et al. to Schäffer, 18 Jan. 1950, BAK, B 126/5693; [Landesvorsitzenden Grossing, ZvD], "Stellungnahme zum Lastenausgleich," 23 Dec. 1952, 4, BAK, B 136/7324; second quote: Gustav Dücker to Finanz Minister, 19 June 1950, BAK, B 126/5701.

16. Ida Garolick to Bundeskanzler, 28 Nov. 1950, BAK, B 126/5704; for quote: Lieschen Schnittka to Herr Direktor! 15 Nov. 1950, BAK, B 136/1186; Verband der Lebensversicherungsunternehmen to Verwaltung für Finanzen, 25 Aug. 1949, BAK, B 102/8227-1.

17. Andreas Huber to Finanzausschuß beim Wirtschaftsrat, 5 July 1948, BAK, B 126/5703; Julius Mangelsdorf to BmF Schäffer, 4 Mar. 1951 and 30 Sept. 1951, in BAK, B 126/5760; see the similar attitude of World War I–era rentiers: Führer, "Für das Wirtschaftsleben 'mehr oder weniger wertlose Personen,'" 169–70.

18. Bayerische Aufwertungs- und Interessengemeinschaft für Wertpapierbesitzer to Dr. Kaess [sic], 7 Apr. 1952, BAK, B 126/27886; for quote: Hellmuth Wissmann to BmF, 11 Aug. 1954, BAK, B 126/27887.

19. First quote: Wieder-Gutmachungs-Interessengemeinschaft der Total-Flieger- u. Währungsgeschädigten in Bayern to Adenauer, 16 Jan. 1952, BAK, B 148V/22; Dr. Karl Metzger to Direktor der Verwaltung der Finanzen, 27 June 1948, BAK, NL Holzapfel, no. 112; second quote: Otto Hermann Becker to Erhard, 4 May 1952, BAK, B 102/8227-2.

20. "Vorgefechte um den Lastenausgleich," *Selbsthilfe* 25, no. 8 (2. Apr. Ausg. 1951): 2; Oskar Wackerzapp, "Soforthilfe aus dem Lastenausgleich," *Ostvertriebenen-Korrespondenz* 1, no. 7 (5 Oct. 1948): 4.

21. Kather, "Die Mindestforderungen," 4 May 1952, in Kather, *Eingliederung durch Lastenausgleich*, 9; Diehl, *Thanks of the Fatherland*, 141–62; Wengst, *Beamtentum*.

22. O. Wackerzapp, "Lastenausgleich," *Das Blatt der Ostvertriebenen* 1948, no. 1, in BAK, B 126/5680; second quote: "Zusammenstellung von Äußerungen . . . [zum] Lastenausgleich," 11 May 1950, 7, BAK, B 136/7324; [Robert Wolf, Vorsitzer, Flüchtlingsausschuß Flensburg], "Vorschläge zum Lastenausgleich," [early 1950], BAK, B 126/5695; "Lastenausgleich (Alle sollen an Gesetzen mitarbeiten)," [1950?], BAK, B 150/3293; Kreisverband der Heimatvertriebenen Prüm/Eifel to Bundespräsidenten, [Nov. 1950], BAK, B 126/5696; Schelsky, *Wandlungen der deutschen Familie*, 192–218.

23. Philologenverband Niedersachsen, Arbeitsgemeinschaft der Kriegsverdrängten, to Flüchtlingsausschuß des Vereinigten Wirtschaftsrates, 22 Oct. 1948, BAK, B 126/5704; Dr. Fauser, "Grundlagen des endgültigen Lastenausgleichs," [Feb. 1950?], BAK, B 126/5678; Nahm, . . . *doch das Leben ging weiter*, 34; Seuffert and Gille in [Disputation], 34, 36, P-A, I 332/B 9.

24. For traditional poor relief, see Steinmetz, *Regulating the Social*, 157–63, passim; Kather, *Gerechter Lastenausgleich!* 3; "Fliegergeschädigte gründen Zentralverband," *Selbsthilfe* 21, no. 15 (15 Sept. 1947): 1; Deutscher Rentnerbund, "Der Vorrang der Alterssicherung und die Verrentung," [Jan. 1954?], BAK, B 126/27887.

25. Quote: Eugen Rapp, "Vorschläge zur Währungsreform und Lastenausgleich zur Herbeiführung gerechter, solider und beständiger Verhältnisse," 9 July 1948, BAK, B 126/5726; Tilly, "Moral Standards and Business Behavior," 190–93; Geyer, "Teuerungsprotest," 198–99, passim; Davis, "Home Fires Burning," 158–69.

26. First set of quotes: Eugen Rapp, "Vorschläge zur Währungsreform und Lastenausgleich zur Herbeiführung gerechter, solider und beständiger Verhältnisse," 9 July 1948, BAK, B 126/5726; second set of quotes: A. Bauser, "Grundrechte," *Selbsthilfe* 20, no. 12 (15 Sept. 1946), Bauser, "Abwertung oder Blockierung?" ibid. 22, no. 3 (1 Feb. 1948), and W. Mattes, "Währungsgeschädigte in Gefahr," ibid. 24, no. 13 (1. Juli Ausg. 1950). For recurrence of anti-Semitism, Karl Zaiger to Schäffer, 9 Feb. 1950, BAK, B 126/5679.

27. "Sozialdemokratische Grundsätze zum Lastenausgleich," [summer 1948], BAK, NL Blücher, no. 325; Verwaltung für Finanzen, "Volkswirtschaftliche Überlegungen zum endgültigen Lastenausgleich," 1 June 1949, 22, BAK, B 126/5686.

28. BmVt, "Entwurf. An das Zentralkommittee des Deutschen Katholikentages," 25 Aug. 1950, BAK, B 150/4820; Linus Kather in "Zweiter Parteitag der CDU für die britischen Zone, 28–29 Aug. 1948," in Pütz, ed., *Konrad Adenauer und die CDU*, 605; Adolf Bauser, "Lastenausgleich," *Selbsthilfe* 22, no. 10 (25 May 1948); Nöll von der Nahmer in "Der Proletarier als Bürger," ibid. 23, no. 14 (2. Juli Ausg. 1949).

29. Deutscher Rentnerbund, "Entwurf für Sofortprogramm," 19 June 1951, BAK, B 126/27886; Karl Wilhelm Böttcher, "Die deutschen Flüchtlinge als europäisches Problem," *Frankfurter Hefte* 3, no. 7 (July 1948): 602; Oskar Wackerzapp, "Sozialer oder sozialistischer

Ausgleich," *VK* 2, no. 4 (27 Jan. 1951): 15. See here Geyer, "Teuerungsprotest," 182–83; Ryan, *Property and Political Theory.*

30. "Begriff und Grenzen des Eigentums," *Selbsthilfe* 22, no. 5 (1 Mar. 1948): 2; Kops, von Brühl, and Wackerzapp, *Notwendiges Vertriebenenrecht,* 7, in BAK, Z 20/100.

31. Albert Schnell, "Lastenausgleich, die große Aufgabe," [early 1948], BAK, Z 32/39; quotes from Mattes, "Verbesserte Aussichten," *Selbsthilfe* 24, no. 12 (2. Juni Ausg. 1950), and Mattes, "Währungsgeschädigte in Gefahr," ibid. 24, no. 13 (1. Juli Ausg. 1950).

32. For fortuitousness, among hundreds of examples, Gerhard Jaeck, [received 7 May 1948], 1, BAK, Z32/47; F. Pratje to O. A. de Kat, 10 May 1949, ASD, NL Weisser, no. 456; R. Scholl, "Ist ein Lastenausgleich möglich?" [summer 1948], ACDP, NL Binder, 044 C II 3B; see here also Jolles, *Zur Soziologie der Heimatvertriebenen,* 43, 108–9, 361–62; for relative innocence, A. Bauser, "Innere Wiedergutmachung," *Selbsthilfe* 21, no. 8 (1 June 1947): 2; for state intervention, [Dr. Hinz], "Betr.: Lastenausgleich," [May 1950], BAK, B 150/4820. World War I–era rentiers devastated by inflation used similar terminology of relative innocence: Crew, " 'Wohlfahrtsbrot ist bitteres Brot,' " 219.

33. Sombart, *Die vorkapitalistische Wirtschaft,* 183, 185–87, 188–93, 204–8, passim; Walker, *German Home Towns,* 101, passim; Stürmer, *Herbst des alten Handwerks,* 16, 107–9.

34. See, e.g., Frey, *Der reinliche Bürger,* 156–57, 255–56, passim; Münch, *Ordnung, Fleiß und Sparsamkeit,* 9–26, passim.

35. Thompson, "Moral Economy of the English Crowd," 79 (quote); [Schäffer] to Staatssekretär des Innern im Bundeskanzleramt, 8 May 1950, BAK, B 126/5682.

36. Dr. H. E., "Schuldner Staat," *Selbsthilfe* 24, no. 8 (2. Apr. Ausg. 1950): 1; Mattes, "Vortrag," 9 May 1948, ACDP, NL Binder 044, C II 3 B; Mattes, "Bedenkliche Tendenzen," [Feb. 1950], BAK, B 126/5682.

37. Wengst, *Beamtentum,* esp. 157–61, 174–81.

38. "Hilfen-System wird abgelehnt," *Ost-West Kurier* 3, no. 36 (9–15 Sept. 1950); ZvD, "Stellungnahme zum Regierungsentwurf zum Lastenausgleich," 2 Nov. 1950, BAK, B 126/10433.

39. See chap. 2 above.

40. For other countries, see Schröder, "Kriegsschadenrecht," 434–85, esp. 446–47 for Finland.

41. Arbeitsgemeinschaft ZvD/Vereinigte Ostdeutsche Landsmannschaften, "Die Forderungen der Vertriebenen zum Lastenausgleich," 1 Mar. 1951, BAK, B 136/7324; Bund der Flieger- und Kriegsgeschädigten, Landesverband Bayern, to Adenauer, 18 June 1950, BAK, B 126/5682.

42. See, e.g., D. von Doetinchem-Blankenhagen, "Gedanken zur Verwirklichung eines individuellen Lastenausgleichs," 31 July 1948, BAK, NL Holzapfel, no. 112; F. von Gaertner to Weisser, 5 July 1948, ASD, NL Weisser, no. 1086.II; "Quotal oder Sozial" and "Unser 'Nein,' " *Selbsthilfe* 25, no. 5 (1. März Ausg. 1951): 1. Similarly, war veterans sought to reassert a legal claim to benefits under Nazi legislation: Diehl, *Thanks of the Fatherland,* 143, 147.

43. Interessengemeinschaft der Ostvertriebenen, Stadt Gütersloh, "Resolution," 15 Jan. 1949, BAK, NL Holzapfel, no. 111.

44. For quote: "Eine Aufgabe von fundamentaler Bedeutung," *Ostvertriebenen-Korrespondenz* 1, no. 7 (5 Oct. 1948), BAK, Zsg 1-204/25; E.-A. Köhnke to BmF, 22 Mar. 1952, BAK, B 126/5700. For interwar fear of bureaucratic discretion, see Crew, *Germans on Welfare,* esp. 92–94; Hong, *Welfare, Modernity, and State,* 127.

45. W. Kraft, "Was geht in Bonn vor?" *Stimmen aus dem Osten* no. 11 (June 1950), in BAK, NL Kraft, no. 51; Kather in Friedrich Karrenberg, "Lastenausgleich," *Die Stimme der Gemeinde* 2, no. 12 (Dec. 1950): 8, in BAK, B 126/10444; Blaum in "Tagung des Hauptausschusses in

Stuttgart," *Nachrichtendienst des Vereins für öffentliche und private Fürsorge,* no. 12 (1948): 225, in BAK, B 126/5691; Uwe Kleinert, "Die Flüchtlinge als Arbeitskräfte—zur Eingliederung der Flüchtlinge in Nordrhein-Westfalen nach 1945," in Bade, *Neue Heimat im Westen,* 56.

46. Peukert, *Weimar Republic;* Crew, *Germans on Welfare,* esp. 4, 9.

47. For prewar property distribution, Moeller, *Protecting Motherhood,* 86; for postwar conflicts over reestablishing traditional gender relationships, see ibid., 188, 201, 207; Frevert, *Women in German History,* 255–86.

48. Gerhard Wahrig, "*Opfer,*" *Das große deutsche Wörterbuch; Selbsthilfe,* 1946–48.

49. Eghigian, "Politics of Victimization," 382–83, passim.

50. Goschler, *Wiedergutmachung;* Herbst and Goschler, *Wiedergutmachung;* Whalen, *Bitter Wounds;* Diehl, *Thanks of the Fatherland;* and Hudemann, "Kriegsopferpolitik nach beiden Weltkriegen."

51. Arbeitsgruppe "Lastenausgleich" des "Ständigen Ausschusses für Selbsthilfe," "Entschließung," 5 May 1949, BAK, B 150/8013-2; Arbeitsgemeinschaft der Chemie-Industrie to BmF, 22 May 1950, BAK, B 126/5715.

52. Erich Dederra, "Die gesamtdeutsche Aufgabe des Zentralverbandes der vertriebenen Deutschen," *VK* 1, no. 16 (11 Nov. 1950): 2; Kather, "Die Mindestforderungen," 4 May 1952, in Kather, *Eingliederung durch Lastenausgleich,* 20; Lehmann, *Im Fremden ungewollt,* 207 (quote), 39–41, 206–7, 221–27.

53. For reparation generally, see Goschler, *Wiedergutmachung,* 218–19, passim, and the articles in Herbst and Goschler, eds., *Wiedergutmachung;* for rape victims, see Sander and Johr, *BeFreier und BeFreite,* and Lehmann, *Im Fremden ungewollt,* 151–53, 158; for job, see, e.g., Dr. Hans Goll, "Zwei Aufgaben des Lastenausgleichs!" June 1949, 2, BAK, B 148V/20.

54. Cupit, *Justice,* 76–77; for Germany, Kriegssachschädenverordnung, § 6; for other countries' war-damages legislation, Schröder, "Kriegsschadenrecht," 440, 450, 457; for war-damaged, "Gesetzentwurf, § 10," *Selbsthilfe* 22, no. 10 (25 May 1948): 3.

55. For quote: Prof. Dr. Wilhelm Weizsäcker, "Zur Vorgeschichte der Deutschenaustreibung aus den Sudetenländern," *Archiv: Informationsdienst des Göttinger Arbeitskreises* (29 Sept. 1949): 1; [Hugo Mezger], "Sanierungs-Vorschlag," 1 Sept. 1947, BAK, Z 32/36; Hausbesitz Vereinigung "Lastenausgleichschutz" to Schäffer, 22 Feb. 1950, BAK, B 126/5726.

56. The organized war-damaged came from the lower-middle to upper-middle classes who had disproportionately voted for Hitler in the early 1930s: see, e.g., Childers, *Nazi Voter,* 262–65, passim, and Hamilton, *Who Voted for Hitler?;* for broad support among Germans for Hitler and his war: Bankier, *Germans and Final Solution,* 101–56; Kershaw, *The "Hitler Myth,"* esp. 155–60, and Steinert, *Hitler's War and the Germans,* 41, 50, 57–58, 65–72, 118–21, 133–37, 140–45; for German participation in Nazi atrocities: Bartov, "Savage War" and *Hitler's Army.*

57. For quote: L. Jerschabek to Fr. Blücher, 24/3/47, THA, FDP no. 8; Eugen Kogon, "Der Kampf um Gerechtigkeit," *Frankfurter Hefte* 2, no. 4 (Apr. 1947): 373; Kather, *Gerechter Lastenausgleich!* 16.

58. "Protokoll, erste Sitzung, Unterausschuß Lastenausgleich [CDU]," 29 July 1948, ACDP, NL Binder, 041 C II B; Notgemeinschaft der Bombengeschädigten, Evakuierten und Währungsgeschädigten e. V., Paderborn, to Schäffer, 8 Jan. 1951, BAK, B 126/5727; G. Niedhart, " 'So viel Anfang war nie' oder: 'Das Leben und nichts anderes'—deutsche Nachkriegszeiten im Vergleich," in Niedhart and Riesenberger, eds., *Lernen aus dem Krieg?* 16–17.

59. For absolute innocence, Fritz Seiler to BmF, 25 June 1950, BAK, B 126/5696; for relative innocence, A. Bauser, "Der Zentralverband der Fliegergeschädigten," in Finanzminister a. D. Dr. Mattes, *Wir fordern Gerechtigkeit!* 1948, in BAK, B 126/5680; Walther Meinen to Bundespräsident, 8 Jan. 1952, BAK, B 126/5700; for fortuitousness, for quote: Gerhard Jaeck,

[received 7 May 1948], 1, BAK, Z 32/47; ZvD/ZvF, *Forderungen . . . zum Lastenausgleich,* 5, 8, 10.

60. For quote: Dr. Erich Dederra, "Die gesamtdeutsche Aufgabe des Zentralverbandes der vertriebenen Deutschen," *VK* 1, no. 16 (11 Nov. 1950): 2; "Fliegergeschädigte gründen Zentralverband," *Selbsthilfe* 21, no. 15 (15 Sept. 1947): 1. See also Lehmann, *Im Fremden ungewollt,* 18, 188, 205–7; Trommler, " 'Deutschlands Sieg oder Untergang,' " 220; and Berghoff, "Verdrängung und Aufarbeitung," 103.

61. Quote cited in Scholz, " 'Heraus aus der unwürdigen Fürsorge,' " 340, passim; Crew, " 'Wohlfahrtsbrot ist bitteres Brot,' " 218–20, 227–29, passim; Crew, *Germans on Welfare,* esp. 89–95; Hong, *Welfare, Modernity, and State,* 105–6, 122; Haupt, "Petty Bourgeoisie in France and Germany," 315–16, passim; Ferguson, *Paper and Iron,* 63.

62. See, e.g., Verwaltung für Finanzen, "Memorandum, Vorbereitung, Lastenausgleich," [2d ½ of 1948], 24, BAK, NL Blücher, no. 324; "Geteilter Lastenausgleich," *Deutsche Ztg. und Wirtschafts-Ztg.,* 31 Mar. 1951, P-A, D 515/3. A few did call the game into question, e.g., Westdeutsches Institut für Wirtschaftsforschung, *Der Lastenausgleich wirtschaftlich gesehen!* 7, but they are notable by their scarcity.

63. Henke und Woller, *Politische Säuberung;* Frei, "Problem der NS-Vergangenheit," in Weisbrod, ed., *Rechtsradikalismus;* Herbert, "Rückkehr in die Bürgerlichkeit?" esp. 165; Berghoff, "Verdrängung und Aufarbeitung"; Gerstenmaier, "Hilfe für Deutschland," 1 Jan. 1946, in Gerstenmaier, *Reden und Aufsätze,* 57; Gerstenmaier, "Rede zur Beendigung der Entnazifizierung," 23 Feb. 1950, in ibid., 154–55.

64. Bund der Flieger- und Kriegsgeschädigten, Landesverband Bayern, to Bundeskanzler, 13 Oct. 1949, BAK, B 126/5697; "Vermögensausgleich aus dem Steueraufkommen," *Handelsblatt* no. 2 (8 Jan. 1948), in BAK, Z 32/52; Verwaltung für Finanzen, "Memorandum . . . Lastenausgleich," [late 1948], BAK, NL Blücher, no. 324.

65. Aristotle, *Politics,* book 4, chap. 11; Blackbourn, "The *Mittelstand,*" 412, passim; "Programm der Christlich-Demokratischen Union der britischen Zone, 1 Mar. 1948," in Pütz, ed., *Konrad Adenauer und die CDU,* 133; Giersch, *Ausgleich der Kriegslasten,* 15; "Grundsätze eines sozialen Lastenausgleichs," ASD, NL Seuffert, no. 53; Catholic bishops in "Gerechter Verteilung der Lasten," *Badische Zeitung,* 9 Sept. 1948, in BAK, B 126/5691; "Hamburger Programm: Das Programm der Christlich-Demokratischen Union für den zweiten deutschen Bundestag," 1953, in Heck, ed., *CDU und ihr Programm,* 56; Dietrich, *Eigentum für Jeden.*

66. [German Charitable Organizations], "Währungsreform und Sozialreform," Apr. 1948, BAK, Z 32/21; von der Gablentz, *Über Marx hinaus,* 7–8; Roseman, "Organic Society and 'Massenmenschen,' " 297–301; Grebing, *Konservative gegen Demokratie,* 85–86, 949–97, 102, 215; for the quotation on property and freedom: Hermann-Joseph Wallraff, "Unternehmenseigentum und katholische Sozialethik," in Walter-Raymond-Stiftung, ed., *Eigentum und Eigentümer,* 73; Röpke, *Humane Society,* 71.

67. Arbeitsgemeinschaft der Chemie-Industrie, "Lastenausgleich und andere Steuerprobleme 1949," BAK, B 102/8215-2; Verwaltung für Finanzen, "Memorandum . . . Lastenausgleich," [late 1948], 25, BAK, NL Blücher, no. 324; Erhard, *Kriegsfinanzierung,* 80.

68. "Lastenausgleich—Aufgabe ohne Beispiel," *Christ und Welt* 1, no. 7 (17 July 1948): 1, ACDP, NL Theiss, 015/III; "Hilfe für die Vertriebenen," *SPD Informationen für die Flüchtlingsausschüsse der Ortsvereine* no. 1 (July 1947): 1, in BAK, Z 2/100; Gerstenmaier (CDU) in "Tagung über Fragen des Lastenausgleichs, Karlshöhe, 13.–15. August 1948," 5, in NL Binder 044 C II 3 B; G. Weisser, "Endgültiger Lastenausgleich," [ca. Sept. 1950], and J. Kunze, "Erste Aufgabe für den Bundestag," *Freie Presse* [July 1949], both in ASD, NL Weisser, no. 1080.

69. "Vier Forderungen zum Lastenausgleich," *Christ und Welt* 1, no. 7 (17 July 1948): 6,

in BAK, B 126/5691; "Wo stehen wir?" *Industrie-Kurier,* 3 Feb. 1951, P-A, D 515/3; von der Gablentz, "1. Diskussionsgrundlage," 27 July 1948, 3, ACDP, NL Binder, 044 C II/3 B; for 1920s civil servants' similar sentiments about inflation-impoverished rentiers: Führer, "Für das Wirtschaftsleben 'mehr oder weniger wertlose Personen,'" 173.

CHAPTER 6

1. Becker, *Property Rights,* 83–86.

2. Ibid., 81–83; Bolte, *Leistung und Leistungsprinzip,* 24, 36–37; Cupit, *Justice,* 39–40.

3. [CDU/CSU Arbeitsgemeinschaft der Landesflüchtlingsausschüsse], "Abschrift! Entschließung," 14 Jan. 1950, BAK, B 126/5682; ZvD/ZvF, *Forderungen . . . zum Lastenausgleich,* [Jan. 1949], 8, 10, BAK, B 126/5681.

4. ZvD/ZvF, *Forderungen . . . zum Lastenausgleich,* [Jan. 1949], 8, 11.

5. "Bundeskabinett gegen Kriegsgeschädigten," *Selbsthilfe* 24, no. 21 (1. Nov. Ausg. 1950): 1; Otto Lindemann, "Der Lastenausgleich ohne Last?" *Ost-West Kurier* 3, no. 10 (11–17 Mar. 1950).

6. Oskar Wackerzapp, "Sozialer oder sozialistischer Lastenausgleich," *VK* 2, no. 4 (27 Jan. 1951): 15 (his emphasis), P-A, D 515/3; Wilhelm Mattes, "Für und wider den Lastenausgleich," *Selbsthilfe* 22, no. 8 (15 Apr. 1948): 1.

7. Crafts and Toniolo, *Economic Growth in Europe,* 467, 475–76; Abelshauser, *Wirtschaftsgeschichte,* 97–98; Giersch, *Ausgleich der Kriegslasten,* 77; Herbert Kriedemann, "SPD: Lastenausgleich—Koalition: Laßt den Ausgleich!" *Neuer Vorwärts,* 14 Aug. 1953, P-A, D 515/11.

8. Ludwig Düchting to BmF, 8 Mar. 1950, BAK, B 102/8215-3; Eugen Rapp, "Vorschläge zur Währungsreform und Lastenausgleich," 9 July 1948, BAK, B 126/5726.

9. "Zwei Bedingungen," *Selbsthilfe* 23, no. 4 (2. Feb. Ausg. 1949); Bayerische Aufwertungs- und Interessengemeinschaft für Wertpapierbesitzer to BmF, 6 June 1951, BAK, B126/5701.

10. Arbeitsgemeinschaft der Chemie-Industrie, "Lastenausgleich und andere Steuerprobleme 1949," 3, 7 Jan. 1949, BAK, B 102/8215-2; "Schattenquote—erster Akt des Lastenausgleichs," *Deutsche Zeitung und Wirtschaftszeitung* (3 Sept. 1949), in BAK, B 126/5702.

11. For quote: Dr. Hans Fülster, "Wirkt der Lasten-Ausgleich produktionshemmend?" *Deutscher Kurier* (30 Sept. 1951), in BAK, B 126/5714 (his emphasis); see also Lukaschek to President, Deutsche Bauernverbände, 12 Aug. 1950, BAK, B 150/4820.

12. Heinrich Troeger, "10 Thesen zum Lastenausgleich," 2 July 1948, reprinted in Troeger, *Interregnum,* 173; [Wirtschaftsausschuß der CDU/BBZ], "Die Vermögensabgabe bei Kapitalgesellschaften," 21 July 1950, 6, P-A, I 332/B 5.

13. Paul Sedlag to Bundestag, 27 May 1950, BAK, B 126/5731; W. Mattes, "Vermögenszuwachsabgabe für den Lastenausgleich," 21–22, 1950, BAK, B 136/7314; Deutscher Rentnerbund, "Entwurf für Sofortprogramm für die währungsgeschädigten Altrentner," 19 June 1951, BAK, B 126/27886.

14. "Vermögensumschichtung fördert Aufbau," *Ost-West Kurier* 2, no. 40 (21 Oct. 1949); Hans Schneider, "Lastenausgleich durchführbar trotz fehlendem Steueraufkommen," 1 June 1950, P-A, I 332/B 9.

15. Dr. Wilhelm von Rheinbaben, "Ein Vorschlag zum Lastenausgleich," *Ostvertriebenen-Korrespondenz* 1, no. 8 (20 Oct. 1948): 2; "Stop, Dr. Erhard!" *Selbsthilfe* 22, no. 16 (2. Aug. Ausg. 1948): 1; ZvD/ZvF, *Forderungen . . . zum Lastenausgleich,* [Jan. 1949], 12, in BAK, B 126/5681.

16. [Unsigned], "Die Meinung des Volkes," 12 Mar. 1950, BAK, B126/5731; Kather, *Gerechter Lastenausgleich!* 11.

17. "Ein Hohn für die Geschädigten!" *Selbsthilfe* 24, no. 9 (1. Mai Ausg. 1950): 1; "Die große Lüge," ibid. 24, no. 10 (2. Mai Ausg. 1950): 4; Karl Palmedo to BmF, 26 Mar. 1950, BAK, B 126/5698.

18. Hughes, *Paying for Inflation*, 44–46; Luther, *Feste Mark—Solide Wirtschaft*, 24–26, 30–32; Feldman, *Great Disorder*, 198–99, 347–48, 429; Holtfrerich, *German Inflation*, 128–29, 134–35; Möller, *Vorgeschichte der Mark*, 421, 427–28; Special Agency meetings, esp. the Eighth, Eighteenth, Twenty-sixth, Thirty-first, Thirty-second, and Thirty-third Sessions, in IfZ, Sammlung Möller, Protokolle der Sonderstelle Geld und Kredit; for Finland, see Bundestagskommission in Finnland, "Lastenausgleich und Bodenreform in Finnland," [1951], in BmI, ed., *Lastenausgleichsgesetze*, 4/1:404–5, 415.

19. Friedrich Gabbe to Wirtschaftsrat, 14 Sept. 1948, BAK, B 126/5726; "Währungs-geschädigte in Gefahr," *Selbsthilfe* 24, no. 13 (1. Juli Ausg. 1950); C. Fischer and W. Budczies, "Erster Entwurf, Begründung zum Gesetz zur Neuordnung des Geldwesens," 1 Apr. 1948, 66, IfZ, Sammlung Möller, Begründung zum Gesetz zur Neuordnung des Geldwesens; "Lastenausgleich auf individueller Grundlage," *FDK* 1, no. 8 (9 Feb. 1950): 4.

20. Deutscher Industrie- und Handelstag to BmF Schäffer, 24 Nov. 1949, BAK, B 126/5706; BmF (signed Vangerow) to Bundeskanzler, 5 May 1950, BAK, B 126/5714; F. Kärcher, "Gedanken zum endgültigen Lastenausgleich," [Winter 1949?], 3, in ACDP, NL Binder, 044 C II 3 B.

21. "Beitrag zu der Rede des Herrn Ministers [Schäffer] in Hamburg, Betrifft: Lasten-ausgleich," 6 Oct. 1949, 3, BAK, B 126/5678; for quotes: "Schattenquote—erster Akt des Lastenausgleichs," *Deutsche Zeitung* (3 Sept. 1949), in BAK, B 126/5702.

22. "33. Sitzung, SGK," 13 Jan. 1948, 2–3, IfZ, Sammlung Möller, SGK Protokolle; Verwaltung für Finanzen, "Endgültige Gestaltung des Lastenausgleichs," 30 May 1949, BAK, NL Blücher, no. 337; [BmF], "Allererste Gedanken, Alt-Währungsgeschädigte . . . des Lastenausgleichs," 22 Sept. 1949, 2–3, BAK, B 126/12738.

23. "Stellungnahme des 4. Unterausschusses zur Frage des Lastenausgleichs," 10 Jan. [1950], ASD, NL Weisser, no. 404; "Niederschrift über die 1. Sitzung des Wissenschaftlichen Beirats der BmF," 23–24 Mar. 1950, 16–25, BAK, B 126/10431.

24. Milward, *Reconstruction of Western Europe*, 72–87, 115–18, 466–69, passim; Hogan, *Marshall Plan*, 1–27.

25. Calleo, *German Problem*, esp. 16–22, 164–69; Henke, *Die amerikanische Besetzung*, 470; Abelshauser, *Wirtschaftsgeschichte*, 147–54; Berghahn, "Resisting the Pax Americana?"

26. Crafts and Toniolo, *Economic Growth in Europe;* Milward, *Reconstruction of Western Europe.*

27. See here Klotzbach, *Weg zur Staatspartei*, 237–39, 247, 254–55.

28. Campbell, *Joy in Work*, 317, 337–42; Latzel, " 'Freie Bahn dem Tüchtigen!' " esp. 340–41; Michael Prinz, "Die soziale Funktion moderner Elemente in der Gesellschaftspolitik des Nationalsozialismus," in Prinz and Zitelmann, eds., *Nationalsozialismus und Modernisierung*, esp. 301–2, 308.

29. Friedrich Tenbruck, "Alltagsnormen und Lebensgefühle in der Bundesrepublik," 290–99; Latzel, " 'Freie Bahn dem Tüchtigen!' " esp. 341; Schelsky, *Wandlungen der deutschen Familie;* Bolte, *Leistung und Leistungsprinzip*, 11–12, 14, 19, 21–28, passim; for postwar emphasis on production, see, e.g., Bauser and Kaufmann, "Denkschrift zur Währungs- und Finanzreform," Apr. 1947, BAK, Z 1/311.

30. Bolte, *Deutsche Gesellschaft*, 259–60, 305; Bolte, *Leistung und Leistungsprinzip*, 14, 27–28, 37; Horst Reimann, "Pro und Contra zum Leistungsprinzip," in Friedrich, ed., *Leistungsprinzip*, esp. 91; Claessens, Klönne, and Tschoepe, *Sozialkunde*, 270, 293; Kreckel, "Statusinkonsistenz," 33–34, 36–37; Sweeney, "Work, Race, and Culture."

31. Hughes, *Paying for Inflation,* 88.

32. Clay for Byrnes, 20 Apr. 1945, and Clay to McCloy, 26 Apr. 1945, in Smith, ed., *Papers of General Clay,* 5–8; "Wann endgültiger Ausgleich?" *Selbsthilfe* 22, no. 24 (2. Dez. Ausg. 1948): 1.

33. L. Wolkersdorf, "Der Leidensweg des endgültigen Lastenausgleichs," [May 1950], 2–3, B 126/5683; [SPD] "Grundsätze eines sozialen Lastenausgleichs," [early 1950], ASD, NL Seuffert, no. 53; Hockerts, "Integration der Gesellschaft," 33.

34. Hochstein, *Ideologie des Überlebens,* 94–95, 98–100; Braun, "Streben nach 'Sicherheit,'" 285–86, 302; Ott, *Wirtschaftskonzeption,* 239–41.

35. Large, *Germans to Front,* 65–66; Kleßmann, *Die doppelte Staatsgründung,* 230–31; Mastny, *Cold War,* 91–111.

36. Abelshauser, *Wirtschaftsgeschichte,* esp. 63–70; Kollmer von Oheimb-Loup, "Wirtschaftspolitik Erhards als Fessel," 459–77; Nicholls, *Freedom with Responsibility,* esp. 222–31, 270–99; Hockerts, "Integration der Gesellschaft," 29.

37. Abelshauser, *Wirtschaftsgeschichte,* 85–98; Eichengreen, *Europe's Postwar Recovery;* Crafts and Toniolo, *Economic Growth in Europe.*

38. Nicholls, *Freedom with Responsibility,* esp. 299.

39. Dr. Kurt Friedrich, "Lastenausgleich — eine Notlösung," *Schwäbische Landeszeitung* (26 Feb. 1952), P-A, D 515/5; Fritz Brühl, "Lastenausgleich — Moral," *Süddeutsche Zeitung* (3 Apr. 1952), P-A, D 515/6; Diefendorf, *Wake of War,* 282.

40. "Dies Land ist unser," *Der Landesbote,* [ca. Oct. 1950], in BAK, B 126/5731; "Blutspender tot — Patient lebt," *Neue Presse* (Coburg), 13 Feb. 1951, in BAK, B 126/5703.

41. Haus- und Grundeigentümerverein des Siegerlandes und Sauerlandes, "Unsere Meinung zum Lastenausgleich," [22 Mar. 1951], BAK, B 126/5727; Report no. 28 (14 Nov. 1946) [OMGUS poll], in Merritt and Merritt, *Public Opinion in Germany,* 112–13; Frantzioch, *Die Vertriebenen.*

42. Dr. Hans R. Eckstein, "Kampf um das Recht!" *Selbsthilfe* 23, no. 18 (2. Sept. Ausg. 1949); Kather to Bundeskanzler, 20 Sept. 1951, BAK, B 136/645.

43. For poll, Stern, *Whitewashing Yellow Badge,* 372; Kather, *Gerechter Lastenausgleich!* 1–2.

44. "Lastenausgleich vor neuer Phase," *DUD,* Ausgabe A, 4, no. 6 (9 Jan. 1950): 1; "Erste Stellungnahme des Deutschen Städtetages zum Lastenausgleich," 5 Oct. 1948, 1, BAK, NL Blücher, no. 334.

45. Kather, *Gerechter Lastenausgleich!* 1–2; M. Bott-Bodenhausen, "Gedanken zum Lastenausgleich," [23 Mar. 1949], ACDP, NL Binder, 014 B I 4; Kather at Pressekonferenz, 3 Nov. 1950, 9–10, BAK, B 145/I-9.

46. "Lastenausgleich durch Realabgabe," *Wirtschafts- und Finanzzeitung* (29 Oct. 1948), in BAK, B 126/5759; Wirtschaftswissenschaftliches Institut der Gewerkschaften, "Die Gewerkschaften zur Währungs- und Finanzreform," [Spring 1948], 24–25, BAK, Z 32/46; for SPD, see, e.g., "Die nächste Aufgabe: Der Lastenausgleich," *Stuttgarter Nachrichten* (29 July 1948), in ASD, NL Weisser, no. 1244.

47. Oskar Wackerzapp, "Entwurf zu einer Stellungnahme," [Feb. 1950], BAK, B 126/5682.

48. "Niederschrift über eine Besprechung über das Zertifikatsproblem im endgültigen Lastenausgleich," 3 May 1950, BAK, B 126/5759.

49. "Auszug aus dem Vortrag . . . Otto Pfleiderer," 16 Sept. 1948, BAK, NL Blücher, no. 333; O. Wackerzapp, "Sozialer Lastenausgleich durch naturale Lieferungen und Leistungen," [Fall 1949], 4–5, BAK, B 126/5681.

50. Westdeutsches Institut für Wirtschaftsforschung, "Betr.: Bemerkungen zur endgültigen Gestaltung des Lastenausgleichs," 18 May 1949, BAK, NL Blücher, no. 334.

51. See, e.g., Dr. von Neuhoff, ZvD, to Lukaschek, 25 May 1950, BAK, B 150/3294.

52. Ibid.; ZvD, "Memorandum zum Regierungsentwurf für den Lastenausgleich," 6 Nov. 1950, P-A, I 332/B 8; Kather, *Gerechter Lastenausgleich!* 12.

53. Friedrich Gabbe to Erhard, 20 June 1949, BAK, B 126/5698; Landesausschuß "Heimatvertriebenes Landvolk" im Landesverband der Ostvertriebenen, Nordrhein-Westfalen to Schäffer, 31 May 1950, BAK, B 126/5682.

54. 68. Kabinettssitzung (23 May 1950) and 70. Kabinettssitzung (31 May 1950) in Enders and Reiser, eds., *Kabinettsprotokolle der Bundesregierung,* 2:399–401, 417.

55. "Lastenausgleich—gestrichen?" *Süddeutsche Zeitung* (5 Dec. 1951), P-A, D 515/5; "Episkopat und Lastenausgleich," *VK* 1, no. 6 (2 Sept. 1950): 9.

56. See, e.g., [Bayerischer Bauernverband], "Lastenausgleich und Landwirtschaft," [Jan. 1949], BAK, B 126/5715; "Gutachten des Unterausschusses III 'Steuerpolitik und Kapitalbildung' des Finanzpolitischen Beirates zur Soforthilfe und zum Lastenausgleich," [early 1949], BAK, B 126/5681.

57. See, e.g., DIHT et al. to BmF, 7 Feb. 1951, BAK, B 126/5705; Arbeitsgemeinschaft der Chemie-Industrie to BmF, 22 May 1950, BAK, B 126/5715.

58. "Lastenausgleich wirtschaftlich gesehen," *Finanz-Zeitung,* 1 Oct. 1948, BAK, B 126/5691; "Lastenausgleich," *Deutsche Wirtschaft* (24 Sept. 1948), BAK, B 126/5685; Hughes, "Wer bezahlt die Rechnung?"

59. H. Kriedemann, "Betr.: Lastenausgleich," [Summer 1951], ACDP, NL Seuffert, no. 53; *Lastenausgleich! Gründe und Gegengründe der SPD,* NL Weisser, no. 1080; L. Wolkersdorf to Weisser, 20 Aug. 1948, ASD, NL Weisser, no. 1086.I; chap. 7 below.

60. Lorenz Wolkersdorf, "Stellungnahme zum Gesetzentwurf des Allgemeinen Gewerkschaftsbundes Rheinland-Pfalz über den Lastenausgleich," 30 Nov. 1949, 3, 13, BAK, B 126/5759; H. Baumgarten, "Des anderen Last," *Frankfurter Allgemeine Zeitung* (8 May 1952), P-A, D 515/7; Deutscher Gemeinschaftsblock der Heimatvertriebenen und Entrechteten, "Zum Lastenausgleich," 10 Dec. 1951, P-A, D 515/5.

61. Dr. Bodsch to [Kunze], 2 Feb. [1952], BAK, B 102/8223-3.

62. Schillinger, *Entscheidungsprozeß beim Lastenausgleich,* 279; Seuffert in 209. Sitzung (8 May 1952), *VerhBT, Sten. Ber.,* 11:9167; Wackerzapp, "Sozialer oder sozialistischer Lastenausgleich," *VK* 2, no. 4 (27 Jan. 1951), P-A, D 515/3; "Stellungnahme des Deutschen Gewerkschaftsbundes zum Allgemeinen Lastenausgleich," [10 Mar. 1951], P-A, I 332/B 7; Verwaltung für Finanzen, "Volkswirtschaftliche Überlegungen zum endgültigen Lastenausgleich," 1 June 1949, 11–12, 20, BAK, B 126/5686; Berghahn, "Ideas into Politics: The Case of Ludwig Erhard."

63. "Über 4 Millionen Hauptanträge auf Soforthilfe," *Archiv: Informationsdienst des Göttinger Arbeitskreises* 28, no. 50 (13 July 1950); Verwaltung für Finanzen, "Volkswirtschaftliche Überlegungen zum endgültigen Lastenausgleich," 1 June 1949, 11–12, 18, BAK, B 126/5686; Ernst Hafter, "Gefahren des Lastenausgleichs," *Der Volkswirt,* no. 46 (1950): 12, in BAK, B 126/5683; Kriedemann in 209. Sitzung (8 May 1952), *VerhBT, Sten. Ber.,* 11:9155; ZvF, "Vorschläge . . . zum Entwurf eines Gesetzes über einen Allgemeinen Lastenausgleich," [17 Mar. 1951], 6, BAK, B 126/5699.

64. Dr. Gernot Gather, "Vortrag, Tagung der Wirtschaftspolitischen Gesellschaft von 1947," 21 Oct. 1948, BAK, B 126/5759; "Stellungnahme des Zentralbankrates der Bank deutscher Länder," 14–15 Mar. 1951, BAK, B 126/10436; Westdeutsches Institut für Wirtschaftsforschung, *Lastenausgleich wirtschaftlich gesehen!* 9–10, 16; Davis, "Food Scarcity and the Empowerment of the Female Consumer in World War I Berlin," 287–89, passim; Carter, *How German Is She?* 41, passim.

65. See also Hughes, "Wer bezahlt die Rechnung?"

CHAPTER 7

1. "Johannes Kunze" and Kunze, "Erste Aufgabe für den Bundestag," both in *Freie Presse,* [July 1949], in ASD, NL Weisser, no. 1080; [Transcript, Disputation, im Auftrag des Wirtschaftswissenschaftlichen Clubs], 33, P-A, I 332/B 9; [CDU/CSU], "Soforthilfe und Lastenausgleich," [early 1950], BAK, B 126/5682; Kunze in "Sitzung führender Politiker der CDU/CSU," 31 Aug. 1949, in Wengst, ed., *Auftakt zur Ära Adenauer,* 122; Schillinger, *Entscheidungsprozeß beim Lastenausgleich,* 184.

2. Kunze, *Lastenausgleich vor der Entscheidung,* 5, BAK, B 136/7314; Kunze, "Allgemeiner Bericht," *VerhBT, Sten. Ber.,* 11:9014–16; "Protokoll über die Tagung des Zonenausschusses der CDU für die britische Zone," 1–2 Aug. 1946, in Pütz, ed., *Konrad Adenauer und die CDU,* 179; Binder and Vockel in "1. Sitzung, Unterausschuß Lastenausgleich [CDU]," 29 July 1948, ACDP, NL Binder, 041, C II B; [Abg. Braun], "Der Lastenausgleich. Beitrag zu einer Diskussion des Problems," 29 July 1948, ACDP, NL Binder, 044, C II 3 B.

3. For quote: Kunze, *Lastenausgleich vor der Entscheidung,* 7–8; Kunze, "Erste Aufgabe für den Bundestag," *Freie Presse,* [July 1949], in ASD, NL Weisser, no. 1080.

4. "Das dritte Gesetz zur Währungsreform," *DUD,* no. 104 (29 June 1948): 1; "Wie wünscht die CDU/CSU den Lastenausgleich?" *DUD* 4, no. 100 (22 May 1950): 2–3; Hockerts, "Integration der Gesellschaft," 30.

5. Kunze in 115. Sitzung (31 Jan. 1950), *VerhBT, Sten. Ber.,* 6:4344; "Wird es doch besser als sein Ruf?" *Stimme der Vertriebenen* (20 Jan. 1952), P-A, D 515/5; for poll, "Die dringlichsten Aufgaben der neuen Bundesregierung," [summer 1949], BAK, NL Schäffer, no. 30.

6. [Disputation], 18, P-A, I 332/B 9; P.-P. Nahm, "Über die Bedeutung der 8. Novelle zum LAG," NDR, 27 July 1957, P-A, D 515/Ordner 9.

7. H. Kriedemann, "Novellen-Trost und Wirklichkeit," *Neuer Vorwärts,* 23 May 1952, P-A, D 515/8; Krause, *Flucht vor Bombenkrieg,* 239–40.

8. For undamaged businessmen, see, e.g., the correspondence between the Binder brothers (Paul, CDU politician, and Odilo, business official) in ACDP, NL Binder, 014, B I 3; for war-damaged businessmen, see, e.g., Frhr von Senfft to Holzapfel, 30 July 1948, BAK, NL Holzapfel, no. 112.

9. Walter-Raymond-Stiftung, *Eigentum und Eigentümer,* esp. 34–35, 73–75, 94–97; "Stellungnahme des Vertriebenen-Ausschusses zur Frage der Unterhaltshilfe, der Entschädigungen und der Finanzierungsfrage," [1951], THA, FDP Parteiakten, A-13, no. 4; "Programm der Christlich-Demokratischen Union der britischen Zone," 1 Mar. 1946, in Pütz, ed., *Konrad Adenauer und die CDU,* 133; [D. von Doetinchem-Blankenhagen], "Gedanken zur Verwirklichung eines individuellen Lastenausgleichs," 31 July 1948, BAK, NL Holzapfel, no. 112.

10. "Protokoll über die Fraktionssitzung," 21 Oct. 1949, THA, NL Blücher, no. 11; for quote: "Protokoll über die Sitzung des Vertriebenen-Ausschusses am 2. April 1952," THA, FDP Parteiakten, A-13, no. 4; Hein, *Zwischen liberaler Milieupartei,* esp. 192–93, 352–53.

11. Kunze in [Disputation], 22, P-A, I 332/B 9.

12. "Notgemeinschaft der Fliegergeschädigten," *Selbsthilfe* 20, no. 4 (15 May 1946): 1; A. Bauser, "Der Zentralverband der Fliegergeschädigten," in Finanzminister a. D. Mattes, *Wir fordern Gerechtigkeit!* 29–31, BAK, B 126/5680; Kather, *Gerechter Lastenausgleich!* 7.

13. Hochstein, *Ideologie des Überlebens,* 7, 45–49, 98, 142–43, 257–63; Merritt, *Democracy Imposed,* 328–31; Hudemann, *Sozialpolitik im deutschen Südwesten,* 415–16.

14. Krause, *Flucht vor Bombenkrieg,* 233–37, 242–46; Steinert, *Vertriebenenverbände;* Breitling, *Verbände in der Bundesrepublik,* esp. 71, 73–77.

15. "Lastenausgleich—unsere letzte Hoffnung!" *Der Neubürger* 2, no. 8 (Aug. 1948), in

ACDP, NL Theiss, 015/III; "Almosen oder Rechte," *VK* 3, no. 17 (3 May 1952); Mattes in ZvD/ZvF, *Forderungen . . . zum Lastenausgleich* [1949], 5.

16. Mattes in "Es liegt in unserer Hand!" *Selbsthilfe* 23, no. 2 (2. Jan. Ausg. 1949): 1; Pascal cited in "Nicht müde werden!" ibid. 23, no. 3 (1. Febr. Ausg. 1949): 1; "Wachsende Empörung der Heimatvertriebenen," from Pressedienst der Heimatvertriebenen, 2 Feb. 1950, in BAK, B 136/6569.

17. For creditors, see Hughes, *Paying for Inflation,* esp. chap. 9.

18. Krause, *Flucht vor Bombenkrieg,* 239–40; Arbeitsgemeinschaft der Kriegsgeschädigten Sitz Köln, "Einladung . . . Protest-Kundgebung," May 1952, ACDP, NL Kuntscher 008/1; "Und abermals nach 25 Jahren," *Selbsthilfe* 24, no. 8 (2. Apr. Ausg 1950): 1; Manfred-Gerhard Giesel, "Unfähigkeit," *Ost-West Kurier* 3, no. 5 (4–10 Feb. 1950): 2.

19. For BHE leadership and supporters, see Neumann, *Block der Heimatvertriebenen,* 21–25, 57–63, 303–5; Kather to Kraft, 18 Jan. 1950, ASD, Parteivorstand, no. 846; Lukaschek in Protokoll, no. 24 (15 July 1953), in Buchstab, ed., *Adenauer. "Es muß alles neu gemacht werden,"* 636.

20. Prof. Dr. Oberländer, "Mein Lieber Wähler!" 17 June 1954, and "Uns hilft kein Kampf der Klassen und Parteien," both in BAK, Zsg 1-54/15; "Die Grundgedanken des Parteiprogramms," *BHE Informationsdienst,* no. 2 (1950): 2–3.

21. "Die Fronten im Lastenausgleich," "Staat 12 jetzt 3," *BHE Informationsdienst* 3, no. 7 (5 Apr. 1952): 2; Kraft in "Abschrift aus Sitzungsbericht des Deutschen Bundesrates vom 19.1.1951," in BAK, NL Kraft, no. 38.

22. "Kraft warnt vor Radikalismus," *Frankfurter Allgemeine Zeitung* (9 Mar. 1951), P-A, D 515/3; Günther Ziehm, "BHE im Kampf," [1953 election], BAK, Zsg 1-54/15; Neumann, *Block der Heimatvertriebenen,* 24–25, 325–34; Grosser, *Bonner Demokratie,* 153–54; "Die Mühlen mahlen langsam," *Der Spiegel* 50, no. 18 (29 May 1996): 18.

23. See the articles in *BHE Informationsdienst,* no. 3 (1950): 2–18.

24. Neumann, *Block der Heimatvertriebenen,* 35, 69–72, 306, passim.

25. The trade unions apparently disposed of their Lastenausgleich records in the 1960s.

26. Wolkersdorf, "Stellungnahme zum Gesetzentwurf des Allgemeinen Gewerkschaftsbundes Rheinland-Pfalz über den Lastenausgleich," 30 Nov. 1949, BAK, B 126/5759; Wolkersdorf, "Der Leidensweg des endgültigen Lastenausgleichs," [May 1950], in BAK, B 126/5683.

27. Grote-Mißmahl in ZvD/ZvF, *Forderungen . . . zum Lastenausgleich,* 5–6, BAK, B 126/5681; Grote-Mißmahl, "Grundsätze eines sozialen Vermögensausgleichs," [Apr. 1950], BAK, B 126/5705.

28. "Stellungnahme des Deutschen Gewerkschaftsbundes . . . zum Allgemeinen Lastenausgleich," [10 Mar. 1951], P-A, I 332/B 7.

29. Weisser, "Soforthilfe und Lastenausgleich," [May 1949?], ASD, NL Weisser, no. 466; SPD Parteivorstand, "Protokoll der Lastenausgleichstagung," 6 Feb. 1950, ASD, NL Seuffert, no. 53.

30. Klotzbach, *Weg zur Staatspartei,* 27–29, passim; Dr. Troeger, "Sozialer oder quotaler Lastenausgleich?" [ca. 6 Nov. 1950], ASD, NL Seuffert, no. 53; Weisser to Schumacher, 7 Aug. 1948, ASD, NL Weisser, no. 855; "Gespräche über den Lastenausgleichsentwurf mit Abgeordneten Dr. Kunze und Seuffert," NWDR, 24 Jan. 1951, ASD, NL Seuffert, no. 53.

31. Seuffert, "Wo stehen wir mit dem Lastenausgleich?" *Der Betriebs-Berater* 4, no. 30 (30 Oct. 1949): 601–2; Weisser to Schumacher, 7 Aug. 1948, ASD, NL Weisser, no. 855; "Niederschrift über eine Besprechung des Entwurfes eines Lastenausgleichsgesetzes am 21. Aug. 1950," ASD, NL Seuffert, no. 53; for quote: "Lastenausgleich: Gründe und Gegengründe der Sozialdemokratie," ASD, NL Weisser, no. 1080.

32. Grebing, *Flüchtlinge und Parteien*, 11–15, 19, 51–55, 102–3, 117–18; Schillinger, *Entscheidungsprozeß beim Lastenausgleich*, 253–54; "Sitzung des Parteivorstandes am 30. März 1951," ASD, Partei-Vorstand, no. 6.

33. Schumacher, "Kontinentale Demokratie," 4 Apr. 1946, in Schumacher, *Reden und Schriften*, 422; Klotzbach, *Weg zur Staatspartei*, 61–63; Edinger, *Schumacher*, 79, 90; see the virtually identically worded, untitled memoranda, dated 25/26 May 1951, in BAK, NL Kraft, no. 51, and ASD, NL Seuffert, no. 53.

34. "Tauziehen um den Lastenausgleich," *Rheinischer Merkur* (22 June 1951), P-A, D 515/4; Kriedemann, "Betr.: Lastenausgleich, vertraulich," [summer 1951], ASD, NL Seuffert, no. 53, "5.6.1951: Fraktionssitzung," Weber, *SPD-Fraktion*, 1:279.

35. "Sitzung des Parteivorstandes am 22. und 23. Feb. 1952" and "Sitzung des Lasten-ausgleich-Ausschusses mit Vertretern aus den Bezirken und Landtagen am 8. und 9. Feb. 1952," both in ASD, Parteivorstand, no. 7; Kather, *Die entscheidenden Jahre*, 176; for continued cooperation in committee, see Atzenroth (FDP) in 207. Sitzung (6 May 1952), *VerhBT, Sten. Ber.*, 11:8982; Klotzbach, *Weg zur Staatspartei*, 253–54.

36. "Die Vernunftehe SPD-BHE in Niedersachsen," *Sozialdemokratischer Pressedienst* [Politik] 6, no. 133 (12 June 1951).

37. Kunze to Seuffert, 2 June 1950, ASD, NL Seuffert, no. 53; "Maßgeblicher CDU-Abgeordneter: Schadenfeststellung nicht vordringlich," 21 June 1950, in BmVt, ed., *Lasten-ausgleichsgesetze*, 1/1:161; Kunze to Bundeskanzler, 3 Oct. 1951, BAK, B 136/645.

38. [Disputation], [early 1951], P-A, I 332/B 9 (for Seuffert defense of Kunze, 41; for Gille quote, 14); "Kunze auf der Pressekonferenz am 16. 2.," in BAK, NL Kather, 03/3; Atzenroth (FDP) in 207. Sitzung (6 May 1952), *VerhBT, Sten. Ber.*, 11:8982.

39. Diehl, *Thanks of the Fatherland*, 241–42; Hockerts, *Sozialpolitische Entscheidungen*, 90, 428; Schulz, *Wiederaufbau in Westdeutschland*, 324; Kralewski and Neunreither, *Oppositionelles Verhalten*, 84–85.

40. "Die Maske fiel vorm Mikrophon," in BAK, NL Kather, 03/3.

41. "Die Meinung des Volkes," 12 Mar. 1950, BAK, B 126/5731; "Stellungnahme des BHE gegen den Luxus," *BHE Informationsdienst* 2, no. 11 (10 Nov. 1951); Richard Christer to alle Bundes- und Landtagsabgeordnete, 20 June 1950, BAK, B 126/5703; Peter Ogermann to Bundesfinanzminister, 21 Aug. 1950, BAK, B 126/5699. For other legislation, see Wengst, *Beamtentum*; Diehl, *Thanks of the Fatherland*; Hockerts, *Sozialpolitische Entscheidungen*; and Goschler, *Wiedergutmachung*.

42. For war-damaged suspicions, see, e.g., Bund der Fliegergeschädigten und Vertriebenen in Baden, Kreisverband Hochschwarzwald, et al. to Bundestagsabgeordnete, 20 Jan. 1951, P-A, I 332/B 7; Jakob Fromm to Hauptvorstand der Sozialdemokratischen Partei, 16 Feb. 1950, BAK, B 126/5714; for government desire to put issue behind them, see 68. Kabinettssitzung (23 May 1950) in Enders and Reiser, eds., *Kabinettsprotokolle der Bundesregierung*, 2:399; Schäffer to Blücher, 28 July 1950, BAK, B 126/10432.

43. "Unkel, 13–14 May 1950," and Kunze, [untitled], 1 June 1950, "Bericht über die Ver-handlungen des Unkeler Kreises vom 3.–5.8.50," all in BAK, B 126/10431; "Kurzbericht über die Tagung den Koalitionsparteien angehörigen Mitglieder des Lastenausgleichsausschusses des Bundestages am 17. u. 18. Apr. 1950," BAK, B 102/8223-1; for Schäffer's views and con-flict with Unkeler Circle, see, e.g., his letters, May–November 1950, in BAK, B 126/51552. Schillinger, *Entscheidungsprozeß beim Lastenausgleich*, 171–218.

44. Hockerts, *Sozialpolitische Entscheidungen*, 124–30; Bohn and Bruhn, *Lastenausgleich*, 1:315–424.

45. "Die dringlichsten Aufgaben der neuen Bundesregierung. Eine öffentliche Befragung des Bielefelder Instituts 'EMNID,'" BAK, NL Schäffer, no. 30.

46. See, e.g., [Niederbayerische Landwirtschaft], "Resolution," 19 Sept. 1948, BAK, B 126/5715; Arbeitsgemeinschaft chemische Industrie to Schäffer, 22 May 1950, ibid.; Straubinger Hausbesitz, "Entschließung," 19 Oct. 1950, BAK, B126/5726.

47. Paul Binder to Odilo Binder, 13 Nov. 1948, in ACDP, NL Binder, 014, B I 3; Dr. Hz., "Betrifft: Lastenausgleich," 8 Sept. 1950, BAK, B 150/4820.

48. Schillinger, *Entscheidungsprozeß beim Lastenausgleich,* 202; Wiesen, "Overcoming Nazism," 202 (his emphasis); Prowe, "Democratization as Restabilization," 312–15, 325–26.

49. "Wirtschaft in der Entscheidung," *Selbsthilfe* 23, no. 14 (2. Juli Ausg. 1949): 1.

50. See the two very different versions of "Versandliste für den Bericht, 'Der endgültige Lastenausgleich,' " in BAK, B 126/5679; Dr. Eckstein in "Stenographische Niederschrift der gemeinsamen Sitzung des Ausschusses für den Lastenausgleich und des Ausschusses für Heimatvertriebene am Mittwoch, 20. Sept. 1950," 7, B 126/10448; Dr. Hinz, "Besprechung des Lastenausgleichs, 14. Sept. 1950," 18 Sept. 1950, BAK, B 150/4820; Diehl, *Thanks of the Fatherland,* 240–41.

51. "Lastenausgleich — Erfüllung einer Staatsschuld," *Selbsthilfe* 24, no. 5 (1. März Ausg. 1950): 1; "Bundes-Innenminister auf der Großkundgebung in Hannover," ibid. 26, no. 3 (1. Feb. Ausg. 1952): 1–2; "Empfang durch Bundeskanzler," ibid. 25, no. 14 (2. Juli Ausg. 1951): 1; "Die Vertriebenen beim Kanzler," *VK* 2, no. 11 (24 Mar. 1951): 3; 70. Kabinettssitzung (31 May 1950) in Enders and Reiser, eds., *Kabinettsprotokolle der Bundesregierung,* 2:417.

52. Adolf Krauss to Schäffer, 4 June 1950, BAK, B 126/5704; Bruno Steffan to Bundesregierung, 21 Dec. 1949, BAK, B 126/5698; "Ringen um Aufwertung," *Selbsthilfe* 23, no. 23 (1. Dez. Ausg. 1949): 2; "Heimatvertriebene fordern Lastenausgleich," *Ost-West Kurier* 3, no. 13 (1–7 Apr. 1950).

53. For a more detailed discussion, see Hughes, "Restitution and Democracy."

54. Numerous announcements of and articles about demonstrations in *Selbsthilfe, VK,* and *Ost-West Kurier,* among them "Weitere Lastenausgleichs-Kundgebungen," *VK* 2, no. 9 (10 Mar. 1951): 3, and "Großkundgebung mit Dr. Mattes in München," *Selbsthilfe* 25, no. 18 (2. Sept. Ausg. 1951): 1.

55. 129. Kabinettssitzung (16 Feb. 1951) in Hüllbüsch, ed., *Kabinettsprotokolle der Bundesregierung,* 4:164; Kather et al., "Protestaktion der Vertriebenen zum Lastenausgleich," *VK* 2, no. 3 (20 Jan. 1951): 1–2; C. Neumann, "Alarmstufe I," *VK* 2, no. 7 (24 Feb. 1951): 1–3.

56. "Kurz kommentiert," *Tages-Anzeiger* Regensburg (7 Mar. 1951), and "Politik mit Flüchtlingen," *Welt der Arbeit* (16 Mar. [1951]), both in BAK, NL de Vries, no. 6; "Der ZvD und Bonn," *SPD Pressedienst* (19 Feb. 1951), in BAK, B 126/5693. For postwar fears of mass democracy, Mommsen, "Von Weimar nach Bonn"; Poiger, "Rebels with a Cause?" 108–13.

57. "Protokoll, Gesamtvorstand, ZvD, 15 Dec. 1953," in BVD-A, Protokolle des Präsidiums und Gesamtvorstandes des ZvD, 1950–53; Krause, *Flucht vor Bombenkrieg,* 233, 236; "Vermerk über die Sitzung des Ausschusses für Heimatvertriebene," 21 Feb. 1951, BAK, B 126/10435.

58. "Vermerk über die Sitzung des Ausschusses für Heimatvertriebene," 21 Feb. 1951, BAK, B 126/10435; C.J.N., "Alarmstufe I," *VK* 2, no. 7 (24 Feb. 1951): 3.

59. No documents available to me suggest that subsidies were actually cut, and the BvD was still receiving subsidies in the mid-1950s ("Protokoll, Gesamtvorstand, ZvD, 15 Dec. 1953," in BVD-A, Protokolle des Präsidiums und Gesamtvorstandes des ZvD, 1950–53); Breitling, *Verbände in der Bundesrepublik,* 70.

60. "Zur Bonner Demonstration gegen den Lastenausgleich," *Union in Deutschland* 5, no. 16 (24 Feb. 1951): 2–3; "Ein gefährlicher Weg," *Stuttgarter Zeitung* (27 Feb. 1951), P-A, D 515/3.

61. For first quote: C.J.N., "Alarmstufe I," *VK* 2, no. 7 (24 Feb. 1951): 1–3 (his emphasis); for second quote: "Nachspiel," *VK* 2, no. 10, in BAK, NL Kather, no. 14/1; Linus Kather, "Der Weg

der Geschädigten," *Die Welt* (20 Mar. 1951), P-A, D 515/3; "Kontrollorgan Wähler," *Selbsthilfe* 23, no. 21 (1. Nov. Ausg. 1949): 4.

62. "Vorschläge des ZvF . . . Gesetz . . . Lastenausgleich," [17 Mar. 1951], 25–26, BAK, B 126/5699; Kreisverband der Vertriebenen, Saulgaus, "Resolution," 2 Apr. 1949, BAK, B 148/V/20; Crew, *Germans on Welfare*, 99–104; Diehl, *Thanks of the Fatherland*, 110, 111, 113, passim; Prowe, "Foundations of West German Democracy," 114–18. Cf., though, notions of participatory or direct democracy (1918/19, 1968ff.): Grube and Richter, *Demokratietheorien*, 169–220.

63. For committees, see Lastenausgleich Law, §§ 309, 314.

64. Kather quote: "Die Güter dieser Welt," *Der Spiegel* 5, no. 12 (21 Mar. 1951): 27; for second quote: Arbeitsgemeinschaft der Kriegssachgeschädigten- und Evakuierten-Verbände des Bundesgebietes to Bundesregierung, 22 Dec. 1950, BAK, B 126/5697; Kreisgemein-schaft der Ostvertriebenen und Evakuierten, Rinteln, "Resolution," 7 May 1950, BAK, B 126/5695; Schwarz, "Die ausgebliebene Katastrophe," esp. 153–54, 161; Braun, "Streben nach 'Sicherheit.' "

65. First quote: "Die Aufwertungsvorlage," *Beamtenbund* 9, no. 40 (4 Apr. 1925); Kather, *Gerechter Lastenausgleich!* 7; Mattes, "Verbesserte Aussichten," *Selbsthilfe* 24, no. 12 (2. Juni Ausg. 1950): 1.

66. For Luther, see Hughes, *Paying for Inflation*, 29–30, 119, 139; for Adenauer, see Large, *Germans to the Front*, 269, passim; Adenauer, "Grundsatzrede des 1. Vorsitzenden der Christlich-Demokratischen Union für die Britische Zone in der Aula der Kölner Universität," 24 Mar. 1946, in Adenauer, *Reden*, 95, 100–101, and Schulz, "Konrad Adenauers gesellschafts-politische Vorstellungen," 161–63; Adenauer to Schäffer, 4 Dec. 1950, BAK, B 126/51552; for Schäffer in 1945, see Niethammer, "Die amerikanische Besatzungsmacht," 186–87; for Schäffer quote: "Pressekonferenz," 8 Dec. 1950, 2, BAK, B 145/I-10.

67. Hughes, "Restitution and Democracy"; cf. Merritt, *Democracy Imposed*.

68. "Pressekonferenz," 8 Dec. 1950, BAK, B 145/I/10; "Niederschrift über die Beratun-gen in der 47. Sitzung des Bundesrates am 19.1.1951" and "Bekanntgabe der Beschlüße des Bundesrates an die Bundesregierung vom 19.1.1951," in BmI, ed., *Lastenausgleichsgesetze*, 1/3:63–147; Kather in 115. Sitzung (31 Jan. 1951), *VerhBT, Sten. Ber.,* 6:4353–57; Dr. Eckstein, "Ein Dokument schlechten Willens," *Selbsthilfe* 24, no. 24 (2. Dez. Ausg. 1950): 1–2.

CHAPTER 8

1. Schillinger, *Entscheidungsprozeß beim Lastenausgleich,* 187–282.

2. "Kurzprotokoll, 28. Sitzung, Ausschuß für den Lastenausgleich," 9 Feb. 1951, BAK, B 126/10448; Kunze, "Allgemeiner Bericht," *VerhBT, Sten. Ber.,* 11:9014–15; Kunze in [Dispu-tation], P-A, I 332/B 9, 31; for inventory levy, 208. Sitzung (7 May 1952), *VerhBT, Sten. Ber.,* 11:9099.

3. Dr. Linus Kather, "Der richtige Weg," *VK* 2, no. 10, 16, in ACDP, NL Kather, 14/1; "Die Fiktion der 50-%igen Vermögensabgabe," *VK* 2, no. 39, P-A, D 515/4; "Der Lastenausgleich — das große Problem," *Rheinische Zeitung* (Koblenz), 6 May 1952, P-A, D 515/7.

4. ZvD, "Stellungnahme zum Regierungsentwurf zum Lastenausgleich," 2 Nov. 1950, BAK, B 126/10433; "Niederschrift, 10. Sitzung des Ausschusses für Flüchtlingsfragen, Bundesrat," 31 Aug. 1950, 7, BAK, B 136/7324.

5. Kather at Pressekonferenz, 3 Nov. 1950, 3, 5, BAK, B 145/I-9; Kather, *Gerechter Lastenausgleich!* 11–12.

6. Mattes in "Niederschrift, Besprechung mit Organisationen der Abgabepflichtigen und der Geschädigten," 14 Sept. 1950, BAK, B 126/10433.

7. Schäffer to Kunze, 9 Nov. 1951, BAK, B 102/8223-3; Kunze, "Allgemeiner Bericht," *VerhBT, Sten. Ber.*, 11:9015; Kriedemann, "Betr.: Lastenausgleich," [Summer 1951], 3, ASD, NL Seuffert, no. 53.

8. "Vermerk, Vertriebenenforderungen—Lastenausgleich," 17 July 1950, BAK, B 136/6569; BmF, "Zur Ablösung der Lastenausgleichs-Abgaben," 17 Jan. 1952, BAK, B 126/5758; "Ein Ja mit Zähneknirschen," *Aachener Nachrichten* (5 Apr. 1952), P-A, D 515/6.

9. W. Mattes, "Verfälschter Lastenausgleich," *Selbsthilfe* 23, no. 1 (1. Jan. Ausg. 1949): 1–2; Kreisverband der Heimatvertriebenen, Saulgau, "Resolution des Kreisverbandes Saulgau," 2 Apr. 1949, BAK, B 148V/20.

10. For social concerns, see the numerous petitions in BAK, B 126/5726 and B 126/5731; for practical difficulties, BmF, *Der endgültige Lastenausgleich,* 21; for working- and lower-middle-class support for a Lastenausgleich, "Report no. 169, German Appraisals of Lastenausgleich," 6 May 1949, IfZ, OMGUS, DK 110.001, 9; Bohn and Bruhn, *Lastenausgleich,* 105–6, 116–18.

11. Kunze, "Der deutsche Lastenausgleich im Entwurf," *Die Neue Zeitung* (26/27 Jan. 1952), and Prof. Dr. Nöll von der Nahmer, "Wie weit ist der Lastenausgleich?" [ca. 28 Feb. 1952], both in P-A, D 515/5; Bohn and Bruhn, *Lastenausgleich,* 107–11, 332–33.

12. [Dr. Hans von Neuhoff], "Vorschläge zur Heranziehung des Hausrats zum Lastenausgleich," [Aug. 1950], BAK, B 126/5705; ZvF, "Forderungen zum Allgemeinen Lastenausgleich," 3 Mar. 1952, BAK, B 126/5700; "Kurzprotokoll, 32. Sitzung, Ausschuß für den Lastenausgleich," 23 Feb. 1951, BAK, B 126/10448; "Kurzprotokoll, 52. Sitzung, Ausschuß für den Lastenausgleich," 16 May 1951, BAK, B 126/10449; Kunze and Seuffert vs. Gille, [Disputation], 39–42, P-A, I 332/B 9.

13. "Stellungnahme des Hauptausschusses der Bombengeschädigten Berlin-Charlottenburg zur Frage der Hausratsentschädigung," [7 May 1951], P-A, I 332/B 7; Interessengemeinschaft der Fliegergeschädigten, Düsseldorf, [early 1951], BAK, B 126/5699; "Stellungnahme zum Regierungsentwurf zum Lastenausgleich," 2 Nov. 1950, BAK, B 126/10433.

14. Kunze, "Allgemeiner Bericht," *VerhBT, Sten. Ber.*, 11:9015; Mattes, "Die Vermögenszuwachs-Abgabe," *Selbsthilfe* 24, no. 17 (1. Sept. Ausg. 1950): 1–2.

15. "Äusserung der Bundesregierung zu der Stellungnahme des Bundesrates . . . zum Entwurf," [Jan. 1951], BAK, B 126/10445, 3–4; Kunze, "Allgemeiner Bericht," *VerhBT, Sten. Ber.*, 11:9015–16.

16. See §§ 229, 232, 233, 373 of the Lastenausgleich Law.

17. Kunze, "Allgemeiner Bericht," *VerhBT, Sten. Ber.*, 11:9016–18; for quotes: Kunze, "Leitgedanken für die Beratung . . . betr. . . . Lastenausgleich," 3 May 1952, 4, 19, BAK, B 126/10451.

18. Kather to Bucerius, 13 Nov. 1948, BAK, NL Holzapfel, no. 111; Schäffer in "Niederschrift, Besprechung, BmF mit Vertretern der Bundestagsfraktionen der Regierungskoalition . . . Lastenausgleich," 15 Nov. 1950, 3, BAK, B 126/51552; "Almosen oder Rechtsanspruch?" *Die Freiheit* (10 Oct. 1951), P-A, D 515/4.

19. Horst von Zitzewitz, "Die Alten dürfen nicht hungern," *Die Stimme der Vertriebenen* (24 June 1951), in BAK, B 126/5760; Kunze, "Allgemeiner Bericht," *VerhBT, Sten. Ber.*, 11:9016; Dr. Weber (FDP), "Kriegsschadenrente," ibid., 11:9037–40.

20. Kunze, "Leitgedanken für die Beratung . . . betr. . . . Lastenausgleich," 3 May 1952, 28–29, and Kunze, "Zu den vorliegenden Abänderungsanträgen," 3 May 1952, 8, BAK, B 126/10451; Kunze quote in "Pressekonferenz," 8 Dec. 1950, 20, BAK, B 145/I/10.

21. "Stellungnahme des Hauptausschusses der Bombengeschädigten Berlin-Charlottenburg zur Frage der Hausratsentschädigung," [7 May 1951], P-A, I 332/B 7; [totally bomb-damaged women], "An die Mitglieder des Ausschusses für den Lastenausgleich," [Feb. 1951?], and Interessengemeinschaft der Fliegergeschädigten, Düsseldorf, [Resolution], [Mar. 1951], BAK,

B 126/5699; Dr. Wilhelm Grotkopp, "Die Klippe der 8000 Mark," *Die Welt* (12 Feb. 1952), P-A, D 515/5.

22. "Äusserung der Bundesregierung zu der Stellungnahme des Bundesrates," [Jan. 1951], BAK, B 126/10445; 40. Sitzung (30 Mar. 1951) and 46. Sitzung (27 Apr. 1951), Ausschuß für den Lastenausgleich, BAK, B 126/10448; "Kurzprotokoll, 79. Sitzung des Ausschusses für den Lastenausgleich" (including Anlage), 29 Nov. 1951, BAK, B 126/10449; Schütz, "Eingliederungsdarlehen," *VerhBT, Sten. Ber.*, 11:9037; "Nach wie vor unannehmbar," [ca. 25 Feb. 1952], P-A, D 515/5; "Einheitswert nur mit Zuschlägen!" *Die Stimme der Vertriebenen* (2 Mar. 1952), P-A, D 515/6; ZvF, "Änderungsvorschläge zum Ausschußentwurf des Bundestages v. 15 Feb. 1952," 7, Mar. 1952, BAK, B 148V/22.

23. Kather, "Die Mindestforderungen," 4 May 1952, in Kather, *Eingliederung durch Lastenausgleich*, 9; Karl Wilhelm Böttcher, "Die deutschen Flüchtlinge als europäisches Problem," *Frankfurter Hefte* 3, no. 7 (July 1948): 609–10; Adenauer in "Erster Parteitag der CDU der britischen Zone," 15 Aug. 1947, in Pütz, ed., *Konrad Adenauer und die CDU*, 341; Landesausschuß "Heimatvertriebenes Landvolk" im Landesverband der Ostvertriebenen Nordrhein-Westfalen to Schäffer, 31 May 1950, BAK, B 126/5682.

24. Kather, *Gerechter Lastenausgleich!* 9; for quote (his emphasis), Dr. Koops to Landesverband, CDU, 8 Jan. 1949, BAK, NL Holzapfel, no. 111; "Vorschläge des Zentralverbandes der Fliegergeschädigten und Währungsgeschädigten zum Entwurf eines Gesetzes über einen Allgemeinen Lastenausgleich," [17 Mar. 1951], 5, BAK, B 126/5699.

25. Verwaltung für Finanzen, "Volkswirtschaftliche Überlegungen zum endgültigen Lastenausgleich," 1 June 1949, 20, BAK, B 126/5686; Der Bundesminister für Wohnungsbau to BmF, 19 Oct. 1950, BAK, B 136/7323.

26. Kunze, "Zum Lastenausgleich," 10 Aug. 1950, 9, P-A, I 332/B 2; Meyer, "Wohnraumhilfe," *VerhBT, Sten. Ber.*, 11:9041.

27. J. Kunze, "Erste Aufgabe für den Bundestag," *Freie Presse* [July 1949], in ASD, NL Weisser, no. 1080; "Vorschlag Weisser für eine gerechte Bemessung der Entschädigungsansprüche," BAK, B 150/8013-1; BmI to BmF, 25 Aug. 1950, BAK, B 136/7323; Schelsky, *Wandlungen der deutschen Familie*, 180–84.

28. [SPD], "Grundsätze eines sozialen Lastenausgleichs," [early 1950], 5, ASD, NL Seuffert, no. 53; "Die Nichtgeschädigten im Lastenausgleich," *VK* 1, no. 11 (7 Oct. 1950): 8; Kunze in 115. Sitzung (31 Jan. 1950), *VerhBT, Sten. Ber.*, 6:4347; Lastenausgleich Law § 302.

29. Schillinger, *Entscheidungsprozeß beim Lastenausgleich*, 218–29, 251 (n. 75), 256–63; Fritz, *Schadenfeststellung;* "Schematische Gerechtigkeit," *Frankfurter Neue Presse* (29 June 1951), P-A, D 515/4; "Erhöhung der Altmieten?" *Frankfurter Allgemeine Zeitung* (1 June 1951), P-A, D 515/3.

30. "Sitzung des Lastenausgleichs-Ausschusses mit Vertretern aus den Bezirken und Landtagen am 8. und 9. Feb. 1952," 2–3, ASD, Parteivorstand, no. 7; 79. Sitzung (26 July 1950), *VerhBT, Sten. Ber.*, 4:2857; [Kunze/Seuffert Disputation], 30–31, 34, P-A, I 332/B 9; W. Seuffert to R. Neumann, 4 May 1951, ASD, NL Seuffert, no. 13.

31. Gille in [Kunze/Seuffert Disputation], 36, P-A, I 332/B 9; Interessenverein kriegsgeschädigte Wirtschaft, "Vorschläge für die Ausgestaltung und Durchführung des Lastenausgleichs," Apr. 1950, and Landesausschuß "Heimatvertriebenes Landvolk" im Landesverband der Ostvertriebenen Nordrhein-Westfalen to Schäffer, 31 May 1950, both in BAK, B 126/5682.

32. Schillinger, *Entscheidungsprozeß beim Lastenausgleich*, 223–29, 256–63; 200. Sitzung (20 Mar. 1952), *VerhBT, Sten. Ber.*, 11:8564–65, 8580–81; Feststellungsgesetz in Bohn and Bruhn, eds., *Lastenausgleich*, 2:383–97; Ministerialrat von Aulock, "Das Feststellungsgesetz," *Sparkasse* Heft 12 [1952], 183–85, P-A, D 515/6.

33. Michael Horlacher in 115. Sitzung (31 Jan. 1950), *VerhBT, Sten. Ber.*, 6:4357–58; "Bewertungsprobleme im Lastenausgleich," *Handelsblatt* (14 Sept. 1948), in BAK, B 126/5758.

34. Direktor, Verwaltung für Finanzen, to Kriedemann, 30 Sept. 1948, and tables of *Einheitswerte* and immediate post–currency reform market values, BAK, B 126/5757; ZvD, "Memorandum zum Regierungsentwurf für den Lastenausgleich," 6 Nov. 1950, 2, 4, P-A, I 332/B 8; [Disputation], [early 1951], 31–32, P-A, I 332/B 9.

35. [SPD Flüchtlingsvertreter], "Grundsätze eines sozialen Lastenausgleichs," [early 1950], ASD, NL Seuffert, no. 53; Kunze, Pressekonferenz, 1 June 1950, 3–4, 7, BAK, B 145/I/6; Lastenausgleich Law, §§ 243–52; Schütz, "Hauptentschädigung," *VerhBT, Sten. Ber.*, 11:9035–36.

36. CDU/CSU, "Soforthilfe und Lastenausgleich," [Spring 1950], 4, BAK, B 126/5682; H. Kriedemann, "Dritte Lesung — und was dann?" *SPD Pressedienst — Politik* 7, no. 110 (13 May 1952): 2; [Disputation], 32, P-A, I 332/B 9.

37. ZvD/ZvF, *Forderungen . . . zum Lastenausgleich*, 11; Kather, *Gerechter Lastenausgleich!* 2, 8; Kunze, "Grundsatzfrage . . . Bericht des Ausschusses für den Lastenausgleich," 31 Mar. 1952, 8–9, ACDP, NL Kuntscher 008/2; Schütz, "Hauptentschädigung," *VerhBT, Sten. Ber.*, 11:9035–36.

38. Dr. Kitz, [no title], [mid-1949], 28, BAK, NL Blücher, no. 338; "Lastenausgleich auf individueller Grundlage," *FDK*, no. 8 (9 Feb. 1950): 4; O. Wackerzapp, "Altspareraufwertung durch Sondergesetz oder im Zuge des allgemeinen Lastenausgleichs?" [7 June 1951], BAK, B 126/27887; BmF to Staatssekretär in der Bundeskanzlei, 2 Oct. 1952, BAK, B 136/1188.

39. For ZvF history, see its periodical *Selbsthilfe*, 1946–53; "Die Forderungen des Deutschen Rentnerbundes an den Lastenausgleich," June 1951, BAK, B 126/27886.

CHAPTER 9

1. Kleßmann, *Die doppelte Staatsgründung*, 255–57; for a polemical but evocative study, Hannover, *Politische Diffamierung;* Kreisverband der Ostvertriebenen, "Zum Lastenausgleich," 12 June 1950, BAK, B 126/5693; Neumann, *Block der Heimatvertriebenen*, esp. 11–12; Wilfried Loth, "Der Koreakrieg und die Staatswerdung der Bundesrepublik," in Foschepoth, ed., *Kalter Krieg*, 348–49. For East Germany, see chap. 4 above.

2. "Neue kommunistische Störungsversuche," *Selbsthilfe* 26, no. 2 (2. Jan. Ausg. 1952): 2, " 'Einheitsverband' entlarvt," *Selbsthilfe* 26, no. 6 (2. März Ausg. 1952): 3, and Krause, *Flucht vor Bombenkrieg*, 242–46; Westdeutscher Flüchtlingskongreß, "Erklärung," 22 May 1955, BAK, B 150/3293; Kather, "Die Mindestforderungen," 4 May 1952, in Kather, *Eingliederung durch Lastenausgleich*, 7; "Neue Warnung vor kommunistischer Wühlarbeit," *VK* 3, no. 8 (23 Feb. 1952): 4; "Auf Dummenfang," *Union in Deutschland* 7, no. 65 (1953): 3.

3. Kleßmann, *Die doppelte Staatsgründung*, 255–57 (quote: 257); for second paired quotes, Doering-Manteuffel, "Strukturmerkmale der Kanzlerdemokratie," 14.

4. Neumann, *Block der Heimatvertriebenen*, 12, 67; Merritt, *Democracy Imposed*, 94–107, 394; Schwarz, "Die ausgebliebene Katastrophe."

5. Abelshauser, *Wirtschaftsgeschichte*, 74–84; Friedrich-Wilhelm Henning, "Konrad Adenauer und die soziale Marktwirtschaft bis 1956," in Pohl, ed., *Adenauers Verhältnisse*, 26–27; Nicholls, *Freedom with Responsibility*, 270–99; Dickhaus, "Bank deutscher Länder," 176–78; for a taste of contemporary concerns, see, e.g., "Ernste Lage," hvp Kommentare, *Archiv: Informationsdienst des Göttinger Arbeitskreises* 10, no. 51 (8 Mar. 1951): 1.

6. Abelshauser, *Wirtschaftsgeschichte*, 74–84; Temin, " 'Korea Boom' in West Germany"; Nicholls, *Freedom with Responsibility*, 293–99.

7. Clemens J. Neumann, "Der Standpunkt der Katholischen Kirche zum Lastenausgleich,"

VK 3, no. 16 (26 Apr. 1952): 9 (his emphasis); "Stellungnahme des Katholischen Flüchtlingsrats zum Lastenausgleich," in BmVt, "Mitteilung für die Presse," 15 Mar. 1952, BAK, B 150/3293.

8. Wildt, *Beginn der "Konsumgesellschaft,"* 45–47, 67, passim; Schillinger, *Entscheidungsprozeß beim Lastenausgleich,* 270 (n. 144); Kramer, *West German Economy,* table 5.6.

9. Hockerts, *Sozialpolitische Entscheidungen,* 184, 195–97, 202–3; "Erklärung der Bundesregierung zur zweiten Lesung . . . Lastenausgleich," 6 May 1952, BAK, B 126/10450.

10. Adenauer, "Ansprache vor dem Bundesparteiausschuß der CDU in Bonn, 6. September 1952," in Adenauer, *Reden,* 266–67; Goschler, *Wiedergutmachung,* esp. 257–305; Rudolf Huhn, "Die Wiedergutmachungsverhandlungen in Wassenaar," in Herbst and Goschler, eds., *Wiedergutmachung,* 139–60; Stern, *Whitewashing Yellow Badge,* esp. 349–56, 365–85; Pross, *Wiedergutmachung,* 52–53, 57–72, passim.

11. Schwarz, *Wiederherstellung des Kredites,* esp. 14–15, 32–34, 40–41, 51–55, 59–61; Adenauer, "Ansprache vor dem Bundesparteiausschuß der CDU in Bonn, 6. September 1952," in Adenauer, *Reden,* 266.

12. Large, *Germans to the Front,* 32–45, 62–65, 82–97.

13. "Di-visionen," *Selbsthilfe* 24, no. 17 (1. Sept. Ausg. 1950): 1; Mattes, "Kriegsgeschädigte und Sicherheitspolitik," *Selbsthilfe* 24, no. 20 (2. Okt. Ausg. 1950): 1; Fritz Brühl, "Rangordnung der Lasten," *Süddeutsche Zeitung* (2 Feb. 1951), P-A, D 515/3; "Unannehmbar!" *Ost-West Kurier* (14 Mar. 1952), P-A, D 515/6.

14. Breitling, *Verbände in der Bundesrepublik,* 77; Krause, *Flucht vor Bombenkrieg,* 235–41, passim; "5 Jahre Zentralverband," *Selbsthilfe* 26, no. 13 (1. Juli Ausg. 1952): 1.

15. Breitling, *Verbände in der Bundesrepublik,* 74; Lodgman, Sudetendeutsche Landsmannschaft, "Lastenausgleich, ZvD—Landsmannschaften," 8 Nov. 1950, BAK, B 126/5683; Kather correspondence with de Vries in BAK, NL de Vries, no. 6; Kather, *Die entscheidenden Jahre,* 167–70, 186–87; "10. 1. 53. Sitzung des Bundesvorstandes," in Wengst, ed., *FDP-Bundesvorstand,* 784–85; Ahonen, "Domestic Constraints," 34.

16. "Mittelstand und Lastenausgleich," *VK* 2, no. 10, 13, ACDP, NL Kather, 14/1; "Die Fliegergeschädigten verloren viel—die Vertriebenen alles," *VK* 3, no. 15 (19 Apr. 1952): 4–5; for moderating influence: expellee leader Wilfried Keller, cited in Neumann, *Block der Heimatvertriebenen,* 49; for bomb-damaged anger, see, e.g., Ortsverband Forchheim, Bund der Flieger- und Kriegsgeschädigten, to Bundeskanzler, 27 Feb. 1950, BAK, B 126/5698; Mattes, "Gleiches Recht für alle Geschädigten," *Selbsthilfe* 25, no. 22 (2. Nov. Ausg. 1951): 1; "Der Bonner Lastenausgleich und die Parteien," *Selbsthilfe* 26, no. 11 (1. Juni Ausg. 1952): 1.

17. "Heimatvertriebene fordern Lastenausgleich," *Ost-West Kurier* 3, no. 13 (1–7 Apr. 1950); L. Kather, "Weshalb ich Ja sagte," in Kather, *Eingliederung durch Lastenausgleich,* 27.

18. "Soforthilfe endlich genehmigt," *Selbsthilfe* 23, no. 16 (2. Aug. Ausg. 1949): 1; "Noch ist es nicht zu spät," *VK* 3, no. 8 (23 Feb. 1952): 2.

19. Kunze, "Allgemeiner Bericht," *VerhBT, Sten. Ber.,* 11:9017–18; "Vermerk," 20 July 1950, BAK, B 136/6569; Kather cited in Kunze, "Niederschrift, Besprechung betr. Lastenausgleich," 26 Oct. 1951, P-A, I 332/B 5; "Staatssekretär Oberländer verneint Möglichkeit eines echten Lastenausgleichs," *Die Neue Zeitung* (4 Dec. 1951), P-A, D 515/5.

20. Clemens J. Neumann, "Vorfinanzierung des Lastenausgleichs," *Ost-West Kurier* (8 Feb. 1952), P-A, D 515/5; BVD/ZvD, "Unannehmbar!" *Ost-West Kurier* (14 Mar. 1952), P-A, D 515/6; "Kurzprotokoll über die Gesamtvorstandsitzung," 4–5 Apr. 1952, BVD-A, Protokolle des Präsidiums und Gesamtvorstandes der ZvD, 1950–53; BVD, [press release], 5 Apr. 1952, ACDP, NL Kuntscher 008/1.

21. Josef Foschepoth, "Westintegration staat Wiedervereinigung: Adenauers Deutschlandpolitik 1949–1955," in Foschepoth, ed., *Adenauer und deutsche Frage,* 34, passim; Large,

Germans to the Front, 45–47, 51–56, 74–81, passim; "Manöver," *Selbsthilfe* 23, no. 18 (2. Sept. Ausg. 1949): 3.

22. For quote: Karola Piontek, "Betr. Lastenausgleich Hausratentschädigung," 27 Nov. 1950, BAK, B 126/5760; Kather, "Die Mindestforderungen," 4 May 1952, in Kather, *Eingliederung durch Lastenausgleich!* 8–9; Kather to Bundeskanzler, 20 Sept. 1951, BAK, B 136/645; "Kriegsgeschädigte und Sicherheitspolitik," *Selbsthilfe* 24, no. 20 (2. Okt. Ausg. 1950): 1.

23. Adenauer, *Tee-Gespräche,* 1:113; von Brentano to Adenauer, 25 Apr. 1952, in Baring, ed., *Sehr verehrter Herr Bundeskanzler!* 93; 210. Kabinettssitzung (25 Mar. 1952), in von Jena, ed., *Kabinettsprotokolle der Bundesregierung,* 5:192–93; Lenz, *Zentrum der Macht,* 274–77, 330–33; Birke, *Nation ohne Haus,* 280–320; "Das heiße Eisen: Geben und Nehmen," *Rhein Zeitung* (17 May 1952), P-A, D 515/7; BDI, *Jahresbericht,* 1 June 1951–30 Apr. 1952, 68.

24. Noelle and Neumann, *Jahrbuch der öffentlichen Meinung,* 172–73, 252–53; Birke, *Nation ohne Haus,* 353–59; "Lastenausgleich — Grundgesetz," *Ost-West Kurier* 5, no. 21 (May 1952 Folge 4); "Im Zeichen der Vertriebenenstimmen," *Badische Neueste Nachrichten* (19 May 1952), P-A, D 515/7; Schillinger, *Entscheidungsprozeß beim Lastenausgleich,* 274; Henzler, *Fritz Schäffer,* 347–48; Blücher in 210. Kabinettssitzung (25 Mar. 1952), in von Jena, ed., *Kabinettsprotokolle der Bundesregierung,* 5:192.

25. Hockerts, "Adenauer als Sozialpolitiker," 469–70; Wenzel, *Adenauer,* 20, 56, 71–72, 98–99, 128–29; Schulz, "Konrad Adenauers gesellschaftspolitische Vorstellungen," 179.

26. For Kunze quote: [Disputation], [early 1951], 40, P-A, I 332/B 9; for Weimar Republic, see chap. 1 above; [petitions from expellee groups from late April and early May 1952 in] ACDP, NL Kuntscher, 008/1; Ollenhauer (SPD), 211. Sitzung (14 May 1952), *VerhBT, Sten. Ber.,* 11:9263–65; Kunze in 213. Sitzung (16 May 1952), ibid., 11:9391; "Lastenausgleich — Anfang, nicht Abschluß," *Rhein-Zeitung* (Koblenz) (24 May 1952), P-A, D 515/8. See here similarly the union leader quoted in Abelshauser, *Die langen fünfziger Jahre,* 46.

27. For SPD anger at defending bill, see, e.g., Seuffert in 208. Sitzung (7 May 1952), *VerhBT, Sten. Ber.,* 11:9095–96; for Seuffert quote: 212. Sitzung (15 May 1952), ibid., 11:9316; see Diehl, *Thanks of the Fatherland,* esp. 241–42.

28. "Erklärung der Fraktionen der CDU/CSU, FDP, und DP zu der Beratung des Lastenausgleichsgesetzes," 6 May 1952, BAK, B 126/10450; Hughes, *Paying for Inflation,* 134–35, 152, 156.

29. "Die dramatische Endphase der dritten Lesung," *Ost-West Kurier* 5, no. 21 (May 1952 Folge 4); "Annahme des Lastenausgleichsgesetzes im Bundestag gesichert," *Frankfurter Rundschau* (16 May 1952), P-A, D 515/7; "Neue Bewährungsprobe des Bundestages," *Union im Deutschland* 6, nos. 41/42 (23 May 1952): 2; 212. Sitzung (15 May 1952), *VerhBT, Sten. Ber.,* 11:9320.

30. Schillinger, *Entscheidungsprozeß beim Lastenausgleich,* 277–78, reports on Schäffer's resistance, though he gives no source; Wenzel, *Adenauer,* 25, 27–28; Abs in Schwarz, *Wiederherstellung des Kredites,* 56; Schwarz, *Adenauer,* 647–48.

31. "Protokoll über die Gesamtvorstandssitzung des BVD/ZvD am 26. Mai 1952," and [press release], 28 May 1952, BVD-A, Protokolle des Präsidiums und Gesamtvorstandes der ZvD, 1950–53.

32. "Protokoll über die Gesamtvorstandssitzung des BVD/ZvD am 26. Mai 1952," BVD-A, Protokolle des Präsidiums und Gesamtvorstandes der ZvD, 1950–53; Gille to Kraft, 25 June 1952, and Landesverband der vertriebenen Deutschen/Vereinigte Landsmannschaften Schleswig-Holstein (signed Gille), "Zur Entschließung des BVD-Vorstandes vom 26.5.1952," 9 June 1952, in BAK, NL Kraft, no. 38; "Nach Canossa gehen wir nicht!" *Ostdeutsche Zeitung. Die Stimme,* no. 21 (25 May 1952).

33. CJN, "Erfolg," *VK* 3, no. 19 (19 May 1952): 1–4; Horst von Zitzewitz, "Keine Kraft mehr

zu warten!" *Die Stimme der Vertriebenen* (31 May 1952), P-A, D 515/8; "Nach Canossa gehen wir nicht!" *Ostdeutsche Zeitung. Die Stimme,* no. 21 (25 May 1952).

34. "Was haben wir 1951 erreicht?" *Selbsthilfe* 26, no. 1 (1. Jan. Ausg. 1952): 2; "Erfolge des Zentralverbandes," ibid. 26, no. 8 (2. Apr. Ausg. 1952): 1; Mattes, "Lastenausgleich ohne Gleichberechtigung," ibid. 26, no. 10 (2. Mai Ausg. 1952): 1; "Der Bonner Lastenausgleich und die Parteien," ibid. 26, no. 11 (1. Juni Ausg. 1952): 1; "5 Jahre Zentralverband," ibid. 26, no. 13 (1. Juli Ausg. 1952): 1; *Total-Flieger- und Währungs-Geschädigten in Bayern,* 1952, 5–6, BAK, B 126/10444.

35. "86. Sitzung des deutschen Bundesrates," 6 June 1952, "Kurzprotokoll der 37. Sitzung des Vermittlungsausschusses," 7 July 1952, and "Mündlicher Bericht des Vermittlungsausschusses," 4 July 1952, in BmI, ed., *Lastenausgleichsgesetze,* 1/3:1070–1102, 1130–37, and 1138–46; "Die Entscheidung," *VK* 3, no. 26 (5 July 1952): 1–2.

36. O. Wackerzapp, "Altspareraufwertung durch Sondergesetz oder im Zuge des allgemeinen Lastenausgleichs?" [June 1951], BAK, B 126/27887; BmF to Frau Minna Lotz, 15 Nov. 1951, BAK, B 126/5703; Lastenausgleich Law, §§ 228, 261, 272, 365.

37. BmF, *Der endgültige Lastenausgleich,* 65; BmF to Staatssekretär in der Bundeskanzlei, 2 Oct. 1952, BAK, B 136/1188; ZvF: Mattes, "Währungsgeschädigte in Gefahr," *Selbsthilfe* 24, no. 13 (1. Juli Ausg. 1950): 1; Deutscher Rentnerbund, "Vorschläge, Beseitigung der Währungsschäden," Nov. 1953, BAK, B 126/27887; "Niederschrift, Sitzung des Ausschusses für den Kapitalmarkt," 23 Oct. 1952, BAK, B 126/27886.

38. Deutscher Rentnerbund, "Entwurf für Sofortprogramm für die währungsgeschädigten Altrentner," 19 June 1951, and Dr. F. W. Kärcher, "Nur die quotale Altsparerentschädigung kann den Kapitalmarkt retten," [1952], in BAK, B 126/27886; Zorn quoted in " 'Stiefkinder des Staates' sorgen für ihr Recht," *Frankfurter Rundschau* (15 Oct. 1952), P-A, D 515/9; "Verbitterte Altsparer," *Aachener Nachrichten* (23 Apr. 1953), P-A, D 515/11.

39. BmF to Staatssekretär des Bundeskanzleramts, 2 Oct. 1952, BAK, B 126/27887; "Die 'Schattenquote' aus der Geldreform wird realisiert," *Frankfurter Rundschau* (24 Apr. 1953), P-A, D 515/11.

40. BmF to Staatssekretär des Bundeskanzleramts, 2 Oct. 1952, BAK, B 126/27887; "Altsparer und Pfandbriefbesitzer dürfen wieder hoffen," *Der Kommentar,* no. 202 (10 Jan. 1952), BAK, B 126/27886; "Unsere Mindestforderungen," *Selbsthilfe* 27, no. 3 (1. Feb. Ausg. 1953): 1; "Die 'Schattenquote' aus der Geldreform wird realisiert," *Frankfurter Rundschau* (24 Apr. 1953), and "Altsparer sollen 13,5 v. H. erhalten," *Ruhr-Nachrichten* (26 Apr. 1953), P-A, D 515/11; "Altsparergesetz," in Bohn and Bruhn, eds., *Lastenausgleich,* 2:415–40.

41. See here Reismann (FU) and Tichi (Indep.) in 115. Sitzung (31 Jan. 1951), *VerhBT, Sten. Ber.,* 6:4378, 4362; Douglas, *How Institutions Think,* 4; Amato, *Victims and Values,* 209–14.

42. Dr. Atzenroth (FDP), "Schlechter Kompromiß im Lastenausgleich," *FDK* 3, no. 46 (8 July 1952): 9; "Neue Bewährungsprobe des Bundestages," *Union im Deutschland* 6, nos. 41/42 (23 May 1952): 2; Blücher in 207. Sitzung (6 May 1952), *VerhBT, Sten. Ber.,* 11:8968; Falter, "Kontinuität und Neubeginn."

43. Kather, *Die entscheidenden Jahre,* 229–30; [various CDU-Bundesvorstand Sitzungen], in Buchstab, ed., *Protokolle des CDU-Bundesvorstandes,* 76, 146–47, 335, 343, 636–39; Neumann, *Block der Heimatvertriebenen,* 91–92, 96, 296–97, 303–6.

44. "ZvD. Verbesserungen des Lastenausgleichs," *Ost-West Kurier* (25 Feb. 1954), P-A, D 515/12; "Betr. 8. Gesetz zur Änderung des Lastenausgleichsgesetzes," 27 Sept. 1956, BAK, B126/10483; "Kurzprotokoll über die Besprechung am 23. März 1956 . . . betr. ein Lastenausgleichsschlußgesetz," BAK, B 150/2600.

45. "Stand der Hausratentschädigung," *VdL Informationen* 5, no. 38 (24 Sept. 1956): 6; "Entwurf eines 8. Gesetzes zur Änderung des Lastenausgleichsgesetzes," ibid. 5, no. 25

(25 June 1956): 11; "Die soziale Bilanz muß stimmen," *Deutsche Einheit* (15 Dec. 1956), P-A, D 515/15; "Machtvolle Demonstration der Einheimischen," *Selbsthilfe* 29, no. 13 (1. Juli Ausg. 1955): 1; "Kurzprotokoll über die Besprechung am 23. März 1956 . . . betr. ein Lastenausgleichsschlußgesetz," BAK, B 150/2600.

46. Paul Ittner to Präsidenten, Bundesausgleichsamt, 3 July 1953, BAK, B 126/12676; "Neues Unrecht droht!" *Selbsthilfe* 27, no. 3 (1. Feb. Ausg. 1953): 1; Neumann, *Block der Heimatvertriebenen*, 96, passim.

47. Peter Paul Nahm, "Kriegsschaden und Mittelstand," in BmVt, ed., *Dokumente Kriegsschäden*, 1:x–xi; Nahm, . . . *doch das Leben ging weiter*, 36; quotation cited in Lehmann, *Im Fremden ungewollt*, 100.

48. "Um die Verantwortung des Verbandes," *Selbsthilfe* 30, no. 9 (1. Mai Ausg. 1956): 1; Bund der Westvertriebenen, Mannheim-Sanhofen, to Oberbürgermeister der Stadt Heidelberg, 4 Mar. 1957, BAK, B106 (150)/22863; Kai-Uwe von Hassel in "Protokoll des CDU-Bundesvorstandes," 11 Mar. 1953, in Buchstab, ed., *Protokolle des CDU-Bundesvorstandes*, 610.

49. For quote: Athen., "Unsere Weltanschauung ist das Recht," *GB/BHE Nachrichtendienst der Partei* 4, no. 1 (2 Jan. 1953): 5; Allemann, *Bonn ist nicht Weimar*, 275, 296–99; Prof. Dr. Ziegler, "Sozialer Verband oder Interessenorganisation?" *Selbsthilfe* 29, no. 1 (1. Jan. Ausg. 1955): 1; "Die Verbesserung des Lastenausgleichs," ibid. 31, no. 8 (2. Apr. Ausg. 1957): 1.

50. Gille to Kraft, 25 June 1952, BAK, NL Kraft, no. 38; Neumann, *Block der Heimatvertriebenen*, 78, 348–51; [Protokoll], 29 Aug. 1957, BVD-A, Protokolle des Präsidiums und Gesamtvorstandes, BVD, 1954–58; Krause, *Flucht vor Bombenkrieg*, 236–37; Koopmans, *Democracy from Below*, 26.

51. "Der Staat und die einheimischen Geschädigten," *Selbsthilfe* 27, no. 12 (2. Juni Ausg. 1953): 2; "Lastenausgleich und Verteidigung," *VK* 8, nos. 8/9 (30 Mar. 1957): 5; Baring, *Im Anfang Adenauer*, 317.

52. Norbert Frei, "Das Problem der NS-Vergangenheit in der Ära Adenauer," in Weisbrod, ed., *Rechtsradikalismus*, 29; Herbert, "Rückkehr in die Bürgerlichkeit?" 167–68; Günther Ziehm, "BHE im Kampf," BAK, Zsg 1-54/15; Athen., "Demokratie — aber demokratisch!" *GB/BHE Nachrichtendienst der Partei* 4, no. 5 (27 Feb. 1953); "10. Jahrestag der ausgebombten Städte," *Selbsthilfe* 29, no. 8 (2. Apr. Ausg. 1955): 1.

53. "Protokoll der 66. Sitzung des Lastenausgleichsausschusses des BVD," 15 Mar. 1955, BAK, B 126/10473; "Das war die Abschlußlesung," *Selbsthilfe* 29, no. 6 (2. März Ausg. 1955): 1; "19. August 1952," ibid. 27, no. 16 (2. Aug. Ausg. 1953): 1; "Frau Müller weiß Bescheid," ibid., 3.

54. For the statistics, see Dr. Klötzer (BHE), "8. LAG-Novelle statt Lastenausgleichsschlußgesetz," *GB/BHE Nachrichtendienst der Partei* 7, no. 13 (Anfang Juli 1956); Abelshauser, *Wirtschaftsgeschichte*.

55. Braun, "Streben nach 'Sicherheit,'" esp. 293; Wildt, *Beginn der "Konsumgesellschaft"*; Schwarz, "Die ausgebliebene Radikalisierung"; Birke, *Nation ohne Haus*, 372–73.

56. Dietrich Thränhardt, "Wahlen und Wiedervereinigung: Die Absicherung des Weststaats," in Foschepoth, ed., *Adenauer und deutsche Frage*.

57. Diehl, *Thanks of the Fatherland;* Wengst, *Beamtentum;* Hockerts, *Sozialpolitische Entscheidungen*.

58. For Gille quote: "Grundsätze der Geschädigtenpolitik," *GB/BHE Nachrichtendienst der Partei* 5, no. 10 (25 May 1954): 7; "Der Topf des Lastenausgleichs," *Selbsthilfe* 30, nos. 15/16 (Aug. Ausg. 1956): 1; "Kurzprotokoll über die Besprechung . . . im BmVt," 23 Mar. 1956, BAK, B 150/2600.

59. Dr. Klötzer, "8. LAG-Novelle statt Lastenausgleichsschlußgesetz," *GB/BHE Nachrichtendienst der Partei* 7, no. 13 (Anfang Juli 1956).

60. "Kurzprotokoll über die 48. Kabinettsausschuß-Sitzung am 17. Mai 1956," BAK, B 126/10483.

61. "Der Topf des Lastenausgleichs," *Selbsthilfe* 30, nos. 15/16 (Aug. Ausg. 1956): 1; ZvF to Staatssekretär Dr. Hartmann, 1 Oct. 1956, BAK, B 126/10484; "Soziale Neugliederung des deutschen Volkes," *GB/BHE Nachrichtendienst der Partei* 5, no. 12 (25 June 1954); "10. Jahrestag der ausgebombten Städte," *Selbsthilfe* 29, no. 8 (2. Apr. Ausg. 1955): 1; "Ist das wirklich ein gerechter Lastenausgleich?" *VdL Informationen* 6, no. 27 (5 July 1957): 7; Interessengemeinschaft heimatvertriebener Selbständiger und Unterhaltsempfänger, Marburg, to Schäffer, [Oct. 1955], BAK, B 126/10482.

62. The Finance Ministry simply stopped preserving most individual letters and local- and regional-group petitions once the Lastenausgleich Law had been promulgated, presumably because ministry officials thought the heat would be off. See, though, Interessengemeinschaft heimatvertriebener Selbständiger und Unterhaltsempfänger to BmF, [Oct. 1955], BAK, B 126/10482; "Denkschrift der Vertretung der heimatvertriebenen Wirtschaft, Landesverband Nordrhein-Westfalen, zur 8. Novelle," [mid-1956], P-A, II 443/2.

63. "Kein Lastenausgleichs-'Schlußgesetz,'" *Selbsthilfe* 30, no. 7 (1. Apr. Ausg. 1956): 1; "Kurzprotokoll über die Besprechung am 23 März 1956," BAK, B 150/2600.

64. "Verbesserung des Lastenausgleichs gefordert," *Sicht des Gesamtdeutschen Blocks/BHE* (19 June 1954): 1–3; "Lastenausgleich und Verteidigung," *VK* 8, nos. 8/9 (30 Mar. 1957): 5.

65. "Kein Lastenausgleichs-'Schlußgesetz,'" *Selbsthilfe* 30, no. 7 (1. Apr. Ausg. 1956): 1; Dr. Klötzer, "8. LAG-Novelle statt Lastenausgleichsschlußgesetz," *GB/BHE Nachrichtendienst der Partei* 7, no. 13 (Anfang Juli 1956): 13; "Die soziale Bilanz muß stimmen," *Deutsche Einheit* (15 Dec. 1956), P-A, D 515/15.

66. "Kein Lastenausgleichs-'Schlußgesetz,'" *Selbsthilfe* 30, no. 7 (1. Apr. Ausg. 1956): 1; "Einigkeit aller Geschädigtenverbände über das sogenannte Lastenausgleichsschlußgesetz," *VdL Informationen* 5, no. 17 (30 Apr. 1956): 11.

67. Dr. Blaum, "'Rechtstitel' oder Wahlpropaganda?" *Selbsthilfe* 30, no. 9 (1. Mai Ausg. 1956): 1; "Denkschrift, Geschädigten-Verbände, 8. Gesetz zur Änderung des Lastenausgleichsgesetzes," [mid-1956], P-A, II 443/2; Theodor Oberländer, "Soziale Waffen im Kalten Krieg," *GB/BHE Nachrichtendienst der Partei* 6, no. 6 (20 Mar. 1955): 4.

68. "Die Entscheidung ist gefallen!" *Selbsthilfe* 31, no. 7 (1. Apr. Ausg. 1957): 1; Prof. Dr. Wilhelm Ziegler, "Was erwarten wir in 1957?" ibid. 31, nos. 1/2 (Jan. Ausg. 1957): 1; "MdB Joh. Kunze über Probleme des Lastenausgleichs," Stuttgart [radio], 3 Apr. 1957, P-A, D 515/Ordner 9.

69. "Auszug, Kurzprotokoll, 48. Kabinettsausschußsitzung," 17 May 1956, and "Kurzprotokoll über die 137. Kabinettssitzung," 6 June 1956, BAK, B 126/10483.

70. "Die Politik der neuen Bundesregierung," *Bulletin* (Presse und Informationsdienst der Bundesregierung), no. 203 (30 Oct. 1957): 1859–60; [Dr. Czaja (CDU)], "Begründung," [1956], BAK, B 150/2600; [Staatssekretär Dr. Peter Nahm], "Die Neugestaltung des Lastenausgleichs," *Ost-West Kurier* (1 June 1957), P-A, D 515/Ordner 9; "Oberländer in Stuttgart!" *Selbsthilfe* 30, no. 13 (1. Juli Ausg. 1956): 1; Dietrich, *Eigentum für Jeden.*

71. "Denkschrift, Geschädigten-Verbände, 8. Gesetz zur Änderung des Lastenausgleichsgesetzes," [mid-1956], P-A, II 443/2; "Forderungen zum Lastenausgleichsschlußgesetz," *Selbsthilfe* 30, no. 6 (2. März Ausg. 1956): 1; Staatssekretär Dr. Peter Nahm, "Über die Bedeutung der 8. Novelle zum LAG," Norddeutsche Rundfunk, (27 July 1957), P-A, D 515/Ordner 9; "Auszug, Kurzprotokoll, 48. Kabinettsausschußsitzung," 17 May 1956, BAK, B 126/10483.

72. Hockerts, *Sozialpolitische Entscheidungen,* 320–425.

73. "Forderungen zum Lastenausgleichsschlußgesetz," *Selbsthilfe* 30, no. 6 (2. März Ausg.

1956): 1; Dr. Hans von Neuhoff, "Die verbesserte Kriegsschadenrente," *Ost-West Kurier* (4 May 1957), P-A, D 515/Ordner 9; "Denkschrift, Geschädigten-Verbände, 8. Gesetz zur Änderung des Lastenausgleichsgesetzes," [mid-1956], and "Zweite Denkschrift, Geschädigten-Verbände, 8. Gesetz zur Änderung des Lastenausgleichsgesetzes," 4 Dec. 1956, P-A, II 443/2.

BIBLIOGRAPHY

ARCHIVAL SOURCES

Archiv für Christlich-Demokratische Politik, Sankt-Augustin
  Deutschland-Unions-Dienst: 1947/48–53
  Union in Deutschland: 1950–53
  I 105 — Nachlaß Binder: 007, A I/14–15; 013, B I/1–2; 014, B I/3–4; 016, B I/7; 039, C I/12B;
    040, C I/2C, C I/14; 041, C II/1A, 2B; 042, C II/2A; 043, C II/3A–3B; 044, C II/4–5; 090,
    F I/71
  I 337 — Nachlaß Kather: 02/3, 03/1–4, 6, 04/3, 10/13, 14/1
  I 202 — Nachlaß Kuntscher: 00312, 008/1–2, 2616
  I 401 — Nachlaß Rock: 025/3
  I 151 — Nachlaß Thiess: 005/II, 015/II–III
Archiv der sozialen Demokratie, Bonn
  Büro Schumacher: J 86/1–2, J 88
  Nachlaß Seuffert: 13, 19, 20, 25, 37, 53, 65
  Nachlaß Weisser: 404, 456–57, 466, 845, 855, 1040, 1079–82, 1085, 1086.I–II, 1089, 1091, 1220,
    1244, 1519, 1710
  Partei-Vorstand
    Neuer Bestand: 846
    Protokolle: 3–12 (1948–57)
  SPD — Pressedienst
    Politik, Vols. 3–9 (1948–55)
    Volkswirtschaft, Vols. 3–12 (1948–57)
  Zeitungs-Ausschnitte (K 291/I): 1947–52
Bund der vertriebenen Deutschen — Archiv, Bonn
  Protokolle des Präsidiums und Gesamtvorstandes des ZvD, 1950–53
Bundesarchiv Koblenz
  Z 1 — Länderrat, Amerikanische Besatzungszone: 294, 309, 311, 341, 345
  Z 2 — Beirat, Britische Besatzungszone: 53, 95, 101
  Z 3 — Wirtschaftsrat: 85, Anhang N 1, Anhang N 7
  Z 4 — Länderrat, Bi-Zone: 48, 530–31, 542, 551, 554

Z 13 — Direktorialkanzlei des Verwaltungsrates des Vereinigten Wirtschaftsgebietes: 858

Z 32 — Sonderstelle Geld und Kredit: 12–14, 21, 25, 27, 30–55

B 102 — Bundesministerium der Wirtschaft: 8215/1–3, 8223/1–3, 8227/1–3

B 126 — Bundesministerium für Finanzen: 5678–83, 5685–93, 5695–5706, 5712, 5714–15, 5726–27, 5730–31, 5757–63, 5769, 10431–54, 10473–84, 12676–77, 12738, 27886–87 51552

B 136 — Bundeskanzlei: 644–46, 651, 1167, 1186, 1188, 1193, 6569, 7314, 7323–24

B 145/I — Pressekonferenzen: 5–6, 9–10, 16

B 148 — Lastenausgleichbehörden: V/20–22, 44

B 150 — Bundesministerium für Vertriebene: 480, 2600, 2669–70, 3293–94, 4790/1–2, 4791/1–2, 4820, 8013/1–2 22778, 22863

Zsg 1 — Zeitgeschichtliche Sammlung: 54, 112, 118, 204, 238, 305

Nachlaß Blücher: 231, 324–27, 329, 331, 333–34, 336–39, 352, 354

Nachlaß de Vries: 6, 9

Nachlaß Holzapfel: 41, 105, 111–12, 187

Nachlaß Kraft: 38, 51

Nachlaß Schäffer: 30, 33

Deutscher Bundestag — Parlamentsarchiv, Bonn

D 515 — Zeitungs-Ausschnitte, Lastenausgleich: 1–15, Ordner 9–10

I 332 — Lastenausgleichs-Ausschuß: A 1, B 1–9

II 443 — Lastenausgleichs-Ausschuß: B 2

Institut für Zeitgeschichte, Munich

OMGUS: DK 110.001

Sammlung Möller

National Archives and Records Service, Washington, D.C./Suitland, Md.

RG 59 — Department of State: 734, 3764A, 3769–70, 3792A, 3794, 3797A, 6576–76

RG 107 — War Department: 7–8

RG 165 — War Department: 233, 407, 555

RG 200 — General Lucius Clay, Personal Papers: 1–2

RG 260 OMGUS: 1, 24–26, 33, 66, 72, 74, 91, 93, 95, 99–100, 102, 106, 117, 119, 151, 153, 276, 366, 543

SWNCC: 303

Theodor Heuss Archiv, Gummersbach

Blücher — *Kurze Nachrichten,* 1948–49

Freie Deutsche Korrespondenz, 1950–52

FDP Akten:

Gesamtvorstand Sitzungen, 1949–50

Parteiakten: 565, A 13

Sachakten: 8

Nachlaß Becker: 41, 51

Nachlaß Blücher (A-3): 1, 28, 35–36, 44, 47, 54, 56, 66, 73

Nachlaß Blücher (N 37): 11–13, 24–25

Nachlaß Dehler: 941, 989, 993, 998, 1076, 1147, 3111–13

PERIODICALS

Archiv. Informationsdienst des Göttinger Arbeitskreises, 1949–55

BHE — Dienst, 1951–52

Flüchtlings-Kurier, 1948–49

Frankfurter Hefte, 1946–49

Gesamtdeutscher Block/BHE Nachrichtendienst der Partei, 1953–56
Nachrichtenblatt der Partei (Gesamtdeutscher Block/BHE), 1953
Ostdeutsche Zeitung. Die Stimme, 1952–53
Ostvertriebenen-Korrespondenz, 1948
Ost-West-Kurier, 1950, 1952–53
Selbsthilfe, 1946–57
Die Sicht des Gesamtdeutschen Blocks—BHE, 1953–56
VdL Informationen, 1954–57
Vertriebenen-Korrespondenz, 1950–52, 1957
Völkischer Beobachter, 1941–44
Wall Street Journal, 1946–49

PRINTED PRIMARY SOURCES

Adenauer, Konrad. *Briefe, 1945–1947.* Edited by Hans Peter Mensing. Rhöndorfer Ausgabe. N.p.: Siedler Verlag, 1983.

―――. *Briefe, 1949–1951.* Edited by Hans Peter Mensing. Rhöndorfer Ausgabe. N.p.: Siedler Verlag, 1985.

―――. *Briefe, 1951–1953.* Edited by Hans Peter Mensing. Rhöndorfer Ausgabe. N.p.: Siedler Verlag, 1987.

―――. *Erinnerungen 1945–1953.* Stuttgart: Deutsche Verlags-Anstalt, 1965.

―――. *Reden 1917–1967: Eine Auswahl.* Edited by Hans-Peter Schwarz. Stuttgart: Deutsche Verlags-Anstalt, 1975.

―――. *Tee-Gespräche.* Vol. 1. N.p.: Siedler Verlag, 1984.

Arendt, Hannah. "The Aftermath of Nazi Rule: Report from Germany." In Hannah Arendt, *Essays in Understanding, 1930–1954,* edited by Jerome Kohn, 248–64. New York: Harcourt, Brace, 1993.

Aristotle. *Politics.* Translated by Benjamin Jowett. Chicago: The Great Books Foundation, 1966.

Baring, Arnulf, ed. *Sehr verehrter Herr Bundeskanzler! Heinrich von Brentano im Briefwechsel mit Konrad Adenauer, 1949–1964.* Hamburg: Hoffmann und Campe, 1974.

Bauser, Adolf. *Für Wahrheit und Recht.* Stuttgart: Verlag Württemberger Sparerbund, 1927.

Blumenberg-Lampe, Christine, ed. *Der Weg in die soziale Marktwirtschaft.* Stuttgart: Klett-Cotta, 1986.

Boberach, H., ed. *Meldungen aus dem Reich.* Neuwied: Luchterhand Verlag, 1965.

Boelcke, Willi, ed. *Kriegspropaganda, 1939–1941.* Stuttgart: Deutsche Verlags-Anstalt, 1966.

Bohn, A., and J. W. Bruhn, eds. *Der Lastenausgleich.* 2 vols. Baden-Baden: Verlag E. Bohn, 1952/53.

Breloer, Heinrich, ed. *Mein Tagebuch. Geschichten vom Überleben, 1939–1947.* Cologne: Verlagsgesellschaft Schulfernsehen, 1984.

Buchstab, Günter, ed. *Adenauer: "Es mußte alles neu gemacht werden." Die Protokolle des CDU-Bundesvorstandes 1950–1953.* Stuttgart: Klett-Cotta, 1986.

Bundesministerium des Innern, ed. *Die Lastenausgleichsgesetze.* Vol. 1/3. Würzburg: Bergstadtverlag Korn, 1991.

―――. *Die Lastenausgleichsgesetze.* Vol. 4/1. Bonn: n.p., 1964.

―――. *Die Lastenausgleichsgesetze.* Vol. 4/2. Bonn: n.p., 1973.

Bundesministerium für Finanzen. *Der endgültige Lastenausgleich.* Bonn: n.p., 1949.

Bundesministerium für Vertriebene, Flüchtlinge, und Kriegsgeschädigte, ed. *Dokumente deutscher Kriegsschäden.* 4 vols. Bonn: n.p., 1960–79.

————. *Die Lastenausgleichsgesetze.* Vol. 1/1. Bonn: n.p., 1962.

————. *Die Lastenausgleichsgesetze.* Vol. 1/2. Bonn: n.p., 1964.

————. *Die Lastenausgleichsgesetze.* Vol. 2/1. Bonn: n.p., 1962.

CDU. "Ahlener Programm," 3 Feb. 1947. In *Die Parteien der Bundesrepublik Deutschland,* edited by Ossip Flechtheim. Hamburg: Hoffmann und Campe, 1973.

Chambers, S. P. "Post-War German Finances." *International Affairs* 24, no. 3 (July 1948): 364–76.

Clay, Lucius D. *Decision in Germany.* Garden City, N.Y.: Doubleday, 1950.

Colm, Gerhard, Raymond Goldsmith, and Joseph Dodge. "A Plan for the Liquidation of War Finance and the Financial Rehabilitation of Germany." *Zeitschrift für die gesamte Staatswissenschaft* 111, no. 2 (1955): 205–43.

Danckelmann, Bernhard. *Kriegssachschädenrecht.* 3d ed. Munich: C. H. Beck Verlag, 1944.

Der endgültige Lastenausgleich. Bericht der Gutachterkommission für den Lastenausgleich. 2d ed. Bonn: n.p., 1950.

Der wissenschaftliche Beirat bei der Verwaltung für Wirtschaft des Vereinigten Wirtschafts-gebietes. *Gutachten,* 1948–May 1950. Göttingen: Verlag Otto Schwartz, 1950.

Enders, Ulrich, and Konrad Reiser, eds. *Die Kabinettsprotokolle der Bundesregierung, 1949.* Vol. 1. Boppard: Harald Boldt Verlag, 1982.

————. *Die Kabinettsprotokolle der Bundesregierung, 1950.* Vol. 2. Boppard: Harald Boldt Verlag, 1985.

Entwurf eines Gesetzes zur Neuordnung des Geldwesens (Homburg Plan). Heidelberg: Springer Verlag, 1948.

Erhard, Ludwig. *The Economics of Success.* Translated by J. A. Arengo-Jones and D. J. S. Thomson. Princeton, N.J.: D. Van Nostrand, 1963.

————. *Kriegsfinanzierung und Schuldenkonsolidierung: Faksimiledruck der Denkschrift von 1943/44.* Frankfurt/M: Propyläen Verlag, 1977.

————. *Prosperity through Competition.* Translated by Edith Roberts. London: Thames and Hudson, 1958.

Fallada, Hans. *Little Man—What Now?* Translated by Eric Sutton. New York: Simon & Schuster, 1933.

Fendt, Franz. *Lastenausgleich: Die soziale und wirtschaftliche Kernfrage unserer Zeit.* Munich: Plum Verlag, 1948.

Friedrich, Heinz. *Mein Kopfgeld: Die Währungsreform: Rückblicke nach vier Jahrzehnten.* Munich: Deutscher Taschenbuch Verlag, 1988.

Gelberg, Karl-Ulrich, ed. *Das Kabinett Schäffer: 28. Mai bis 28. September 1945.* Munich: Oldenbourg Verlag, 1995.

————. *Kriegsende und Neuanfang in Augsburg, 1945.* Munich: Oldenbourg Verlag, 1996.

Gessner, Herbert. *Kommentare.* 2 vols. Munich: Freitag Verlag, 1946.

Giersch, Herbert. *Der Ausgleich der Kriegslasten vom Standpunkt der sozialen Gerechtigkeit.* Dortmund: Verlag "Soziale Welt," 1948.

Goebbels, Joseph. *Reden.* Vol. 2, *1939–1945.* Edited by Helmut Heiber. Düsseldorf: Droste Verlag, 1972.

Güstrow, Dietrich. *In jenen Jahren. Aufzeichnungen eines "befreiten" Deutschen.* Munich: Deutscher Taschenbuch Verlag, 1985.

Gut, Fritz. *Leitfaden durch das gesamte Kriegsschädenrecht.* 2d ed. Karlsruhe: Verlag G. Braun, 1944.

Hammer, Ingrid, and Susanne zur Nieden, eds. *"Sehr selten habe ich geweint": Briefe und Tagebücher aus dem Zweiten Weltkrieg von Menschen aus Berlin.* Zurich: Schweizer Verlagshaus, 1992.

Heck, Daniel, ed. *Die CDU und ihr Programm: Programme Erklärungen Entschließungen.* Melle: Verlag Ernst Knoth, 1979.

Hielscher, Erwin. *Das Jahrhundert der Inflation. Ein Beitrag aus der Bundesrepublik Deutschland.* Munich: Olzog Verlag, 1967.

――――. *Der Leidensweg der deutschen Währungsreform.* Munich: R. Pflaum Verlag, 1948.

Hildebrandt, Horst. *Quellen zur Verfassungsgeschichte.* Vol. 1. Paderborn: Verlag Schöningh, 1954.

Hitler, Adolf. *Es spricht der Führer: 7 exemplarische Hitler-Reden.* Edited by Hildegard von Kotze and Helmut Krausnick. Gütersloh: Signert Mohn Verlag, 1966.

Huber, Anton. *Die Ordnung der finanziellen, wirtschaftlichen und sozialen Verhältnisse in Deutschland.* Stuttgart: n.p., 1947.

Hüllbüsch, Ursula, ed. *Die Kabinettsprotokolle der Bundesregierung, 1951.* Vol. 4. Boppard: Harald Boldt Verlag, 1988.

Jaeger, Richard. "Auf dem Weg zur Demokratie." In *Lehrjahre der CSU,* edited by K.-D. Henke and H. Woller. Stuttgart: Deutsche Verlags-Anstalt, 1984.

Jaspers, Karl. *The German Question.* New York, 1964.

Jünger, Ernst. *Jahre der Okkupation.* Stuttgart: Ernst Klett Verlag, 1958.

Kaff, Brigitte, ed. *Die Unionsparteien, 1946–1950: Protokolle der Arbeitsgemeinschaft der CDU/CSU Deutschlands und der Konferenzen der Landesvorsitzenden.* Düsseldorf: Droste Verlag, 1991.

Kather, Linus. *Eingliederung durch Lastenausgleich.* Frankfurt: Wegweiser für Heimatvertriebene Verlag, 1952.

――――. *Die entscheidenden Jahre.* Vol. 1 of *Die Entmachtung der Vertriebenen.* Munich: Günter Olzog Verlag, 1965.

――――. *Gerechter Lastenausgleich!* Hamburg: Neuer Ostdeutscher Verlag, [1951].

Kogon, Eugen. "Das Recht auf den politischen Irrtum." *Frankfurter Hefte* 2 (1947): 641–55.

Kreikamp, Hans-Dieter, ed. *Akten zur Vorgeschichte der Bundesrepublik Deutschland.* Vol. 5. Munich: Oldenbourg Verlag, 1981.

Lenz, Otto. *Im Zentrum der Macht: Das Tagebuch vom Staatssekretär Lenz, 1951–1953.* Edited by Klaus Gotto, Hans Otto Kleinmann, and Reinhard Schreiner. Düsseldorf: Droste Verlag, 1989.

Luther, Hans. *Feste Mark—Solide Wirtschaft.* Berlin: O. Stollberg, 1924.

Meyers kleines Lexikon. Vol. 8. Leipzig: Bibliographisches Institut, 1940.

Military Government—Germany. United States Area of Control. *Laws no. 61–63: First–Third Laws for Monetary Reform. Law no. 64: Provisional Revision of Tax Legislation.* Washington, D.C.: Department of the Army, Public Information Division, 1948.

Möller, Hans. *Der Lastenausgleich.* Hamburg: Reich und Heidrich Evangelischer Verlag, n.d.

Möller, Hans, ed. *Zur Vorgeschichte der Deutschen Mark: Die Währungsreformpläne, 1945–1948.* Basel: Kyklos Verlag, 1961.

Moeller, Hero. "Geldabschöpfung und Geldüberhang." *Zeitschrift der Akademie für deutsches Recht* 10, no. 11 (10 Aug. 1943): 1–3.

Nahm, Peter-Paul, ed. *Sie haben sich selbst geholfen: Tatsachenberichte aus chaotischer Zeiten.* N.p.: n.p., n.d.

Noelle, Elisabeth, and Erich Neumann, eds. *Jahrbuch der öffentlichen Meinung, 1947–1955.* 2d ed. Allensbach: Verlag für Demoskopie, 1956.

Picker, Henry, ed. *Hitlers Tischgespräche im Führerhauptquartier.* 3d ed. Stuttgart: Seewald Verlag, 1976.

Plum, Günter, ed. *Akten zur Vorgeschichte der Bundesrepublik Deutschland.* Vol. 3. Munich: Oldenbourg Verlag, 1982.

Pütz, Helmut, ed. *Konrad Adenauer und die CDU der britischen Besatzungszone.* Bonn: Eichholz Verlag, 1975.

Ritter, Gerhard A., and Merith Niehuss. *Wahlen in der Bundesrepublik Deutschland. Bundestags- und Landtagswahlen 1946–1987.* Munich: Beck Verlag, 1987.

Röpke, Wilhelm. *A Humane Economy: The Social Framework of the Free Market.* Translated by Elizabeth Henderson. Chicago: Henry Regnery, 1960.

Salin, Edgar. "Währungsexperimente und Währungsreformen, 1945–1948." *Kyklos* 3, no. 2 (1949): 97–115.

Schieder, Theodor, ed. *Die Vertreibung der deutschen Bevölkerung aus den Gebieten östlich der Oder-Neisse.* Vol. 1/1–2. Bonn: n.p., 1953.

Schröder, H. A. O. "Das Kriegsschadenrecht in der Gesetzgebung Deutschlands und des Auslands." In *Lastenausgleichsgesetze,* vol. 4/1, edited by Bundesministerium des Innern, 435–85.

Schulze, Rainer, ed. *Unruhige Zeiten: Erlebnisberichte aus dem Landkreis Celle, 1945–1949.* 2d ed. Munich: Oldenbourg Verlag, 1991.

Schumacher, Kurt. *Reden und Schriften.* Edited by A. Scholz and W. Oschilewski. Berlin: arani Verlag, 1962.

Schwerin von Krosigk, Lutz Graf. *Staatsbankrott: Die Geschichte der Finanzpolitik des Deutschen Reiches von 1920 bis 1945.* Göttingen: Musterschmidt, 1974.

Smith, Jean, ed. *The Papers of General Lucius D. Clay.* 2 vols. Bloomington: Indiana University Press, 1974.

Sombart, Werner. *Händler und Helden.* Munich: Duncker & Humblot, 1915.

Soyka, Theodor. *Währung und Wiederaufbau.* Berlin, 1947.

SPD. *Lastenausgleich!* N.p., [1950?].

Thorwald, Jürgen. *Die große Flucht.* Stuttgart: Steingrüben Verlag, 1962.

Troeger, Heinrich. *Interregnum: Tagebuch des Generalsekretärs des Länderrats der Bizone, 1947–1949.* Edited by Wolfgang Benz and Constantin Goschler. Munich: Oldenbourg Verlag, 1985.

United States. Department of State. *Foreign Relations of the United States, 1947.* Vol. 2. Washington, D.C.: U.S. Government Printing Office, 1972.

——— . *Foreign Relations of the United States, 1948.* Vol. 2. Washington, D.C.: U.S. Government Printing Office, 1973.

United States. Senate Committee on Foreign Relations. *Documents on Germany, 1944–1959.* Washington, D.C.: U.S. Government Printing Office, 1959.

Vaubel, Ludwig. *Zusammenbruch und Wiederaufbau.* Edited by Wolfgang Benz. Munich: Oldenbourg Verlag, 1984.

Verhandlungen des Deutschen Bundestages: Anlage. Bonn: n.p., 1949–57.

Verhandlungen des Deutschen Bundestages: Stenographische Berichte. Bonn: n.p., 1949–57.

Vogel, Walter, and Christoph Weisz, eds. *Akten zur Vorgeschichte der Bundesrepublik Deutschland.* Vol. 1. Munich: Oldenbourg Verlag, 1976.

von der Gablentz, Otto. *Über Marx hinaus.* Berlin: Wedding Verlag, 1946.

von Jena, Kai, ed. *Die Kabinettsprotokolle der Bundesregierung, 1952.* Vol. 5. Boppard: Harald Boldt Verlag, 1988.

Walter-Raymond-Stiftung, ed. *Eigentum und Eigentümer in unserer Gesellschaftsordnung.* Cologne: Westdeutscher Verlag, 1961.

Weisser, Gerhard. "Die Gesetzgebung über den Lastenausgleich." *Finanzarchiv* NF 16, no. 1 (1955): 62–80.

Weisz, Christoph, ed. *Akten zur Vorgeschichte der Bundesrepublik Deutschland.* Vol. 4. Munich: Oldenbourg Verlag, 1983.

Wengst, Udo, ed. *Auftakt zur Ära Adenauer: Koalitionsverhandlungen und Regierungsbildung, 1949*. Düsseldorf: Droste Verlag, 1985.

————. *FDP-Bundesvorstand. Die Liberalen unter dem Vorsitz von Theodor Heuss und Franz Blücher: Sitzungsprotokolle, 1949–1954*. Düsseldorf: Droste Verlag, 1990.

Werner, Wolfgang, ed. *Akten zur Vorgeschichte der Bundesrepublik Deutschland*. Vol. 2. Munich: Oldenbourg Verlag, 1979.

Westdeutsches Institut für Wirtschaftsforschung. *Der Lastenausgleich wirtschaftlich gesehen!* Essen: Im Westverlag, 1948.

Wirtschaftwissenschaftliches Institut der Gewerkschaften. *Stellungnahme zur Währungs- und Finanzreform*. Cologne: Bund Verlag, 1948.

Wolf, Eduard. "Geld- und Finanzprobleme der deutschen Nachkriegswirtschaft." In *Die deutsche Wirtschaft zwei Jahre nach dem Zusammenbruch*, edited by Deutsches Institut für Wirtschaftsforschung, 196–261. Berlin: Albert Nauck, 1947.

Wörtliche Berichte und Drucksachen des Wirtschaftsrates des Vereinigten Wirtschaftsgebietes 1947–1949. Vols. 2, 4, 5. Edited by Christoph Weisz and Hans Woller. Munich: Oldenbourg Verlag, 1977.

Yeager, General Chuck. *Yeager: An Autobiography*. Toronto: Bantam Books, 1985.

Zentralverband vertriebener Deutschen/Zentralverband der Fliegergeschädigten. *Die Forderungen der Heimatvertriebenen, Kriegssach- und Währungsgeschädigten zum Lastenausgleich*. N.p., [Jan. 1949].

SECONDARY SOURCES

Abelshauser, Werner. *Die langen fünfziger Jahre: Wirtschaft und Gesellschaft der Bundesrepublik Deutschland, 1949–1966*. Düsseldorf: Schwann, 1987.

————. *Wirtschaftsgeschichte der Bundesrepublik Deutschland, 1945–1980*. Frankfurt/M: Edition Suhrkamp, 1983.

————. "Erhard oder Bismarck? Die Richtlinienentscheidung der deutschen Sozialpolitik am Beispiel der Reform der Sozialversicherung in den Fünfziger Jahren." *Geschichte und Gesellschaft* 22, no. 3 (July–Sept. 1996): 376–92.

————, ed. *Die Weimarer Republik als Wohlfahrtsstaat: Zum Verhältnis von Wirtschafts- und Sozialpolitik in der Industriegesellschaft*. Stuttgart: Franz Steiner Verlag, 1987.

Ahonen, Pertti. "Domestic Constraints on West German *Ostpolitik:* The Role of the Expellee Organizations in the Adenauer Era." *Central European History* 31, nos. 1–2 (1989): 31–64.

Allemann, Fritz R. *Bonn ist nicht Weimar*. Cologne: Kiepenheuer & Witsch, 1956.

Allen, William Sheridan. *The Nazi Seizure of Power: The Experience of a Single German Town, 1922–1945*. Rev. ed. New York: Franklin Watts, 1984.

Amato, Joseph. *Victims and Values: A History and Theory of Suffering*. New York: Greenwood, 1990.

Ambrosius, Gerold. *Die Durchsetzung der Sozialen Marktwirtschaft in Westdeutschland, 1945–1949*. Stuttgart: Deutsche Verlags-Anstalt, 1977.

Bade, Klaus. *Neue Heimat im Westen: Vertriebene Flüchtlinge Aussiedler*. Münster: Westfälischer Heimatbund, 1990.

Bajohr, Franz. "Leybuden, Laubenkolonien, Nissenhütten: Wohnen in der Zusammenbruchgesellschaft." In *Improvisierter Neubeginn*, edited by Detlev Peukert, 70–77.

Bankier, David. *The Germans and the Final Solution: Public Opinion under Nazism*. Oxford: Blackwell, 1996.

Baranowski, Shelley. *The Sanctity of Rural Life*. New York: Oxford University Press, 1995.

Baring, Arnulf. *Im Anfang war Adenauer: Die Entstehung der Kanzlerdemokratie.* Munich: Deutscher Taschenbuch Verlag, 1982.

Bartov, Omer. *Hitler's Army.* New York: Oxford University Press, 1991.

——. "Savage War." In *Confronting the Nazi Past: New Debates on Modern German History,* edited by Michael Burleigh, 125–39. New York: St. Martin's Press, 1996.

Becker, Lawrence C. *Property Rights.* London: Routledge & Kegan Paul, 1977.

Bennett, David. *Demagogues in the Depression.* New Brunswick, N.J.: Rutgers University Press, 1969.

Benz, Wolfgang. "Konzeptionen für die Nachkriegsdemokratie." In *Deutschland nach Hitler,* edited by Thomas Koebner, Gert Sautermeister, and S. Schneider-Grube, 201–13.

——. *Von der Besatzungsherrschaft zur Bundesrepublik: Stationen einer Staatsgründung, 1946–1949.* Frankfurt/M: Fischer Verlag, 1985.

——. *Zwischen Hitler und Adenauer: Studien zur deutschen Nachkriegsgesellschaft.* Frankfurt/M: Fischer Taschenbuch Verlag, 1991.

——, ed. *Die Vertreibung der Deutschen aus dem Osten: Ursachen, Ereignisse, Folgen.* Frankfurt/M: Fischer Taschenbuch Verlag, 1985.

Berger, Helga, and Albrecht Ritschl. "Die Rekonstruktion der Arbeitsteilung in Europa. Eine neue Sicht des Marshallplans in Deutschland, 1947–1951." *Vierteljahrshefte für Zeitgeschichte* 43, no. 3 (July 1995): 473–519.

Berghahn, Volker. *The Americanisation of West German Industry, 1945–1973.* Cambridge: Cambridge University Press, 1986.

——. "Ideas into Politics: The Case of Ludwig Erhard." In *Ideas into Politics,* edited by R. J. Bullen, H. Pogge von Strandmann, and A. B. Polonsky, 178–92. London: Croom Helm, 1984.

——. "Resisting the Pax Americana? West German Industry and the U.S., 1945–1955." In *America and Shaping of German Society,* edited by Michael Ermarth, 85–100.

——. "West German Reconstruction and American Industrial Culture, 1945–1960." In *The American Impact on Postwar Germany,* edited by Reiner Pommerin, 65–82. Providence, R.I.: Berghahn Books, 1995.

Berghoff, Hartmut. "Zwischen Verdrängung und Aufarbeitung: Die bundesdeutsche Gesellschaft und ihre nationalsozialistische Vergangenheit in den Fünfziger Jahren." *Geschichte in Wissenschaft und Unterricht* 49 (1998): 96–114.

Birke, Adolf M. *Nation ohne Haus: Deutschland, 1945–1961.* N.p.: im Siedler Verlag, [1989].

Blackbourn, David. "The *Mittelstand* in German Society and Politics, 1871–1914." *Social History* 2, no. 1 (Jan. 1977): 409–33.

Boehling, Rebecca. *A Question of Priorities: Democratic Reforms and Economic Recovery in Postwar Germany.* Providence, R.I.: Berghahn Books, 1996.

——. "Symbols of Continuity and Change in Postwar German Liberalism. Wolfgang Haußmann and Hildegard Hamm-Brücher." In *In Search of a Liberal Germany,* edited by Konrad Jarausch and Larry Eugene Jones, 361–87. New York: Berg, 1990.

——. "U.S. Military Occupation, Grass Roots Democracy, and Local German Government." In *American Policy and Reconstruction,* edited by Jeffrey Diefendorf, Axel Frohn, and H.-J. Rupieper, 281–306.

Boelcke, Willi. *Die Kosten von Hitlers Krieg.* Paderborn: Ferdinand Schöningh, 1985.

——. *Der Schwarzmarkt, 1945–1948: Vom Überleben nach dem Kriege.* Braunschweig: Westermann Verlag, 1986.

Bolte, Karl Martin. *Deutsche Gesellschaft im Wandel.* Opladen: Leske Verlag, 1967.

——. *Leistung und Leistungsprinzip: Zur Konzeption, Wirklichkeit und Möglichkeit eines gesellschaftlichen Gestaltungsprinzips.* Opladen: Leske Verlag, 1979.

Botting, Douglas. *From the Ruins of the Reich: Germany, 1945–1949.* New York: Meridian Books, 1985.

Bracher, Karl Dietrich. "Die Kanzlerdemokratie." In *Die zweite Republik,* edited by Richard Löwenthal and Hans-Peter Schwarz, 179–202.

Brackmann, Michael. *Vom totalen Krieg zum Wirtschaftswunder: Die Vorgeschichte der westdeutschen Währungsreform, 1948.* Essen: Klartext, 1993.

Braun, Hans. "Das Streben nach 'Sicherheit' in den 50er Jahren: Soziale und politische Ursachen und Erscheinungsweisen." *Archiv für Sozialgeschichte* 18 (1978): 279–306.

Breitling, Rupert. *Die Verbände in der Bundesrepublik: Ihre Arten und ihre politische Wirkungsweise.* Meisenheim am Glan: Verlag Anton Hain, 1955.

Breuilly, John. *The State of Germany.* London: Longman, 1992.

Brooks, Peter. *The Melodramatic Imagination.* New York: Columbia University Press, 1985.

Broszat, Martin, Klaus-Dietmar Henke, and Hans Woller, eds. *Von Stalingrad zur Währungsreform: Zur Sozialgeschichte des Umbruchs in Deutschland.* Munich: Oldenbourg Verlag, 1989.

Brubaker, Rogers. *Citizenship and Nationhood in France and Germany.* Cambridge, Mass.: Harvard University Press, 1992.

Buchheim, Christoph. "Marshall Plan and Currency Reform." In *American Policy and Reconstruction,* edited by Jeffrey Diefendorf, Axel Frohn, and H.-J. Rupieper, 69–83.

———. "Die Währungsreform 1948 in Westdeutschland." *Vierteljahrshefte für Zeitgeschichte* 36, no. 2 (April 1988): 189–231.

Burleigh, Michael, and Wolfgang Wippermann. *The Racial State: Germany, 1933–1945.* Cambridge: Cambridge University Press, 1991.

Cahn, Hans J. *Das Kriegsschadenrecht der Nationen.* Zurich: Europa Verlag, 1947.

Calleo, David. *The German Problem Reconsidered: Germany and the World Order, 1870 to the Present.* Cambridge: Cambridge University Press, 1982.

Campbell, Joan. *Joy in Work, German Work: The National Debate, 1800–1945.* Princeton, N.J.: Princeton University Press, 1989.

Carter, Erica. *How German Is She? Postwar West German Reconstruction and the Consuming Woman.* Ann Arbor: University of Michigan Press, 1997.

Cary, Noel D. *The Path to Christian Democracy: German Catholics and the Party System from Windhorst to Adenauer.* Cambridge, Mass.: Harvard University Press, 1996.

Chapman, John W. "Justice, Freedom, and Property." In *Nomos* 22: 289–324. New York: New York University Press, 1980.

Childers, Thomas. *The Nazi Voter.* Chapel Hill: University of North Carolina Press, 1983.

Claessens, Dieter, Arno Klönne, and Armin Tschoepe. *Sozialkunde der Bundesrepublik Deutschland.* Düsseldorf: Diederichs Verlag, 1968.

Connelly, John. "The Uses of *Volksgemeinschaft:* Letters to the NSDAP Kreisleitung Eisenach, 1939–1940." *Journal of Modern History* 68, no. 4 (Dec. 1996): 899–930.

Connor, Ian. "The Refugees and the Currency Reform." In *Reconstruction in Postwar Germany,* edited by Ian Turner, 301–24. Oxford: Berg, 1989.

Crafts, Nicholas, and G. Toniolo, eds. *Economic Growth in Europe since 1945.* New York: Cambridge University Press, 1996.

Crew, David F. *Germans on Welfare: From Weimar to Hitler.* New York: Oxford University Press, 1998.

———. "'Wohlfahrtsbrot ist bitteres Brot': The Elderly, the Disabled and the Local Welfare Authorities in the Weimar Republic, 1924–1933." *Archiv für Sozialgeschichte* 30 (1990): 217–45.

Cunliffe, Marcus. *The Right to Property: A Theme in American History*. Leicester: Leicester University Press, 1974.

Cupit, Geoffrey. *Justice as Fittingness*. Oxford: Clarendon Press, 1996.

Dahrendorf, Ralf. *Democracy and Society in Germany*. New York: W. W. Norton, 1968.

Davis, Belinda. "Food Scarcity and the Empowerment of the Female Consumer in World War I Berlin." In *The Sex of Things: Gender and Consumption in Historical Perspective*, edited by Victoria de Grazia and Ellen Furlough. Berkeley: University of California Press, 1996.

———. "Home Fires Burning: Politics, Identity and Food in World War I Berlin." Ph.D. diss., University of Michigan, 1992.

Davison, W. Phillips. *The Berlin Blockade: A Study in Cold War Politics*. Princeton, N.J.: Princeton University Press, 1958.

de Zayas, Alfred. *The German Expellees: Victims in War and Peace*. New York: St. Martin's Press, 1993.

———. *Nemesis at Potsdam: The Anglo-Americans and the Expulsion of the Germans*. London: Routledge & Kegan Paul, 1979.

Deighton, Anne. *The Impossible Peace: Britain, the Division of Germany, and the Origins of the Cold War*. Oxford: Clarendon Press, 1990.

Deutsche Bundesbank, ed. *Währung und Wirtschaft in Deutschland, 1876–1975*. Frankfurt: Fritz Knapp Verlag, 1976.

Dickhaus, Monika. "Fostering 'the Bank That Rules Europe': The Bank of England, the Allied Banking Commission, and the Bank deutscher Länder, 1948–1951." *Contemporary European History* 7, no. 2 (1998): 161–79.

Diefendorf, Jeffry M. *In the Wake of War: The Reconstruction of German Cities after World War II*. New York: Oxford University Press, 1993.

Diefendorf, Jeffry M., Axel Frohn, and H.-J. Rupieper, eds. *American Policy and the Reconstruction of West Germany, 1945–1955*. Cambridge: Cambridge University Press, 1993.

Diehl, James M. *The Thanks of the Fatherland: German Veterans after the Second World War*. Chapel Hill: University of North Carolina Press, 1993.

Diestelkamp, Bernhard. "Rechtsgeschichte als Zeitgeschichte: Historische Betrachtungen zur Entstehung und Durchsetzung der Theorie vom Fortbestand des Deutschen Reiches als Staat nach 1945." *Zeitschrift für neuere Rechtsgeschichte* 7, nos. 3/4 (1985): 181–207.

Dietrich, Yorck. *Eigentum für Jeden: Die vermögenspolitischen Initiativen der CDU und die Gesetzgebung, 1950–1961*. Forschung und Quellen zur Zeitgeschichte, vol. 29. Düsseldorf: Droste Verlag, 1996.

Dilcher, Gerhard. "Das Gesellschaftsbild der Rechtswissenschaft und die soziale Frage." In *Das wilhelminische Bildungsbürgertum: Zur Sozialgeschichte seiner Ideen*, edited by Klaus Vondung, 53–66. Göttingen: Vandenhoeck & Ruprecht, 1976.

Doering-Manteuffel, Anselm. "Deutsche Zeitgeschichte nach 1945: Entwicklung und Problemlagen der historischen Forschung zur Nachkriegszeit." *Vierteljahrshefte für Zeitgeschichte* 41, no. 1 (Jan. 1993): 1–30.

———. "Strukturmerkmale der Kanzlerdemokratie." *Der Staat* 30, no. 1 (1991): 1–18.

Douglas, Mary. *How Institutions Think*. Syracuse, N.Y.: Syracuse University Press, 1986.

Drexler, Alexander. *Planwirtschaft in Westdeutschland, 1945–1948*. Wiesbaden: Steiner Verlag, 1985.

Edinger, Lewis. *Kurt Schumacher*. Stanford, Calif.: Stanford University Press, 1965.

Eghigian, Greg. "The Politics of Victimization: Social Pensioners and the German Social State in the Inflation of 1914–1924." *Central European History* 26, no. 4 (1993): 376–403.

Eichengreen, Barry, ed. *Europe's Postwar Recovery*. New York: Cambridge University Press, 1995.

Eisenberg, Caroline. *Drawing the Line: The American Decision to Divide Germany.* Cambridge: Cambridge University Press, 1996.

Enssle, Martin. "Five Theses on German Everyday Life after World War II." *Central European History* 26, no. 1 (1993): 1–20.

Ermarth, Michael, ed. *America and the Shaping of German Society, 1945–1955.* Providence, R.I.: Berg, 1993.

Falter, Jürgen. "Kontinuität und Neubeginn: Die Bundestagwahl 1949 zwischen Weimar und Bonn." *Politische Vierteljahresschrift* 22, no. 3 (1981): 236–63.

Feldman, Gerald D. *The Great Disorder: Politics, Economics, and Society in the German Inflation, 1914–1924.* New York: Oxford University Press, 1993.

Ferguson, Niall. *Paper and Iron: Hamburg Business and German Politics in the Era of Inflation, 1897–1927.* Cambridge: Cambridge University Press, 1995.

Fisch, Jörg. *Reparationen nach dem Zweiten Weltkrieg.* Munich: C. H. Beck, 1992.

Fischer, Wolfram, ed. *Währungsreform und soziale Marktwirtschaft: Erfahrungen und Perspektiven nach 40 Jahren.* Schriften des Vereins für Sozialpolitik, NF, vol. 190. Berlin: Duncker & Humblot, 1989.

Foschepoth, Josef. "Zur deutschen Reaktion auf Niederlage und Besatzung." In *Westdeutschland,* edited by Ludolf Herbst, 151–65.

———, ed. *Adenauer und die deutsche Frage.* Göttingen: Vandenhoeck & Ruprecht, 1988.

———. *Kalter Krieg und deutsche Frage.* Göttingen: Vandenhoeck & Ruprecht, 1985.

Francke, Hans-Hermann, and Harald Nitsch. "Der Beitrag der Währungsumstellung zur Finanzierung der deutschen Einheit." In *Finanzierungsprobleme der deutschen Einheit.* Vol. 1, edited by Alois Oberhauser. Berlin: Duncker & Humblot, 1993.

Frantzioch, Marion. *Die Vertriebenen: Hemmnisse und Wege ihrer Integration.* Berlin: Dietrich Reimer Verlag, 1987.

Frevert, Ute. *Women in German History: From Bourgeois Emancipation to Sexual Liberation.* Translated by Stuart McKinnon-Evans. New York: Berg, 1989.

Frey, Manuel. *Der reinliche Bürger: Entstehung und Verbreitung bürgerlicher Tugenden in Deutschland, 1760–1860.* Göttingen: Vandenhoeck & Ruprecht, 1997.

Friedrich, Otto, ed. *Das Leistungsprinzip in unserer Zeit.* Berlin: Beuth Verlag, 1974.

Fritz, Rudolf. *Der Einfluß der Parteien und Geschädigtenverbände auf die Schadenfeststellung im Lastenausgleich.* Berlin: n.p., 1964.

Führer, Karl Christian. "Für das Wirtschaftsleben 'mehr oder weniger wertlose Personen': Zur Lage von Invaliden- und Kleinrentnern in den Inflationsjahren, 1918–1924." *Archiv für Sozialgeschichte* 30 (1990): 145–80.

Gall, Lothar. *The Deutsche Bank, 1870–1995.* London: Weidenfeld & Nicolson, 1995.

Geschichtliche Grundbegriffe. Vol. 2. Stuttgart: Klett Cotta, 1975.

Geyer, Martin H. "Teuerungsprotest, Konsumentenpolitik und soziale Gerechtigkeit während der Inflation: München, 1920–1923." *Archiv für Sozialgeschichte* 30 (1990): 181–215.

Geyer, Michael. "Ein Vorbote des Wohlfahrtsstaates. Die Kriegsopferversorgung in Frankreich, Deutschland und Großbritannien nach dem Ersten Weltkrieg." *Geschichte und Gesellschaft* 9 (1983): 230–77.

Gimbel, John. *The Origins of the Marshall Plan.* Stanford, Calif.: Stanford University Press, 1976.

Goschler, Constantin. *Wiedergutmachung: Westdeutschland und die Verfolgten des Nationalsozialismus.* Munich: Oldenbourg Verlag, 1992.

Gottlieb, Manuel. "Failure of Quadripartite Monetary Reform, 1945–1947." *Finanzarchiv* 17 (1956/57): 398–417.

————. *The German Peace Settlement and the Berlin Crisis*. New Brunswick, N.J.: Transaction Books, 1960.

Grebing, Helga. *Flüchtlinge und Parteien in Niedersachsen*. Hannover: Verlag Hahnsche Buchhandlung, 1990.

————. *Konservative gegen die Demokratie: Konservative Kritik an die Demokratie in der Bundesrepublik nach 1945*. Frankfurt/M: Europäische Verlagsanstalt, 1971.

Grosser, Alfred. *Die Bonner Demokratie*. Düsseldorf: Karl Raucher Verlag, 1960.

Grube, Frank, and Gerhard Richter, eds. *Demokratietheorien*. Hamburg: Hoffmann & Campe, 1975.

Hamby, Alonzo. *Beyond the New Deal*. New York: Columbia University Press, 1973.

Hamilton, Richard. *Who Voted for Hitler?* Princeton, N.J.: Princeton University Press, 1981.

Hannover, Heinrich. *Politische Diffamierung der Opposition im freiheitlich-demokratischen Rechtsstaat*. Dortmund-Barop: im Verlag Pläne, 1962.

Hansemeyer, Karl-Heinrich, and Rolf Caesar. "Kriegswirtschaft und Inflation (1936–1948)." In *Währung und Wirtschaft*, edited by Deutsche Bundesbank, 367–429.

Hardach, Gerd. *Der Marshallplan: Auslandshilfe und Wiederaufbau in Westdeutschland, 1948–1952*. Munich: Deutscher Taschenbuch Verlag, 1994.

Haupt, Heinz-Gerhard. "The Petty Bourgeoisie in Germany and France in the Late Nineteenth Century." In *Bourgeois Society*, edited by Jürgen Kocka and Alan Mitchell, 302–22.

Hazard, Paul. *European Thought in the Eighteenth Century*. Cleveland and New York: Meridian Books, 1969.

Hein, Dieter. *Zwischen liberaler Milieupartei und nationaler Sammlungsbewegung. Gründung, Entwicklung und Struktur der Freien Demokratischen Partei, 1945–1949*. Düsseldorf: Droste Verlag, 1985.

Henderson, W. O. *The Rise of German Industrial Power, 1834–1914*. Berkeley: University of California Press, 1975.

Henke, Klaus-Dietmar. *Die amerikanische Besetzung Deutschlands*. Munich: Oldenbourg Verlag, 1995.

————. "Die Trennung vom Nationalsozialismus: Selbstzerstörung, politische Säuberung, 'Entnazifizierung,' Strafverfolgung." In *Politische Säuberung in Europa: Die Abrechnung mit Faschismus und Kollaboration nach dem zweiten Weltkrieg*, edited by Klaus-Dietmar Henke and Hans Woller, 21–83. Munich: Deutscher Taschenbuch Verlag, 1991.

Henzler, Christoph. *Fritz Schäffer, 1945–1967*. Munich: Hanns Seidel Stiftung eV, 1994.

Herbert, Ulrich. "Rückkehr in die Bürgerlichkeit? NS-Eliten in der Bundesrepublik." In *Rechtsradikalismus in der Nachkriegszeit*, edited by Bernd Weisbrod, 159–73.

Herbst, Ludolf. *Der totale Krieg und die Ordnung der Wirtschaft*. Stuttgart: Deutsche Verlags-Anstalt, 1982.

————, ed. *Westdeutschland, 1945–1955: Unterwerfung, Kontrolle, Integration*. Munich: Oldenbourg Verlag, 1986.

Herbst, Ludolf, and Constantin Goschler, eds. *Wiedergutmachung in der Bundesrepublik Deutschland*. Munich: Oldenbourg Verlag, 1989.

Herf, Jeffrey. *Divided Memory: The Nazi Past in the Two Germanys*. Cambridge, Mass.: Harvard University Press, 1997.

————. "Late Victory of Lost Causes." In *Heidelberg 1945*, edited by Jürgen Heß, Hartmut Lehmann, and Volker Sellin, 387–90. Stuttgart: Franz Steiner Verlag, 1996.

————. "Multiple Restorations: German Political Traditions and the Interpretation of Nazism, 1945–1946." *Central European History* 26, no. 1 (1993): 21–56.

Hochstein, Beatrix. *Die Ideologie des Überlebens. Zur Geschichte der politischen Apathie in Deutschland*. Frankfurt/M: Campus Verlag, 1984.

Hockerts, Hans Günter. "Adenauer als Sozialpolitiker." In *Konrad Adenauer und seine Zeit,*
edited by Dieter Blumenwitz, 466–87. Stuttgart: Deutsche Verlags-Anstalt, 1976.
———. "Integration der Gesellschaft: Gründungskrise und Sozialpolitik in der frühen
Bundesrepublik." *Zeitschrift für Sozialreform* 32, no. 1 (Jan. 1986): 25–41.
———. *Sozialpolitische Entscheidungen im Nachkriegsdeutschland: Alliierte und deutsche
Sozialversicherungspolitik.* Stuttgart: Klett-Cotta, 1980.
Hogan, Michael. *The Marshall Plan: America, Britain, and the Reconstruction of Western
Europe, 1947–1952.* Cambridge: Cambridge University Press, 1987.
Holtfrerich, Carl-Ludwig. "Die Deutsche Bank, 1945–1957." In Gall, *The Deutsche Bank,
1870–1995.*
———. *The German Inflation.* Translated by Theo Balderston. Berlin and New York: W.
deGruyter, 1986.
Hong, Young-Sun. *Welfare, Modernity, and the Weimar State, 1919–1933.* Princeton, N.J.:
Princeton University Press, 1998.
Hudemann, Rainer. "Kriegsopferpolitik nach den beiden Weltkriegen." In *Staatliche, städ-
tische, betriebliche und kirchliche Sozialpolitik vom Mittelalter bis zur Gegenwart,* edited by
Hans Pohl, 269–93. Stuttgart: Fritz Steiner Verlag, 1991.
———. *Sozialpolitik im deutschen Südwesten zwischen Tradition und Neuordnung, 1945–1953.*
Mainz: von Hase Koehler Verlag, 1988.
Hughes, Michael L. "Hard Heads, Soft Money? West German Ambivalence about Currency
Reform, 1944–1948." *German Studies Review* 21, no. 2 (May 1998): 309–27.
———. "Lastenausgleich unter Sozialismusverdacht: Amerikanische Besorgnisse, 1945–1949."
Vierteljahrshefte für Zeitgeschichte 39, no. 1 (Jan. 1991): 37–53.
———. *Paying for the German Inflation.* Chapel Hill: University of North Carolina
Press, 1988.
———. "Restitution and Democracy in Germany after Two World Wars." *Contemporary
European History* 4, no. 1 (Mar. 1994): 1–18.
———. "Wer bezahlt die Rechnung? Die Kosten des Regimewechsels im Deutschland
des 20. Jahrhunderts." *Geschichte in Wissenschaft und Unterricht* 43, no. 9 (Sept. 1992):
538–56.
Jolles, Hiddo M. *Zur Soziologie der Heimatvertriebenen und Flüchtlinge.* Cologne: Kiepenheuer
& Witsch, 1965.
Kaes, Anton, Martin Jay, and Edward Dimendberg, eds. *The Weimar Republic Sourcebook.*
Berkeley: University of California Press, 1994.
Kamenka, Eugene, and Alice Tay, eds. *Justice.* New York: St. Martin's Press, 1980.
Keegan, John. *The Second World War.* New York: Viking Press, 1990.
Kershaw, Ian. *The "Hitler Myth": Image and Reality in the Third Reich.* Oxford: Clarendon
Press, 1987.
———. *The Nazi Dictatorship.* 3d ed. London: Edward Arnold, 1993.
Kimball, Warren F. *Swords or Ploughshares? The Morgenthau Plan for Defeated Nazi Germany,
1943–1946.* Philadelphia: Lippincott, 1976.
Kindleberger, Charles. *A Financial History of Western Europe.* 2d ed. Oxford: Oxford
University Press, 1993.
Kitchen, Martin. *Nazi Germany at War.* London: Longman, 1995.
Kitterer, Wolfgang. "Rechtfertigung und Risiken einer Finanzierung der deutschen Einheit
durch Staatsverschuldung." In *Finanzierungsprobleme der deutschen Einheit,* edited by
Alois Oberhauser. Vol. 4. Berlin: Duncker & Humblot, 1996.
Kleßmann, Christoph. *Die doppelte Staatsgründung: Deutsche Geschichte, 1945–1955.* Göttingen:
Vandenhoeck & Ruprecht, 1989.

Klotzbach, Kurt. *Der Weg zur Staatspartei.* Berlin and Bonn: Dietz Verlag, 1982.

Knapp, Manfred. "Das Deutschlandproblem und die Ursprünge des europäischen Wiederaufbauprogramms." In *Marshallplan und westdeutscher Wiederaufstieg,* edited by H.-J. Schröder, 22–31.

———. "Deutschland und der Marshallplan." In *Marshallplan und westdeutscher Wiederaufstieg,* edited by H.-J. Schröder, 35–59.

Kocka, Jürgen, and Allen Mitchell, eds. *Bourgeois Society in Nineteenth-Century Europe.* Oxford: Berg, 1993.

Koebner, Thomas, Gert Sautermeister, and S. Schneider-Grube, eds. *Deutschland nach Hitler: Zukunftspläne im Exil und aus der Besatzungszeit, 1939–1949.* Cologne and Opladen: Westdeutscher Verlag, 1987.

Koerfer, Daniel. *Kampf ums Kanzleramt: Erhard und Adenauer.* Stuttgart: Deutsche Verlags-Anstalt, 1987.

Kollmer von Oheimb-Loup, Gert. "Die Wirtschaftspolitik Erhards als Fessel des wirtschaftlichen Aufschwungs." *Vierteljahrschrift für Sozial- und Wirtschaftsgeschichte* 82, no. 4 (1995): 459–77.

Koopmans, Ruud. *Democracy from Below: New Social Movements and the Political System in West Germany.* Boulder, Colo.: Westview, 1995.

Kralewski, Wolfgang, and Karlheinz Neunreither. *Oppositionelles Verhalten im ersten Deutschen Bundestag.* Cologne and Opladen: Westdeutscher Verlag, 1963.

Kramer, Alan. *The West German Economy, 1945–1955.* New York: Berg, 1991.

Krause, Michael. *Flucht vor dem Bombenkrieg. "Umquartierungen" im Zweiten Weltkrieg und die Wiedereingliederung der Evakuierten in Deutschland, 1943–1963.* Düsseldorf: Droste Verlag, 1997.

Kreckel, Reinhard. "Statusinkonsistenz und Statusdefizienz in gesellschaftstheoretischer Perspektive." In *Sozialstruktur im Umbruch,* edited by Stefan Hradil, 29–47. Opladen: Leske Verlag, 1985.

Krohn, Claus-Dieter. *Intellectuals in Exile: Refugee Scholars and the New School for Social Research.* Translated by Rita and Robert Kimber. Amherst: University of Massachusetts Press, 1993.

LaFeber, Walter. *America, Russia, and the Cold War, 1945–1980.* 4th ed. New York: Wiley & Sons, 1980.

Large, David. *Germans to the Front: West German Rearmament in the Adenauer Era.* Chapel Hill: University of North Carolina Press, 1996.

Latzel, Klaus. " 'Freie Bahn dem Tüchtigen!' Kriegserfahrung und Perspektiven für die Nachkriegszeit in Feldpostbriefen aus dem Zweiten Weltkrieg." In *Lernen aus dem Krieg?* edited by Gottfried Niedhart and Dieter Riesenberger, 331–43.

Laufer, Jochen. "Die UdSSR und die deutsche Währungsfrage, 1944–1948." *Vierteljahrshefte für Zeitgeschichte* 46, no. 3 (July 1998): 455–85.

Leffler, Melvyn P. *The Struggle for Germany and the Origins of the Cold War.* German Historical Institute, Occasional Paper no. 16. Washington, D.C.: German Historical Institute, n.d.

Lehmann, Albrecht. *Im Fremden ungewollt zuhaus: Flüchtlinge und Vertriebene in Westdeutschland, 1945–1990.* 2d ed. Munich: C. H. Beck, 1993.

Lemberg, Eugen, and Friedrich Edding, eds. *Die Vertriebenen in Westdeutschland: Ihre Eingliederung und ihr Einfluß auf Gesellschaft, Wirtschaft, Politik und Geistesleben.* 3 vols. Kiel: Ferdinand Hirt, 1959.

Loth, Wilfried. "Die Deutschen und die deutsche Frage. Überlegungen zur Dekomposition der deutschen Nation." In *Die deutsche Frage,* edited by Wilfried Loth.

———. "Die Historiker und die deutsche Frage." In *Die deutsche Frage,* edited by Wilfried Loth.

———, ed. *Die deutsche Frage in der Nachkriegszeit.* Berlin: Akademie Verlag, 1994.

Löwenthal, Richard, and Hans-Peter Schwarz, eds. *Die zweite Republik: 25 Jahre Bundesrepublik Deutschland—eine Bilanz.* Stuttgart: Seewald Verlag, 1974.

Lübbe, Hermann. "Der Nationalsozialismus im deutschen Nachkriegsbewußtsein." *Historische Zeitschrift* 236 (1983): 579–99.

Mai, Gunther. *Der Alliierte Kontrollrat in Deutschland, 1945–1948: Alliierte Einheit—deutsche Teilung?* Munich: Oldenbourg Verlag, 1995.

Maier, Charles S., ed. *The Origins of the Cold War and Contemporary Europe.* New York: New Viewpoints, 1978.

Manuel, Frank E., and Fritzie P. Manuel. *Utopian Thought in the Western World.* Cambridge, Mass.: Belknap Press of Harvard University Press, 1979.

Marrus, Michael. *The Unwanted: European Refugees in the Twentieth Century.* Oxford: Oxford University Press, 1985.

Mastny, Vojtech. *The Cold War and Soviet Insecurity: The Stalin Years.* New York: Oxford University Press, 1996.

Merkatz, H. J., ed. *Aus Trümmern wurden Fundamente.* Düsseldorf: W. Rau, 1979.

Merritt, Richard L. *Democracy Imposed: U.S. Occupation Policy and German Public Opinion, 1945–1949.* New Haven, Conn.: Yale University Press, 1995.

Milward, Alan. *The Reconstruction of Western Europe.* Berkeley: University of California Press, 1984.

Mintzel, Alf. "Der akzeptierte Parteienstaat." In *Zäsuren nach 1945,* edited by Martin Broszat. Munich: Oldenbourg Verlag, 1990.

Mitchell, Maria D. "Materialism and Secularism: CDU Politicians and National Socialism, 1945–1949." *Journal of Modern History* 67, no. 2 (June 1995): 278–308.

Mitscherlich, Alexander, and Margarete Mitscherlich. *The Inability to Mourn.* New York: Grove Press, 1975.

Moeller, Robert G. *Protecting Motherhood: Women and the Family in the Politics of Postwar West Germany.* Berkeley: University of California Press, 1993.

———. "War Stories: The Search for a Usable Past in the Federal Republic of Germany." *American Historical Review* 101, no. 4 (Oct. 1996): 1008–48.

Möller, Hans. "Die westdeutsche Währungsreform von 1948." In *Währung und Wirtschaft in Deutschland, 1876–1975,* edited by Deutsche Bundesbank, 433–83.

Mommsen, Hans. "Der lange Schatten der untergehenden Republik: Zur Kontinuität politischer Denkhaltungen von der späten Weimarer Republik zur frühen Bundesrepublik." In Hans Mommsen, *Der Nationalsozialismus und die deutsche Gesellschaft,* 362–404. Hamburg: Rowohlt Taschenbuch Verlag, 1991.

———. "Von Weimar nach Bonn: Zum Demokratieverständnis der Deutschen." In *Modernisierung im Wiederaufbau,* edited by Axel Schildt and Arnold Sywottek, 745–58.

Morsey, Rudolf. "Konrad Adenauer und der deutsche Bundestag." In *Konrad Adenauer und der Deutsche Bundestag,* edited by Hans Buchheim, 14–27. Bonn: Bouvier Verlag, 1986.

Müller, Ingo. *Hitler's Justice: The Courts of the Third Reich.* Translated by Deborah Schneider. Cambridge, Mass.: Harvard University Press, 1991.

Münch, Paul, ed. *Ordnung, Fleiß und Sparsamkeit. Texte und Dokumente zur Entstehung der "bürgerlichen Tugenden."* Munich: Deutscher Taschenbuch Verlag, 1984.

Nahm, Peter Paul. *. . . doch das Leben ging weiter.* Cologne: Grote Verlag, 1971.

———. "Lastenausgleich und Integration der Vertriebenen und Geflüchteten." In *Die zweite Republik,* edited by Richard Löwenthal and Hans-Peter Schwarz, 817–42.

Naimark, Norman M. *The Russians in Germany: A History of the Soviet Occupation Zone, 1945–1949.* Cambridge, Mass.: Belknap Press of Harvard University Press, 1995.

Nawratil, Heinz. *Die deutschen Nachkriegsverluste unter Vertriebenen, Gefangenen und Verschleppten.* Munich: Herbig Verlagsbuchhandlung, 1986.

Neumann, Franz. *Der Block der Heimatvertriebenen und Entrechteten, 1950–1960.* Meisenheim: Verlag A. Hain, 1968.

Nicholls, A. J. *The Bonn Republic: West German Democracy, 1945–1990.* London: Longman, 1997.

———. *Freedom with Responsibility: The Social Market Economy in Germany, 1918–1963.* Oxford: Clarendon Press, 1994.

Niedhart, Gottfried, and Dieter Riesenberger, eds. *Lernen aus dem Krieg? Deutsche Nachkriegszeiten, 1918/1945.* Munich: C. Beck Verlag, 1992.

Niethammer, Lutz. "Die amerikanische Besatzungsmacht zwischen Verwaltungstradition und politischen Parteien in Bayern 1945." *Vierteljahrshefte für Zeitgeschichte* 15, no. 2 (Apr. 1967): 153–210.

———. "Privat-Wirtschaft: Erinnerungsfragmente einer anderen Umerziehung." In *"Hinterher merkt man, daß es richtig war, daß es schiefgegangen ist": Nachkriegs-Erfahrungen im Ruhrgebiet,* edited by Lutz Niethammer, 17–105. Berlin: Dietz Verlag, 1983.

———. "Structural Reform and a Compact for Growth: Conditions for a United Labor Movement in Western Europe after the Collapse of Fascism." In *Origins of Cold War,* edited by Charles S. Maier, 201–43.

Niethammer, Lutz, and Alexander von Plato. *"Wir kriegen jetzt andere Zeiten": Auf der Suche nach der Erfahrung des Volkes in nachfaschistischen Ländern.* Berlin: Dietz Verlag, 1985.

Ott, Erich. *Die Wirtschaftskonzeptionen der SPD nach 1945.* Marburg: Verlag Arbeiterbewegung und Gesellschaftswissenschaft, 1978.

Overesch, Manfred. "Einheit oder Teilung? Westdeutsche Entscheidungsträger vor der gesamtdeutschen Frage, 1945–1947." In *Kalter Krieg,* edited by Joseph Foschepoth, 269–90.

Overy, R. J. *The Air War, 1939–1945.* New York: Stein & Day, 1980.

Overy, Richard. *War and Economy in the Third Reich.* Oxford: Clarendon Press, 1994.

Paterson, Thomas G. *Meeting the Communist Threat: Truman to Reagan.* New York: Oxford University Press, 1988.

Petzina, Dietmar, ed. *Ordnungspolitische Weichenstellungen nach dem Zweiten Weltkrieg.* Schriften des Vereins für Sozialpolitik, NF Bd. 203. Berlin: Duncker & Humblot, 1991.

Peukert, Detlev. "Hamburg in den Jahren 1943 bis 1953. Das Jahrzehnt einer unfreiwilligen Revolution." In *Improvisierter Neubeginn,* edited by Detlev Peukert, 9–18.

———. *Inside Nazi Germany: Conformity, Opposition, and Racism in Everyday Life.* Translated by Richard Deveson. New Haven, Conn.: Yale University Press, 1987.

———. *The Weimar Republic.* Translated by Richard Deveson. New York: Hill & Wang, 1993.

———, ed. *Improvisierter Neubeginn: Hamburg, 1943–1953.* Hamburg: Ergebnisse Verlag, 1989.

Plumpe, Werner. *Vom Plan zum Markt. Wirtschaftsverwaltung und Unternehmerverbände in der britischen Zone.* Düsseldorf: Verlag Schwann, 1987.

Pohl, Hans, ed. *Adenauers Verhältnisse zu Wirtschaft und Gesellschaft.* Bonn: Bouvier Verlag, 1992.

Poiger, Uta G. "Rebels with a Cause? American Popular Culture, the 1956 Youth Riots, and the New Conception of Masculinity in East and West Germany." In *The American Impact on Postwar Germany,* edited by Reiner Pommerin, 93–124. Providence, R.I.: Berghahn Books, 1995.

Prinz, Michael, and Rainer Zitelmann, eds. *Nationalsozialismus und Modernisierung.* Darmstadt: Wissenschaftliche Buchgesellschaft, 1991.

Prowe, Diethelm. "Foundations of West German Democracy: Corporatist Patterns in the Post-1945 Democratization Process." In *Coping with the Past: Germany and Austria after 1945,* edited by Kathy Harms, Lutz-Rainer Reuter, and Volker Dürr, 105–29. Madison: University of Wisconsin Press, 1990.

———. "German Democratization as Conservative Restabilization: The Impact of American Policy." In *American Policy and Reconstruction,* edited by Jeffry M. Diefendorf, Axel Frohn, and H.-J. Rupieper, 307–29.

Rogers, Daniel E. "Transforming the German Party System: The United States and the Origins of Political Moderation." *Journal of Modern History* 65, no. 3 (Sept. 1993): 512–41.

Roseman, Mark. "The Organic Society and the 'Massenmenschen': Integrating Young Labour in the Ruhr Mines, 1945–1958." In *West Germany under Construction: Politics, Society, and Culture in the Adenauer Era,* edited by Robert G. Moeller, 287–320. Ann Arbor: University of Michigan Press, 1997.

Rumpf, Hans. *The Bombing of Germany.* Translated by Edward Fitzgerald. New York: Holt, Rinehart & Winston, 1962.

Ryan, Alan. *Property and Political Theory.* New York: Basil Blackwell, 1984.

Sachße, Christoph, and Florian Tennstedt. *Fürsorge und Wohlfahrtspflege, 1871–1929.* Vol. 2 of *Geschichte der Armenfürsorge in Deutschland.* Stuttgart: Verlag Kohlhammer, 1988.

Sander, Helke, and Barbara Johr, eds. *BeFreier und BeFreite: Krieg, Vergewaltigungen, Kinder.* Munich: Verlag Antje Kunstmann, 1992.

Schelsky, Helmut. *Wandlungen der deutschen Familie in der Gegenwart.* Stuttgart: Enke Verlag, 1960.

Schildt, Axel, and Arnold Sywottek, eds. *Massenwohnung und Eigenheim.* Frankfurt: Campus Verlag, 1988.

———. *Modernisierung im Wiederaufbau.* Bonn: J. Dietz, 1993.

Schillinger, Reinhold. *Der Entscheidungsprozeß beim Lastenausgleich, 1945–1952.* St. Katharinen: Scriptura Mercaturae Verlag, 1985.

Schlatter, Richard. *Private Property: The History of an Idea.* New Brunswick, N.J.: Rutgers University Press, 1951.

Schmidt, Theodoric. *Graslitz: Die Bevölkerung einer sudetendeutschen Stadt einst und jetzt.* Karlstein am Main: Kolb-Verlag, 1983.

Scholz, Robert. " 'Heraus aus der unwürdigen Fürsorge': Zur sozialen Lage und politischen Orientierung der Kleinrentner in der Weimarer Republik." In *Gerontologie und Sozialgeschichte: Wege zu einer historischen Betrachtung des Alters,* edited by Christoph Conrad and Hans-Joachim von Kondratowitz, 319–50. Berlin: DZA, 1983.

Schornstheimer, Michael. *Bombenstimmung und Katzenjammer: Vergangenheitsbewältigung: Quick und Stern in den 50er Jahren.* Cologne: Pahl-Rugenstein, 1989.

Schroeder, Gregory. "The Long Road Home: German Evacuees of the Second World War, Postwar Victim Identities, and Social Policy in the Federal Republic." Ph.D. diss., Indiana University, 1997.

Schröder, H.-J., ed. *Marshallplan und westdeutscher Wiederaufstieg.* Stuttgart: Steiner Verlag, 1990.

Schulz, Günther. "Konrad Adenauers gesellschaftspolitische Vorstellungen." In *Adenauers Verhältnisse,* edited by Hans Pohl, 157–79.

———. *Wiederaufbau in Deutschland: Die Wohnungsbaupolitik in den Westzonen und der Bundesrepublik von 1945 bis 1957.* Düsseldorf: Droste Verlag, 1994.

Schulze, Rainer, Doris von der Brelie-Lewen, and Helga Grebing, eds. *Flüchtlinge und*

Vertriebene in der westdeutschen Nachkriegsgeschichte. Hildesheim: Verlag August Lax, 1987.

Schwarz, Hans-Peter. *Adenauer.* Vol. 1. Stuttgart: Deutsche Verlags-Anstalt, 1986.

———. "Die ausgebliebene Katastrophe. Eine Problemskizze zur Geschichte der Bundesrepublik." In *Den Staat denken: Theodor Eschenburg zum Fünfundachtzigsten,* edited by Hermann Rudolph, 151–74. N.p.: Siedler Verlag, 1990.

———. "Modernisierung oder Restauration? Einige Vorfragen zur sozialgeschichtlichen Forschung über die Ära Adenauer." In *Rheinland-Westfalen im Industriezeitalter,* vol. 3, edited by Kurt Düwell and W. Köllmann. Berlin: Ullstein Verlag, 1984.

———. *Die Wiederherstellung des deutschen Kredites.* Stuttgart: Belser Verlag, 1982.

Scott, Craig Dee. "Money Talks: The West German Currency Reform of 1948." Ph.D. diss., University of Wisconsin–Madison, 1995.

Seraphim, Peter-Heinz. *Die Heimatvertriebenen in der Sowjetzone.* Berlin: Duncker & Humblot, 1954.

Siegel, Tilla. *Leistung und Lohn in der nationalsozialistischen "Ordnung der Arbeit."* Opladen: Westdeutscher Verlag, 1989.

Skran, Claudena M. *Refugees in Interwar Europe: The Emergence of a Regime.* Oxford: Clarendon Press, 1995.

Smith, Woodruff. *The Ideological Origins of Nazi Imperialism.* New York: Oxford University Press, 1986.

Sombart, Werner. *Die vorkapitalistische Wirtschaft.* Munich: Duncker & Humblot, 1928.

Soutou, Georges-Henri. "Frankreich und die Deutschlandfrage." In *Ende des dritten Reiches,* edited by Hans-Erich Volkmann.

Steinert, Johannes. *Vertriebenenverbände in Nordrhein-Westfalen.* Düsseldorf: Schwann Verlag, 1986.

Steinert, Marlis. *Hitler's War and the Germans: Public Mood and Attitude during the Second World War.* Translated by Thomas E. J. de Witt. Athens: Ohio University Press, 1977.

Steinmetz, George. *Regulating the Social: The Welfare State and Local Politics in Imperial Germany.* Princeton, N.J.: Princeton University Press, 1993.

Stern, Frank. *The Whitewashing of the Yellow Badge: Antisemitism and Philosemitism in Postwar Germany.* Translated by William Templer. Oxford: Pergamon Press, 1992.

Stolleis, Michael. "Gemeinschaft und Volksgemeinschaft. Zur juristischen Terminologie im Nationalsozialismus." In *Recht im Unrecht. Studien zur Rechtsgeschichte des Nationalsozialismus,* edited by Michael Stolleis, 94–125. Frankfurt/M: Suhrkamp, 1994.

———. "Rechtsordnung und Justizpolitik 1945–1949." In *Recht im Unrecht. Studien zur Rechtsgeschichte des Nationalsozialismus,* edited by Michael Stolleis, 249–74. Frankfurt/M: Suhrkamp, 1994.

Stürmer, Michael. *Herbst des alten Handwerks.* Munich: Deutscher Taschenbuch Verlag, 1979.

Sweeney, Dennis. "Work, Race, and the Transformation of Industrial Culture in Wilhelmine Germany." *Social History* 23, no. 1 (Jan. 1998): 31–62.

Temin, Peter. "The 'Korea Boom' in West Germany: Fact or Fiction?" *Economic History Review* 48, no. 4 (Nov. 1995): 737–53.

Tenbruck, Friedrich. "Alltagsnormen und Lebensgefühle in der Bundesrepublik." In *Die zweite Republik,* edited by Richard Löwenthal and Hans-Peter Schwarz, 289–310.

Ther, Philipp. "The Integration of the Expellees in Germany and Poland after World War II: A Historical Reassessment." *Slavic Review* 55, no. 4 (Winter 1996): 779–805.

Thompson, E. P. "The Moral Economy of the English Crowd in the Eighteenth Century." *Past and Present* 50 (Feb. 1971): 76–136.

Tilly, Richard. "Moral Standards and Business Behavior in Nineteenth-Century Germany and Britain." In *Bourgeois Society*, edited by Jürgen Kocka and Allen Mitchell, 179–206.

Trommler, Frank. "'Deutschlands Sieg oder Untergang': Perspektiven aus dem Dritten Reich auf die Nachkriegsentwicklung." In *Deutschland nach Hitler*, edited by Thomas Koebner, Gert Sautermeister, and S. Schneider-Grube, 214–28.

Turner, Ian. "Great Britain and the Post-War German Currency Reform." *Historical Journal* 30 (1987): 685–708.

Volkmann, Hans-Erich, ed. *Ende des dritten Reiches—Ende des zweiten Weltkrieges. Eine perspektivische Rückschau.* Munich: Piper Verlag, 1995.

von Plato, Alexander. "Fremde Heimat. Zur Integration von Flüchtlingen und Einheimischen in die Neue Zeit." In *"Wir kriegen jetzt andere Zeiten,"* edited by Lutz Niethammer and Alexander von Plato, 172–219.

―――, ed. *"Der Verlierer geht nicht leer aus": Betriebsräte geben zu Protokoll.* Berlin: Verlag Dietz Nachf., 1984.

Waldron, Jeremy. *The Right to Private Property.* Oxford: Clarendon Press, 1990.

Walker, Mack. *German Home Towns: Community, State, and General Estate, 1648–1871.* Ithaca, N.Y.: Cornell University Press, 1971.

Wallich, Henry. *Mainsprings of the German Revival.* New Haven, Conn.: Yale University Press, 1955.

Wambach, Manfred. *Verbändestaat und Parteienoligopol: Macht und Ohnmacht der Vertriebenenverbände.* Stuttgart: Enke Verlag, 1971.

Wandel, Eckhard. *Die Entstehung der Bank deutscher Länder und die deutsche Währungsreform, 1948.* Frankfurt/M: Fritz Knapp Verlag, 1980.

Weisbrod, Bernd, ed. *Rechtsradikalismus in der politischen Kultur der Nachkriegszeit: Die verzögerte Normalisierung in Niedersachsen.* Hannover: Verlag Hahnsche Buchhandlung, 1995.

Welch, David. *The Third Reich: Politics and Propaganda.* London: Routledge, 1993.

Wengst, Udo. *Beamtentum zwischen Reform und Tradition: Beamtengesetzgebung in der Gründungsphase der Bundesrepublik Deutschland, 1948–1953.* Düsseldorf: Droste Verlag, 1988.

Wenzel, Rolf. *Konrad Adenauer und die Gestaltung der Wirtschafts- und Sozialordnung im Nachkriegsdeutschland.* Flensburg: IPSE, 1983.

Werner, Wolfgang. "Belastungen der deutschen Arbeiterschaft in der 2. Kriegshälfte." In *Über Leben im Krieg: Kriegserfahrungen in einer Industrieregion, 1939–1945,* edited by U. Borsdorf and M. Jamin, 33–42. Reinbek: Rowohlt, 1989.

Whalen, Robert Weldon. *Bitter Wounds: German Victims of the Great War, 1914–1939.* Ithaca, N.Y.: Cornell University Press, 1984.

Wieacker, Franz. *Privatrechtsgeschichte der Neuzeit.* Göttingen, 1967.

Wiesemann, Falk, and Uwe Kleinert. "Flüchtlinge und wirtschaftlicher Wiederaufbau im britischen Besatzungsgebiet." In *Wirtschaftspolitik im britischen Besatzungsgebiet, 1945–1949,* edited by Dietmar Petzina, 297–326. Düsseldorf: Pädagogischer Verlag Schwann, 1985.

Wiesen, S. Jonathan. "Overcoming Nazism: Big Business, Public Relations, and the Politics of Memory, 1945–1950." *Central European History* 29, no. 2 (1996): 201–26.

Wildt, Michael. *Am Beginn der "Konsumgesellschaft": Mangelerfahrung, Lebenshaltung, Wohlstandshoffnung in Westdeutschland in den fünfziger Jahren.* Hamburg: Ergebnisse Verlag, 1994.

―――. *Der Traum vom Sattwerden: Hunger und Protest, Schwarzmarkt und Selbsthilfe.* Hamburg: VSA Verlag, 1986.

Wille, Manfred. "Die Zentralverwaltung für Deutsche Umsiedler: Möglichkeiten und Grenzen ihres Wirkens." In *Sie hatten alles verloren: Flüchtlinge und Vertriebene in der sowjetischen Besatzungszone Deutschlands,* edited by Manfred Wille, Johannes Hoffmann, and Wolfgang Meinicke. Wiesbaden: Harrassowitz Verlag, 1993.

Winkel, Harald. *Die Wirtschaft im geteilten Deutschland, 1945–1970.* Wiesbaden: Steiner Verlag, 1974.

Woller, Hans. "Germany in Transition from Stalingrad to Currency Reform." In *America and Shaping of German Society,* edited by Michael Ermarth, 23–34.

————. *Gesellschaft und Politik in der amerikanischen Besatzungszone.* Munich: Oldenbourg Verlag, 1986.

Wünsche, Horst. *Ludwig Erhards Gesellschafts- und Wirtschaftskonzeption: Soziale Marktwirtschaft als politische Ökonomie.* Stuttgart: Bonn Aktuell, 1986.

Yergin, Daniel. "Shattered Peace: The Origins of the Cold War and the National Security State." In *Origins of Cold War,* edited by Charles S. Maier, 107–42.

INDEX

Colm, Gerhard, 44–46
Colm-Dodge-Goldsmith Plan, 44–48, 50, 54, 70
Communism and Communists, 30, 76, 144, 193; general fears of, 23, 26–27, 44, 46, 52–56, 64–65, 115, 117–18, 146, 147, 165–67, 182; and Lastenausgleich, 70, 132, 138, 147, 149, 159, 166, 182, 186, 188, 190, 194. *See also* East Germany; Union of Soviet Socialist Republics
Community: "racial," 1, 3, 9–10, 24, 38–39, 40, 115–16, 190; of risk, 37–42, 94–96, 112–13, 120–21, 127, 153, 178, 185, 188, 190–91; West German, 98, 178, 198
Compensation: instead of Lastenausgleich, 94–96, 152, 185–87; for war-damaged not to be lower than for other war victims, 185–87
— limits on: graduated rates, 138, 157, 163, 186, 187; maximum for recompensable losses, 157–58, 163, 174
Compromise, political, 97, 179; by economic elites, 143–44; by parties, 76, 141, 149–50, 159, 172–75, 194; by war-damaged, 149, 165, 171–77, 182–83, 194
Connolly, John, 40
Consumption: as economically problematic, 10, 28, 31, 88, 111, 113, 122, 124, 126, 156, 157, 177, 187, 193; as stimulus to economic growth, 57, 66, 110, 193
Cooperation: between government and opposition parties, 80, 140–42, 173–75, 197; and conflict among war-damaged groups, 80, 135, 169–70
Corporatist democracy, 26, 84, 148
Credit and credit policy, 45, 49, 56–59, 66–68, 110–11, 118, 169, 177–78, 191
Creditors. *See* Savers
Currency-damaged, 51, 75, 77, 94, 163–64, 177–78. *See also* Savers
Currency reform, 5, 37, 130, 190, 192; American policies, 44–47, 53–63, 191; economic growth after, 65, 67, 119; economic problems after, 67, 68, 69, 73–74, 88, 91, 109; German preferences, 32–33, 47–63 passim, 105, 112–14, 178; need for, 29, 31–32, 34, 44
Currency-reform levy, 74, 155
Czechoslovakaia: and expulsion of Germans, 18–20; 1948 crisis in, 54

Debt: domestic private, 58, 60, 62, 74; prewar foreign, 169, 175, 195; Reich (war), 1–3, 5, 12–13, 31–33, 38, 45, 47, 49–50, 56, 59, 61, 62
Dederra, Erich, 99
Deflation, 48, 52, 56–59, 67–68, 118
Democratization in postwar Germany: general development of, 25–26, 37, 83–86, 133, 140, 141, 183–84; in context of Lastenausgleich, 81–82, 129, 133–34, 143–50, 173–84 passim, 194–98. *See also* Allies: promotion of parliamentary democracy in West Germany
Demonstrations, political, 145–48
De-Nazification, 25, 36–37, 103–4, 136. *See also* National Socialism
Division of Germany, steps toward, 23, 43–55 passim, 64–65
Dodge, Joseph, 44
Douglas, Mary, 178

East Germany (German Democratic Republic), 3, 52, 70, 117–18, 132, 144, 159, 165–66, 178, 182, 190, 193, 194, 198
Economic conditions in postwar West Germany, 28–33, 53, 65, 67–68, 71, 111–12, 118–19, 142, 166–68, 183–84, 186–88
Economic controls and decontrol, 10, 12, 28–29, 34, 46, 65–67, 115, 117–18, 119, 167
Economic Council, 48, 52, 66–68, 73–82; Lastenausgleich Advisory Commission, 76
Economic expediency: as key criterion in Lastenausgleich, 8, 85–87, 107–8, 121–32 passim, 142, 150–53, 155, 159, 167, 168, 193–94
Economic growth. *See* Economic conditions in postwar West Germany
Economic Institute of the Trade Unions, 137
Economic policies: Allied, 23, 29, 30, 44–45, 66, 114–15; Nazi, 12; West German, 26–28, 65–67, 108–11, 115–18, 166–67, 188, 193
Education and training: in Lastenausgleich legislation, 72–73, 78, 156, 159–60, 180
Eghigian, Greg, 98
Elections, federal: in 1949, 84; in 1953, 136, 141, 179, 182–84, 186, 194; in 1957, 180, 183, 184, 188
Enssle, Martin, 30
Entitlement or legal claim to a Lastenausgleich: assertion one existed on basis of War-Damages Decree, 1, 5–8, 10, 41–42, 68–69, 74, 94–97, 99, 102, 135, 137, 185, 191, 192; grants of, in legislation,

Rechtsstaat: and right to Lastenausgleich, 37
Red Army, 18–19, 65, 117–18, 165, 195
Reparations, 23, 29, 39–40, 117, 161
Responsiveness of political system, 143–45,
    149–50, 197
Restitution: for Nazi crimes, 168–69
Restoration through a Lastenausgleich, 70,
    73, 189; of children's status, 159–60; of
    prewar economic structure, 125–26, 131,
    158, 185; of prewar moral order, 6, 88,
    96, 113, 185, 189, 192; of prewar social
    status/honor, 83, 88, 90, 94, 108, 123, 138,
    158, 161, 189, 192; of prewar wealth, 10,
    41, 78–79, 83, 88, 108, 120, 192
Revaluation and 1920s currency stabiliza-
    tion, warnings about and memories
    of: among 1920s creditors, 11–12, 176;
    among Nazis, 12; among post-1945
    war-damaged, 3, 13, 32–33, 88; among
    undamaged, 33, 42–55 passim, 74, 112,
    143–44, 190
Right, radical. *See* Neo-Nazis and radical
    Right
Röpke, Wilhelm, 105
Rothwesten Conclave, 57–59, 63
Royall, Kenneth, 56, 81

Sacrifice: as basis of community, 178;
    demands for, in Lastenausgleich, 9–10,
    40, 123; growing unwillingness to, in
    Lastenausgleich, 86, 119–29 passim, 143
Savers (creditors): activism and organiza-
    tion among, 32–33, 133–34, 163–64, 177;
    and currency reform, 58, 61, 62, 72; and
    exclusion from Lastenausgleich Law,
    163–64; in 1920s, 11, 134, 149; and Old
    Saver Law, 177–78; self-perception of,
    12–13, 37, 88, 89, 96–97, 164. *See also*
    Currency-damaged
Saving, willingness for, 109–10, 177–78
Schäffer, Fritz: Lastenausgleich preferences
    of, 34, 86–87, 94, 113, 126, 130, 142–
    44, 153, 156, 168, 172, 174, 187, 188; and
    Old Savers Law, 178; political views of,
    85–87, 149–50, 175
Schillinger, Reinhold, 62, 76, 85, 130, 144,
    151, 160
Schumacher, Kurt, 36, 84, 85, 139–40, 141,
    150
Schütz, Hans, 146–47
Schwarz, Hans-Peter, 42, 149
Security, perceptions of personal, 70, 72–73,
    83, 180, 191

Seiler, Fritz, 102
Selbsthilfe, 94, 108, 134, 176, 182–83, 184
Seuffert, Walter, 8, 35, 90, 125, 139–40,
    141–42, 161–62, 174
Shift of levy costs to consumers and
    taxpayers, 124–25, 135, 136–39, 174,
    177
Social Democratic Party (SPD), 8, 40, 44,
    69, 88, 90, 110, 118, 130, 195; agreement
    with BHE, 139–40; attitude toward street
    demonstrations, 146, 147; cooperation
    with CDU, 80, 140–42, 172–74, 197; and
    education in Lastenausgleich, 160; and
    First Lastenausgleich Law, 75, 80, 129;
    and forward-looking Lastenausgleich,
    24; general policy preferences, 26, 66,
    84, 119, 172–74; and Lastenausgleich
    Law, 155, 173–74, 176–77; and Nazi
    responsibility for financing Lasten-
    ausgleich, 36; preference for social
    Lastenausgleich, 70–73, 91–92, 106,
    131, 132, 138–39, 150, 161–63, 176–77;
    productionism, 109, 117, 121, 124, 125–
    26, 137, 153, 158; shifting of burden as
    danger, 125, 137; support for private
    property, 104, 136–37, 140; views welfare
    as humiliating, 106, 156
Social-market economy, 64, 117, 126; and
    currency reform, 75–76; general devel-
    opment of, 27, 66–67, 84, 115, 166–67;
    Lastenausgleich in, 3, 27–28, 119, 167,
    168, 185–97 passim
Social policy in early West Germany: gen-
    eral, 85, 87, 89–90, 115, 131, 168, 172, 173,
    183–84, 195; regarding social insurance
    system, 62, 89, 183, 188; regarding war
    victims, 86–87, 98, 142, 183–84
Sovereignty, West German, 23, 34, 83, 169,
    172, 183
Special Agency for Money and Credit,
    48–52, 57–59, 61, 75, 112, 113–14
Stalin, Joseph, 52, 54, 118, 146, 182
State Department, U.S., 46, 54, 55, 81
Status, social, 4, 29–30, 41, 47, 96, 161,
    165–66; achievement as basis for, in
    West Germany, 116; household goods
    as basis for, 154–55, 157–58; rejection
    of welfare to preserve, 90–91, 138, 196.
    See also Restoration: of prewar social
    status/honor
Stech, Paul, 147
Subsidies: from government for interest
    groups, 146–47, 181–82